CW00434479

Leonid Trofimov

26.12.08

RUSSIA
in War and Revolution,
1914–1922
A Documentary History

RUSSIA
in War and Revolution, 1914–1922
1914–1922
A Documentary History

Edited and Translated,
with an Introduction, by

JONATHAN DALY
and
LEONID TROFIMOV

Hackett Publishing Company, Inc.
Indianapolis/Cambridge

14 13 12 11 10 09   1 2 3 4 5 6 7

For further information, please address
    Hackett Publishing Company, Inc.
    P.O. Box 44937
    Indianapolis, Indiana 46244-0937

    www.hackettpublishing.com

Cover design by Abigail Coyle
Interior design by Elizabeth L. Wilson
Composition by Agnew's, Inc.
Printed at Victor Graphics, Inc.

Library of Congress Cataloging-in-Publication Data
Russia in war and revolution, 1914–1922 : a documentary history / edited and
translated, with an introduction, by Jonathan Daly and Leonid Trofimov.
        p. cm.
    Includes bibliographical references and index.
    ISBN 978-0-87220-987-9 (pbk.) — ISBN 978-0-87220-988-6 (cloth)
    1. Soviet Union—History—Revolution, 1917–1921—Sources.   2. Russia—
History—Nicholas II, 1894–1917—Sources.   3. World War, 1914–1918—
Russia—Sources.   4. World War, 1914–1918—Soviet Union—Sources.
I. Daly, Jonathan W.   II. Trofimov, Leonid.
    DK265.A54155 2009
    947.084'1—dc22   2009012040

The paper used in this publication meets the minimum requirements of American
National Standard for Information Sciences—Permanence of Paper for Printed Library Materials, ANSI Z39.48–1984.

Every reasonable effort has been made to trace the owners of copyright materials in
this book, but in some instances this has proven impossible. The author and publisher will be glad to receive information leading to more complete acknowledgments
in subsequent printings of the book and in the meantime extend their apologies for
any omissions.

CONTENTS

Chapter 3: The Bolsheviks' Revolution and the Road to a New World

Building Socialism

Soviet Russia and the World

Chapter 4: Popular Opposition and Civil Wars   205

The Fate of the Constituent Assembly

Worker Unrest

IMAGES

MAPS

PREFACE

The Russian Revolution set in motion much of 20th-century history. It brought a mighty empire to collapse and opened the door to takeover by Communists with their stunningly ambitious attempt to refashion the Russian people and ultimately the world. Fear of the "red menace" gave a boost to the political fortunes of both the fascists and Nazis, as well as a host of lesser right-wing demagogues, like Senator Joseph McCarthy. Admiration of, and revulsion toward, Communist achievements spurred governments in capitalist lands to implement comprehensive social legislation. Hostility toward "Jewish Bolsheviks" drove Hitler's Operation Barbarossa, which resulted in the Nazis' subsequent defeat at the hands of the Soviet Army. Decolonization drew strong inspiration from the anti-imperialist banner hoisted first by Soviet Communists. Finally, the Cold War, that geopolitical stalemate dominating world history for more than 40 years, stemmed largely from a deep rift between the capitalist West and a communist East that began to yawn in the years following the Russian Revolution.

Clearly, therefore, understanding the whirlwind of events that shook Russia in 1917 is important for students of history and educated people in general. Providing a comprehensive, readable, detailed, inexpensive, and up-to-date selection of sources on those events is our goal. We believe that the Russian Revolution did not erupt out of nowhere. World War I served as its catalyst and cradle. Nor did the Revolution end with the Tsar's fall. In fact, it took its most breathtaking turns later that year, when the Bolshevik Party and its supporters seized power in Petrograd and began their pursuit of a radically different concept of society, which provoked gradually expanding forms of resistance and ultimately a civil war. For 3 years diverse movements, armies, regions, and governments struggled to defend their power, their rights, and their visions for the future. Ultimately, by 1922, the Bolshevik sociopolitical system had triumphed: a one-party dictatorship state grudgingly tolerating elements of a market economy, yet ready to proceed with ambitious social engineering projects. Still, the voices and hopes of millions of people who imagined the revolutionary outcome differently should not be forgotten. Their experiences and aspirations are articulated throughout this volume.

A Note on the Sources

Many millions of original documents date from Russia's time of war, revolution, and Communist consolidation. A vast number appeared immediately in newspapers and journals, government decrees and pre-1917 parliamentary records, collected works by Communists, and émigré publications. Over the following seven decades, Soviet scholars published hundreds of carefully vetted collections of documents relating to the period. These collections omitted materials casting a bad light on the Communist system and were generally accompanied by highly biased commentary, yet they remain historically valuable. During these years, Russian émigrés published many important documents, especially memoirs and letters. A fuller account of the events covered in the present volume, however, only became feasible with the fall of Communism in Russia and the consequent opening of the archives. Over the past two decades, Russian scholars have scoured the formerly secret vaults and restricted special collections, including many in the provinces, and have brought out dozens of volumes brimming with materials illuminating nearly every aspect of the Russian Revolution from the fall of the Romanov dynasty to the rise of the Communist regime. The present volume draws on documents from all of the foregoing sources but most heavily from recently published collections.

The editors have provided fresh translations of most selections. In each case, we sought both faithfulness to the authors' intentions and clarity of meaning. At times reconciling both goals proved difficult. Prerevolutionary bureaucratic prose was often florid and dense; writings from the "lower depths," essential to any study of the revolutionary events, usually ignored grammatical niceties. In order to capture the flavor and feel of such documents, it seemed necessary to preserve some irregularities of style and examples of officialese.

The number enclosed in square brackets following each document title refers to the bibliographical entry from which the document was excerpted. Volume and page numbers are included as necessary.

Calendrical Problems

Until the time of Peter the Great, Russia followed the Jewish calendar, which counted each year from the putative creation of the world 3,760 years before the birth of Christ. On January 1, 1700, Peter imposed the Julian calendar, then still used in Protestant European countries, even though the Catholic world had already adopted the more accurate Gregorian calendar in 1582. Until February 1, 1918, when the new government abandoned the Julian system, moving the country ahead to February 14, Russia's annual reckoning trailed Western Europe's by 13 days in the 20th century. Thus, the February Revolution occurred in March by the Gregorian reckoning and the October Revolution in November. All dates in this volume follow the

Julian system until the end of 1917, except in references to the outside world. Then, a distinction will be made between old Russian style (O.S.) and the European "New Style" (N.S.)

Terminology

Although Nicholas II was technically an emperor, we use "tsar" and "emperor" interchangeably but prefer the former since it is better known, more storied, and captures some of the distinctiveness of Russia in the European context.

The Russian term vlast' stems from the Slavic roots "vlad," and "volod," meaning power, control, command, rule. The term, used occasionally before 1917 to mean authority, government, and/or rule, occurred ubiquitously after the Romanov dynasty fell and especially after the Bolsheviks came to power, especially in the phrase Soviet power (*Sovetskaia vlast'*). Vlast' in this usage has a raw quality, like an authority with popular support but not fully institutionalized, apparently more informal than traditional governments. We choose to translate the term variously, depending on the context, as government, rule, authority, or power.

Other Technical Matters

Ellipsis points standing alone stem from the original documents (some are in the Russian style of three points without spaces); we have added those enclosed in square brackets. Words italicized for emphasis throughout the documents always reflect the original usage. The spelling of words in some documents already translated into English has occasionally been Americanized or altered to achieve consistency. Finally, Russian words have been transliterated following the Library of Congress system (minus diacritical marks), except for a few commonly known words and names, for example Trotsky instead of Trotskii.

Russian Pronunciation

The "e" in Russian is pronounced "yeh." So, the newspaper title *Rech* sounds like "ryech."

ACKNOWLEDGMENTS

We wish to express gratitude to those who inspired our efforts—our students—and to those whose suggestions, advice, and criticism much improved the resulting volume. Among these were our two expert and diligent anonymous reviewers. We were delighted to learn, quite by chance, that one was Rex Wade. One cannot imagine a more knowledgeable or perceptive critic. We are further grateful to him for allowing us to include the excellent map of Petrograd in 1917 from his book *The Russian Revolution* in ours. Additional thanks to David Chandler, the cartographer for all the other maps. Our gratitude also goes out to Michael Melancon, who read our entire manuscript and provided several of the documents included in this collection; to Paul Simmons for expert advice on the Russian military; to Gregory Freeze for valuable references; to Julia Sergeeva-Albova for linguistic advice; to Page Herrlinger and Aleksander Kravetskii for advice about documents; to Christina Kowalewski for obtaining permission to publish copyrighted documents; to Liz Wilson for shepherding the book smoothly through production; and to Rick Todhunter, our wonderfully helpful editor.

For my children, J.D.
For my son Maxim, L.T.

INTRODUCTION

Historical Background

The Russian Revolution can trace its origins to deep historical trends, impersonal social and economic processes, concrete events, and specific actions of human agents. Russia was on the edge of Europe, both influenced by European history and relatively untouched by such seismic changes as the Renaissance and the Reformation. In the early 1700s, Peter the Great sought to transform his country technologically, militarily, administratively, and culturally—ultimately to make it European. His successors carried forward his legacy, especially in the cultural sphere. Thus Catherine the Great, in the late 1700s, corresponded with Voltaire and granted some civil rights to the elites. Russia was undoubtedly a great European power when its troops took part in the military coalitions that destroyed Napoleon's armies in 1813–1815.

Yet Russia's rulers had a deeply held belief that Russia was a unique country, a civilization unto itself and thus had resisted key changes intimately linked to Europe's dynamism and material success. Guarantees of individual liberty and political participation, in particular, were off the table. The narrow civil rights enjoyed by nobles were bestowed through imperial generosity, not respected as inhering in the very nature of humankind. Literary and philosophical experimentation, while tolerated beginning in the late 18th century, were regarded with suspicion, especially when resulting in political demands or proposals. Even technological developments, like building railroads, were opposed up to 1855 by Nicholas I as liable to shake up the social life of the country. At the same time, both general and technical education continued to expand. By the 1840s, there emerged elites known as "intelligentsia," who were often highly educated but also alienated from the existing order. While denied any political representation or power by the autocratic regime, many of them developed a sense of moral responsibility for the future of the Russian people. From among their ranks arose radical elements committed to social and political change.

The "men of the 1840s," very few in number, read Hegel and the French socialists and formed discussion circles. Despite their relative quietism, they faced ferocious persecution from the secret police, especially when revolution swept Europe in 1848. "Nihilists" in the 1860s theorized about conspiracy and the destruction of what they believed was an oppressive and unjust regime. Hundreds of idealistic young people, Populists, "went to the people" in the early 1870s in order to learn from them and to inspire them to rebel. Largely rejected by the peasants they sought to influence, most faced persecution, including prison and Siberian exile. Later in the decade, dozens of activists formed secret organizations aimed at fomenting revolution by means of political terror. In March 1881, one group, which called itself "People's Will," succeeded in killing Tsar Alexander II.

This outcome would have been unexpected from the vantage point of 1861 when that sovereign, against the will of the Russian nobility, had liberated 40 million serfs (but had kept them bound to agricultural communes). Indeed, the era of "Great Reforms" also included the establishment of institutions of local self-government in localities both rural (zemstvos) and urban (town dumas) and the creation of an entirely independent judiciary. On the eve of his death, when the terrorists seemed under control, he was even on his way to sign a decree in effect yielding to the elite demand for a consultative assembly. Alas, it was not to be. Instead, his son Alexander III rolled back some of the reforms and clamped down hard on intellectual life. At the same time, however, he accelerated the industrialization drive launched modestly by his father. By the 1890s, the Russian economy was growing slower only than that of the United States.

The Russian Empire appeared to be on the rise. Yet the emergence of an industrial economy naturally gave rise to a new set of social and economic tensions associated with an industrial workforce, which the latest avatar of the revolutionary intelligentsia interpreted through the lens of Marxism. Unlike the Populists and their ideological heirs the Socialist-Revolutionaries, who focused on peasant conditions and enfranchisement, a reasonable proposition for a country overwhelmingly rural, the Russian Marxists drew upon world-renowned texts (the first foreign translation of *Das Kapital* was into Russian) offering an allegedly scientific solution to Russia's woes. Karl Marx[1] had purported to prove that each society must pass through a series of developmental stages, and that while industrialization was inevitable, factory workers could subsequently bring people to the reign of justice through socialism. Russia might be developmentally backward, its government autocratic, and its society weak, yet fundamental social revolution was not beyond reach; in fact, it was only a matter of time in Russia, as well as all over the world. At least this is what the country's Social Democrats, or Marxists,

---

1. Karl Marx (1818–1881) was a German political philosopher, radical journalist, and political leader. Facing political persecution at home, he spent much of his life living in France and Great Britain. A prolific writer, he contributed important ideas to three major fields. His sociology holds that all societies are divided into irreconcilable classes based on economics and that all social, political, and cultural realities are determined by their interrelations. Struggle among these classes drives all of human history, according to his theory of history. Finally, as an economic theorist, Marx argued that capitalism was highly progressive in its promotion of new technology and industrial methods but at the same time led to an ever-growing gap in the distribution of wealth and would at some point exhaust its productive capacity, giving way to a more efficient and equitable socialist system.

believed. It was precisely Marxism's apparent usefulness in addressing these grave problems that won so many fervent Russian intellectual converts.

The Social Democratic movement emerged, along with a welter of other revolutionary organizations, in the early years of the reign of Russia's last Tsar, Nicholas II. He was a weak man, of small stature, sensitive and well educated, but stubborn and unshakably committed to fulfilling his father's death-bed demand in 1894 that he uphold political absolutism. Soon after taking the throne, he dismissed as "senseless dreams" the request of moderate and radical zemstvo activists from Tver province for the creation of a consultative assembly. His German-born wife, Alexandra, the favorite granddaughter of Queen Victoria, an extremely shy and superstitious woman, steadfastly urged him to remain implacably opposed to political change. Yet some things were beyond Nicholas' control. Carrying forward his father's policy of industrialization demanded the continued expansion of education and dramatically undermined the system of political absolutism by fostering an unprecedented growth of social institutions, forces, and organizations. Their exclusion from political power, along with wrenching and often painful economic changes, gave rise to a spectacular concatenation of public protests, revolutionary agitation, incidents of rebellion, and acts of political terrorism after the turn of the century.

Russia faced major strikes in St. Petersburg in 1896 and 1897, massive student demonstrations and strikes across European Russia in 1899 and 1900, the assassination of the minister of education in 1901 and the minister of the interior in 1902, huge peasant uprisings in Poltava and Kharkov provinces in 1902, a murderous anti-Jewish pogrom in Kishinev in 1903, along with the formation of a half-dozen major political parties throughout these years, of diverse viewpoints but all devoted to toppling the autocratic government, which completely discredited itself in the eyes of the many in the unsuccessful war with Japan that began in 1904.[2] The autocracy was under siege. A touch of political imbecility plunged Russia into revolution and the near collapse of the state in 1905.

On January 9, following weeks of serious labor unrest, a couple hundred thousand protesters peacefully approached the Winter Palace. Their leaders demanded amnesty for political prisoners, full civil liberties, better working conditions, the right to strike, and an end to the war. Aware of the impending demonstration, Nicholas had nevertheless foolishly departed from the capital, leaving orders to prevent any disturbances. As the crowd massed, troops fired. Some 200 died and 800 were gravely wounded. The remainder

---

2. The first war in history when a European power was defeated by a developing country, the Russo-Japanese War (1904–1905) undermined the Russian government's prestige and deepened the country's political and social crisis in 1905.

of the year witnessed almost ceaseless protests—by workers, peasants, intellectuals, soldiers, sailors, students, and ethnic minorities. The government held on to power only because these various social forces never coalesced and erupted all at the same time. The closest calls came in October and December. On October 17, amid a general strike that paralyzed the economy, Nicholas signed the October Manifesto, which promised civil liberties and representative government. Nicholas expected and indeed had been assured by his advisors that unrest would immediately dissipate. In reality, anti-Jewish violence flared up in cities, and peasant mobs rampaged in the countryside. In December, insurgents seized control of large sectors of Moscow and launched an armed uprising. Artillery fire and street-by-street combat crushed the insurgency but also killed 424 people, mostly bystanders. The first Russian Revolution was over.

The next 8 years saw the emergence of a constitutional order. Even Nicholas admitted he had granted Russia a constitution by enacting the Fundamental Laws of April 23, 1906. Henceforth, all citizens had the right to assembly, to form unions and associations, to foreign travel, to free speech, to property, and to conscience; homes could be searched and persons detained only "as prescribed by the law"; and finally, laws could be enacted only with the approval of both legislative chambers and the emperor. Deputies of the lower chamber, the Duma, were elected by restricted franchise but generally expressed popular opinion. Quite radical in its first year, the Duma grew moderate and even relatively conservative in later years, thanks in part to an unconstitutional modification of the electoral law on June 3, 1907. Half the members of the State Council, or upper chamber, were appointed by the Tsar, making the body a bulwark of conservatism. Gridlock was a major feature of Russian political life in these years and relatively little major legislation was passed. Major exceptions were laws allowing peasants to leave the commune (1906), expanding primary education (1908), and establishing a health-insurance system for workers (1912).

These interwar years witnessed cultural vibrancy, government repression, and political scandal. The Russian *Ballets Russes* took Europe by storm. Igor Stravinsky's *Firebird* (1910) and *The Rite of Spring* (1913) stunned audiences. One critic called these performances "dazzling, intoxicating, enchanting, seductive." Russian modernist painters—Leon Bakst, Marc Chagall, Vasily Kandinsky, Kazimir Malevich—were among Europe's most influential artists of the time. Literacy in Russia increased, from 28 percent in 1897 to 40 percent in 1914. Newspaper publication expanded tenfold in these years to 1,158 with a daily circulation of 3 million, while other periodicals soon numbered over 3,000. The police actively clamped down on publications deemed "subversive," though aside from the trade-union press they little affected the availability of information from diverse points of view. Even the most radical wing of the Russian Social Democratic Party, the Bolshe- viks, was able to publish a daily newspaper in 1912–1914. At the same time, trade unions faced continuous harassment, and all the political parties to the left of the moderately conservative Octobrists remained technically illegal outside the Duma, though elite associations generally avoided persecution. Neither the government nor the dynasty enjoyed strong public support, thanks in part to political gridlock, police repression, and unsavory persons linked publicly to the royal family. Chief among these was Grigorii Rasputin. Alexandra relied on him for healing and comforting her only son, Aleksei, a hemophiliac born in 1904. Government officials sought to keep the Siber- ian peasant away from the Winter Palace, but Nicholas forbade meddling with what he considered his private affairs.

War

World War I was disastrous for all Europe and for no country more so than Russia. Locked into an alliance with France, facing in Germany a re- doubtable foe more similar to Russia in political and social life than its ally, and feeling a "pan-Slavic" obligation toward a Serbia squeezed between hostile empires in the Balkans, Russia entered the fight. From the start, the powerful German army defeated the poorly equipped and badly com- manded Russian forces. From time to time, Germany would send divisions to the Western Front in the hope of gaining advantage against France and Britain.[3] Then Russia could advance against the weaker Austrian army. Yet each time the German divisions would return and restabilize the Eastern Front.

Elite public opinion waxed patriotic early on but grew critical as the de- feats multiplied. On August 8, the Duma assembled briefly, voted almost unanimously in favor of war credits, and then dissolved itself. "We would only get in the way," declared one prominent deputy. A week earlier, zem- stvo activists had founded the All-Russian Zemstvo Union for providing aid to sick and wounded soldiers. Over the next year, several more nongovern- mental organizations sprang up to assist in the war effort, including the All- Russian Union of Town Dumas and the War-Industries Committees, as well as five public-private organizations, called special councils, which for the first

---

3. The two blocs of belligerent countries were the Triple Entente (France, Great Britain, and Russia; the United States joined them in 1917) and the Central Powers (Germany, Austria-Hungary, the Ottoman Empire, and Bulgaria).

time in Russian history brought together on an equal footing representatives of both the government and the private sector. The members of all these organizations began with disinterested commitments to the war effort but many gradually allied their work with active opposition to government policies. Public activists, many concluded, could more effectively prosecute the war than the stodgy bureaucrats. The latter, for their part, were generally suspicious of the public activists and sometimes impeded their work. The activists nevertheless helped solve the crisis in the supply of shells and other military equipment by mid-1915.

Early that summer, to appease public opinion, the Tsar appointed several liberal ministers to the government. Still unsatisfied, in July politicians from diverse political parties formed the Progressive Bloc within the Duma and demanded a "ministry enjoying the confidence of the Duma." Their plea fell on deaf ears. Against the advice of his government but in response to further military reversals and in particular the evacuation from Warsaw in July, in late August 1915 Nicholas resolved to take symbolic personal command of the armed forces at General Headquarters in Mogilev. Then, over the next few months, he dismissed each of the new ministers. With Nicholas absent from Petrograd, Alexandra's influence on policy and official appointments grew, as did that of Rasputin on her. A succession of shady figures, schemers, and incompetents rose to the highest positions in government. Henceforth, mutual distrust and suspicion reigned between government and the elite public.

Although Nicholas began 1916 with the conciliatory gesture of personally convening the Duma, animosity toward the sovereign only increased. Structural and policy troubles contributed to this trend. The railroad system gradually buckled under the strain of overuse. Printing money to pay for war materiel fueled inflation, despite Russia's huge gold reserves. Toward the end of the year, food and fuel shortages made life in urban areas difficult. In June, General Aleksei Brusilov launched a mighty offensive against Austrian positions in an effort to relieve the Allies, then under siege at Verdun. Initially successful, the offensive raised public spirits in Russia but then dashed them as once again German reinforcements repulsed the advance. The appointment of the politically moderate but mentally erratic Aleksandr Protopopov, an ally of Rasputin, as minister of the interior in September further soured relations with society. In early November, from the rostrum of the Duma, Pavel Miliukov, the widely respected historian and a leader of the liberal Constitutional Democratic Party, denounced Prime Minister Boris Shtiurmer, rhetorically inquiring whether "stupidity or treason" on his part had occasioned Russia's political and military misfortunes. In mid-December, conservative elites murdered Rasputin in the hope that his death would bring Nicholas closer to high society. It did not.

The Year of Revolutions

Amid rumors of impending revolution and fears of inadequate food supplies, the year 1917 began with massive strikes, demonstrations, and general disaffection. Strategic arrests of radical activists by police from early January to mid-February availed nothing: in late February mass unrest in Petrograd drew enormous crowds into the streets. Their numbers swelled day by day. Reserve troops left massed in the capital against expert advice rebelled on February 27 and joined the opposition. Immediately, the police fled, and jails, prisons, police stations, and court houses were looted and ransacked. On March 2, the Tsar abdicated. The regime had fallen.

Already on February 27, two separate bodies claiming legitimacy and authority sprang up. This was the so-called Dual Power. Leading Duma deputies, liberals along with one socialist, formed the Provisional Government. The Allies quickly recognized precisely this body, Russia's face to the developed world. Socialist activists meanwhile organized hundreds of delegates from factories and military units into a Soviet, or council. Able to call huge crowds into the street at any moment, this body held both veto power and strong influence over the quasi-official liberal government. Thus, the new era's first official decree, Order No. 1, which increased soldiers' rights and stripped officers of power, originated in the Soviet.

Russia's new leaders agreed on an agenda of liberation. In a paroxysm of euphoria, they freed prisoners, abolished police institutions, eliminated ethnic and religious discrimination, and lifted the remaining restrictions on civil liberties. An investigating commission was instituted to look into alleged crimes of the Old Regime. Hundreds of political activists streamed back to Russia from exile in Siberia and abroad. Before even setting foot in the country, Vladimir Lenin (1870–1924),[4] the Bolshevik leader, admitted it was the "freest of all the belligerent countries." Ordinary people across Russia were involved in forming soviets at every level of government: in villages, districts, cities, and provinces. Committees of soldiers sprang up in most military units. Workers set up committees, trade unions, armed bands, regional brotherhoods, and diverse cultural organizations. Congresses of peasants, of ethnic minorities, and of other population groups were convened. Many localities, regions, and former provinces declared political autonomy. Parishes declared their administrative autonomy from dioceses. Democracy had apparently triumphed.

Yet clashes soon broke out between and among the diverse political factions, the rival powers, and competing local institutions, classes, ethnic groups, and regions. Mass demonstrations in Petrograd in late April provoked a

4. For a brief biography of Lenin, see Document 6, p. 14, n. 8.

political crisis and led to the formation of a coalition government composed of six socialists and nine liberals. Lenin, who had returned in early April, appealed to ordinary people's growing frustrations with crime, economic hardship, and the Provisional Government's failure to stop the war, undertake land reform, or hold elections to a Constituent Assembly. Under the slogans "Peace, Land, Bread" and "All Power to the Soviets," Lenin and other Bolsheviks, along with other radical left leaders, including Left Socialist-Revolutionaries and left-wing Mensheviks, steadily won support in elections to the soviets in Moscow and Petrograd. Since the Bolsheviks were the best organized and most united radical party, they played a leading role over the following weeks. The failed military offensive, launched by the new minister of war, Alexander Kerensky,[5] on June 18, fueled popular discontent and further increased support for the radical left. Huge demonstrations in Petrograd on June 18 and July 3–4 rocked the government. The arrest of key Bolshevik leaders, accused of being German agents, slowed the party's élan, though only temporarily. Another political crisis resulted in the formation on July 24 of a second coalition government with a majority of socialists and Kerensky as prime minister.

Propertied and educated elites gathered in Moscow on August 8–10 to propose solutions to the deepening crisis. Decrying the economic, military, and governmental breakdown, they called on "all statesmanlike elements" to join forces in order to forge a strong national authority. Almost simultaneously and also in Moscow, the Provisional Government convened some 2,600 representatives of nearly all political parties (though not the Bolsheviks) and institutions, economic interests, national minorities, and intellectual elements in the country. Many speakers, including Kerensky, also argued passionately in favor of restoring order, curtailing the power of the Petrograd Soviet, and restoring capital punishment for heinous crimes. The most conservative elements in society, coalescing around the newly appointed supreme commander, Lavr Kornilov, therefore had reason to imagine that the prime minister favored their hard-line intentions. Yet when Kornilov sought to lead troops into the capital, Kerensky denounced him as a traitor and reached out to the left by amnestying the Bolshevik leaders and arming red guard units. The attempted coup was thwarted, but Kerensky's victory rang hollow as it revealed that the prime minister now lacked any support base of his own.

---

5. Alexander Kerensky (1881–1970) was a politically engaged socialist lawyer, who had defended revolutionaries in court and served as a deputy in the Fourth Duma. The only member of the First Provisional Government who also served in the Executive Committee of the Petrograd Soviet, he acted as an intermediary between the far left and the liberal and moderate-right elements in revolutionary Russia.

Meanwhile, the Bolsheviks kept gaining in popularity, both by blaming economic hardship and social disorder, which continued to deepen, on "capitalists" and other privileged groups and by promising an end to the war, the distribution of all the land to the peasantry, and worker control of factories. Other far-left activists also gained ground, but lacking the strict discipline of the Bolsheviks, they played at best a supporting role in the coming events. By September the far-left bloc was winning majorities or big pluralities in the city and urban district soviets and in many trade unions, factory committees, and other elections in Petrograd and Moscow. In this context, a "Democratic Conference" of socialists was held on September 14–19 in Petrograd in order to push for the formation of an all-socialist government. Divisions among the socialists, however, allowed the creation of a third liberal-socialist "coalition" government.

By late September, lower-class opinion ran solidly toward a new socialist system of "All Power to the Soviets," while Lenin demanded his party orchestrate an armed seizure of power in the name of the soviets. The convening of a "Preparliament" intended to unite all political forces, both liberal and socialist, behind the government in early October laid bare the deep divisions among the socialists when the Bolshevik delegates stormed out.

From mid-September, Lenin began vehemently pressing for a Bolshevik seizure of power. In mid-October he began, within Bolshevik circles, to advocate immediately launching an armed uprising to that end. Yet other Bolshevik leaders balked, including Lev Kamenev and Grigorii Zinoviev, who publicly denounced this plan. Leon Trotsky, who was elected chairman of the Petrograd Soviet on September 25, came up with a different plan, proposing that the coming All-Russian Congress of Soviets should be used by the Bolsheviks and other leftists to transfer power to the soviets. It did not hurt that the Petrograd Soviet had at its disposal the Military Revolutionary Committee (MRK), an institution created on October 12 to defend against military threats.

On the morning of October 24, the Kerensky (third coalition) government gave the Bolsheviks an excuse to seize power by sending military cadets to seize the press and editorial offices of their newspaper, *Pravda*. That night the Military Revolutionary Committee took control of all the main centers of power in the name of the All-Russian People's Congress of Soviets, scheduled to meet the following day. When the Bolshevik leaders presented a fait accompli to the congress, most other socialists walked out, leaving the Bolshevik-dominated body to nationalize all the land, to promise an end to the war, and to form a new government, the Council of People's Commissars (SNK), headed by Lenin. Within days, the new body abolished ranks, titles, and privileges; ended the special legal position of the Russian Orthodox Church; and granted national minorities the right to secession. Despite resistance from civil servants, most political parties, and some trade unions, the new government won the right to govern by decree. Among its early acts were decreeing worker control over factories, the nationalization of private business, the abolition of the judicial system and its replacement by elective courts and revolutionary tribunals, and starting peace talks with Germany.

On December 10, the Left Socialist-Revolutionaries joined the Bolsheviks as coalition partners, and relatively free elections to a Constituent Assembly were allowed to go forward. Yet when the elections, despite some restrictions on electoral campaigning and harassing of opposition candidates, gave the Bolsheviks only a quarter of the votes, Russia's new leaders permitted the assembly to meet only briefly in early January and then shut it down at gunpoint. Popular demonstrations in support of the institution were also suppressed by force.

The Bolsheviks were at this time an embattled minority. Most of their leaders—and indeed most of the educated elites—doubted they could hang on to power. They were eager to build socialism but exerted almost no influence in the countryside where peasants were busily seizing all the land or on the periphery where entire regions and former provinces, like Ukraine, Poland, and Finland and later the Caucasus, moved toward independence. A plethora of self-styled independent territories appeared and disappeared all across the former Russian Empire—more than sixty by the end of 1917—with exotic names like the Estland Workers' Commune, the Tanu-Tuvinskaia Popular Republic, the Ural-Volga States (attempting to unite the Tatar and Bashkir peoples), and the Rudobel'skaia Partisans Republic. The major cities still faced looting and criminality on a huge scale. The creation in early December of the Extraordinary Commission, or Cheka, a secret police and forerunner of the KGB, was intended in part to help restore civil order. Moreover, when the Bolsheviks, despite the Russian army's disintegration, were unwilling to make significant concessions at the negotiating table, Germany and Austria launched a broad offensive against Russia. Fearful of political collapse, the government empowered the Cheka to shoot "enemies of the people" on the spot and in early March signed the Treaty of Brest-Litovsk, ceding one-third of European Russia to the enemy. While many rank-and-file Bolsheviks and all Left Socialist-Revolutionaries considered this deal all but treasonous, Lenin and other leading Bolsheviks believed that the toiling masses of Europe would rise up and overthrow their own governments at any moment, thus rendering any concessions to Imperial Germany null and void. They also considered hanging onto power more important than preserving Russian territory, a view many other leading Bolsheviks found hard to accept. The government retreated to Moscow in mid-March, as German military forces approached Petrograd.

Around the same time, modest Allied forces began landing on Russia's periphery—in the far north and far east—in order to keep weaponry shipped to Russia from falling into enemy hands but also, if readily possible, to replace the government with one willing to carry on fighting the war. In the south, Cossacks[6] rebelled against Bolshevik forces, and the anti-Bolshevik Volunteer Army began to take shape. Thus, the Bolsheviks were embattled geopolitically. They responded, in April 1918, by creating military commissars to keep tabs on officers and by establishing universal military training.

According to orthodox Marxism, peasants by nature are "petty-bourgeois" and therefore counterrevolutionary. Since the Bolsheviks came to power in an overwhelmingly peasant country (at most one in twenty was an industrial worker), a tactical adjustment was necessary. Thus, from 1917 Lenin advocated a union (also called *smychka*) of the workers and peasants. Government policies of forced grain requisition begun in May 1918, to prevent urban starvation and to extend their vision of socialism to the countryside, all but sundered that union in practice.

Civil War

The spark that set it off was the "mutiny" of the 40,000-man Czechoslovak Legion, a well-trained military force seeking to evacuate through Siberia and via the United States so as to resume fighting in France against the Central Powers in pursuit of Czech and Slovak independence. When the German authorities demanded the Legion's disarmament and the Bolshevik government sought to comply in late May, the Czechs rebelled and had soon seized control of the Trans-Siberian Railroad, followed by major towns in the Urals. When the Czechs occupied Samara, on June 8, leaders of the disbanded Constituent Assembly, mainly Socialist-Revolutionaries, formed a committee claiming to be the legitimate government of Russia (*Komuch*) and immediately declared armed struggle against the Bolsheviks. Beginning on July 6, simultaneously but independently, Left and Right Socialist-Revolutionaries launched unsuccessful anti-Bolshevik rebellions in Moscow and other cities. Furthermore, peasant uprisings broke out across the country in July and August.

The Bolshevik government, for its part, declared martial law and a universal military draft in late May and, in early June, held a congress of Military

---

6. Cossacks were peoples of Russian, Ukrainian, and other ethnic backgrounds who began settling on Russia's southern frontiers in the 1300s and formed communities from the mid-1500s. Gradually incorporated into the Russian state, they enjoyed greater autonomy than other subjects of the Tsar and in exchange provided loyal military service.

comissars and reintroduced capital punishment. In mid-July, as the
Czechoslovaks drew closer to Ekaterinburg, where the Tsar, his immediate
family, and their entourage were imprisoned, Bolshevik officials murdered
them all, in cold blood and in the dead of night. The next day, Bolshevik officials killed several other members of the Tsar's family, further north in the
Ural Mountains. Their purpose, it seems, was to prevent their enemies gaining a royal standard-bearer.

When, on August 30, unaffiliated Socialist-Revolutionaries killed the
Cheka boss in Petrograd and wounded Lenin in Moscow, the regime set in
motion a policy of "Red Terror." Decrees were issued in rapid succession declaring Russia "a single military camp," ordering the taking of hostages, and
calling for mass terror against "class enemies." Within days, 1,400 people
were shot in Petrograd and Kronstadt. Over the next few months, thousands
more people were shot without trial. Ironically, the victims were generally
defined as "bourgeois" or other elites and not Socialist-Revolutionaries, who
at that point constituted the greatest political and strategic threat to the new
regime. The Bolsheviks adopted this policy, it seems, in order to demoralize
anti-Bolshevik socialists and to appropriate for themselves the rhetoric and
identity of "revolution." In view of the Socialist-Revolutionaries' feeble resistance to the Bolsheviks throughout the Civil War, it would appear that
they succeeded in achieving both goals.

The Civil War was a complicated, shifting congeries of struggles, threats,
battles, and fronts. The Communists, or Reds,[7] were surrounded on almost
all sides—Whites[8] to the west, south, and east—and at the very least symbolic foreign threats in every cardinal direction. They also faced many internal enemies and much popular discontent, including peasant partisans,
or Greens. Yet all these enemies were divided geographically, ideologically,
politically, even ethnically and linguistically. There were socialists, liberals,
and monarchists; Georgians, Poles, Ukrainians, and many other peoples.
They had little in common aside from opposition to the government in
Moscow. The Communists, by contrast, were all concentrated in the Russian heartland, with control over the main railroad lines. Perhaps most important, they knew what they wanted: to forge a bright socialist future, in
which all people would live in peace and prosperity, where distinctions and
hierarchies based on wealth, nationality, and religion would be no more.

7. For centuries a symbol of defiance, the red flag was adopted by French revolutionaries
in 1793 and by subsequent political radicals in Europe. Red was also a popular color in
east Slavic culture; the Russian words for "beautiful" and "red" derive from the same root.
8. The name "Whites" was something of a misnomer, since it implies support for monarchism, whereas few anti-Bolshevik forces supported a restoration of the emperor or the
dynasty.

Considering themselves true Marxists, the Bolsheviks believed that private property and markets inevitably lead to inequality, exploitation, and ultimately economic crises, stagnation, and general impoverishment. Thus, central to their vision was the abolition of private property and the free market and their replacement by rational central economic planning. A series of decrees, beginning almost immediately, sought to fulfill this goal and came to be known under the term "War Communism." In summer 1918, the government nationalized heavy industry, railroads, and steam plants and abolished the right to own urban real property. Large apartments and houses of the wealthy and middle class were confiscated, and many new tenants were "compressed" into them. Apartment buildings, granted by the state to major factories and plants and offering communal services like cafeterias and day care, were considered the wave of the future. In the fall, decrees made it illegal for people without jobs to obtain food, imposed a one-time 10-billion-ruble contribution on the urban and village "bourgeoisie," banned all retail and wholesale commerce, and established a universal labor obligation for people ages 16–50. Then in early 1919, the Bolsheviks instituted a confiscatory tax in kind (*prodrazverstka*) across the entire country and nationalized all consumer cooperatives and compelled all citizens to join them. All of these policies taken together, along with the hardships imposed by the war itself, drastically lowered agricultural and industrial output, drove millions of city dwellers into the countryside, caused the ruble to collapse, forced most people to rely on barter, and engendered a huge black market. In fact, illegal black-market trade in grain and other food items helped millions of people escape starvation. As people ate less, they fell ill, and epidemics of typhus and other diseases struck broadly in the population.

As the Civil War gained intensity and threatened the very existence of Soviet power, the Communist leadership strived to mobilize the entire country for battle. Decrees issued in March and June 1919 on fighting desertion, as well as the creation in March of Cheka offices in all armies and fronts, were aimed in large part at stanching the flood of recruits out of military units. The authorities counted nearly two million deserters in 1919; during 7 months of that year, 95,000 soldiers were sentenced for desertion; 600 of them were shot. Decrees in April 1919 mobilized volunteers for the defense of the rear and created forced-labor camps. The leading Communists believed moreover that their revolution would fail without mobilizing proletarians to support them in the major industrialized European countries. Thus, in early March 1919 Moscow hosted the First Congress of the Comintern, or Communist International, in order to promote revolution in those countries.

The anti-Communist forces—never a fully developed coalition and never even a relatively coordinated bloc—at various points from fall 1918 to spring

1920 scored signal gains and suffered bitter reversals. A few salient points can be mentioned. From June to September 1918, the Committee of the Constituent Assembly (*Komuch*), which was dominated by Socialist-Revolutionary deputies to the suppressed Constituent Assembly, governed several provinces in the Volga and Ural regions; they enforced civil rights and adopted pro-market policies. Thereafter, Komuch was replaced by the Directory of Ufa (later based in Omsk). A celebrated naval officer, Aleksandr Kolchak, dominated this body as a dictator beginning in November. Also in late fall 1918, World War I ended and the Communist forces invaded German-occupied Byelorussia and Ukraine, Cossack offensives in the south and White forces led by Kolchak in the east pushed forward, and Ukrainian forces commanded by the Ukrainian nationalist Simon Petliura pressed hard against Moscow's army. These and other peasant and Cossack forces fighting against the Communists in the south, such as those of Nestor Makhno and Nikifor Grigoriev, never made common cause with the White army in the south led by General Denikin, much to the benefit of Moscow.

Many of the anti-Communist military forces, especially those commanded by Grigoriev, participated to varying degrees in anti-Jewish violence that took at least 75,000 lives. While these deaths resulted from uncoordinated, generally random acts, a government order signed by Lenin on January 24, 1919, led directly to the execution of some 8,000 Cossacks in mid-March. The victims of the Civil War, then, suffered on ethnic as well as ideological grounds.

Throughout the Civil War, government policies toward the main opposition socialist parties shifted repeatedly. Leniency usually followed military victories, while defeats brought on persecution. In November 1918, the Mensheviks were allowed to stand for election to the soviets, in exchange for political cooperation, and in February 1919, the Socialist-Revolutionary party was legalized. Yet repression fell heavily on both parties in March 1919. Denikin's occupation of the Don region, the Donbass (the Donets Basin), Tsaritsyn, and part of Ukraine in June 1919 coincided with the expulsion of Mensheviks and Socialist-Revolutionaries from the All-Russian Central Executive Committee,[9] as well as with an order empowering the Cheka to shoot "bandits" on the spot, whereas Red Army success in taking several major Ural cities in July triggered a general political amnesty. Late September until mid-October 1919 marked the most desperate time for Soviet power. During that 2-week period, anarchists managed to explode a bomb at a party meeting at Leontievskii Lane in Moscow killing twelve Bolshevik leaders, Denikin's

---

9. The All-Russian Central Executive Committee was the executive board elected by the Congress of Soviets and charged in principle with governing the country. In practice, the Politburo and Central Committee of the Communist Party were the true executive branch.

forces aimed at threatening Moscow, the White General Nikolai and Iudenich drew close to Petrograd. Yet over the next few weeks, the tide turned decisively in favor of Moscow, so much so that the government commemorated the second anniversary of the October Revolution with a general amnesty. By late November, the Red Army was unleashing a general offensive on all its fronts.

Although Soviet power went from strength to strength in late 1919 and early 1920, control over the labor force actually intensified. Decrees issued in November 1919 specified a punishment of 6 months in a labor camp for breaches of labor discipline and authorized the "militarization" of state institutions and enterprises. This latter idea, the brainchild of Trotsky, was followed in January 1920 by a decree on the creation of "labor armies" and another in February establishing a universal labor obligation. The purpose of these measures was to use the momentum and the methods of the Civil War in order to rebuild a country shattered by years of wrenching violence, political chaos, and economic breakdown and bring it closer to socialism. (The labor armies were disbanded at the end of 1921.)

So, the Bolsheviks won the Civil War because of their united political leadership, their stronger military organization, and their control of Russia's heartland—which gave them control of most of the country's industry, railroads, and ethnically homogeneous population. Perhaps just as important, the Whites lost because they never managed to unite their disparate forces or to win broad-based support among the population and indeed alienated much of it. Even the conservative Russian nationalist Vasilii Shulgin believed that the Whites began their struggle practically as saints and ended it almost as bandits. The Whites were too closely associated in the eyes of most people with the old order. They never captured the imagination of millions with the promise and vision of a new and better life. The Bolsheviks managed to do just that. Their enormous, modern propaganda machine, which in the absence of free speech, flooded Soviet Russia with inspiring posters, staged performances, "agit trains," booklets, and newspapers all aimed at promoting their vision of socialism, while stirring up class hatred. Completely outclassed in the realm of public relations, the Whites hardly knew what had hit them.

After winning the Civil War the Bolsheviks tried to present their victory as inevitable and as an ultimate justification of their right to power. Yet there was nothing inevitable about their victory, as Lenin and others admitted at the time. The Brest-Litovsk Peace Treaty is one milestone that should dilute any sense of inevitability, both in terms of how vulnerable the Bolshevik regime was and how uncertain key Bolsheviks were about whether to pursue peace on German terms. Likewise, in many instances in 1918, their opponents overturned Bolshevik control with similar ease, as was the case with the Czechoslovak mutiny in the Volga region. Finally, when Denikin's forces were approaching Moscow in summer 1919, the Bolsheviks began to make earnest preparations for going "underground." With the White forces all but destroyed in early 1920 (mopping-up operations continued in the south and east into the spring, and the White remnants were driven from the Crimea only in November), Soviet power faced two more armed threats: peasant rebellions and a Polish invasion. Peasants were now willing to violently oppose the Communists, whom they generally loathed, with little fear of playing into the hands of the Whites, whom they mistrusted even more. The uprisings began in February 1919 in the Volga region and spread across a swath of territory from Kazan to Saratov by April. Gradually, some Bolshevik commanders, like A. P. Sapozhkov, a Socialist-Revolutionary sympathizer who rejected the government's policies toward peasants, joined the rebellion. By August the famous "antonovshchina," led by the Left Socialist-Revolutionary Aleksandr Antonov, had erupted in Tambov province. Meanwhile, Poland launched an invasion into Ukraine in late April. By early May, the Polish army had seized Kiev. The Red Army quickly undertook a counteroffensive and by midsummer was threatening Warsaw. The Poles managed to hold the line, and the war ended in October.

As the Civil War was ending, the leaders of Soviet Russia adopted ever more ambitious and far-reaching measures. In March 1920, steps toward the abolition of money were undertaken, such as providing free mail, cable, and phone service to Soviet institutions. The party congress in early April voted to abolish all private property and to militarize the economy. Later in the month, the government decreed a universal food-rationing system for all laborers. In early May fares on public transportation were abolished. Then in July, all Soviet and public institutions and organizations were prohibited to use money for any purchases. November saw a decree nationalizing all small businesses. Finally, in December the government declared its intention to distribute food and other necessary goods for free, and in January 1921 housing was also proclaimed a free benefit. A month later, the State Planning Agency (Gosplan) was created as the chief governing body for the state economy.

The Bolsheviks proclaimed their commitment to human liberation from the old order and eagerly extended their reach beyond economic matters. The Provisional Government had abolished many gender-based restrictions. Women had been admitted to the bar in June 1917, the electorate in July, and the civil service in August. The Communists went farther still, seeking to efface any distinctions between men and women. Decrees immediately after the Bolshevik coup gave women the right to full participation in political life in the workplace and 16 weeks' maternity leave. The Family Code of 1918 abolished the idea of illegitimacy but also forbade adoption, ascribed to civil marriage sole legal validity, and gave women the right to keep their maiden names. Women's departments, set up in fall 1919 and directed by the Central Committee, were tasked with winning support among women for the new regime and with developing institutions, such as day-care centers and public cafeterias, to liberate women from patriarchal relationships and the drudgery of traditional domestic work. Few such institutions actually received funding, however. Abortion and contraception were legalized in 1920. Common-law marriages grew in popularity, which apparently encouraged many men to shed responsibility for their children. By 1921, partly in consequence of this tendency but also due to social and economic devastation brought on by war and revolution, there were some 7 million abandoned children and few orphanages to care for them.

Women's leadership roles improved but remained weak. By 1924 only 8.2 percent of party members were women. They held very few senior positions; only one, Alexandra Kollontai, held a cabinet post and then only briefly. Women served as military officers during the Civil War but not afterward.

Internal political opposition and resistance actually intensified as the Civil War wound down. Back in May 1920, a political faction within the Communist Party, the Workers' Opposition, denounced the "bureaucratization" of the Soviet system and complained that the number of paid officials, many if not most uncommitted to Communist ideals, had multiplied like mushrooms after a summer's rain. The country faced other major problems, too, chief among them economic hardship and collapse. With the threat of political restoration safely behind them, ordinary urban dwellers now dared to express frustration and anger about poor living conditions and the lack of civil liberties. In late February and early March 1921, factory workers went on strike in Petrograd. The authorities tamped down that fire with ample supplies of food and clothing. Simultaneously and more menacingly, Kronstadt sailors—formerly the staunchest advocates of Bolshevism who were stationed at the fortress protecting Petrograd in the Gulf of Finland—rebelled, demanding free and fair elections to the soviets. Delegates of soldiers, sailors, and workers adopted a platform of demands, including free and fair elections to the soviets, civil liberties, the right of peasants to sell grain and artisans to sell their products, and an end to the Communist Party's monopoly of power. The delegates, representing some 18,000 inhabitants of the island, including 9,000 sailors, also voted to create a provisional revolutionary committee.

The authorities responded to these challenges with both carrots and sticks. Among the former the most far-reaching and desperately welcome was the New Economic Policy (see below). More immediately, in the first days of March 1921 they launched a propaganda barrage denouncing the rebels as Socialist-Revolutionaries allied with White Guards and lackeys of foreign bourgeois governments. Political activists believed to be sympathetic

toward the rebels were arrested all across the region; some individuals in contact with them were shot; many people related to known rebels were seized
as hostages to be killed in case the rebels should harm Communists. A first
military offensive, sent across the ice by Mikhail Tukhachevskii on March 7,
failed. More preparations were furiously undertaken. Both sides urgently
pleaded for support and recognition. Cheka officials swarmed into military
units to prevent defections. A second offensive began on the 9th. Pitched
battles ensued for over a week. Finally, about 8,000 rebels fled to Finland.
At least 1,000 lay dead on each side. The Communist authorities spent several months investigating the rebellion and sentenced to death over 2,000
and to various terms of prison and exile over 6,000.

Economic Retreat, Political Crackdown

The Tenth Party Congress, which happened to be meeting at the time, proclaimed both further political control and economic liberalization. On the
one hand, the Workers' Opposition was condemned and factions in the
Communist Party were banned. This meant that even party members could
no longer join together to support diverging political causes. Party membership also grew more demanding: in 1921 roughly a quarter of all members were "purged," or expelled, from the party. Moreover, the party's power
increased further over the next months. In June, the courts lost the right to
try Communists without party sanction, and decrees in September 1921 and
November 1922 forbade state institutions to refer to higher party decisions
in their official minutes or to copy resolutions of the Central Committee or
of local party committees. On the other hand, in a belated realization of the
catastrophic state of the Soviet economy and following Lenin's lead, the
Congress proclaimed a New Economic Policy (NEP) allowing peasants to
trade their produce and small-scale entrepreneurs to set up businesses and
even to hire laborers. More important still, perhaps, the confiscatory grain
procurements were replaced by a defined, relatively modest tax in kind. In
May, partial denationalization of businesses began, in July tariffs were
reestablished for public transportation and postal-telegraph services, and in
October the autonomy of cooperatives was restored and state enterprises
were permitted a limited trade in goods at market prices. Even the labor
armies were disbanded in December. In time, these policies exerted a positive effect. By 1926, Russia's economic output had almost returned to its
1913 level.

   Society changed dramatically in Soviet Russia during the NEP. Educational opportunities expanded enormously. The number of junior high
schools more than tripled. So almost did schools for vocational training. The

Rabfak, a department for remedial education created in most institutions of higher learning to prepare young adult peasants and workers for entrance into accelerated programs of study in higher education, opened the door to rapid economic and social advancement for hundreds of thousands of lower-class people. The educational system in fact began to discriminate in their favor. After vocational training and a few years of factory work, the most talented "proletarians" were encouraged to earn university degrees, often with the help of an extensive support network, and then drawn up the ladder of power and status. Highly influential in developing social cohesion and the desired outlook among the upwardly mobile was the Communist Youth League, or Komsomol, which emerged in 1917–1918 as an urban voluntary association with over 1 million members, mostly peasants, but was co-opted by the Communist Party in 1919. The organization's purpose was to train future leaders, to inculcate Communist values, and to prepare activists for party membership. While members of the lower classes thus enjoyed un-precedented upward mobility, hundreds of thousands of former petty traders and shop clerks emerged as a significant economic force in the guise of "NEP-men." These were not industrialists or financiers but rather shop owners, retailers, restaurateurs, and other service-oriented business people. They grew relatively well-to-do, much to the consternation of Bolshevik activists and Civil War veterans. Finally, later in the decade the NEP became the "golden age of the peasantry." Millions and millions of peasants planted, harvested, and traded mostly freely. They also dominated the countryside, had little to do with the Communist authorities, and upheld their traditional ways.

In the meantime, Soviet society was rocked by two cataclysmic developments: peasant rebellion and famine. The two were tightly linked, since drastic grain seizures drove the peasantry to sow less and to rise up. The re-bellions, isolated and ill equipped, were doomed to fail. The Tambov uprising, which had slowly gathered force, posed the greatest challenge. A huge military force, deploying heavy artillery, armored trains, and poison gas, took several months starting in late June 1921 to quell it. Far more lethal than peasant partisans was the famine that erupted in summer 1921 in the Volga region and southern Ukraine. The government refused to allow either public activists or the Church to organize famine relief, and its own Central Commission on Famine Relief (*Pomgol*), created in July, apparently was relatively ineffectual. Despite the herculean efforts of foreign relief agencies, including the American Relief Administration, which at the peak of its activity was feeding nearly 11 million people a day, as many as 5 million lost their lives to hunger and disease by the time the famine ended in 1922. The foreign relief efforts ceased in 1923, after reports about Soviet exports of grain emerged.

The Communist authorities moreover used the famine as a pretext for a powerful assault against the church. As an independent institution, the

Russian Orthodox Church had no rivals, with over 200,000 parish and monastic clergy, 31,000 parishes, more than 75,000 churches and chapels, over 1,100 monasteries, some 37,000 primary schools, 57 seminaries and 4 university-level academies, and thousands of orphanages, old people's homes, and hospitals. Its powerful worldview, mostly diametrically opposed to that of the Bolsheviks, rendered the church a dire enemy for the Communist leadership. Lenin and many of his colleagues had ambivalent feelings and ideas about how to get rid of religion. Some believed that economic and social progress would simply make it go away. Others argued that religion was so deeply rooted in popular ignorance and superstition that more drastic measures were required. Already in January 1918, a decree on the "separation of church and state" had aimed to undermine ecclesiastical authority and to strip the church of its traditional privileges. During the Civil War, the government often violently persecuted individual clergy and laypeople but avoided a frontal assault on the church as a whole. Then in summer 1921, one slowly began. In July, a decree ordered the "liquidation" of saints' remains across the country. The procedure usually took the form of demonstratively proving that these relics were not the uncorrupted objects as alleged but decomposed body parts, straw, or bricks. The next month, the party excluded religious believers from its ranks.

The real assault, "storming the last citadel," began in early 1922. On February 23, the government decreed the confiscation of church valuables, including sacred vessels, allegedly in order to feed the starving. It was a win-win situation. The state would gain what they supposed to be a huge fund of wealth, religious leaders would probably balk at the procedure and therefore call upon themselves justified criticism and persecution, and the church would come out of the conflict weaker, divided, and poorer. Within days, Patriarch Tikhon protested the confiscation decree, declaring that sacred objects would be sacrificed but only voluntarily. Initial confiscation efforts, accompanied by a huge propaganda campaign, indeed encountered resistance. Lenin exulted. In mid-March, he urged a "decisive attack" on the church "with such brutality that it will not forget it for decades to come." The plan had three parts. First, a propaganda campaign dominating major dailies to discredit the church as allegedly greedy and hard-hearted. Second, efforts to split the church into "progressive," in practice calling themselves "Renovationist," and "reactionary" clergy. Finally, show trials leading to death sentences to terrorize religious believers and leaders. Numerous such trials took place, most famously in Moscow, beginning in late April, and in Petrograd, starting in June. The latter resulted in four death sentences and executions. Overall, in the course of 1922 and 1923, roughly 8,000 priests, monks, and nuns were killed by government forces.

The regime and its supporters cracked down on opposition political and cultural leaders as well.

Some of the Bolsheviks' opponents in the Menshevik and the Socialist Revolutionary (SR) party had hoped that they would be allowed to operate more freely after the end of the Civil War. This was not to be. Already in early January 1922, ten anarchist leaders were expelled from Russia. At the same time, measures were taken to banish Menshevik leaders from Moscow, Petrograd, and other major cities and to settle them in distant provincial towns. In early June 1922, Soviet Russia received its first criminal code— drafted specifically for the up-coming trial of thirty-four Right Socialist-Revolutionary leaders, which ran into August. For weeks a huge propaganda campaign had accused the defendants of counterrevolutionary activities. The trial lacked any normal judicial procedure, a mob hurling abuse at the defendants was admitted to the courtroom, European socialist defense attorneys were prevented from defending their clients, and death sentences were a foregone conclusion. Bowing to international pressure, the Communist leadership agreed to commute these sentences to lengthy terms of imprisonment, contingent on good behavior.

Despite their rhetoric of class division, the Bolshevik leaders realized fully that, just as they could not hope to win the Civil War without the knowledge and assistance of military professionals, they could not rebuild the country and turn it into a modernized socialist state simply by relying on industrial workers. New cadres of educated professionals were required, but they could not emerge overnight. Thus along with vigorous efforts to expand basic literacy and higher education, especially in technical fields and among the formerly underprivileged, the government developed a two-pronged approach to the surviving members of the educated elites. Those who agreed to cooperate and add their expertise to the Bolshevik vision of socialism would gain privileges, subsidies, jobs, and other signs of favor. All the main branches of intellectual activity would win such perks as state-sponsored unions and clubs, each with access to scarce material goods and services. For example, in June 1922, a House of Scholars opened in Moscow (similar clubs for architects, filmmakers, authors, and composers were set up in the 1930s). Yet beginning in August, not a single organization, union, or association could exist in Soviet Russia without the permission and close oversight of the People's Commissariat for Internal Affairs (NKVD). Moreover, from late August through December as many as 400 (but probably closer to 160) scholars, philosophers, and professors, mostly in the humanities, were placed on ships and banished from Russia, never to return. Finally, everything that was printed in the country, right down to playing cards and matchboxes, from June 1922 had to be inspected and approved by the new censorship agency called Glavlit (the first novel it banned was *We* by Evgenyi Zamiatin).

In 1918, the Bolshevik government had repudiated Imperial Russia's huge debts to foreign creditors, especially France and the United Kingdom. In late August, the authorities arrested some 200 French and British nationals in Moscow and killed the British naval attaché, Captain Francis Cromie, during an attack on the British Embassy; in the fall the Allies imposed a blockade on Russia and broke off all diplomatic relations with the new regime. Furthermore, they supported, albeit halfheartedly, various anti-Bolshevik forces in the Russian north, south, and the Far East with financial and military assistance. From the standpoint of the Whites they never did enough, yet this assistance fed into the Bolshevik mind-set of encirclement, a belief that the whole old capitalist world had risen in concert against the young Soviet power in order to strangle it "in its cradle." The demand of worldwide Communist parties to subordinate their decision making and interests to Moscow, imposed at the Second Congress of the Comintern (July 1920), further worried established "bourgeois" governments and gave rise to a "red scare" across the Western world. Consequently, France and Britain waited until 1924 to extend diplomatic recognition to Soviet Russia; the United States dragged its feet until 1933. Still, mutually beneficial commercial relations were re-established with the UK and the USA in 1921. Military cooperation with Germany commenced in 1922 as well.

The end of the Civil War also witnessed the consolidation of Moscow's control over most of the territories of the former Russian Empire, despite Communist declarations of support for the self-determination of ethnic minorities and for their right to secede from Soviet Russia. The Communist leaders, especially Lenin, repudiated Russian nationalism, however, and implemented policies aimed at cultivating national identities within Soviet society, including the promotion of minority languages and customs and the elevation of members of minority groups to positions of authority. In time, the country became, as one historian has argued, an "affirmative action empire," though only in cultural matters—not in setting economic policy or in evading political subordination to Moscow. In December 1919, a Ukrainian Soviet Socialist Republic (SSR) was founded and in July 1920 a Byelorussian SSR appeared, followed a month later by a Kirgiz Autonomous SSR. In November 1920 and February 1921, an Armenian SSR and a Georgian SSR were created. The Bolshevik leaders appealed to the peoples of all continents but especially to those under colonial domination urging them to rise up against their imperialist overlords, for example at the Congress of Peoples of the East held in Baku in September 1920. For similar reasons, a Communist University of National Minorities opened in September 1922 in Petrograd. Of all the territories of the former Russian Empire, only Finland,

Poland, the Baltic provinces, most of Bessarabia, and small parts of Ukraine and Byelorussia did not join Soviet Russia. Nearly all, except Finland and most of Poland, were obliged to do so during and after World War II.

Struggle for Power

Despite a stroke suffered in May 1922, Lenin, always the undisputed leader, continued to try to control political events. Yet mastery gradually slipped from his hands and fell into those of Stalin, Kamenev, and Zinoviev. Fear of Trotsky, in whom everyone saw a potential Napoleon, drew them together. Stalin brilliantly feigned modesty and acted like a team player. So, in April 1922 his colleagues elected him general secretary of the Central Committee. This role, added to his positions on the Politburo and the Orgburo, enabled him to control the exponentially multiplying patronage jobs throughout the party bureaucracy. When the crunch came, the party apparatus would side with him. Stalin was also the commissar for nationalities. In August 1922, Lenin instructed him to draw up plans to clarify relations between the RSFSR and the various national states and territories. Stalin proposed subordinating them to it. Lenin favored instead a supranational entity standing above all the national republics and making them co-equal, albeit in a purely formal sense, including the RSFSR. Stalin backed down and laid the groundwork for the new state, the Union of Soviet Socialist Republics, which came into existence on December 30, 1922. This was Lenin's last victory. On December 15 he suffered another stroke. A week or so later, with his right arm and leg paralyzed, he began to dictate letters and an article rejecting Stalin's nationalities policies, character, and style of leadership. The letters, known to posterity as Lenin's "Testament," urged the party leadership to remove Stalin as secretary-general of the Central Committee. Yet Lenin did not single out a worthy successor; he damned each one in turn. Thus, the contenders all agreed to keep the letters secret. The rest of the decade witnessed a contest to see which of them would come out on top. But for now the Revolution was over.

CHAPTER 1
War and Social Unrest

Historians have discussed the role of World War I in bringing about the Russian Revolution. Some claim that Russian society was so highly polarized that major political and social upheaval was unavoidable anyway. Others argue that by sparking patriotic sentiment the war actually delayed the inevitable. Such scholars point to evidence like Document 1 as proof of an unbridgeable gulf between social classes, groups, and milieus. Still others, often called optimists, believe that Russia was progressing relatively well and was on the eve of World War I a "member of the European family," given its improved civil rights record, establishment of constitutional government, cultural achievements, and economic development. For these scholars, the war strained Russia's social institutions and resources and plunged the country into severe political distress.

The Romanov dynasty celebrated its 300th anniversary in 1913 amid grand pomp and circumstance. It was a joyous time for Tsar Nicholas II and his immediate relations. The educated elites were largely excluded from the festivities, however, and most of them, even many conservatives, had lost faith in the monarch and in the political system, which seemed to most observers inextricably linked to a security police apparatus run amok and other scandalous and outrageous phenomena. Among these were the obvious ascendancy of Grigorii Rasputin at court, the emperor's high-handed attitude toward the representative institutions, ceaseless government interference in the activities of trade unions and publishers, and the gunning down by government forces of some 200 striking workers in the Lena Goldfields in April 1912. It certainly did not help that the interior minister, Aleksandr Makarov, an "honest and decent" lawyer, declared in the Duma in regard to the massacre that in all such cases the troops have "no choice but to fire. That is how it has always been and will be in the future."

Ironically, Russia was less consistently repressive than it seemed or than contemporaries believed it to be. The most prominent revolutionary leaders

1

The Russian Empire, ca. 1914.

could indeed scarcely set foot inside the country, yet a huge underground reservoir of lesser organizers, agitators, and activists managed to operate more or less with impunity. One such person was Nikolai Sukhanov. Although wanted by the police for various subversive activities, he found employment throughout World War I in a minor department in the bureaucracy under his true name, Himmer, while publishing articles using his pseudonym in Maxim Gorky's antiwar journal *Letopis,* which the government allowed to appear from late 1915 onward.

It was a fine line to tread for a government that wished to encourage further development of the economy while thwarting an expansion of political and social opposition movements. Many senior officials in charge of homeland security recognized the precariousness of domestic tranquility under such circumstances. In fact, some clearly spelled out the danger to the Russian state of becoming entangled in a major European war, as Document 2 indicates. Such a war, unavoidably, would exert a powerful strain on social relations and political institutions. Tensions indeed flared as millions of soldiers were killed, wounded, or taken prisoner; the rate of inflation spiraled upward; food and fuel periodically grew scarce; and the Russian army retreated unrelentingly on the battlefield. Documents 3, 4, and 5 reflect popular reactions to these unwelcome conditions.

Vladimir Lenin, the Bolshevik leader who had been living abroad since 1906, viewed World War I as a sign of the bankruptcy of the European state

Grigorii Rasputin and High Society Ladies, Imperial Palace at Tsarskoe Selo. *Liberty's Victorious Conflict: A Photographic History of the World War* (Chicago: The Magazine Circulation Co., Inc., 1918), 51. It has been argued that Rasputin's proximity to the Imperial Court contributed to undermining the prestige and legitimacy of the Russian monarchy.[1]

and economic system (Document 6). The war, he argued, was an imperialist conflict waged by rapacious powers seeking to expand their global influence. As such, the oppressed classes and their defenders should offer no support for the conflict, and instead should seek by revolutionary means both to end it and to overthrow the capitalist order. The experience of the government ministers, as exemplified in Document 7, suggested on the contrary that the state and the military, far from serving the interests of capital, were hopelessly divided among themselves. Indeed, the military commanders, who arrogated to themselves nearly absolute power in the huge swath of territory along the front lines, seemed to be acting entirely without regard to state, society, or economy. Yet as Document 8 suggests, the senior commanders at the military's General Headquarters were neither entirely competent nor in firm control of the situation. Finally, the emperor and empress (see Document 9) seemed to be guided more by petty personal considerations and intrigues than concern for winning the war or the higher interests of state.

By fall 1916, Russia's social fabric had begun to unravel, as an economic crisis began to grip the country. Document 10, for example, reflects the harsh reality most people faced of higher prices, stagnant wages, foodstuffs disappearing from stores, and a general demoralization and foreboding regarding the coming winter. Contemporary security police reports submitted

1. Anna Vyrubova (1884–1964), a lady-in-waiting and confidante of Empress Alexandra, is fifth from the left, looking upward.

Russia in World War I.

for Petrograd in October 1916 warned of impending unrest, possible hunger riots, and even the danger of revolution.

Activist elites sought to forestall the worst outcomes and to bring about national salvation. In early November, Pavel Miliukov, the respected liberal parliamentarian, denounced the head of the government from the rostrum of the State Duma in an act (Document 11) that he later considered the starting point of the revolution. A month later, a rich nobleman and a right-wing Duma deputy carried out a violent act, described in Document 12, that some observers viewed as another step toward revolution: the murder of Grigorii Rasputin. By eliminating an object of almost universal derision and contempt, the perpetrators of this murder hoped to stop the rapid decline of the monarchy's prestige. It was too late.

1. Anonymous Letter by a Soldier, December 22, 1913
[51, pp. 79–80]

On December 15, 1913, the official newspaper of the Russian army, Russkii invalid, *published an official announcement that the scheduled discharge into the reserves of active-duty soldiers would be delayed for 6 months, until new recruits could be called up, so as not to undermine the military's battle readiness, given "the intensive increase in the size of western European military forces."* Russkoe chtenie, *a right-wing publication edited by General Dmitrii Dubenskii, reprinted the announcement, noting that the measure was "very important and very timely" and would be greatly appreciated by all of Russia, including its lower classes and soldiers. A flood of letters to the contrary obliged him to warn the defense minister of profound discontent within the military ranks. One such letter is excerpted below.*

Dear editor, in November your newspaper—I don't remember which issue—published an article about postponing the discharge of lower-rank servicemen who are subject to discharge into the reserves this year. You write there that not a single ordinary soldier will be offended that he will have to serve a few extra months for the glory of the Russian army. [. . .] Whoever wrote this article was completely unfamiliar with the views of the lower ranks; therefore, *as a member of the lower ranks on active duty, I will express my view.*[2]

First of all, I will say that *day after day, since I entered military service, I have been cursing the day I was born.* Having entered military service, I found villainy, theft, and injustice everywhere. As soon as I arrived in the unit, *they tried to beat all human feelings out of me,* every superior scolds and punishes me without sorting out whether I am right or not, but just because he has a right to. I also see that what I have endured myself is less than what my comrades have endured. Now think for yourself *what can be expected from a soldier who is used to hating every superior as his worst enemy, whom he would pay back a hundred times at the earliest convenience.* You are writing that adding to the service term would increase the size of the army and give it strength and power. *I say this will bring the same result as the year 1905, which will sooner or later come back, and then the Russian peasant will sweep like dust all the scum that live off his sweat and blood,* violate him, consider him to be their slave, which god[3] created for their needs. *The very first war, the very first*

2. All italics in the text appear in the original.
3. Soviet publications usually began the word *God* with a lowercase letter, whatever the author's intentions.

disturbance inside the state, and the Russian lower-rank serviceman will prove that he also has human rights and feelings, and then woe to all the scum that robs and torments the Russian peasant. I know that you are thinking that the Russian peasant is stupid enough not to ever do this for fear of the punishments of hell, which priests use to frighten him. They do so in vain. *At the present time, every peasant views priests as Pharisees and views the martyrs who have struggled for his freedom as the followers of Christ* who laid down his life for the truth, while those peasants who become soldiers, even the strongest believers, will have no faith left in about a year: religious oppression, coerced church attendance, and other such escapades of their superiors will extinguish it. [. . .]

[. . .] as in Paris during the St. Bartholomew's Day Massacre when no Huguenots were left,[4] in Holy Rus there will remain none of the scum that lives off the sweat and blood of the Russian peasant, whose fathers, grandfathers, and great grandfathers also lived off the sweat and blood of the Russian peasant. [. . .]

Forgive that I write completely illiterately, but you will nevertheless read it, and if not, then you are more illiterate than any peasant, even though you deem yourselves literate! I will also remind you that the peasant now understands what is a lie and what is truth, and your newspaper circulates only in the army where people have no choice but to read such junk. Once again I am telling you that if the soldiers got their hands on whoever increased their term of service, they would do to him what the Drevlians did to Igor.[5]

2. P. N. Durnovo Memorandum to Nicholas II, February 1914   [24, pp. 3–23]

Born in 1842 to a landless old noble family, Pyotr Nikolaevich Durnovo headed the Police Department from 1884 to 1893. Appointed minister of the interior in October 1905, he almost single-handedly pulled Russia back from the brink of social collapse, largely by demanding harsh repression from local officials. "Take the most energetic measures in struggling against the

---

4. The author is referring to the massacre of Huguenots, during the French Wars of Religion, by Catholic mobs beginning on August 24, 1572 (the feast of Bartholomew the Apostle). The violence spread throughout the country, leaving tens of thousands of Protestants dead.

5. Prince Igor of Kiev was killed by the East-Slavic Drevlians in 945 when he attempted to collect tribute from them.

revolutionary movement," ignoring all obstacles he wrote to Russia's governors. "Remember! I will take full responsibility upon myself [for your actions]." Appointed to the State Council, Russia's upper parliamentary chamber, in 1906, he led the rightist group from 1908 until 1915, when he died. Not opposed to democracy in principle, he believed that the vast majority of Russians, including most of the educated elites, were far from prepared to govern themselves. He was deeply pessimistic about human nature in general and acutely aware of the immense threats to the existing political order in Russia. Durnovo's memorandum called for extreme caution in the face of a possible war with Germany, arguing that its impact on the empire could be devastating. Although delivered to Nicholas II in February 1914, it achieved no apparent effect. It was published by the Bolsheviks in 1922.

The central factor of the period of world history through which we are now passing is the rivalry between England and Germany. This rivalry must inevitably lead to an armed struggle between them, the issue of which will, in all probability, prove fatal to the vanquished side. The interests of these two powers are far too incompatible, and their simultaneous existence as world powers will sooner or later prove impossible. [. . .]

The Russo-Japanese War radically changed the relations among the great powers and brought England out of her isolation. As we know, all through the Russo-Japanese War, England and America observed benevolent neutrality toward Japan, while we enjoyed a similar benevolent neutrality from France and Germany. Here, it would seem, should have been the inception of the most natural political combination for us. But after the war, our diplomacy faced abruptly about and definitely entered upon the road toward rapprochement with England. France was drawn into the orbit of British policy; there was formed a group of powers of the Triple Entente, with England playing the dominant part; and a clash, sooner or later, with the powers grouping themselves around Germany became inevitable. [. . .]

Are we prepared for so stubborn a war as the future war of the European nations will undoubtedly become? This question we must answer, without evasion, in the negative. That much has been done for our defense since the Japanese war, I am the last person to deny, but even so, it is quite inadequate considering the unprecedented scale on which a future war will inevitably be fought. [. . .]

[. . .] It should not be forgotten that Russia and Germany are the representatives of the conservative principle in the civilized world, as opposed to the democratic principle, incarnated in England and, to an infinitely lesser degree, in France. Strange as it may seem, England, monarchist and conservative to the marrow at home, has in her foreign relations always acted as the protector of the most demagogical tendencies, invariably encouraging all popular movements aiming at the weakening of the monarchical principle.

From this point of view, a struggle between Germany and Russia, regardless of its issue, is profoundly undesirable to both sides, as undoubtedly involving the weakening of the conservative principle in the world, of which the above-named two great powers are the only reliable bulwarks. More than that, one must realize that under the exceptional conditions that exist, a general European war is mortally dangerous both for Russia and Germany, no matter who wins. It is our firm conviction, based upon a long and careful study of all contemporary subversive tendencies, that there must inevitably break out in the defeated country a social revolution which, by the very nature of things, will spread to the country of the victor.

During the many years of peaceable neighborly existence, the two countries have become united by many ties, and a social upheaval in one is bound to affect the other. [. . .]

The peasant dreams of obtaining a gratuitous share of somebody else's land; the workman, of getting hold of the entire capital and profits of the manufacturer. Beyond this, they have no aspirations. If these slogans are scattered far and wide among the populace, and the Government permits agitation along these lines, Russia will be flung into anarchy, such as she suffered in the ever-memorable period of troubles in 1905–1906. War with Germany would create exceptionally favorable conditions for such agitation. As already stated, this war is pregnant with enormous difficulties for us, and cannot turn out to be a mere triumphal march to Berlin. Both military disasters —partial ones, let us hope—and all kinds of shortcomings in our supply are inevitable. In the excessive nervousness and spirit of opposition of our society, these events will be given an exaggerated importance, and all the blame will be laid on the Government. [. . .]

If the war ends in victory, the putting down of the Socialist movement will not offer any insurmountable obstacles. There will be agrarian troubles, as a result of agitation for compensating the soldiers with additional land allotments; there will be labor troubles during the transition from the probably increased wages of wartime to normal schedules; and this, it is to be hoped, will be all, so long as the wave of the German social revolution has not reached us. But in the event of defeat, the possibility of which in a struggle with a foe like Germany cannot be overlooked, social revolution in its most extreme form is inevitable.

As has already been said, the trouble will start with the blaming of the Government for all disasters. In the legislative institutions a bitter campaign against the Government will begin, followed by revolutionary agitations throughout the country, with Socialist slogans, capable of arousing and rallying the masses, beginning with the division of the land and succeeded by a division of all valuables and property. The defeated army, having lost its most dependable men, and carried away by the tide of primitive peasant desire for land, will find itself too demoralized to serve as a bulwark of law and order. The legislative institutions and the intellectual opposition parties, lacking real authority in the eyes of the people, will be powerless to stem the popular tide, aroused by themselves, and Russia will be flung into hopeless anarchy, the issue of which cannot be foreseen. [. . .]

3. Antiwar Appeal of Soldiers of the 437th Chernigov Infantry Brigade, February 1915   [68, p. 71]

As in the rest of Europe, the use of corporal punishment as a judicial penalty in Russia had been gradually restricted. The lash had been abolished in 1863 and replaced by the use of birch rods, a bundle of leafless sticks. This method of judicial punishment was abolished in 1904 for all segments of the population except prisoners, though it remained broadly used in peasant culture and in the military. In November 1914, however, the commander of the southwestern front, General N. I. Ivanov, complained that no adequate methods of punishment were available to stem the huge tide of deserters from military service. His request for the authority to reintroduce corporal punishment, though rejected at the time, was apparently granted on an ad hoc basis thanks to a law of December 29, 1914, which allowed the supreme commander of the Russian armies to impose harsher punishments as he saw fit.

Comrade Soldiers!

On orders from the Supreme Commander, henceforth the vilest and most inhumane type of punishment will be applied to you, peasant and worker folk—birch rods. The whip drove us here, tore us away from our beloved fields, from our wives and children, so that two or three weeks later another shipment of human flesh could be sent to face the German bullets. They want to beat a spirit of obedience and patriotism in you by means of the rods. What does the Russian government care about the grief, the insults, the dignity of the Russian people?! Following orders, the police used to flog Russian peasants seeking land and freedom. Now rods are used to punish the Russian soldier wordlessly giving his life for a cause that is not his own, a cause he was dragged into by the Russian autocracy and the government of officials and landlords.

Soldiers, you are the people's offspring! Who among you would allow yourself or your comrade to be insulted by a disgraceful punishment! Let those who live off the people's tears and woes try and forge new chains and new insults for you. You will respond to them as the Russian peasants and workers responded in the glorious days of the 1905 revolution: "We will not take it!"

Enough of tormenting us and crippling Russia! We refuse to be cannon fodder anymore! We reject the war launched by the Russian government!

Long live the friendship of all peoples!

Land and freedom to the Russian people!

Long live free Russia!

Long live revolution!

United Group of Social-Democrats and Socialist-Revolutionaries

4. A Textile-Workers Strike in Kostroma, June 1915
[31, pp. 8, 12]

During World War I, as economic conditions gradually worsened, an empirewide strike movement gathered steam. An important step, though by no means the first, in this movement was the textile-worker strike in Kostroma some 230 miles north of Moscow. It began with purely economic demands on June 2. The document below shows how the factory administration responded to those demands. By the next day all 6,000 employees of the Great Kostroma Flax Factory—who were largely unskilled, young, of peasant origin, and often female—had laid down their tools. That day, the governor-general threatened to deploy military force should the strike continue, given the factory's military contracts. By June 5th, other factories had joined the walkout, and workers began to construct defensive barricades. Police and soldiers undertook arrests and fired on strikers, killing or gravely wounding twelve workers (five of them girls or young women), including a 10-year-old and three younger than 17. Over the next several days, factories throughout the region joined the protest. Gradually it wound down and dissipated. Historians have noted that "subsistence riots," usually spearheaded by women, were common during both the French Revolution and World War I in Russia. Also, since most workers in Russia retained strong ties to the countryside, this unrest was probably strongly influenced by the Russian peasant custom of banding together to resist outside interference.

Announcement of the administration to the workers of the Great Kostroma Flax Factory Company, June 2, 1915. [. . .]

1) In February and May without any requests by workers, a pay raise was issued at the company's factory totaling 25%. There will be no further raises.

2) The factory at this time is working almost entirely for the army, and therefore work stoppage at the factory would cause a delay in supplying the army with munitions and would benefit our enemies.

Moreover, because of the military contracts, the government issued an exemption to the conscripts working at the factory. In the event of a stoppage, this waiver will be lost.

The menacing times our fatherland is enduring demand intense work and complete calm within the country.

This is not the time to strike—this is the time to work.

Proclamation of Kostroma women workers to soldiers, June 1915.

To a Russian soldier from a Russian woman.

Soldiers! We are asking you for help. Defend us. Our fathers, sons, and husbands were taken and sent to war, while we, defenseless and unarmed, are being shot at by healthy well-fed police guards. There is nobody to defend us. You defend us!

They say: work calmly, but we are hungry and we cannot work. We asked but were not heard; we began to demand, and they shot at us. They say there is no bread. Where is it then? Or is it only for the Germans that the Russian land produces?[6]

Soldiers!

What are we to do? Teach us, help us! We have no relatives.

Women workers

5. Excerpts from Soldiers' Letters, Intercepted by Censors, 1915–1917   [9, pp. 126–7, 129, 131–2, 136, 142–3]

Like all the belligerent societies, Russia's subjects and rulers imagined the war would end quickly and victoriously. Yet, the Russian soldiers were sent poorly clothed, armed, trained, and commanded against a far superior foe. The shell shortage of spring 1915, largely solved by summer, nevertheless provoked a political and military crisis. Military defeats engendered discontent among the soldiery, which mirrored discontent within the broader population. These sentiments did not go unnoticed by government censors. For decades, postal workers had secretly intercepted private correspondence in order to combat

6. During the Russian retreat from Latvia and Poland in early 1915, the army was forced to abandon millions of pounds of grain to the Germans.

revolutionary activists; this work expanded during the war as a means to ascertain the "mood" of soldiers and civilians. Excerpts from some intercepted letters are provided below. They were sometimes copied and then sent to their destination or, rarely, confiscated. Government censors prepared official summaries of such letters but during the war often downplayed the level of discontent they revealed, so as not to alarm senior officials.

A. Novikov to A. I. Ivanova, Moscow

The elation that the troops felt earlier is no more. [. . .]

In Lvov, before the eyes of 28 thousand soldiers, five people were flogged for leaving their courtyard without permission to buy white bread.

Anon. to A. P. Nechaeva, Kharkov, July 15, 1915

Cholera is ravaging the entire area. Every day a hundred people are brought from the front; the nearby inhabitants are also sick. The death rate is astronomical.

[. . .] I will describe to you the conditions and the treatment of the sick: all of them lie on straw, without mattresses or pillows. There is no disinfection; those who die are buried nearby, behind the huts of the Galicians. There are two doctors and four physicians for 500 sick people. The medical personnel are completely exhausted. Several nurses grew sick from exhaustion and died.

The sick are not isolated; the contagion is spreading. [. . .]

Efim D. Chernyshev, Belostok, to Aleksandr A. Belikov, Village of Druzhkovka, Factory of the Toretskii Company

We are now so consumed with work day and night that there is no time to look up at the sky, but we are gradually retreating. We have retreated from Lomzha to Belostok. Dear brother, if you could only see what is going on here! The military transports have stretched over a hundred *versts,*[7] but most of the people traveling are civilians leaving their homes and going not knowing where, giving themselves up to the mercy of fate. It is a sorry sight to look at: they are driving along cows and pigs, taking whatever they can and leaving the rest for somebody else. You can see children crying, and in some instances parents lose their children, and everywhere you hear the weeping and wailing of the poor Poles, because they are being moved out, and their grain and houses are being burned, so as to leave nothing to the Germans.

---

7. A *verst* was equal to one kilometer, or 0.6 miles.

Anon. to N. V. Pudulova, Moscow
[. . .] We are still experiencing shortages of shells and rifle bullets. We are all in a bad mood now: it is very unpleasant that the enemy is driving us back. It was fun and good when we were chasing them. We all appreciate that you all, the civilian population, are trying to save Russia and relieve the army, but alas, our superiors are acting in the exact opposite way.

Anon. to S. V. Sukharev, Moscow, November 2, 1916
[. . .] There is some news—the Plastun [Cossack] regiment refused to go on the offensive. They are saying: "We are not going without artillery." I don't know what will happen to them. I am writing about it, but if they open the letter, it won't reach you.

Mikhail Vosvizik to Kuz'ma Vosvizik, Village of Kamenets
Tell our relatives and friends to fear military service like fire, because there is neither good footwear, nor clothing, nor food. They don't give us even meat and instead they give us rotten fish and mushrooms with worms. I buy a few things myself, because by sticking to the rations you can die quickly.

Anon. to Novikova, Romanovka, Suburb of Odessa
I am alive, thank god, and the devils haven't taken me. Some people are fortunate—they get wounded after two days on the front line. But here it is as if the bullets can't strike you. I am so tired of this dog's life.

Kh. Grishin to Agaf'ia M. Grishina, Village of Beguny
[. . .] Others think war is just as inevitable as death is inevitable, but I think this is not so, since death is the natural end of existence and creatures, whereas war is an artificial extermination of everything in general and not just of people. I am writing this to you, my dear, so that you will have a correct understanding of war and not think that war is sent by god. War is the result of cunning people's minds and actions, who hold power and, either because they do not know how to use this power properly or for reasons of their own selfish gain, direct matters in such a way that war flares up.

6. V. I. Lenin,[8] *Imperialism, the Highest Stage of Capitalism: A Popular Outline*   [44, vol. 22, pp. 298–304]

Early on Lenin became a confirmed and passionate proponent of revolutionary Marxism with its apocalyptic vision of an impending capitalist collapse and global revolutionary transformation. By the 1900s, Marx's vision of the spiraling immizeration of industrial workers, the narrowing of the propertied classes, and an unavoidable "proletarian revolution" had failed to materialize. Labor unions, social legislation, and huge economic expansion had resulted in higher wages and better working conditions, as well as the dynamic growth of the middle class in most European societies. Consequently, revisionist theories had emerged arguing that socialism could be achieved by evolution. Revolutionary Marxism was rapidly losing adherents. Vladimir Lenin's Imperialism, the Highest Stage of Capitalism *(written in 1916; first published in April 1917 in Petrograd), aimed to revitalize that cause by seeking to demonstrate that the economic and social position of the laboring and middle classes in capitalist societies had improved only at the expense of exploited colonies in the developing world. The day of reckoning—the proletarian revolution—was still imminent, except that its main agents would be not only factory workers in the most advanced countries but also the "thousand million people" in Europe's colonies.*

Chapter X. The Place of Imperialism in History

We have seen that in its economic essence imperialism is monopoly capitalism. This in itself determines its place in history, for monopoly that grows out of the soil of free competition, and precisely out of free competition, is the transition from the capitalist system to a higher socio-economic order. We must take special note of the four principal types of monopoly, or principal

---

8. Vladimir Il'ich Lenin (1870–1924), whose older brother was hanged for plotting to kill the Tsar in 1887, was expelled from the University of Kazan in 1887 for political activity. He passed the law exam as an external student in 1891 at the University of St. Petersburg and was admitted to the bar. He practiced law for two years in Samara and then devoted the rest of his life to revolutionary affairs. After three years in Siberian exile, in 1900 he emigrated to Europe where he cofounded the Social Democratic newspaper *Iskra* and created the breakaway fraction of Bolsheviks. Aside from the period 1906–1907, he lived abroad until 1917. Throughout these years, Lenin devoted most of his energy to study, writing, and political organizing. Lenin's version of Marxism is often considered unorthodox, because from 1901 on, he strongly emphasized that professional revolutionaries coordinate the activities of rebellious workers, and in 1917 argued that Russia should pass directly to the "socialist phase" of revolution without passing first through the predicted "bourgeois phase."

manifestations of monopoly capitalism, which are characteristic of the epoch we are examining.

Firstly, monopoly arose out of the concentration of production at a very high stage. This refers to the monopolist capitalist associations, cartels, syndicates, and trusts. We have seen the important part these play in present-day economic life. At the beginning of the twentieth century, monopolies had acquired complete supremacy in the advanced countries, and although the first steps towards the formation of the cartels were taken by countries enjoying the protection of high tariffs (Germany, America), Great Britain, with her system of free trade, revealed the same basic phenomenon, only a little later, namely, the birth of monopoly out of the concentration of production.

Secondly, monopolies have stimulated the seizure of the most important sources of raw materials, especially for the basic and most highly cartelized industries in capitalist society: the coal and iron industries. The monopoly of the most important sources of raw materials has enormously increased the power of big capital and has sharpened the antagonism between cartelized and non-cartelized industry.

Thirdly, monopoly has sprung from the banks. The banks have developed from modest middleman enterprises into the monopolists of finance capital. Some three to five of the biggest banks in each of the foremost capitalist countries have achieved the "personal link-up" between industrial and bank capital, and have concentrated in their hands the control of thousands upon thousands of millions which form the greater part of the capital and income of entire countries. A financial oligarchy, which throws a close network of dependence relationships over all the economic and political institutions of present-day bourgeois society without exception—such is the most striking manifestation of this monopoly.

Fourthly, monopoly has grown out of colonial policy. To the numerous "old" motives of colonial policy, finance capital has added the struggle for the sources of raw materials, for the export of capital, for spheres of influence, i.e., for spheres for profitable deals, concessions, monopoly profits, and so on, economic territory in general. When the colonies of the European powers, for instance, comprised only one-tenth of the territory of Africa (as was the case in 1876), colonial policy was able to develop—by methods other than those of monopoly—by the "free grabbing" of territories, so to speak. But when nine-tenths of Africa had been seized (by 1900), when the whole world had been divided up, there was inevitably ushered in the era of monopoly possession of colonies and, consequently, of particularly intense struggle for the division and the redivision of the world.

The extent to which monopolist capital has intensified all the contradictions of capitalism is generally known. It is sufficient to mention the high cost of living and the tyranny of the cartels. This intensification of contradictions constitutes the most powerful driving force of the transitional period of history, which began from the time of the final victory of world finance capital.

Monopolies, oligarchy, the striving for domination and not for freedom, the exploitation of an increasing number of small or weak nations by a handful of the richest or most powerful nations—all these have given birth to those distinctive characteristics of imperialism which compel us to define it as parasitic or decaying capitalism. [. . .]

The receipt of high monopoly profits by the capitalists in one of the numerous branches of industry, in one of the numerous countries, etc., makes it economically possible for them to bribe certain sections of the workers, and for a time a fairly considerable minority of them, and win them to the side of the bourgeoisie of a given industry or given nation against all the others. The intensification of antagonisms between imperialist nations for the division of the world increases this urge. [. . .]

From all that has been said in this book on the economic essence of imperialism, it follows that we must define it as capitalism in transition, or, more precisely, as moribund capitalism. [. . .]

7. Notes from Meetings of the Council of Ministers
[22, pp. 233–7]

From the outset of World War I, an uncle of Nicholas II, Grand Duke Nikolai Nikolaevich, served as supreme commander, a symbolic rather than effective post. In the face of military reversals in 1914 and 1915, especially the evacuation of Warsaw in July 1915, the Tsar resolved personally to replace his uncle at General Headquarters in Mogilev. Nearly all the ministers objected to this plan, arguing that the Tsar should avoid associating himself with potential further defeats. The following is an excerpt from a discussion of this issue in the Council of Ministers, which turned into a passionate confrontation between key ministers and the archconservative Chairman of the Council Ivan Goremykin (1839–1917). The excerpt below is taken from extremely detailed notes kept by Arkadii Nikolaevich Iakhontov (1876–1938), who acted as the council's secretary in 1914–1916.

August 21, 1915

[. . .] [Naval Minister Ivan] Grigorovich: We know that the Emperor is leaving [to assume command of the army]. The situation is worsening. We must present a written report to His Imperial Majesty presenting our opinions about the hopelessness [of the situation], the danger to the dynasty, etc.

Chairman [Ivan Goremykin]: His Imperial Majesty will announce his will at General Headquarters.

Grigorovich: We must speak up about the Grand Duke [Nikolai] and urge a postponement [of the emperor's decision].

[Foreign Minister Sergei] Sazonov: We cannot govern the country.[9] We are powerless to serve, and we cause harm.

Chairman: You want [to give] an ultimatum to the Tsar?

Sazonov: It is not our place to give ultimatums, but supplications. Let us open the Tsar's eyes to the fact that we cannot work. We must write. To warn about the danger and the hopelessness of the situation.

[Interior Minister Nikolai] Shcherbatov: Neither the army, nor the cities, nor the zemstvos,[10] nor the merchants, nor the nobility stand behind the government, so it cannot stand. We are like Don Quixote. [. . .]

Chairman: [. . .] If His Majesty desires to take the risk, it is not up to us to tell him what to do. [. . .]

Chairman: I believe that leftists are using the name of the Grand Duke [Nikolai Nikolaevich] to discredit the Sovereign Emperor.

[Chief Procurator of the Holy Synod Aleksandr] Samarin: The Moscow Duma is not leftist, but everyone is unanimous.

Shcherbatov: I agree. The general tone: lethal fear of all of the Russian public about the decree [on assuming Supreme] Command. [. . .]

Chairman: Let us report to the Sovereign Emperor. He is 47 years old, anointed by God, and embodies Russia. We must obey such a man whatever the consequences. And the will of God will determine the rest.

Shcherbatov: Not a single military commander or commander of a ship would place [his forces] at risk.

Chairman: But what if he, the Supreme Leader, demands it?

[War Minister Aleksei] Polivanov: They will not allow him on the ship.

Sazonov: We have to tell his Imperial Majesty: you are taking yourself to perdition and we cannot help you. Find others to help you. [. . .]

Chairman: The essence of this conversation is that I have an archaic viewpoint. Be so utterly kind: report to His Imperial Majesty that I should be removed. [. . .]

Shcherbatov: I and Samarin are provincial marshals of the nobility.[11] We are not leftist. But I cannot understand how the Sovereign Emperor and the Government are at odds with all of the sensible elements in the country.

---

9. At previous meetings, the ministers lamented the direct administrative control being exercised by the military authorities over a huge swath of territory parallel to the front lines.

10. The *zemstvos*, institutions of rural self-government at the provincial and district level, were mostly dominated by educated elites.

11. Marshals of the nobility were representatives of Russia's nobility, elected every three

Chairman: I do not have the right to tell the Sovereign Emperor: I cannot serve when His Imperial Majesty is in danger.

Shcherbatov: How can one serve, while being aware that it is impossible to serve once the supreme command is changed. Let him select others.

Sazonov: The Tsar is not God; he can make mistakes.

Chairman: But we have no right to leave him. [. . .]

Samarin: I love the Tsar, but I also love Russia. If the Tsar's actions will harm Russia, we cannot go along with him.

Chairman: To resign or disobey is unpatriotic (perhaps my view is archaic, but I cannot change it).

Samarin: Your remarks yesterday suggested a painful sentiment that the Tsar has toward the Grand Duke—a sentiment of competition.

Sazonov: I saw on the Tsar's face how he became agitated by your words about the triumph of the Grand Duke and about the opposition [to the Tsar's decision] of all those who support the Grand Duke.

Chairman: Report that I am unfit.

Shcherbatov: More broadly, I consider myself unfit too: we have been unable for three weeks to dissuade the Tsar.

[State Controller Peter] Kharitonov: If the Tsar wills us not to abandon Russia then we must obey, but if the will [of the Tsar] is tantamount to harming Russia then we must go: I serve both the Tsar and Russia.

Chairman: These two notions are inseparable.

Kharitonov: I cannot subscribe to what in my view is Russia's perdition.

Sazonov: We can sacrifice everything for the Tsar, but not our conscience.

Samarin: The Tsar needs the service of conscious people, not the slavish carrying out of orders.

Chairman: Those are not my words. I believe that the opinion of the Tsar is equal to the opinion of Russia and that we must obey.

Sazonov: The words of the Tsar are not Gospel. His popularity and authority have been shaken.

Chairman: I think we have to take the Tsar as Gospel.

Sazonov. Then all that is left is to drown ourselves. [. . .]

---

years by assemblies of deputies at both the district and provincial level. This institution was founded by Catherine II in 1766.

8. Description of General Headquarters, March 1916
[43, pp. 648–50]

A left-leaning activist who later supported the Bolshevik regime, Mikhail Konstantinovich Lemke (1872–1923) wrote histories of Russian radical and revolutionary movements of the 20th century. Assigned to a senior clerical position at General Headquarters in September 1915, Lemke found himself in a unique position to observe top-level military planning and the people in charge of it. He kept a minutely detailed diary of all that he observed, despite the risk this posed for a man of German ancestry. He was dismissed from this position in July 1916 as "politically unreliable." In the excerpt below Lemke describes the sense of resigned fatalism that was beginning to set in at General Headquarters.

[. . .] Alekseev[12] entered, greeted me, and sat down asking us to continue our conversation, adding that he had come because there was too much smoke in his office from the stove.

[. . .] "You are probably not too much of a believer?" he asked me.

"He is simply an atheist," laughed Pustovoitenko,[13] thus permitting me not to answer, which would have taken our conversation in a direction of no interest to me.

"Personally, I am happy that I believe and believe deeply in God and that it is in God that I believe and not in some blind and impersonal fate" [Alekseev replied]. "You see, I know that we will lose the war, that we cannot possibly win it, but do you think this in any way lessens the zeal with which I am fulfilling my duty? Not at all, because the country must experience all of the bitterness of its fall and then rise up with the assistance of the hand of God, in order for the people's soul to shine forth in all its splendor. . . ."

"And do you entertain the possibility of a more favorable way out of this war for Russia," [inquired Lemke], "especially with the help of the allies, who need to save us for their own good?"

"No, the allies do not need to save us; they only need to save themselves and destroy Germany. Do you think I trust them in the slightest? Who can

---

12. Mikhail Vasilievich Alekseev (1857–1918), a career army officer who served in senior posts during both the Russo-Japanese War and World War I, was appointed chief of staff of General Headquarters when Nicholas II assumed supreme command in Mogilev in August 1915. It was he who persuaded the Tsar to abdicate. An early organizer of the Volunteer Army, he died of heart failure before the Civil War began in earnest.

13. Mikhail Savvich Pustovoitenko (1865–?) was assistant to the chief of staff of General Headquarters in 1916.

be trusted? Italy? France? England? . . . I would sooner trust America, which does not care about us at all. . . . No, my dear sir, to bear everything to the end—that's our destiny, that's what has been predetermined, if one can speak about it at all."

Together with Pustovoitenko, I remained silent.

"Our army is the mirror image of ourselves. Yes that is so, and thus it should be. With an army like that as a whole, one can only perish. And the whole task of the Command is to make sure it happens with the least possible disgrace. [. . .]

"We are helpless, by any possible measures, to change our fate. The future is terrible, and we must sit with folded arms and simply wait for the moment when everything will start falling apart. And it will fall apart furiously and spontaneously. Do you think I don't spend nights thinking about such things, like the demobilization of the army? . . . It will be an unstoppable flood of wild, unbridled soldiery. I have reported about this several times in general terms; I am told that there will be time to figure everything out, that nothing terrible will happen: everyone, they say, will be so happy to return home that no one will take it into their head to do anything foolish. . . . In the meantime, by the war's end we will have neither railroads nor steamboats, nothing at all—we have worn out and defiled everything with our own hands!"

Somebody knocked the door.

"Enter," answered Alekseev.

"Your Excellency, your office is ready; it has been ventilated," reported a field gendarme.

"Well, I blabbed away with you; it is time to work," said Alekseev and went to his office.

I so wanted to bring this conversation to a more substantive end that my mind filled with curses for the field gendarme's untimely arrival.

"Do you think," asked Pustovoitenko, "that the Chief of Staff of General Headquarters is really going to be working now? No, after such conversations he always has only one wish: to pray." [. . .]

"And what about the Supreme [Commander]?" [asked Lemke].

"He views things from the perspective of those close to him, who, of course, cannot be counted on to reveal to him anything truly negative. Such is not their interest. Everyone, especially those seeking to receive some concrete benefit, tries to assure him that everything is going well under his majestic guidance. Does he understand anything about what is going on in the country?! Does he believe even a single grim word from Mikhail Vasilievich? Should he not therefore fear his daily reports as a freak fears a mirror? [. . .]

"[. . .] Look at the army: they do not see it from here, since parades and [official] visits block the view, and yet there is not a single good boot left or a decent trench. Everything is degraded and defiled. And the rear is no better. There is such chaos there, such bedlam that human powers are not sufficient to put things in order."

"Does the Tsar ever speak about general matters?" [asked Lemke].

"Never. That is the peculiarity of his conversations with his Chief of Staff and with myself: only current business."

9. Selections from the Correspondence of Nicholas and Alexandra   [21, pp. 574–5, 577, 582, 601–2]

Princess Alix of Hesse and by Rhine, born in 1872, was a favored grand-daughter of Queen Victoria. She and Nicholas fell madly in love in 1889. His father, Alexander III, disapproved of her and only allowed them to marry when he grew direly ill in 1894. In preparation, she converted to Russian Orthodoxy and changed her name to Alexandra Fyodorovna. She bore five children, including a son, Aleksei, in 1904. Seeking a cure for his hemophilia, a fatal disease passed to him through her, the empress sought help from many healers and charlatans. In this way, she met Grigorii Rasputin, a Siberian peasant—not a priest or monk—who exerted healing or at least comforting influence on the boy. In time she grew to depend on his advice, especially from September 1915 when Nicholas departed for military headquarters in Mogilev. Alexandra generally referred to Rasputin as "our Friend" and "Grigorii." The imperial couple corresponded in English, their best common language. The excerpts below shed light on how they viewed Rasputin and on Alexandra's growing involvement in the affairs of state.

Alexandra to Nicholas, September 7, 1916

My own Sweetheart,

Tho' I am very tired I must begin my letter this evening, so as not to forget what our Friend told me. I gave yr. message & He sends His love & says not to worry, all will be right.—I told Him my conversation with [Prime Minister Boris] Shtiurmer,[14] who says [Police Department Director Evgenii]

---

14. Boris Shtiurmer (1848–1917) was prime minister from January until November 1916 when he was forced into retirement amid unsubstantiated and almost certainly false rumors of treason. Arrested in February 1917, he died in prison.

Klimovich must absolutely be sent away (he becomes senator) & then old [minister of internal affairs Aleksandr] Khvostov will go, as he cannot get along without him. Khvost. is nervous & feels ill (I know he dislikes Sht, & and so does Klimovich, who is a bad man, hates our Friend & yet comes to him pretending & cringing before him). [. . .] Gregory begs you earnestly to name Protopopov[15] [as minister of the interior]. You know him & had such a good impression of him—happens to be of the Duma (is not left) & so will know how to be with them. Those rotten people came together & want Rodzianko to go to you and ask you to change all the ministers & take their candidates—impertinent brutes![16] [. . .]

[. . .] do listen to Him who only want [sic] yr. good & whom God has given more insight, wisdom & enlightenment than all the military put together. His love for you & Russia is so intense & God has sent Him to be our help & guide & prays so hard for you. [. . .]

Nicholas to Alexandra, September 9, 1916
My very own Lovebird,

Tenderest thanks for your dear long letter in which you give over some messages from our Friend. That Protopopov is, I think, good a [sic] man, but he is much in affairs with fabrics [factories] etc. Rodzianko proposed him long ago as minister of communic.[ations] instead of [Vsevolod] Shakhovskoi.[17] I must think that question over as it takes me quite unexpectedly. Our Friend's idea's [sic] about men are sometimes queer, as you know—so one must be careful especially in nominations of high people. That Klimovich I do not know personally. Is it good to send away both at the same time—I mean the Min. of Int. & and the man at the head of the police? That must all be thought out carefully. And whom to begin by? All these changes exhaust the head. I find they happen much too often. It is certainly not at all good for the interior of the country because every new man brings changes into the administration. I am sorry my little letter has become so tiresome, but I had to answer

15. Aleksandr Protopopov was a member of the moderate Octobrist Party, a wealthy landowner from Simbirsk province, and a successful industrialist. As vice-chairman of the Duma, in summer 1916 he led a Duma delegation to Great Britain where he made an excellent impression on King George V. Far from bridging the gap between government and Duma, Protopopov was viewed by the latter as a traitor to their cause. An official investigation in 1917 revealed a brilliant but erratic mind sometimes unable to focus on his work or the topic at hand. Protopopov had met Rasputin at the office of Petr Badmaev, a Buryat practitioner of herbal medicine.

16. Duma deputies met in the office of Michael Rodzianko, president of the Fourth Duma, on September 6, to discuss an early reconvening of the Duma.

17. In fact, Shakhovskoi was minister of trade and industry.

ʝꙫuɩ ꞯꞟcɪꙇꙫɩɪ. Ꙭꙫu ᛒlᴇss you and the girlies.[18] I kiss you all tenderly. Ever, my sweet Sunny, your own old Nicky.

Alexandra to Nicholas, September 14, 1916
My own beloved angel,
    A lovely sunny, fresh morning. I have not gone to Church, as too tired—was last night for 3/4 of an hour. [. . .] God bless yr. new choice of Protopopov—our Friend says you have done a very wise act in naming him. [. . .][19]

Nicholas to Alexandra, September 23, 1916
My own beloved One,
    Tenderly do I thank you for your dear long letter, explaining so well your conversation with Prot[opopov]. God grant he may be the man we want just now! [. . .] Yes, verily, you ought to be my eye and ear there—near the capital while I have to stick here. That is just the part for you to keep the ministers going hand and hand & like this you are rendering me & our country enormous use. Oh, you precious Sunny, I am so happy you have at last found the right work for yourself. Now I will certainly feel quiet & no more worried, at least for the interior.

10. Economic Conditions in Russia, Fall 1916   [58]

The following description of economic conditions on the eve of the February Revolution appeared in Novoe vremia, *a major mass-circulation, pro-monarchy daily newspaper published in St. Petersburg from 1868 to 1917. Before World War I, skilled industrial workers earned on average 50 rubles monthly. Inflation drove their wages higher during the war. In the major cities, these wages barely kept pace with increased prices for consumer goods. Those who earned less, suffered dramatically.*

[. . .]
    The price for various types of labor, which have been established at plants, factories, and subsequently in the cities, indeed can justify the countryside's flight to the city. Nobody wants to think about the inevitable rise in the cost

18. At this time, Aleksei was with his father at headquarters.
19. Protopopov was appointed acting minister of the interior on September 16 and full minister of the interior on December 20, 1916.

of living as a result of this increase in labor costs: everybody is flocking to this higher pay offered by the city like butterflies flock to fire. [. . .] The average pay in factories and plants today has to be calculated as 5 rubles for eight hours, but wherever you look, it can reach 8 rubles, while no extraordinary expert knowledge or specialty is required; everything depends on the level of each worker's diligence. In some cases, when a specialty is required, the pay rises much higher—to 15 rubles. Counting twenty-six work days per month, a worker's salary is currently between 150 and 200 rubles per month, an amount most of those in the free professions cannot dare to dream of. [. . .]

Let's take people who earn 50–60 rubles per month, who are the majority. How can they live in the city on that money, when even in the remote provinces people are unable to live on such a monthly income! [. . .] I don't know whether cod fish ever appears on your dining table. Many dislike it, because of its sharp smell, but among the needy classes of the population of Petrograd it has always been popular, perhaps because of its low cost. In 1910 a pound [of cod] cost 8–10 kopeks. But since 1914 this food item, highly favored by the proletarian population of Petrograd, began to rise in price. Now cod costs 75 kopeks per pound. After such an escalation of prices, what is left to eat for the poor folk? Herring costs 40 kopeks. Butter has reached 2 rubles 20 kopeks, potatoes have risen in price six times. In 1913 a bag of potatoes cost 70–90 kopeks (a bag contains three measures and therefore three *puds*[20]). Now they ask 4 rubles 50 kopeks for such a bag. [. . .] A pound of cabbage now costs 25 kopeks. Cabbage has been always regarded as the basic staple of the Russian cuisine in the city and in the countryside, both among the affluent and among the poor. [. . .] Cucumbers, which are just such an ingredient of our cuisine as cabbage, now sell for 20–30 kopeks, like oranges. They kept telling us about the wonders and healthiness of a vegetarian diet. Yet what kind of vegetarian diet can one have today at the current prices for vegetables, especially when we are threatened—and quite seriously—to be left without potatoes, cucumbers, and cabbage! [. . .]

11. Pavel Miliukov's Duma Speech of November 1, 1916
[24, pp. 154–66]

Pavel Miliukov (1859–1943) was a prominent historian, a leading liberal politician, a founder and the principal leader of the main liberal political

---

20. A pud weighs 36 pounds.

party, the Constitutional Democratic Party (Kadets), and an influential deputy of the State Duma. The document below is one of Miliukov's most blistering attacks on the government, which was at that time headed by Boris Shtiurmer (1848–1917). The principal target of Miliukov's insinuation of treason, Shtiurmer was removed from office nine days later and replaced by Aleksandr Trepov, in an obvious concession to liberal public opinion. Such a radical speech delivered by a highly respected political figure, according to police reports, made a powerful impression. The speech, copied and passed from hand to hand, circulated illegally throughout the country and further undermined the government's credibility in the public mind.

Gentlemen, Members of the State Duma!

With a heavy heart, I ascend this tribune today. You remember the circumstances under which the Duma met over a year ago, August 1, 1915. The Duma was then suffering from the blows of our military failures. These were due to the scarcity of munitions; and for this scarcity the Minister of War, [Vladimir] Sukhomlinov, was responsible. You recall how at that moment the country, under the influence of the terrible peril that had become obvious to all, demanded a union of the national forces and the formation of a Ministry composed of persons in whom the country had confidence. And you recall how even Minister [Ivan] Goremykin, at that time, admitted from this very platform that "the course of the war demands an immense, extraordinary spiritual and physical effort." You remember that the Government then yielded. The Ministers who were odious to the public were then removed before the convocation of the Duma. Sukhomlinov, whom the country regarded as a traitor, was removed (Cries on the left: "He is a traitor"), and, in response to the demand of the popular representatives, [Aleksei] Polivanov, at the session of August 10 announced to us, amid general applause, as you may recall, that a commission of investigation had been appointed and a beginning made toward bringing the former Minister of War to justice. And, gentleman, the public agitation at that time was not without consequences. Our army obtained what it needed, and the nation entered upon the second year of the war with the same enthusiasm as in the first year.

What a difference, gentlemen, there is now, in the 27th month of the war! [. . .]

We ourselves are the same as before [. . .] we are striving for complete victory. [. . .] But, I must say this candidly: there is a difference in the situation. We have lost faith in the ability of this Government to achieve victory (Cries: "That's true!"). [. . .]

In the French Yellow Book[21] there has been published a German document in which rules are laid down for the disorganization of the enemy's country, showing how to stir up trouble and disorder. Gentlemen, if our own Government wanted deliberately to set itself a task, or if the Germans wanted to employ their own means for the same purpose—the means of influencing and of bribing—they could not do better than to act as the Russian Government has acted. (Cries on the left: "Correct!" [Fyodor] Rodichev: "Unfortunately, that is true.") And now, gentlemen, you have the consequences. As early as the 26th of June, 1915, I uttered a warning from this platform that, "the poisonous seed of suspicion is already yielding abundant fruit," and, "from one end of the Russian land to the other, there are spreading the dark rumors of treachery and treason." I am quoting the very words which I then used. I pointed out at the time—and I am again quoting my own words—that, "these rumors reach high and spare none." [. . .]

It is said that a member of the Council of Ministers, (and this was correctly heard by Duma Member [Nikolai] Chkheidze[22]) on being told that the State Duma would on this occasion speak of treason, exclaimed excitedly: "I may, perhaps, be a fool, but I am not a traitor." (Laughter.) Gentlemen, the predecessor of that Minister was undoubtedly a clever Minister, just as the predecessor of our Minister of Foreign Affairs was an honest Minister. But they are no longer in Cabinet. And, does it matter, gentlemen, as a practical question, whether we are, in the present case, dealing with stupidity or treason? When the Duma keeps everlastingly insisting that the rear must be organized for a successful struggle, the Government persists in claiming that organizing the country means organizing a revolution, and deliberately prefers chaos and disorganization. What is it, stupidity or treason? (A voice from the left: "Treason!" Adjemov: "Stupidity!" Laughter.) Furthermore, gentlemen, when the authorities, in the midst of this general discontent and irritation, deliberately set to work stirring up popular outbreaks, that is to say, when they purposely provoke unrest and outbreaks, —is that being done unconsciously or consciously? We cannot, therefore, find much fault with the people if they arrive at conclusions such as I have

---

21. This was a compendium of documents relating to the movement toward war from 1913 to mid-1914.

22. A leading Menshevik from Georgia, Nikolai Chkheidze (1864–1926), helped introduce Marxism to his native land in the 1890s, served in the Russian State Duma, and chaired the Executive Committee of the Petrograd Soviet in 1917. He supported a policy of "revolutionary defensism," that is, continuing the war solely for defensive purposes. Head of the Democratic Republic of Georgia (1918–1921), he later emigrated to France where he committed suicide.

read here, in the words of those representatives of provincial administrative boards.

You must realize, also, why it is that we, too, have no other task left us today, than the task which I have already pointed out to you: to obtain the retirement of this Government. You ask, "How can we start a fight while the war is on?" But, gentlemen, it is only in wartime that they are a menace. They are a menace to the war, and it is precisely for this reason, in time of war and in the name of war, for the sake of that very thing which induced us to unite, that we are now fighting them. (Cries on the left: "Bravo!" Applause.) [. . .]

And, therefore, gentlemen, for the sake of the millions of victims and the torrents of blood poured out, for the sake of the achievement of our national interests,—which [Boris] Shtiurmer does not promise us—in the name of our responsibilities to that nation which has sent us here, we shall fight on until we achieve that genuine responsibility of government which has been defined by the three points of our common declaration: an equal understanding by all the members of the Cabinet of the immediate problems of the present; their agreement and readiness to execute the program of the majority of the State Duma; their obligation, not only in the realization of this program, but throughout their activity to look to the majority of the State Duma for support. A Cabinet which does not satisfy these three standards does not merit the confidence of the State Duma and must go. (Cries: "Bravo!" Stormy and prolonged applause on the left, in the center, and the left section of the right.)

12. The Murder of Rasputin, December 1916
[89, pp. 59–70, 144–7, 158–82]

On the evening of December 16, 1916, Prince Felix Yusupov (1887–1967), one of the richest men in Russia, joined forces with the right-wing Duma deputy, Vladimir Purishkevich (1870–1920), Grand Duke Dmitrii Pavlovich (1891–1941), the Tsar's cousin, and Dr. Stanislaus de Lazovert, chief surgeon and head of the Russian army's Sanitary Corps, to murder Grigorii Rasputin (1869–1916), in order to salvage the prestige of the dynasty and end what they considered his overweening influence on the Tsar and therefore Russia's political life. Ten years later, as an émigré living abroad, Yusupov tried to explain his motives and provide an account of what happened that night. Contrary to the conspirators' hopes, however, it became almost immediately clear that this act drew Nicholas closer to his wife Alexandra and therefore broadened the gulf between him and society.

In the morning of the 16th [N.S. 29th] of December, during an interval in my work, I drove to our house on the Moika, in order to give final instructions.

The room in which Rasputin was to be received that evening was situated in the basement of the house, and had just been redecorated. It had to be arranged in such a way as to give the impression of being habitually used; otherwise Rasputin's suspicions might be aroused, for it would seem strange to him to be conducted into a cheerless and uncomfortable vault. [. . .]

On entering the house I heard my friends' voices, and the sounds of a popular American song on the gramophone. Rasputin stopped to listen.

"What's this going on? A party?"

"No; my wife has friends with her. They will go away soon, so for the time being let's go down to the dining-room and have some tea."

We went downstairs. Rasputin removed his fur coat and proceeded to scrutinize the room and furniture. [. . .]

[. . .] During the whole of that conversation I had only one idea in my head; to make him drink wine out of those poisoned glasses, and to eat the poisoned cakes. [. . .]

He declined them at first.

"Don't want 'em; they're too sweet," he said.

However, he soon took one, then a second. [. . .] Without moving a muscle I watched him take them and eat them, one after another.

The cyanide should have taken immediate effect; but to my utter amazement he continued to converse with me as if he were none the worse for them.

I then suggested that he should sample our Crimean wines. [. . .]

"Well, let me try it," said Rasputin, stretching out his hand for the wine. It was not poisoned.

Why I first gave him the wine in an unpoisoned glass I am also at a loss to explain.

He drank it with obvious pleasure, praised it, and asked if we had much of it. On hearing that we had a whole cellar full, he showed great astonishment. [. . .]

By an apparent accident, however, I soon managed to knock his glass to the floor, where it smashed.

I took advantage of this to pour wine into one of the glasses containing cyanide of potassium. Having once begun to drink he made no further protest.

I stood in front of him and followed each movement he made, expecting every moment to be his last. [. . .]

The poison still had no effect. The starets continued to walk about the room.

I took no notice of the glass which he held out to me, but seized another poisoned one from the tray. I poured wine into it, and passed it to him.

He drained it: and still the poison had no effect. [. . .]

While I was pouring out tea, he got up and paced the room. His eyes fell upon the guitar, which happened to have been left in the room.

"Play something," he begged. "Play something cheerful. I love the way you sing." [. . .]

My voice sounded strange in my ears. Time passed. [. . .] The hands of the clock pointed to half-past two. This nightmare had lasted over two hours. [. . .]

"What's all that noise?" asked Rasputin, lifting his head.

"Probably it's the guests going away," I replied. "I'll go up and see." [. . .]

"The poison has had no effect," I said.

They gazed at me in mute astonishment.

"Impossible," exclaimed the Grand Duke. "The dose was amply sufficient." [. . .]

We began to discuss what to do next, [. . .]

But finally I took the Grand Duke's revolver and went down to the dining-room. [. . .]

"Grigorii Efimovich, you had better look at the crucifix, and say a prayer before it."

Rasputin looked at me in amazement, and with a trace of fear. [. . .]

"Where shall I shoot?" I thought. "Through the temple or through the heart?"

A streak of lightning seemed to run through my body. I fired.

There was a roar as from a wild beast, and Rasputin fell heavily backwards on the bear-skin rug.

In a few minutes Rasputin became quite still. We examined the wound. The bullet had passed through the region of the heart. There could be no doubt about it; he was dead. [. . .]

We believed that Russia was saved, and that with Rasputin's disappearance a new era had dawned. [. . .]

In the midst of our conversation I was suddenly seized by a vague feeling of alarm; I was overwhelmed by the desire to go down to the dining-room. I went downstairs and unlocked the door.

Rasputin lay motionless, but on touching him I discovered that he was still warm. [. . .]

I cannot explain why, but I suddenly seized him by both arms and violently shook him. [. . .]

[. . .] Suddenly the left eye half-opened. [. . .]

Then the incredible happened. [. . .] With a violent movement Rasputin jumped to his feet. I was horror-stricken. The room resounded with a

wild roar. His fingers, convulsively knotted, flashed through the air. . . .
Like red-hot iron they grasped my shoulder and tried to grip me by the
throat. His eyes were crossed, and obtruded terribly; he was foaming at the
mouth. [. . .]

At that moment I understood and felt in the fullest degree the real power
of Rasputin. It seemed that the devil himself, incarnate in this *muzhik*,[23] was
holding me in vice-like fingers, never to let me go.

But with a supreme effort I tore myself free.

Rasputin groaned, and fell backwards, still gripping my epaulet, which
he had torn off in the struggle. I looked at him; he lay all huddled up, motionless. [. . .]

Suddenly he gathered himself up and made a final leap towards the wicket
door leading to the courtyard. [. . .]

Purishkevich immediately rushed after him. Two shots rang out, re-
sounding all over the yard. [. . .]

A third shot rang out, and a fourth. [. . .]

Rasputin stumbled and fell near a snow-heap. [. . .]

He showed no signs of life. [. . .]

It appeared that the shots had been heard at the district police-
station. [. . .]

As soon as he caught sight of the policeman, Purishkevich quickly went
up to him. [. . .]

"Do you know who I am?" Purishkevich went on, excitedly. "I am
Vladimir Mitrofanovich Purishkevich—Member of the Imperial Duma."

"Those shots which you heard killed Rasputin and if you love your country and your Tsar—you must not breathe a word about it."

On going downstairs, I saw Rasputin lying on the lower landing. [. . .]

I rushed at the body and began battering it with the loaded stick. [. . .]
In my frenzy I hit anywhere. [. . .]

I lost consciousness.

In the meantime the Grand Duke Dmitrii Pavlovich, Captain Sukhotin,
and Dr. Lazovert returned in the closed car.

On hearing from Purishkevich all that had happened, they decided not
to disturb me.

They wrapped the body in a cloth, placed it in the car, and drove off to
Petrovski Island.

From a bridge there, the remains of Rasputin were thrown into the water.

---

23. Russian word for male peasants as well as men of simple background in general; often pejorative.

CHAPTER 2
People's Revolution

On February 22, 1917, Nicholas II departed for the front, having spent two months in Petrograd and Tsarskoe Selo. As commander in chief of the Russian army, he spent much of his time away from the capital at General Headquarters in Mogilev. His letters to his wife and diaries are marked by a sense of great serenity and confidence in his authority and power. Yet a few days later Russia would have no Tsar and the Russian monarchy would collapse, not as a result of a carefully planned conspiracy, but due to a broad and largely spontaneous revolt. Even more remarkable, the collapse of the centuries-old and seemingly unassailable regime was achieved with relatively little violence.

This chapter's first section, "Revolution Triumphs" (Documents 13–21), chronicles the fall of the Old Regime and the birth of the new government. The Revolution began on February 23, International Women's Day. After work, female factory workers formed processions demanding bread. They approached metalworking factories and urged the men to join them (Document 14). Many did, even though most people doubted the radical fervor could be sustained. Yet the crowds and the rallies swelled over the next few days, and the pro-government forces began to break down (Document 15). On the 26th, following orders from the Tsar, troops fired at the demonstrators, killing several hundred. That night, soldiers and noncommissioned officers, mostly appalled by what they had wrought, discussed their next steps. Beginning with elements in the Volynskii Guards Regiment, some soldiers mutinied and turned their weapons against their officers, the police, and the Cossacks. Revolutionary activists urged other soldiers to cross "to the other side of the barricades" and to join the Revolution (see Document 16). By the end of the day, the regime was collapsing, the soldiery was in full mutiny, and the police were fleeing for their lives.

Responding to the crisis—and the opportunity—liberal Duma and radical socialist activists created two competing political institutions, the Provisional

Government and the Soviet (Council) of Workers' and Soldiers' Deputies (Documents 17, 19, and 21). On March 1, the Soviet preempted a possible reassertion of military discipline with its first law, Order No. 1 (Document 18), which established extensive rights for soldiers. Two days later, having learned that all the military commanders considered it to be in the interest of Russia and the war effort, the emperor abdicated (Document 20).

The Revolution quickly spread across the country, as "The Revolution Reaches the Provinces" (Documents 22–24) suggests, though its particular manifestations varied in most localities. When the Revolution began, well-known radical party leaders were absent from the scene. Those who were in Siberian exile immediately created revolutionary institutions similar to those in Petrograd (Document 22). Ethnic-minority leaders organized congresses, political institutions, and breakaway territories and governments in some interior zones and all along the periphery of the Russian Empire, in places such as Transcaucasia and Ukraine (Documents 23 and 24).

The elites of the Russian Empire reacted variously to the establishment of the new political order ("Praise and Criticism of the Revolution," Documents 25–29). Liberals, moderate conservatives, and even most socialists exulted at the triumph of the people and the fall of the monarchy (Documents 25 and 26). In a paroxysm of optimism, Russia's new leaders abolished the police forces and dismissed the governors. A leading Kadet and legal counsel to the Provisional Government, Vladimir Nabokov,[1] recalled a "strange faith that everything would somehow work out fine by itself . . . that the great capital with all its criminal elements could function without a police force." At first, critical voices nearly drowned in the sea of rhetorical praise for the Revolution. As time went on, however, they became more forceful. Some viewed with apprehension the growing social and economic chaos (Documents 27 and 29), while others thought the Revolution did not go far enough. Among the most important negative reactions to the new political order was that of Vladimir Lenin, who traveled with the permission and assistance of the German government across Europe and arrived at the Finland Station in Petrograd in early April. In his April Theses (Document 28), he argued that the proletariat should not support the imperialist war or the government waging it. Peace should be secured right away, land given to the peasantry, and all power transferred to the soviets.

As speeches, articles, and editorials rocked Petrograd and other Russian cities, the peasantry began to take matters into their own hands ("Revolution and the Village," Documents 30–33). For one thing, everywhere they set up village soviets. In many cases, soldiers and sailors on leave exerted a strong influence on this process thanks to their revolutionary experience,

---

1. Vladimir Dmitrievich Nabokov (1870–1922) was a leading Kadet legal scholar and journalist.

Women Demanding Political Rights at a Rally on Nevsky Prospekt, March 19, 1917. TsGAKFFD Sankt-Peterburga. By mid-summer, women had won the full right to vote and to run for office in Russia, one of the first countries in the world to grant these rights to women.

knowledge of the outside world, and political fervor (Document 30). Yet even as the masses of peasants reorganized the agricultural economy, the country's food-supply system was breaking down disastrously, as Finance Minister Andrei Shingarev warned in late May (Document 31). Disgruntlement and anger erupted into violence against nonpeasant landowners in the countryside, where peasants harassed them, busily seized land, and established themselves as the new masters (Documents 32 and 33).

As the section entitled "Revolution and Religion" (Documents 34 and 35) indicates, the revolution transformed even the most conservative institutions and traditions, including those of religion. Thus, parishes and religious communities across the country declared their independence from ecclesiastical structures. Meanwhile, representatives of the former Russian Empire's 14 million Muslims convened the first-ever All-Russian Muslim Congress to articulate and defend their interests and rights in the new state.

The question of Russia's continued involvement in the war created a most bitter division among the supporters of the February Revolution and made empty all the talk of national unity and common purpose. While nearly all the political elites, from liberals to socialists, supported the war effort, as indicated in the next section, "Revolution and the War" (Documents 36–41), by summer the soldiers increasingly rejected the war, hoped for peace, and fraternized with the enemy (Document 36). They also organized themselves into soviets and sent representatives to formal meetings of the Soldiers' Section of the Petrograd Soviet (Document 37). In this volatile situation, the Bolshevik leadership attempted on various occasions to harness discontent in the military ranks for insurrectionary purposes (Document 38). As they

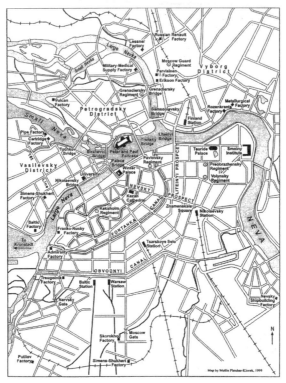

Petrograd in 1917, from Rex A. Wade, *The Russian Revolution, 1917* (Cambridge University Press 2000, 2/e 2005 ISBN 0521841550), p. 30. Reprinted with the permission of Cambridge University Press.

incessantly attacked the Provisional Government for fighting an unpopular war, War Minister Alexander Kerensky managed to launch a major military offensive in June 1917 (see Document 40). This was a disastrous policy, not only because it provoked hostility within many units (see Document 39), but also because it both sparked a massive uprising in Petrograd in early July (Document 41) and ultimately failed militarily.

From this point, one can speak of "The Provisional Government in Decline" (Documents 42 and 43). The Bolsheviks, with their populist slogans of "peace, land, bread," steadily gained support in all the major industrial centers, such as Ivanovo-Voznesensk (Document 42). When conservative elements in the government sought backing among military commanders to "restore order" in the capital, the new prime minister, Kerensky, felt he had no choice but to turn to the left for help, thereby exposing the Provisional Government's growing lack of power and prestige (Document 43).

Revolution Triumphs

13. A Call to Revolution by Mensheviks, January 1917   [20]

The Petrograd Initiative Group, which issued this appeal, was the principal Menshevik organization in the Russian capital.

Proletarians of all countries, unite!

Comrades,

Twelve years ago the streets of Petersburg ran with streams of blood: a three-hundred-thousand-strong proletarian army was subjected to execution by shooting.[2]

It happened on January 9. . . .

Since then every year the working class of Russia leaves their factories and plants on that day and, recalling the mournful day of January 9, celebrates its first mass action on the stage of socio-political struggle.

Calling upon the workers of Petersburg to celebrate this memorable day with a strike as in previous years, we, organized Social-Democrat Mensheviks, propose to connect this mass political action with the greatest events of the present day. We propose to turn our annual mourning celebration into the first resolute action in the struggle for peace.

Enough unnecessary blood! Enough tears!

The moment has come when contrary to the will and wishes of the ruling cliques, which have forced the nations into a fratricidal war, we must stretch out the hand of brotherhood to the proletarians of all countries and proclaim forcefully and loudly:

We do not want war!

Long live peace!

We don't want the government and the bourgeoisie to take advantage of the forced silence of the suppressed people and brazenly substitute their opinions for ours.

We don't want and will not allow our fates to be decided without us, because we believe that the people itself should decide its own fate.

2. The reference is to Bloody Sunday, when on January 9, 1905, peacefully demonstrating workers in central St. Petersburg were fired on, leaving 200 killed and 800 wounded.

Only the clearly expressed will of the proletarians of all countries can halt the present slaughter and achieve the peace that the peoples of Europe desire.

Only peace achieved by the will of the people, and not by Shtiurmer and the Shtiurmerites, can save the peoples from perdition and degeneration.

Thus, when we proclaim the slogan of the struggle for peace and make a show of force on January 9, we know that the path to peace that the people desire is blocked by the obsolete political system in Russia, the hated monarchy. We must also remember that achieving peace is unthinkable without a struggle against the old and obsolete forces.

Our brothers on the other side of the trenches should know that we Russian workers are mobilizing our forces for a struggle against the old regime, standing up for the peace that the international proletariat desires, and thus making common cause with the proletarians of all countries in striving for peace. We therefore expect them to take a similar active stand for peace. We also raise our voice in favor of the convocation of an international worker congress with the participation of representatives from all countries.

Down with the war! Long live peace!

Down with the autocratic regime! Down with the monarchy! Long live democracy! Long live a Democratic Republic!

Long live the struggle for the convocation of an all-national constituent assembly!

Long live the international solidarity of workers!

Long live the struggle for socialism!

14. International Women's Day:[3] The Revolution Begins, February 23–24, 1917   [27, pp. 56–7]

Ilia Mitrofanovich Gordienko, the author of the account of the very first days of the Revolution excerpted below, was a Bolshevik worker-activist working "underground" in the Vyborg Ward of Petrograd on the eve of the February Revolution. Compiled from notes written over the course of many years, his memoir was first published in 1957.

On the morning of February 23, or March 8 [N.S.], we heard female voices in the narrow street by the windows of our shop: "Down with the war! Down with high prices! Down with hunger! Bread to the workers!"

---

3. International Women's Day, February 23, was a socialist holiday first celebrated in the United States in 1909. Its popularity spread across Europe before and during World War I.

Several comrades and I immediately came to the windows. The gates of the First Great Semenovskaia Manufacture were wide open. Masses of women workers in a combative mood spilled into the street. Those who noticed us began to wave their hands and shout: "Come out! Stop working!" Snowballs flew into the windows. We decided to join the rally. We also sent messengers to other shops to find out what they were deciding to do. It turned out that the Mensheviks opposed the strike there and were supported by some workers. It's a women's day, they said, and it was up to them to organize a rally and not our business to get involved. Noise and shouting followed. But at that moment workers from other shops rushed in: "Stop working! Come out!" and the issue was settled.

A brief rally took place near the gates by the main office, and we went out into the street. Women workers met us with shouts of "Hurray!" They took the comrades at the front by their arms and shouting "Hurray!" went together with them toward Bolshoi Sampsonievskii Avenue.

By noon Bolshoi Sampsonievskii Avenue was crammed with workers. Everybody began to move toward the Willie Clinic. Rows of police blocking the way retreated in the face of determined workers. Streetcars stood still in their tracks. Cossacks and Dragoons appeared in the streets. It turned out that the Liteinyi Bridge was occupied by a police unit. But the workers got through to Nevskii Prospect anyway using indirect routes. Clashes with the police took place near the City Duma and in other places, but these were only minor skirmishes. On the Vyborg Side the rallies lasted well into the night.

The same thing happened the next day. Bright and early Bolshoi Sampsonievskii Avenue filled up with workers. The police disappeared, but there were many more Cossacks than the previous day. The situation was tense, clashes unavoidable. Both sides understood this and awaited the outcome. Women workers took the initiative. They surrounded the Cossacks with a dense human chain. "Our husbands, fathers, brothers are at the front!" they shouted. "Here we face starvation, an inordinate workload, insults, humiliation, abuses. You also have mothers, wives, sisters, and children; we demand bread and an end to the war!" Officers, fearing the influence of this agitation on the Cossacks, barked an order. The Cossacks set off toward us. Everyone ran for cover, with a rock or piece of metal ready to throw. But the Cossacks rode right past us without attacking, then turned around and rode back. They were greeted with shouts of "Hurray!" though the heart did not yet believe, and the mind dictated caution.

Then the Cossacks rode past again amid new shouts of "Hurray!" People tossed their hats into the air. The workers, men and women, grew bolder and shouted: "Down with the war! Long live the union of workers and soldiers! Down with the autocracy! Down with the bloodsuckers! Long live the revolution!" Some Cossacks waved their hands and hats in solidarity. This boosted the morale of the people even more. [. . .]

15. Petrograd's Police Chief Describes the Breakdown of Authority   [4]

From 1903 to 1917, Aleksandr Pavlovich Balk (1866–1957) served as a senior police official successively in Warsaw, Moscow, and Petrograd where, in the military rank of major-general, he was the police and administrative chief when the Imperial government collapsed. After three months in prison following the February Revolution, Balk emigrated to Yugoslavia. There, in 1929, he wrote the memoirs excerpted below. While trying to shift the burden of responsibility for failing to deal with the Revolution on the military authorities, Balk nevertheless effectively conveys a profound disconnect between the people of Petrograd and government officials.

February 23, 1917

There were no sinister indications for that day. The day began normally. The weather was excellent, sunny. A temperature of minus 5–6 degrees [Celsius] with no wind whatsoever.

At 10 a.m., while receiving reports in my office, I began to get information by telephone about lively activity on the Liteinyi and Troitskii Bridges, as well as on Liteinyi[4] and Nevskii Avenues. It quickly became clear that this activity was unusual because it was premeditated. The points of attraction: Znamenskaia Square, Nevskii, the State Duma. There were many ladies in the crowd, even more simple women and students, and compared to other such incidents, relatively few workers. The movement of traffic and streetcars was normal. By noon, reports arrived about similar activity on the Petrogradskaia Side [across the Neva River] on Bolshoi and Kamenoostrovksii Avenues. A thick crowd was slowly and calmly moving along the sidewalks, engaged in lively conversation and laughter, and by about 2 p.m. plaintive and depressed voices were heard: bread, bread. . . .

This happened everywhere throughout the day. The crowd chanted, as if moaning: "bread, bread." Yet the faces were lively, cheerful, and apparently pleased with what seemed to them a rather witty and inventive way to protest. [. . .]

---

4. Liteinaia Street in the original.

I immediately gave an order for the next day to occupy, according to the long-established plan, all strategic points in the city by mobilizing all police forces, reinforcing them with Cossack and Cavalry Reserve regiments and the Gendarme Division.[5] [. . .]

Following the meeting, everyone left in a calm mood. The military commanders had complete confidence that the troops, if summoned, would immediately restore order. Upon taking leave, Gen[eral Konstantin] Globachev[6] once again reported to me that the day's rally was a complete mystery to him and that it was possible that nothing would occur the following day.

The night was completely calm.

February 24

After 8 a.m., my secretary A. A. Kutepov and I toured the capital by car. [. . .]

I descended from my car on the [Liteinyi] Bridge and went straight to the crowd, which mostly consisted of simple people standing and looking at the police patrols. I asked them loudly: "Why are you not working, standing here idly?" In response, after some hesitation, four people from among those standing in front began a conversation with me in an entirely seemly fashion. They argued that enough flour was entering the capital but that it was not being given to the population and instead was being sold to speculators. Thus the people were starving, while the speculators grew rich. "Not true," I said and offered to take them with me immediately to the City Governor's Office, where they could see for themselves the Food Department's books and invoices for the daily bread deliveries. One of them could take a seat in the car right away, go together with me to the City Governor's Office, and await the arrival of the others. They thanked me and said that they would come but did not dare to go with me, despite their mutual encouragement. [. . .]

Liteinaia and Znamenskaia Squares, Nevskii Avenue from the Nikolaevskii Train Station to the Politseiskii Bridge, and Sadovaia Street were soon completely filled with masses of people. Streetcar traffic stopped, and more and more the crowd forced passengers to dismount from droshkies [carriages], while near Nikolaevskii Train Station and near Ligovka [Street] hooligans went around knocking cargo down from wagons. The traffic

5. Three gendarme divisions, each employing nearly 500 enlisted men and a few officers, were located in Moscow, St. Petersburg, and Warsaw for crowd control and the maintenance of order in public places.

6. Konstantin Globachev (1870–1941) served as security police chief in several major cities, including in Petrograd from early 1915 until the fall of the dynasty.

across the Neva increased every minute. On the main streets the masses grew thicker, and the police patrols were swallowed up by the crowds. The crowd could get out of control any minute, but just like yesterday there were no leaders, and so far only scattered hooligan mischief occurred.

Procrastination became risky. At 12.30 p.m., I reported to General [S. S.] Khabalov[7] by phone that the police were unable to slow down the movement and concentration of people on the main streets and that, if troops did not take governmental and public institutions under their guard, then I would be unable to maintain order in the capital, especially after dark.

To that, General Khabalov immediately replied: "Therefore, the troops will be brought immediately to the third level [of alert]. Relay to your subordinates that they are to be subordinated to the commanders of the relevant military districts: they should carry out their orders and assist them in troop deployment. I will be in the City Governor's Office in an hour." [. . .]

The daily report to the Tsar, which was prepared in the subsequent days, up to and including the 26th, consisted today, in addition to a brief account of what happened, of reporting that the maintenance of order in the capital had been transferred to the Commander of military forces. A daily report to His Imperial Majesty was written following a special traditional pattern established by Nicholas I. It began with the turnover in hospital beds, then proceeded to a list of accidents involving servicemen, and only at the end briefly mentioned events in the capital. A special clerk with incredibly beautiful handwriting was in charge of writing the report. I signed it never earlier than 12 midnight. The clerk was sincerely aggrieved when I made the report longer than usual, which was against tradition.

Although the movement of people ended early, the Security Bureau Chief reported to me a fact that consoled me little: if the crowds gathered again the next day, then the leftist leaders planned to use this situation for agitation purposes, and if the street responded positively, to launch a disturbance, even an armed uprising, depending on the circumstances. It was not clear what slogans would be thrown at the crowd; that also depended on the circumstances. The leaders themselves, it seemed, could not understand or make sense of the favorable situation, which had fallen into their laps, totally out of the blue.

I reported on this to General Khabalov. The military leadership nevertheless decided for the moment to refrain from resorting to the use of arms.

---

7. Sergei Khabalov (1858–1924) was the commander of the Petrograd military district in 1916 and early 1917.

February 25

[. . .]

Today the factories functioned less intensively than on the previous days. Workers walked off the job in groups, holding rallies as they went. The Police Chief of the Second District, General Grigoriev, reported that in the vicinity of the Putilov Plant crowds of workers were dispersed several times by mounted police patrols.

At 1 p.m., a crowd on Znamenskaia Square unfurled red flags.

The precinct captain of the Aleksandrovskaia precinct, Captain Krylov, an outstanding officer, pushed through the crowd together with a small police patrol, captured the flag bearer, pulled the flag from his hands, and began to move together with the arrested man toward the Nikolaevskii Train Station. The crowd followed, surrounding them tightly. An unknown person came from behind, seized the captain's sword from its scabbard, and dealt him a lethal blow to the head. Although medical assistance was rendered immediately at the train station, Captain Krylov died without regaining consciousness a few minutes later. A large Cossack patrol was nearby but did not provide any assistance, even when mounted police were summoned and began dispersing the crowd on the square.

Speakers emerged in many places calling for the overthrow of the "criminal" government, which had "gone over to the side of the Germans." They also urged the troops to turn their bayonets against the "traitors" and to attack police officials.

The crowd was no longer chanting "bread, bread," and it lacked the joyous mood of the previous days. [. . .]

On the Ekaterininskii Canal near the Church of the Savior on the Blood a detachment of the Pavlovskii Guard Regiment [. . .] halted and began a protest rally. When a mounted police patrol arrived, the soldiers shot at them killing two horses and wounding two mounted policemen. When the commander of the Reserve Battalion of the Pavlovskii Guard Regiment, Colonel Eksten, arrived, the soldiers shouted to him that they [. . .] did not wish to act against the people. Colonel Eksten began to reason with them, when somebody in the crowd shot him from behind with a revolver, gravely wounding him in the neck. The colonel was taken to the regimental barracks, while the detachment continued to demonstrate for a long time, and only the regimental priest was able to convince them to return to their barracks.

Things were now clear. That unpunished attack had great consequences. The [leftist] leaders understood which milieu they should target with all their efforts. As became known later, they used every possible method, including Duma deputies propagandizing troops in the barracks of the Volynskii and Preobrazhenskii Regiments on the night of February 26, and achieved decisive results: the so-called great, bloodless Russian revolution was won with soldiers' bayonets. [. . .]

Throughout the whole course of my joint service with General Khabalov, he impressed me as an accessible, hardworking, and calm person, not without administrative experience, but someone who kept to himself and lacked the ability to influence his subordinates and, most important, to command troops.

The absence of General [Aleksandr] Chebykin,[8] a combat officer from head to toes who intimately knew all the Guard officers of the Petrograd garrison and was able to speak to soldiers and to influence them, had a big impact. [. . .]

16. Revolutionary Appeal to Soldiers, February 27, 1917
[65, p. 79]

The following appeal to soldiers was written and presented by activists of the two most important revolutionary organizations of the time. Formed in 1913, the Inter-District Organization (Mezhraionka) united Bolsheviks and Mensheviks around a centrist Social Democratic position. The Socialist-Revolutionary Party, which drew on huge support among peasants and advocated land redistribution in their favor, was the largest in the country.

By early 1917, Russia had some 7 million frontline soldiers and more than 2 million more stationed in garrisons across the country, including 180,000 in Petrograd itself and another 152,000 in the surrounding suburbs. These soldiers were far from immune to disruptions in supplies and other war-related economic hardships. Many were developing a sense of solidarity with the civilian population. It is that solidarity on which the leaflet below sought to capitalize.

You will gain your rights through struggle!
Proletarians of all countries, unite!

---

8. In 1916–1917, Aleksandr Chebykin (1857–1920) was the commander of the Reserve Guard Battalion in Petrograd. He was on leave when the February Revolution broke out.

COMRADE SOLDIERS!

Driven by hunger, the working class has risen to struggle with your and our enemies, to struggle against the war, against the autocracy of criminal rulers. It has risen to struggle for freedom and land. Comrades! For 22 years you have been suffering in the trenches and in the barracks. For 22 years you have been tormented by inhumane father-commanders. A soldier's lot is hard. A dog is not treated with less honor. Comrades! Brothers! You are our hope! We lay our hopes on you! Toward you we are stretching our calloused hands, crippled by labor! Brothers! Some of you have shot at the people! Workers' blood has been shed! Soldiers! Don't stain your hands with your brothers' blood. Shame on fratricide! Honor and glory to those who have supported the people! Honor to the Cossacks who drove the policemen from Znamenskaia Square.[9] Honor to the soldiers of the Pavlovskii Regiment who took vengeance on policemen for their violence. Brothers! If you are ordered to shoot at the people, shoot at those who are giving you orders. Let your bayonets turn against the violent oppressors. Our starving wives are waiting for your help. Comrades! Read our leaflets! Organize yourselves! Get in touch with the workers! We hold a sacred belief that the soldiers will not betray the people! Brothers! Hear our voice at last! Long live the unity of the army and the people! Down with the autocracy! Down with the war! Long live the revolution! All land to the peasants! All freedom to the people!

Petersburg Inter-District Committee of the RSDRP
Party of Socialist-Revolutionaries

17. A Socialist Describes the Creation of the Executive Committee of the Petrograd Soviet   [76, pp. 40–1, 76–86]

On February 27, mutinous troops and revolutionary crowds liberated socialist activists from prisons. These activists met with public figures, trade-union representatives, and leaders of cooperatives at the Tauride Palace where they formed "the Provisional Executive Committee of the Soviet of Workers' Deputies," which called on workers across the city to vote at 7:00 that evening for a Soviet of Workers' Deputies, set up a commission to feed and care for the scattered soldiers, and summoned officers with democratic leanings to lay plans to defend the Revolution. Perhaps the most well-known and detailed eyewitness account of these days was written by Nikolai Nikolaevich Himmer (pseud.

---

9. This event occurred at midday on February 25.

Sukhanov; 1882–1939).[10] *An expert on economic and agricultural matters and a socialist who had spent four years in prison, he negotiated as a member of the Petrograd Soviet with "bourgeois elements" and thus helped form the Provisional Government. After the Bolsheviks excluded him from the All-Russian Central Executive Committee in June 1918, he began writing voluminous memoirs of the events of 1917.*[11] *In the excerpt below, Sukhanov describes the Executive Committee (Ex. Com.) of the Petrograd Soviet, its composition, and very first steps.*

Having left my office between 12 and 1 o'clock [on February 27], I went out into the streets of the Petersburg Side, to watch the people's revolution being accomplished.

Military detachments were going past, no one knew where to, some with red banners and some without, mingling and fraternizing with the crowd, stopping for conversation, and breaking up into argumentative groups. Faces were burning with excitement. The exhortations of countless street orators to stand with the people and not to go against it to the defense of Tsarist absolutism were received as something self-evident and already assimilated. But the excitement on the soldiers' faces reflected chiefly perplexity and uneasiness: What are we doing and what may come of it? [. . .]

The soldiers' excitement and uneasiness, which arose from the vagueness of the situation, were based in the first place on the fact that their commanders, including the junior officers, were not with them to serve as rudder, and secondly that in those hours only a minority of the garrison were in the streets with the people. The remainder were maintaining at the very least neutrality and an attitude of watchfulness, and some units were still definitely obedient to their commanders.

There were rumors everywhere of clashes on the Liteinyi between Tsarist and revolutionary troops. Of course these were exaggerated. How many loyal troops there were, ready for combat, no one knew. In any case the mutinous soldiers must have felt themselves on the eve of battle.

It was clear to me that I must make my way at once towards the center, to the Tauride Palace. But what I should find there was not clear at all [. . .]

The Provisional Committee of the Duma, in trying to restore the bonds between the officers and the soldiers, wanted those bonds to be just what they had been under Tsarism. It had every reason for hoping that the officers'

10. He remained in Soviet Russia after the Bolshevik takeover and was shot on Stalin's orders in 1939.

11. These memoirs are the only detailed account of these events by an eyewitness. Completed in 1921, they were published in Berlin in 1922–1923.

corps, in joining the revolution and placing itself at the disposition of the Duma, would be making itself a faithful servant of the bourgeoisie; the Provisional Committee, naturally, wanted the "other ranks," in the hands of these officers, to be the passive weapons they had been before and the whole army, thus passing over in its old form from the hands of the Tsar into the hands of an autocratic plutocracy, to be the foundation of its dictatorship in general and of its struggle against the democracy in particular.

It was precisely in the cause of such a bond between the officers' corps and the other ranks that the Duma Committee developed extremely active propaganda from the morning of February 28th on. The watchwords of this propaganda were "order," "discipline," "submission," "obedience," and every other possible variation on the theme of the officer's mailed fist. In this propaganda the bourgeoisie naturally tried to exploit as broadly as possible the efforts of the democratic leaders to restore order and "harmonize relationships" between soldiers and officers. [. . .]

The Soviet Ex. Com. [Ispolkom] immediately took steps to restore the link between the different elements of the army, but it could not allow this link to be the former mechanical discipline, the elemental and absolute obedience of the democratic mass of soldiers to their bourgeois officers. New foundations were being laid for our existence as a state; for the democracy they of necessity presupposed certain new relationships within the army, which would exclude any possibility of exploiting the army against the people for the consummation of the overturn in the narrow class interests of the plutocracy. [. . .]

Civilians were already thronging into the Palace and mingling with the soldiers, and the rooms were beginning to look as they had the day before. People who had come from the city told us that it was still far from restored to order. Shops, warehouses, and flats had been broken into in various places and the destruction was continuing. The criminals released with the political prisoners on the previous day had joined the Black Hundreds[12] and were leading the rioters, pillaging and burning. It was not altogether safe in the streets: police, house-porters, Secret Police, and gendarmes were firing from the attics. They were an incitement to rioting and anarchy. A few fires were burning. [. . .]

The Ex. Com. session could now be opened. Not only were all the elected members gathered together, but the party representatives who were to be included in the Ex. Com. with a vote had also assembled. [. . .]

---

12. The term "Black Hundred," which initially referred to petty urban dwellers in Muscovite Russia, became a general and mostly derogatory name for various monarchist, right-wing, and anti-Semitic organizations that arose primarily in reaction to the Revolution of 1905. Like many revolutionaries, Sukhanov believed that Black Hundreds and regular criminals were likely to act in tandem.

Another trait of the first Ex. Com. leaps to the eye: it was rather poor in personalities. During the first weeks of the revolution not one of the recognized leaders of the Socialist parties or the future central figures of the revolution entered it. Some were in exile, others abroad.

However, in a short time the leaders of the Ex. Com. who had begun the revolution were reduced to a minority and had to pass into opposition. The leading roles were yielded to deserving veteran party leaders. But by then these were representatives of other tendencies who had changed the policy of the Soviet in their own way. It is doubtful whether the revolution gained anything in exchanging its more modest cuckoos for these brilliant hawks.

* * *

It was already about 11 o'clock when the Ex. Com. session opened. I have the impression that during these first days its work went on almost uninterruptedly around the clock. But what work it was! They were not meetings, but a frenzied and exhausting obstacle race.

The agenda had been set up, as pointed out above, in relation to the urgent tasks of the moment. But neither at that session nor in general during the days that followed could there be any question of fulfilling a program of work.

Every five or ten minutes business was interrupted by "urgent announcements," or "emergency reports," "matters of exceptional importance" which couldn't "tolerate the slightest delay," and on which the "fate of the revolution depended," etc. These emergency questions were for the most part raised by the Ex. Com. members themselves, who kept getting some sort of information on the side, or prompted by people who were besieging the Ex. Com. But again and again the petitioners, delegates, and messengers from every possible organization and agency, or simply from the nearby crowds, would themselves burst into the meeting.

In the great majority of cases these emergency matters were not worth a barley-corn. I don't remember what the Ex. Com. did during these hours. I remember only unimaginable hubbub, tension, hunger, and the feeling of irritation at these "exceptional reports." There was simply no way of stopping them.

There was no order even in the meeting itself. There was no permanent chairman. [Nikolai] Chkheidze, who later performed the chairman's duties almost permanently, didn't do much work in the Ex. Com. during its first days. He was constantly being summoned—either to the Duma Committee or the Soviet sessions or, above all, "to the people," the constantly-changing crowd standing in front of the Tauride Palace. He spoke practically without stopping both in the Catherine Hall and in the street, sometimes to workers and sometimes to soldiers. He would scarcely have time to return to the meeting of the Ex. Com. and take his things off before some delegate would burst in with a categorical demand for Chkheidze, sometimes even reinforced by threats, that the mob would break in. And the tired and sleepy old Georgian would get his fur coat on again with a resigned look, put on his hat, and disappear from the Ex. Com.

There was still no permanent secretary, nor were any minutes taken. If they had been taken and preserved, they would not report any "measures" or "acts of state" during these hours. They would reflect nothing but chaos and "emergency reports" about every possible danger and excess we lacked the means to combat. There were accounts of pillage, fires, and pogroms; pogromist Black Hundred leaflets were brought in—handwritten, alas, and thoroughly illiterate. We gave orders not expecting them to be carried out and sent out detachments without any hope that they would really be formed or do their duty. [. . .]

It began to grow noisy in the neighboring hall. The Soviet was assembling. [. . .]

Members of the Ex. Com. were summoned at every minute by every possible delegate from the most unexpected organizations and groups, who had demanded that they should be admitted to the Soviet. [. . .]

Formally the power belonged to the Duma Committee, which displayed considerable activity and quickly distributed departments and functions among deputies of the Progressive Bloc[13] and (very characteristically) some Trudoviks.[14] Besides this, in the course of the day and night of the 28th the Duma Committee found time to publish a whole pile of decrees, appointments, orders, and proclamations. But theirs was only a paper, or if you like a "moral," power; it had authority for all the "statesmanlike" and "right-thinking" elements and served as a fairly reliable protection against the Tsarist counterrevolution. But in these crucial hours of convulsion it was absolutely unable to govern. In particular it had no real validity for the current "technical" tasks—the restoration of order and of normal life in the city.

If anyone had the means to achieve this it was the Soviet, which was beginning to acquire control over the masses of the workers and soldiers. It was clear to everyone that all effective workers' organizations were at the disposal of the Soviet, and that it was for it to set in motion the immobilized tramways, factories, and newspapers, and even to restore order and safeguard the inhabitants from violence.

13. In July 1915, politicians from several moderate and liberal political parties formed the Progressive Bloc within the Duma.

14. The Laborers Group (*Trudovaia gruppa*) was a State Duma fraction composed of diverse pro-peasant socialists; Kerensky was their chairman from 1915.

There is no doubt that if the "conscious" bourgeois-intellectual groups were completely in favor of the Duma Committee's having sole power, the *neutral* petty-bourgeois intelligentsia and the entire Third Estate[15] were indiscriminately forcing their way into our meeting-hall.

I personally received on that day a whole series of this kind of delegation and, not having any constitution to guide me, had neither the powers nor any ground for refusing admission to the Soviet of every kind of delegate, burning with the first ardor of revolution. Other members of the Ex. Com. and our Mandates Commission itself acted in the same way. As a result, a few days later the number of members of the Soviet had reached Homeric and absurd figures, barely short of 2,000. This caused considerable difficulty and unpleasantness for the Ex. Com., which was supposed to set up a correct organization for the Soviet and correct representation in it.

I must note another characteristic thing: to this day I, a member of the Ex. Com., am completely ignorant of what the Soviet was doing in the course of that day. It never interested me, either then or later, simply because it was self-evident that all the practical, pivotal work had fallen on the shoulders of the Ex. Com. As for the Soviet at that moment, in the given situation, with its given quantitative and qualitative composition, it was clearly incapable of any work even as a Parliament, and performed merely *moral functions.*

The Ex. Com. had to accomplish by itself all the current work as well as bring into being a scheme of government. [. . .]

18. Order No. 1, March 1, 1917   [75, vol. 1, pp. 265n1–6n1]

Order No. 1, issued by the Petrograd Soviet, satisfied the desires of many rank-and-file soldiers and was cited by many moderate liberals as evidence that the Petrograd Soviet was grabbing too much power at the expense of the Provisional Government and posed a threat to the integrity of the Russian army. The order formally addressed only the Petrograd garrison, but it had a great appeal outside of Petrograd as well. While some of its provisions sound like mere symbolism, these symbols were rooted in the deeply hierarchical structure of the Russian Imperial Army, which undoubtedly contributed to the growing alienation between the soldiers and their commanding officers. For example,

15. The three traditional social groups into which many European people were legally divided from the Middle Ages into the modern period were the First Estate (the clergy), the Second Estate (the nobility), and the Third Estate (everyone else, though at first mostly the peasantry).

in Russian, as in most European languages other than English, there are two forms of the second person pronoun "you." One is the formal and respectful "vy," and the other is the informal, familiar, and sometimes contemptuous "ty." People in positions of authority under the old regime, especially officials, managers, and officers notoriously used the "ty" form as an expression of disrespect and even insult, much to the anger and resentment of ordinary people. The idea that such lower-class citizens could be addressed as equals seemed to them a huge social triumph, practically a revolution.

To the garrison of the Petrograd District, to all soldiers of the guard, army, artillery, and navy for immediate and precise implementation and to the workers of Petrograd for your information.

The Soviet of Workers' and Soldiers' Deputies decrees:

1. That all companies, battalions, regiments, depots, batteries, squadrons, ships, and individual branches of military agencies shall immediately elect committees of representatives from among the enlisted men of the above-mentioned units.

2. That all military units that have not yet elected their representatives to the Soviet of Workers' Deputies shall elect one representative per company and send them with written credentials to the building of the State Duma on March 2 at 10 a.m.

3. That in all of their political actions military units are subordinate to the Soviet of Workers' and Peasants' Deputies and to their [soldiers'] committees.

4. That the orders of the Military Commission of the State Duma should be complied with, except when they contradict the orders and resolutions of the Soviet of Workers' and Soldiers' Deputies.

5. That weapons of every kind, including rifles, machine guns, armored vehicles, and others, should remain at the disposal and under the control of company and battalion committees [of soldiers], and in no case whatsoever should be given to officers, even at their request.

6. That while on duty and carrying out orders, soldiers must maintain the strictest military discipline, but while off duty and in the capacity of their political, civic, and private life, the civil rights of soldiers cannot in any way be diminished. In particular, that springing to attention and obligatory saluting off duty is abolished.

7. That, moreover, officers shall no longer be addressed as Your Excellency, Your Honor, etc.[16] Instead officers shall be addressed as Mister General,

---

16. Honorific forms of address, such as "Your Honor," were attached to specific ranks, both civil and military, and indicated stature, power, and authority within the governmental

Mister Colonel, etc. The rude treatment of soldiers of any rank and, in particular using the word *ty*, is forbidden, and any violation of this, as well as all misunderstandings between officers and soldiers should be reported by the latter to the company [soldiers'] committees.

This order should be read in all companies, battalions, regiments, crews, batteries, and other combat and noncombat units.

19. Liberal Political Leaders as Russia's Presumptive Government   [65, pp. 154–9]

Miliukov was the leading Kadet, and since the Kadets were the dominant political organization in the government then being formed, he was perhaps the most important member of the Provisional Government, though he held only the foreign ministry portfolio and not the premiership. On assuming his post, Miliukov delivered the following speech at the Tauride Palace on March 2, 1917, detailing the composition and the tasks of the newly formed government to an enthusiastic, yet critical public.

We are witnessing a great historical moment. Just three days ago we constituted a modest opposition, while the Russian government appeared omnipotent. Now this government has fallen into the mud, where it belongs, while we and our friends on the left have been lifted up by the revolution, the army, and the people to a place of honor as members of Russia's first public government. (*Noisy, prolonged applause.*) [. . .] How did it happen that the Russian revolution, which has forever overthrown the old regime, has turned out to be perhaps one of the shortest and most bloodless of all revolutions known to history?!

It happened because history had not known another government as stupid, as dishonest, as cowardly, and treasonous, as that one. [. . .]

[. . .] We have to consolidate our victory. And for that purpose, what we need most of all is to maintain the unity of will and thought that has led us to victory. [. . .]

May you, soldiers and officers of the great and glorious Russian army, also be united, and remember that the army is strong through its internal unity: when it loses this unity and becomes fragmented, it turns into a chaotic mob, and any handful of armed, organized men can master it with bare hands. [. . .]

---

structure. Men serving in ranks three and four, which included major generals and privy counselors, could be called "Your Excellency."

I am being asked: "Who elected you?" Nobody elected us, since if we had waited for a popular election, we would not have snatched power from the hands of the enemy. If we had spent time debating whom to elect, the enemy would have organized itself and defeated both you and us. We were elected by the Russian revolution. [. . .] (*Applause. Shouts: "Who are the ministers?"*).

There can be no secrets for the people. The whole of Russia will know this secret in a few hours, and of course we did not become ministers to be hiding our names. I am going to tell them to you now. The name of the person whom we put at the head of our government symbolizes the organized Russian public (*Shouts: "Property-based!"*), which was so strenuously persecuted by the former government. Prince G. E. Lvov, the head of the Russian zemstvo (*Shouts: "Property-based!"*) will be our Premier and Minister of Interior. You are saying: the property-based public. Yes, but that is the only organized public, which will give other layers of the public the chance to organize themselves. (*Applause.*) But gentlemen, I am happy to tell you that the public without property restrictions also has its representative in our government. I have just received the consent of my comrade A. F. Kerensky to assume a position in the first Russian public cabinet. (*Loud cheers.*) We are eternally joyful to place into the trusty hands of this public activist the ministry that will mete out just retribution to the servants of the old regime, all of these Shtiurmers and Sukhomlinovs. (*Applause.*) These cowardly figures of the days now gone forever, by the will of fate have fallen into the hands not of Shcheglovitovite justice, but of the Justice Ministry of A. F. Kerensky. (*Stormy applause, shouts.*)

Do you want to know other names? (*Shouts: "What about you?"*) My comrades have charged me with supervising Russian foreign policy. (*Noisy, prolonged applause expanding into an ovation to the speaker, who bows in all directions.*) Maybe I will turn out to be a weak minister, but I can promise to you that on my watch the secrets of the Russian people will not fall into the hands of our enemies. (*Stormy, prolonged applause.*) [. . .]

You ask about the dynasty. I know beforehand that my response will not satisfy all of you. But I am going to give it. The old despot who brought Russia to the verge of destruction will voluntarily abdicate or will be deposed. (*Applause.*) The power will go to the regent, Grand Duke Mikhail Aleksandrovich[17] (*Prolonged shouts of indignation, shouts: "Long live the republic!" "Down with the dynasty!" Weak applause overshadowed by another explosion of indignation.*)

Aleksei will be the heir. (*Shouts: "That's the old dynasty!"*)

Yes, gentlemen, that's the old dynasty, which you perhaps do not like and perhaps I do not like. But the matter now is not about who is now liked. We

---

17. Grand Duke Mikhail Aleksandrovich (1878–1918) was the younger brother of Emperor Nicholas II and therefore the next in line to the throne.

cannot leave without response and resolution the question of the nature of
the state order. We view it as a parliamentary constitutional monarchy. Perhaps others view it differently, but if we begin to argue about it instead of
deciding now, then Russia will find itself in the state of a civil war and the
regime that has just been destroyed will be revived. Our responsibility before both you and ourselves forbids this. We do not imagine, however, that
we have settled this issue without any accountability. Our program includes
an item, according to which, as soon as the danger passes and a stable order
is re-established, we will proceed to prepare the convocation of a Constituent
Assembly (*loud applause*), convened on the basis of universal, direct, equal,
and secret balloting. Freely elected representatives of the people will decide
who will express the general opinion of Russia more faithfully: we or our opponents (*Applause, noise, shouts: "Publish the program!"*)

These exclamations remind me of an important question, which the Soviet of Workers' Deputies must resolve, since it speaks on behalf of printing
workers. A free Russia cannot live without the broadest publication and discussion of information, which is at this moment of interest to all of Russia.
I hope that no later than tomorrow the normal publication of periodicals,
now free, will recommence. Gentlemen, I could have mentioned other items
of the program, but I think that those I have mentioned are all of the most
important ones for you; about the others you will learn from the press. I am
losing my voice. It is difficult for me to speak further. Allow me to end my
speech on this note.

20. The Tsar's Abdication, March 2, 1917   [15, pp. 212–41]

*In the excerpt below, Iurii Danilov (1866–?), the general quartermaster of
Headquarters for the Supreme Commander, shares a recollection of the dramatic circumstances that led to Tsar Nicholas II's abdication. It took place
in Pskov to which Tsar Nicholas II's train had been shunted by mutinous soldiers and rebellious railroad workers. There he signed his abdication in
favor of his son, Aleksei, as Danilov's account records. Soon afterward,
fearing for Aleksei's life and health as a hemophiliac, he abdicated the throne
on his behalf, too, and in favor of his own brother, Grand Duke Mikhail
Aleksandrovich.*

Finally, a telegram destined to play a decisive role arrived from General Alekseev for the Sovereign. The telegram relayed verbatim the contents of statements to His Majesty from the commander in chief of the Caucasus Front

Grand Duke Nikolai Nikolaevich,[18] the commander in chief of the South-Western Front General Brusilov, and the commander in chief of the Western Front General [Aleksei] Evert.

In diverse manners, all three of these individuals asked Emperor Nicholas II to accept the conclusion, articulated by the Chairman of the State Duma [to abdicate in favor of Nicholas' son, Aleksei], as the only way to save the Motherland, the dynasty, and the army and to bring the war to a favorable end.

General Alekseev, the Sovereign's chief of staff, on behalf of himself and in addition to communicating these messages, passionately urged Emperor Nicholas II to make a decision about abdication, which, as he put it, "could provide a peaceful and safe resolution to the current, extremely difficult situation."

Sometime later telegrams were received from the commander in chief of the Romanian Front General [Vladimir] Sakharov and the commander in chief of the Baltic Fleet Vice-Admiral [Adrian] Nepenin.

General Sakharov, after a brief and overly florid introduction, which he called "the movement of the heart and of the soul," turned nevertheless to what he called "the logic of reason." In this regard, he also suggested that "perhaps" the most painless solution for the country, and the one likely to preserve its ability to fight the external enemy, was the decision to abdicate, "moving quickly in order to forestall any further vile demands."

Adding his voice to those of the other commanders in chief, Vice-Admiral Nepenin added:

"I am having great difficulty keeping the fleet and the troops entrusted to me in line. . . . If a decision is not made within the next few hours, this will lead to a catastrophe with innumerable consequences for our Motherland."

Thus, all the individuals to whom inquiries were made spoke in favor of Emperor Nicholas II's abdication from the throne with the dominating motive being a desire to secure for Russia the possibility to bring the war to a victorious end. [. . .]

Emperor Nicholas was awaiting our arrival in the green lounge of his dining car, which was well known to us. Outwardly he appeared calm, but he looked paler than usual and had two deep furrows between his eyes indicating a sleepless night and the anxieties he was experiencing. [. . .]

The Tsar warmly greeted us and asked everyone to sit down and smoke, but General [Sergei] Savich[19] and I continued to stand despite ourselves

18. Grand Duke Nikolai Nikolaevich (1856–1929) was Nicholas II's uncle.

19. Sergei Sergeevich Savich (1863–?) was chief of supply for the armies of the front.

because of the extreme burden of the impending conversation. The Tsar himself and commander in chief [Nikolai Ruzskii],[20] weary from all that had happened, sat at the table across from each other. Slowly and clearly, General Ruzskii began to report on all the information received in the previous hours. When the time came to report about the telegram from General Alekseev, along with the conclusions of the commanders in chief, General Ruzskii placed the cable on the desk before the Sovereign and asked him to read it personally.

Having given the Sovereign the time to familiarize himself carefully with the contents of the telegram, General Ruzskii firmly and resolutely expressed his opinion that under the circumstances it was impossible for the Sovereign to make any decision other than the one that followed from the advice of all those consulted.

"But what would the South say?" objected the Tsar, recalling how he had toured the southern cities together with the Empress, where as we were told the royal couple had been received with great enthusiasm. "Finally, how would the Cossacks respond to such an act!" His voice began to tremble, presumably from the bitter recollection of the report he had just read about the Cossacks from his personal guard.

"Your Majesty," General Ruzskii said as he stood up. "I would also request that you listen to the opinion of my aides," and he pointed at us. "They are independent and straightforward men who love Russia deeply; besides, because of their duties they interact with a broader circle of people than I do. Their opinion about the general assessment of the situation will be helpful."

"All right," said the Tsar, "but I am asking you to speak with full candor." We were all very nervous. The Sovereign addressed me first.

"Your Imperial Majesty," I replied. "I know very well the depth of your love for the Motherland. And I am confident that for its sake, for the sake of saving the dynasty and the possibility of bringing the war to a favorable conclusion, you will make the sacrifice that the situation requires from you. I do not see any other solution to this situation except the one outlined by the Chairman of the State Duma and supported by the senior commanders of the armies in the field! . . ."

"And what is your opinion?" the Tsar turned to General Savich who was standing next to me and was apparently having difficulty controlling his agitation.

---

20. Nikolai Vladimirovich Ruzskii (1854–1918) was the commander in chief of the northwestern and the northern fronts.

I am a straight-talking man, as Your Majesty probably heard from General [Vladimir] Dediulin[21] who enjoyed your complete trust. I agree completely with what General Danilov has reported to Your Majesty."

Dead silence followed. . . .

The Tsar went to the desk and several times, apparently without realizing it, looked out the carriage window, which was covered with a curtain. His usually expressionless face became unconsciously distorted by a movement of his lips to the side, which I had never seen before. It was clear that a certain very burdensome decision was ripening in his soul! . . .

Nothing disturbed the silence: the doors and windows were tightly shut. Oh, how I wished this silence to end! . . .

Suddenly Emperor Nicholas abruptly turned back to us and pronounced with a firm voice:

"I have made a decision. I have decided to abdicate the Throne in favor of my son Aleksei." Having said that, he made a broad sign of the cross. We also made the sign of the cross.

"Thank you all for your valiant and loyal service. I hope that it will continue under my son."

This was a profoundly solemn moment.

The Emperor embraced General Ruzskii and warmly shook our hands and then went to his carriage making slow, deliberate steps. [. . .]

21. The Provisional Government's First Steps
[64, pp. 259–65]

The author of this account, Iurii Vladimirovich Lomonosov (1876–1952),[22] was a brilliant railroad engineer and locomotive designer serving as deputy minister of transportation at the time of the February Revolution. The account below comes from unedited notes that Lomonosov jotted down at the end of March 1917. They suggest that Russia's liberal elites had no clear vision for the future, were unwitting and to some extent unwilling revolutionaries, and proved unable to act decisively because of their strict adherence to the principle of the rule of law.

21. Vladimir Aleksandrovich Dediulin (1858–1913) was the Palace Commandant from 1906 to 1913.

22. In 1919–1920, Lomonosov worked for the Soviet railroad system and went abroad to purchase railroad equipment. Recalled to the USSR in 1927, he refused to return and died in emigration.

March 3

I go to the commissars. [Aleksander Aleksandrovich] Bublikov[23] is finishing a phone conversation with somebody, then hangs up and begins to laugh.

"Guess whom I have been speaking with?"

"No idea."

"With former minister [Aleksander Fyodorovich] Trepov.[24] He is asking to be arrested."

"What for?"

"He says he fears that soldiers might break in. [To his subordinates:] Tell the captain to send some soldiers."

"Aleksandr Aleksandrovich, Trepov wants to speak with you again."

"Yes? [Aleksander Vasil'evich] Krivoshein[25] and your brother came to you? I understand. You want me to arrest them too? With pleasure."

In less than an hour our not quite voluntary guests arrived. They were taken to the commissars and offered tea. It was getting late. [. . .] Bublikov began transmitting from the Duma the names of the members of the Provisional Government. [. . .]

Chairman and Interior Minister: Prince [Georgii] Lvov.[26] Foreign Minister: Miliukov. War and Naval Minister: Guchkov. Agriculture: Shingarev. Finance: Tereshchenko. Who? Mikhail Ivanovich? Yes, Tereshchenko. Commerce: Konovalov. Transportation: Nekrasov. Justice: Kerensky. State Controller: Vladimir Lvov. Education: not yet known.

Everybody grew thoughtful.

Krivoshein was the first one to break the silence. Without turning to anyone he said:

"This government has one serious, very serious flaw. It is too rightist. Yes, too rightist. Two months ago it would have satisfied everybody. It would have saved the situation. But today it is too moderate. That is its weakness. And what is needed today is strength. And this way, gentlemen, you are ruining not only your offspring, the Revolution, but also our common fatherland: Russia."

---

23. A. A. Bublikov was a Progressist member of the Fourth Duma.

24. A. F. Trepov was prime minister from November 10 to December 27, 1916.

25. A. V. Krivoshein was a large landowner, a member of the State Council from 1906, and the minister of agriculture in 1908–1915.

26. Of an ancient Russian noble family, Prince Georgii Yevgenievich Lvov (1861–1925) was a Kadet deputy in the First Duma, the chairman of the All-Russian Union of Zemstvos in 1914, and the first prime minister of the Provisional Government. Forced to resign in July, he emigrated and settled in Paris in 1918.

I was struck right then by the words of this experienced old tsarist minister. Not only intelligence, but utter truth resonated in his words. Perhaps my own pride as a practical activist was also hurt, but I did not like the whole composition of this government. What kind of finance minister could Tereshchenko be, a nice, well-cultivated young man, always impeccably dressed, having occupied a ballet-related position and having made a dizzyingly successful impression on the leading lights. What is he to finance and what is finance to him? And this is the Russian financial system, undermined by the war. And what about Nekrasov, a Kadet and an idealist? A professor of construction engineering without scholarly publications, who knows about the transportation system from his student notes and from [membership on the Transportation Committee of] the Duma. [. . .] Finally, Shingarev, who is undoubtedly a clever man but is a doctor by training and dealt with financial matters in the Duma. What does he know about agriculture and agricultural development? [. . .]

[Later the Duma] demanded the original act of Nicholas's abdication for the [first] session [of the Council of Ministers]. [. . .]

[. . .] Prince Lvov arrived around half past ten, frightened and uncertain. He brought the act of the abdication of [Grand Duke] Mikhail. They waited a while for Kerenksy and then sat down. [. . .] They began with the issue of publishing the acts.

"What should these documents be called?"

"In essence, they are manifestos of the two emperors," asserted Miliukov.

"But Nicholas," objected Nabokov, "presented his abdication in a different form, in the form of a telegram addressed to the head of the General Staff. We cannot change this form. . ."

"Perhaps you are right. But it is the abdication of [Grand Duke] Mikhail Aleksandrovich that has decisive importance. [. . .]"

"[. . .] Wait a minute; he never reigned."

A heated debate began.

"From the moment of Nicholas's abdication, Mikhail was the fully legitimate emperor. Mikhail II," Nabokov explained didactically, "had been emperor for almost twenty-four hours. He only refused to assume the supreme authority."

"If there was no authority, there was no reign."

"You are grievously mistaken. What about underage and mentally handicapped monarchs?"

The debate entered into the arcana of constitutional law. Miliukov and Nabokov, with foam at the mouth, argued that Mikhail's abdication could have legal significance only if it were recognized that he had been emperor.

March 4

When midnight struck, the debate was still in progress. Finally, around 2 a.m. agreement was reached. Nabokov wrote the titles of the two acts on two scraps of paper:

Act I: On the abdication of the Tsar Emperor Nicholas II from the Throne of the Russian State in favor of Grand Duke Mikhail Aleksandrovich.

Act II: On the refusal of Grand Duke M. Al. to assume the Supreme authority and on his acknowledgement of the full authority of the Provisional Government, which emerged at the initiative of the State Duma.

These lines could have had the following heading: "The accomplishment of the first six hours of work of the first Provisional Government."

THE REVOLUTION REACHES THE PROVINCES

22. The February Revolution in Irkutsk [53, pp. 93–8]

Located in southeast Siberia on the Angara River, close to Lake Baikal, Irkutsk was an important commercial and administrative center with a population of 515,132 in 1897. It was also a major home of exile for criminals and political dissidents, including Ia. Papernikov, who in the following document describes both the power vacuum in Irkutsk in the wake of the February Revolution and the political exiles' eagerness to fill it.

The February revolution found me in Ikrutsk, to which I had fled from my place of exile. I was working at the Fuks Leather Factory with twelve other political exiles who were living in Irkutsk illegally, like myself. The Police Chief of Irkutsk was well aware of our work and of our living in the city. But since we were working for the defense, so to speak, the police turned a blind eye to our living in Irkutsk. After the revolution we learned that several political exiles, of course with forged documents, even worked in the office of the Governor General of Siberia. In all public organizations without exception, political exiles set the tone, insofar as there was any public activity at all. This was not surprising: in that relatively small city roughly two thousand "politicals" had resided illegally and semi-legally. [. . .]

At the beginning of March, the local newspaper for several days in a row published reports about major strikes breaking out in Piter[27] and other cities. Then wire reports from Piter completely disappeared from the pages of the local newspaper. This caused a lot of talk and rumors among political exiles. But since they were working even in the office of the Governor General and also had contacts in the telegraph office, we learned that major events were unfolding in Piter. What exactly was happening and on what scale we did not know. Governor General [A.] Pil'ts was, of course, well aware that the people had risen against the autocracy in Piter but had decided to conceal it from the population, hoping apparently that the uprising would be crushed.

Nevertheless, the rumors quickly spread across the city. On March 3 the Committee of "the Union of Siberian Workers" issued an appeal to the soldiers calling upon them to support the uprising in Piter and to make every

27. A colloquial name for Petrograd (formerly St. Petersburg).

effort to prevent the local authorities from taking any hostile actions against the newly formed Provisional Government. But Governor General Pil'ts resolved to act forcefully and to the bitter end. Orders were posted all over the city calling upon the population to stay calm and announcing that the most decisive and severe measures would be taken against anyone inciting to mutinies or spreading false rumors. It has to be noted that this order was issued in response to a visit paid to the Governor General by a delegation of local public activists who demanded that he resign from his post voluntarily and temporarily yield power to the City Duma or to the Committee of Public Safety.[28]

A large number of Cossack units patrolled the city. No clashes or misunderstandings occurred, but this made a great impression on the broad masses of the population, which at that point still were not officially informed about the creation of the new government and were prey to diverse rumors. [. . .]

Tension was felt on the streets. Everyone was wondering whether the Governor General would agree to submit peacefully or would try with the help of the Cossacks to drown in blood the fledgling new movement. In the evening, despite the above-mentioned order, the first large, open rally was spontaneously held within the walls of the City Duma, which was filled to overflowing by a huge number of people. As was to be expected, the movement was from the very beginning led and guided by [well-known] political exiles. [. . .] The greatest rejoicing and delight occurred when delegates from various military units of the Irkutsk garrison appeared at the podium and announced their readiness to support the revolution by any and all means. The next day Governor General Pil'ts, along with other police and gendarme officials, was arrested.

Thus the revolution in Irkutsk occurred without a single shot being fired and without any serious clashes, except, it seems, a case when an officer was hit several times near the building of the City Duma. All power in the city now belonged to the Committee of Public Safety. Feverish work began immediately to organize the Soviet of Workers' and Soldiers' Deputies. [. . .] How the events developed further in Irkutsk I do not know, because in two days I left for Moscow. Our departure was organized by the Committee for Assistance to Released Political Prisoners. It is unnecessary to mention that the entire route from Irkutsk to Moscow was for us one big triumphal procession. The train was adorned with banners. At almost every major station celebratory dinners awaited us, where numerous ladies with red bows entertained us.

---

28. When the political exiles in Irkutsk joined forces with other revolutionaries and created a Committee of Public Safety, they were consciously following the example of the French revolutionaries, whose *Comité de salut public* ruled France during the height of the Terror (1793–1794). The adoption of this term, along with many others (such as "commissars"), indicates the extent to which the Russian revolutionaries admired the French Revolution.

23. Description of the February Revolution in Transcaucasia   [86, pp. 344–5]

While in the first few days of the Revolution there was a lot of confusion across the country about what happened in Petrograd, nobody seemed to be more confused than the local authorities. Revolutionary activists quickly moved to take the initiative. At long last they could use their organizational and rhetorical skills to reach out to the people broadly and openly. The author, Socialist-Revolutionary leader Semion Ivanovich Vereshchak, was elected chairman of the Soviet of Soldiers' Deputies formed on March 6, 1917, in Tiflis, Georgia. In the document below he describes the formation of the soviets and their efforts to build on the support of two key groups—workers and soldiers.

The Social-Democrats, with a majority of deputies, dominated the Soviet of Workers' Deputies; there were only a few Socialist-Revolutionaries. In the Soviet of Soldiers' Deputies, however, the greatest influence belonged to the Socialist-Revolutionaries, so that body was considered theirs. Likewise, the influence of these two organizations differed. While the Soviet of Soldiers' Deputies had real military force, which could back up any of its decisions at any time, the Soviet of Workers' Deputies did not have such a force, but its moral and political influence as a worker organization was quite significant.

The Soviet of Workers' Deputies was formed before the Soviet of Soldiers' Deputies. Here is how it happened: on the night of March 3, 1917, Social-Democrats called an organizational meeting on the premises of the "Initiative group for Georgian folkloric performances" (120 Mikhailovskii Prospect). This meeting was semi-legal and was attended by random representatives of districts and individual factories and plants. It was decided at that meeting to create a Soviet of Workers' Deputies. The city was divided into 5 districts. [. . .] An electoral commission was elected to urgently hold the elections. At the same meeting, it was decided to disarm the police and gendarmes and to organize a popular militia. On March 4, the first session of the workers' Soviet took place chaired by Chiaberov (SD), and it was decided to hold a general people's rally in Nakhalovka (a suburb of the city of Tiflis), in order to inform citizens about the unfolding events and to elect a provisional executive committee to be composed of 15 members: 10 elected from the assembled deputies and 5 co-opted from the SD party.

The Soviet of Soldiers' Deputies was organized in March. Before discussing how it was organized, one has to point out that before the coup there were no revolutionary military organizations in Tiflis at all. [. . .]

On 1 March the Commander of the city of Tiflis, General [Vasily] Gabaev, distributed the following phone message: "Secret. No meetings should be allowed. Superiors and commanders are responsible for calm in the units. In the case of revolt of anyone from the lower ranks in units under your command, immediately relay to me their last names." These orders, even though they were secret, nevertheless became known to the broad soldier masses. On the same day a group of Socialist-Revolutionary soldiers organized a rally in the arsenal workshops. Unexpectedly, the whistle signaled the workday's end. The soldiers numbering about 500 people gathered in the courtyard and the rally was held despite threats from the head of the workshops, General [Viacheslav] Rodzevich. At the rally a commission was elected to maintain contacts with other military units, mainly line units, as well as with socialist parties. Simultaneously, an illegal meeting of 20 soldier delegates took place in the engineering workshops located in the arsenal district. That meeting, also led by Socialist-Revolutionaries, was attended by representatives from the headquarters of the corps of engineers, from the engineering workshops, from the arsenal, and from automotive workshops in the rear. The issue of the organized revolt of the Tiflis garrison troops was discussed, and it was decided to immediately begin organizing revolutionary troop cells in line units. [. . .] In the meantime, the city was still in the grips of confusion caused by rumors. The High Command was issuing dreadful orders threatening each and everyone with jail and trial by court-martial, but almost no attention was paid to these orders and threats. Everyone felt that there was no one left to carry out these threats, and those who issued them also, in all likelihood, [felt] that it was their simple and probably final duty to do so. The population was thus kept mired in an atmosphere of rumors and guesses until March 3, when the Viceroy of the Caucasus, former Grand Duke Nikolai Nikolaevich, [. . .] made public the news about the coup d'état in a special announcement. This short announcement was printed and posted all over the city and called on the residents to maintain order and to recognize the Committee of the State Duma as the supreme Russian authority. From that day on, Transcaucasia entered the new era of the all-Russian revolution without any struggle and without shedding a single drop of blood.

24. Ukrainian Declaration and the Provisional Government's Reply, June 1917   [8, vol. 1, pp. 383–6]

A Slavic people predominately of the Eastern Orthodox Christian faith, the Ukrainians, numbering 22 million in 1897, constituted the largest ethnic minority of the Russian Empire. Most of Ukraine was incorporated into Russia with the Treaty of Pereyaslav of 1654 and the Partitions of Poland in the late 1700s. Movements of national consciousness emerged in Ukraine beginning in the 1800, but the government vigorously persecuted them and quite effectively suppressed their associations and publications. Even after the fall of the Tsar, few Russian intellectuals favored the secession of Ukraine.

The Central Council, or Tsentralna Rada, of Ukraine was created on March 17, 1917, on the basis of representatives from diverse political, cultural, and professional organizations. After its reconstitution by the All-Ukrainian National Congress, which met in April, the Rada directed the movement toward national autonomy by means of four major declarations, of which the one below was the first.

The First Universal (Proclamation) of the Ukrainian Rada, June 10, 1917

People of the Ukraine, nation of peasants, workers, and toilers:

By your will you placed us, the Ukrainian Central Rada, as the guardians of the rights and freedoms of the Ukrainian land.

Your best sons, elected by people from the villages, from factories, from soldiers' barracks, from all the large bodies and groups in the Ukraine, have elected us, the Ukrainian Central Rada, and entrusted us to defend these rights and freedoms.

Your elected men expressed their will thus: Let there be a free Ukraine. Without separating from all of Russia, without breaking away from the Russian State, let the Ukrainian people on their own territory have the right to manage their own life. Let a National Ukrainian Assembly (Sejm), elected by universal, equal, direct, and secret suffrage, establish order and a regime in the Ukraine. Only our Ukrainian assembly is to have the right to issue all laws which are to establish this regime. [. . .]

We sent our delegates to Petrograd to present to the Russian Provisional Government our demands.

And the chief demands were as follows:

That the Russian government publicly, by a special act, declare that it is not against the national freedom of the Ukraine, against the right of the people to autonomy.

That the central Russian government have in its cabinet our commissar on Ukrainian affairs for all matters related to the Ukraine.

That local authority in the Ukraine be united in one representative from the central Russian government, that is, by a commissar in the Ukraine elected by us.

That a certain portion of money collected by the central treasury from our people be returned to us, the representatives of this people, for their national and cultural needs.

All these demands of ours the central Russian government rejected. [. . .]
And now, people of the Ukraine, we are forced to create our own destiny. [. . .]

The Central Rada expresses the hope that the non-Ukrainian peoples who live in our land will also be concerned about peace and order in our territory and during this trying time of national disorganization will, in the spirit of friendship, together with us begin the organization of autonomy in the Ukraine.

And after we complete this preparatory organizational work, we shall call representatives from all peoples of the Ukrainian land and will work out laws for her. Those laws, that entire order which we shall prepare, the All-Russian Constituent Assembly must approve by its law.

People of the Ukraine, your electoral organ, the Ukrainian Central Rada, faces a great and high wall which it must demolish in order to lead its people out upon the road of freedom.

We need strength for this. We need strong and brave hands. We need the people's hard work. And for the success of this work we need, first of all, great means (money). Up to this time the Ukrainian people have turned all of their means into the All-Russian central treasury. And the people themselves never had, and have not now, anything in return for it.

The Ukrainian Central Rada consequently orders all organized citizens of villages and towns, all Ukrainian public boards and institutions, beginning with the 1st of July, to tax the population with a special tax for their own affairs and accurately and immediately transmit this tax regularly to the treasury of the Ukrainian Rada.

Ukrainian people! Your future is in your own hands. In this hour of trial, of total disorder and collapse, prove by your unanimity and statesmanship that you, a nation of grain producers, can proudly and with dignity take your place as the equal of any organized powerful nation.

The Provisional Government's Appeal to the Ukrainian People, June 17, 1917

Ukrainian citizens!

In [these] days of great trials the Provisional Government is turning to you in the name of all free Russia.

Russia is passing through grave ordeals to secure the freedom that will bring well-being to the people and the restoration of rights to all the nationalities. The gains of the revolution are in danger.

If the external foe crushes Russia, or if the enemies of freedom emerge triumphant—then the common cause of all the peoples of Russia will be lost.

The Government—the temporary bearer of revolutionary power—has set for itself the task of leading the country through all dangers, and of convoking the National Constituent Assembly, at which all the peoples of Russia will express their will openly and firmly through universal and equal suffrage.

This is your task also, Ukrainian citizens. Are you not a part of free Russia? Is not the fate of the Ukraine inextricably bound up with the fate of all liberated Russia?

Who can doubt that Russia, standing beneath the banner of full popular sovereignty will assure the rights of all the nationalities that form her component parts?

Through their representatives at the Constituent Assembly, the peoples will be able to forge such forms of political and economic organization as will fully answer their national aspirations. [. . .]

But a complete reorganization of the Russian polity and of the structure of the all-Russian army is impossible under the fire of external foes and with the enormous dangers inside the country threatening the cause of freedom.

Brother Ukrainians! Do not take the perilous course of splitting up the forces of emancipated Russia. Do not divorce yourself from our common native land. Do not break up our common army at a time of grave danger. [. . .]

Let all the peoples of Russia stand closer in serried ranks in the fight against the external and internal dangers threatening the country. And let the final decision on all fundamental questions be left to the Constituent Assembly, which is already not far removed in time and where the peoples themselves will decide the fate of their common native land, Russia, and the fate of all her individual regions.

Prince Lvov, Minister-President

PRAISE AND CRITICISM OF THE REVOLUTION

25. "What Is a Revolution?" *Novoe vremia*, March 12, 1917 [8, vol. 1, p. 200]

Excitement about the first revolutionary days was almost universal. Even conservative periodicals like Novoe vremia *joined the revolutionary chorus. As the war raged on, most contributors to the formerly pro-government daily had lost all confidence in the government's ability to resolve the many pressing issues facing the country, including popular unrest, official corruption and ineptitude, and the horrific carnage at the front lines. The document below shows that they, like most people in Petrograd and throughout the country, welcomed the Revolution, praising its lack of violence. Still, the February days were not entirely without bloodshed. Well over 1,000 people were wounded and 169 lost their lives, mostly at the hands of angry individuals and crowds. Policemen, officers, and government officials were especially at risk, though in some cases they too participated in the violence.*

In the minds of frightened people, revolution means "wild destruction. Revolution is a prolonged, hopeless disturbance. Revolution means murder, conflagration, robbery, desecration of temples, infants killed against rocks, rape, disregard of all law, human or divine. The mob gets drunk on liquor and blood, women are transformed into hyenas. The savage rabble carries chopped-off heads on spears in the streets. Self-appointed courts send to the gallows thousands of innocent people. On the plazas guillotines are erected, and their blades know no rest."

That is what revolution was in the imagination of frightened people. This crimson shadow darkened the winds and made hearts contract with horror. For fear of that specter, thousands of decent people who hated the tyranny which hung over our land still reconciled themselves to it in practice. Revolution seemed to them more frightful than the accustomed slavery. [. . .]

By the will of fate, the revolution broke out nonetheless. Let the eternally memorable days of the 27th and 28th of February be blessed. They showed us the real face of the Russian revolution. The peoples' army, the workers and the citizens smashed the idol of autocracy within forty-eight hours. And if unnecessary bloodshed occurred during that time, it was committed by the lackeys of the destroyed despotism, and not by the people. Protopopov,

Shcheglovitov the Cain, Shtiurmer, Makarov—all are alive. Almost all the perfidious lackeys of the ill-fated Emperor are living. He himself is kept under protection and enjoys complete safety. His family lives in its own house in complete inviolability, thirty versts from the center of the revolution.

So where is the axe of the guillotine? Where are the blood-smeared heads on the spears of cannibals? Where are rape, conflagrations, destruction? Where are the maddened furies? Where are the wails for blood and vengeance?

On the contrary, one of the first acts of the new government is the law abolishing the death penalty.

26. Newspaper Editorials on the Abolition of the Death Penalty, March 1917   [8, vol. 1, pp. 200–2]

Immediately upon its establishment, the Provisional Government declared a general amnesty of all political prisoners and fugitives, including terrorists. Yet it was only the first step, followed soon by the realization of the long-cherished dream of Russian liberals and revolutionaries alike, not to mention writers like Leo Tolstoy and Vladimir Korolenko—the abolition of the death penalty. As the selection of enthusiastic editorials indicates, the death penalty had been broadly viewed, at least by the educated public, not only as oppressive but also as fundamentally immoral.

Editorial, *Rech,*[29] March 10, 1917

One item of good news follows the other. Amnesty is followed by the abolition of the death penalty. The death penalty is abolished forever. Only six words, but what a thundering echo they will call forth from the whole Russian land!

The amnesty and the abolition of the death penalty are essentially two sides of the same coin. But here there is no reverse side; they are both equally beautiful, they both call for a new life, they are both building peace and harmony in place of malicious spite and cruel vindictiveness. [. . .]

29. The liberal newspaper, *Rech,* was published from 1906 to 1918 by leaders of the Constitutional Democratic, or Kadet, Party. With an average daily circulation of under 20,000, an often scholarly tone, and unparalleled cultural reporting, the newspaper appealed to intellectuals, the educated middle classes, and political elites. Although Pavel Miliukov was a founder and the political editor of the newspaper, *Rech* was never an official organ of the party.

[I]t would be superfluous to force an open door and to repeat [. . .] the arguments against the death penalty which have already deeply penetrated into everybody's conscience, and this is especially [true] for us, where for the last ten years such energetic propaganda against the death penalty has been carried on, where thousands of signatures covered protests against this terrible form of punishment, where leagues and unions were organized for the fight against this evil.

However, all this shows only how difficult and tenacious was the fight. Therefore, the greatest merit of the revolution is that one of its first achievements has been to abolish the death penalty forever. Forever and ever this act shall remain a solemn evidence, of the greatness of the popular soul and as a manifestation of straightforward nobility. [. . .]

"The Abolition of the Death Penalty," *Rabochaia gazeta,*[30] March 12, 1917

The death penalty—this age-old nightmare of our life—has been abolished. [. . .]

The death penalty, a survival of the ancient blood vendetta, was one of the most terrifying tools of enslavement in the hands of the autocratic government. How many fighters for freedom laid their lives on the chopping block or perished in the hangman's noose![31] And the most awful thing was that these murders were being committed *legally.* The executioners were cloaking themselves with the law. [. . .]

The Provisional Government, which obtained its power from the hands of the revolutionary people, has dissipated this nightmare. It rejected the bloody weapon of the Tsar's government. The death penalty no longer exists.

At the present moment, the people's wrath is hanging over the heads of the former enslavers of the people. The abolition of the death penalty will perhaps bring a sigh of relief to them. But the revolutionary people will find other means to render them harmless for all time to come, and, first of all, it will destroy the conditions which made their domination possible. In these circumstances, the revolutionary people can magnanimously grant them life.

But the death penalty must never again be a *tool* in the hands of the strong against the weak, in the hands of oppressors against fighters for freedom.

---

30. The title of a succession of short-lived and repeatedly suppressed Social Democratic newspapers, beginning with the Russian Social Democratic Labor Party's first organ in 1898, *Rabochaia gazeta* in this avatar first appeared in Petrograd in March 1917. As the official newspaper of the Menshevik Party in this period, it advocated worker moderation, nonconfrontation with employers, and support for the strengthening of civil liberties and the development of political organizations.

31. Twenty-nine people, all regular criminals, were executed in Russia in 1913.

Editorial, *Novoe vremia*, March 18, 1917

The death penalty is abolished in Russia. It is difficult in a few words to express the whole colossal majesty of this act of the Russian governmental power which furnishes from above the most potent evidence of respect, for human personality and for its right to the most valuable entity—human life. [. . .] The great French Revolution of the eighteenth century, while proclaiming its lofty principles of the "rights of man and the citizen," nevertheless did not disdain the inculcation of those principles with the aid of the executioner who bore a sort of honorable title *vengeur public* [public avenger]. The Russian revolution of the twentieth century, in the name of the same principles, begins by taking human life under its protective wing and endeavors to inculcate in the public the realization of the fact that people in the mass must also, following the example of the government, refrain from acts of self-assumed justice and respect the right of every person to life. And in this we see the grandeur of the Russian revolution and of those humane cultural principles which permeate it.

27. A Princess Experiences the Revolution, Early 1917
[29, pp. 348, 354–5, 359–60]

Many observers have noticed a profound gap between how the Russian elites and the majority of the Russian people viewed themselves and the world around them. This gap only widened as those who supported and benefited from the old regime struggled to understand its sudden collapse. Nothing could reconcile the landed noblewoman Princess Nina Pavlova Gruzinskaia to the Revolution.[32] In the excerpt below she tries, in great bewilderment, to make sense of the revolutionary actions and profound resentments of people she knew almost nothing about. In particular, she singles out a Jewish man, whom she refers to as a "Yid" (zhid in Russian), a derogatory but widespread term for Jewish people, implying perhaps that Jews were responsible for the February Revolution. There is, however, no evidence that Jews played a key role in bringing down the imperial regime.

[. . .] I descend from an ancient family of tsars of Georgia, but my mother was Russian (Princess [Anastasiia] Dolgorukaia), and I spent the first three

32. Princess Gruzinskaia emigrated from Russia in 1920 and died in Nice in the early 1930s.

years of the revolution at the estate that I inherited from her and which was located in the Livenskii district of Orel province. [. . .]

In February of the tragic year 1917, I was in Moscow staying in the house of my aunt, Princess Lobanova-Rostovskaia, who at that time lived in Switzerland. [. . .]

And here is what happened to me: one week before the terrible date I walked into a store on the Arbat[33] wishing to buy wallpaper for one of the rooms in the countryside. The store was empty except for the owner and a sales clerk, who began to show me their wares. All of a sudden a big fat merchant came in, clearly a friend of the owner, who began loudly, without any embarrassment to scold (I cannot use a different word) the Empress! He spoke angrily about her actions, repeating outrageous libels about Rasputin, her special telephone to contact the Germans, etc.[34] The owner was silent, only asking him questions. [. . .]

Still under the impression of this incident, which I found outrageous, I walked into a small stationery store. It was run by a boy who looked nineteen years old, undoubtedly a Yid. I asked him to give me postcards with pictures of the Imperial family. To my amazement, this impudent answered me with a look of contempt: "We do not sell them; we do not carry such postcards!" "You do not carry postcards of the Imperial family? Why? Why do you not carry these postcards?" He must have been afraid of my tone, because he did not explain anything, but kept saying: "We don't sell them," shaking his head with disdain. I left, having decided to report these two cases to somebody who could do something about such outrages. Alas, a few days later, the criminal coup occurred and it became clear that these people knew in advance what was being prepared, while we remained in innocent ignorance. [. . .]

28. V. I. Lenin, "The April Theses," April 4, 1917
[44, vol. 24, pp. 21–6]

On the night of April 3, Lenin arrived in Petrograd, having traveled from Switzerland with the full support of the German government, which hoped he would undermine the Russian war effort. The next day, he read his "April The-

33. The Arbat is a storied and prestigious street in Moscow just west of the Kremlin.

34. Alexandra, because she was born in Germany, was often referred to in critical discourse as "the German woman" and was frequently, albeit entirely falsely, accused publicly of supporting the German side in the war.

*ses at the All-Russian Conference of Soviets of Workers' and Soldiers' Deputies.
The text provoked a bitter polemic with fellow Marxists, such as Georgii
Plekhanov,[35] who objected to Lenin's uncompromising stance toward the Provisional Government and his insistence that a proletarian revolution was imminent. Since Marx had argued that such a revolution could occur only in the
most advanced capitalist countries, Lenin's position appeared odd and out of
touch with reality. Yet for Lenin and his supporters, the "April Theses" offered a
clear blueprint for action and became a turning point in their determination
to fight for the next revolution that would bring about an entirely different
kind of society.*

[. . .] 1) In our attitude towards the war, which under the new [Provisional]
government of Lvov and Co. unquestionably remains on Russia's part a
predatory imperialist war owing to the capitalist nature of that government,
not the slightest concession to "revolutionary defensism" is permissible.

The class-conscious proletariat can give its consent to a revolutionary war,
which would really justify revolutionary defensism, only on condition: (a)
that power pass to the proletariat and the poorest sections of the peasants
[that are] aligned with the proletariat; (b) that all annexations be renounced
in deed and not in word; (c) that a complete break be effected in actual fact
with all capitalist interests.

In view of the undoubted honesty of those broad sections of the mass believers in revolutionary defensism who accept the war only as a necessity, and
not as a means of conquest, in view of the fact that they are being deceived
by the bourgeoisie, it is necessary with particular thoroughness, persistence,
and patience to explain their error to them, to explain the inseparable connection existing between capital and the imperialist war, and to prove that
without overthrowing capital it is *impossible* to end the war by a truly democratic peace, a peace not imposed by violence.

The most widespread campaign for this view must be organized in the
army at the front.

Fraternization.

35. Georgii Valentinovich Plekhanov (1856–1918), "the father of Russian Marxism,"
was a political activist who devoted his entire life to expounding and developing the theories of Marx. Following police persecution, he emigrated to Europe in 1880 and only returned to Russia in 1917. Alternately an ally and an opponent of Lenin, he joined the
Menshevik fraction in 1903 and supported the Russian war effort against Germany. He
also supported the Provisional Government and after the October coup moved to Finland
where he died of tuberculosis in May.

2) The specific feature of the present situation in Russia is that the country is *passing* from the first stage of the revolution—which, owing to the insufficient class-consciousness and organization of the proletariat, placed power in the hands of the bourgeoisie—to its second stage, which must place power in the hands of the proletariat and the poorest sections of the peasants.

This transition is characterized, on the one hand, by a maximum of legally recognized rights (Russia is *now* the freest of all the belligerent countries in the world); on the other, by the absence of violence towards the masses, and, finally, by their unreasoning trust in the government of capitalists, those worst enemies of peace and socialism. [. . .]

3) No support for the Provisional Government; the utter falsity of all its promises should be made clear, particularly of those relating to the renunciation of annexations. [. . .]

4) Recognition of the fact that in most of the Soviets of Workers' Deputies our [Bolshevik] Party is in a minority, so far a small minority, as against a bloc of all the petty-bourgeois opportunist elements, from the Popular Socialists and the Socialist-Revolutionaries down to the [Menshevik] Organizing Committee. [. . .] who have yielded to the influence of the bourgeoisie and spread that influence among the proletariat.

The masses must be made to see that the Soviets of Workers' Deputies are the only possible form of revolutionary government, and that therefore our task is, as long as this government yields to the influence of the bourgeoisie, to present a patient, systematic, and persistent explanation of the errors of their tactics, an explanation especially adapted to the practical needs of the masses. [. . .]

5) Not a parliamentary republic—to return to a parliamentary republic from the Soviets of Workers' Deputies would be a retrograde step—but a republic of Soviets of Workers', Agricultural Laborers' and Peasants' Deputies throughout the country, from top to bottom.

Abolition of the police, the army and the bureaucracy.[36]

The salaries of all officials, all of whom are elective and displaceable at any time, not to exceed the average wage of a competent worker.

6) The weight of emphasis in the agrarian program to be shifted to the Soviets of Agricultural Laborers' Deputies.

Confiscation of all landed estates.

Nationalization of *all* lands in the country, the land to be disposed of by the local Soviets of Agricultural Laborers' and Peasants' Deputies. [. . .]

7) The *immediate* union of all banks in the country into a single national bank, and the institution of control over it by the Soviet of Workers' Deputies.

---

36. I.e., the standing army to be replaced by the arming of the whole people. [Footnote added by Lenin.]

8) It is not our immediate task to "introduce" socialism, but only to bring social production and the distribution of products at once under the control of the Soviets of Workers' Deputies. [. . .]

10) A new International

[T]he bourgeois gentlemen who call themselves Social-Democrats, who *do not* belong either to the *broad* sections or to the mass believers in defensism, with serene brow present my views thus: "The banner[!] of civil war" (of which there is not a word in the theses and not a word in my speech!) has been planted(!) "in the midst [!!] of revolutionary democracy . . .". [. . .]

Mr. Plekhanov in his paper called my speech "raving." Very good, Mr. Plekhanov! But look how awkward, uncouth, and slow-witted you are in your polemics. If I delivered a raving speech for two hours, how is it that an audience of hundreds tolerated this "raving"? Further, why does your paper devote a whole column to an account of the "raving"? Inconsistent, highly inconsistent!

It is, of course, much easier to shout, abuse, and howl than to attempt to relate, to explain, to recall *what* Marx and Engels said in 1871, 1872, and 1875 about the experience of the Paris Commune and about the *kind* of state the proletariat needs. [. . .]

Ex-Marxist Mr. Plekhanov evidently does not care to recall Marxism. [. . .]

29. I. Ehrenburg on the Revolutionary Violence, September 1917   [19, pp. 34–5]

Ilya Ehrenburg (1891–1967) was born in Kiev, became a revolutionary in his youth, was arrested in 1908, and emigrated to France the same year. A correspondent for Russian newspapers during World War I, he returned home in July of 1917. In September 1917 he traveled by train from Moscow to the Crimea, a trip he describes in the document excerpted below. The account was first published in October 1917. Ehrenburg rejected Bolshevik radicalism and internationalism in favor of the White movement but grew disillusioned with it in the course of the Civil War and eventually became an obedient mouthpiece for the Stalinist regime.

It began back in Moscow, when the people slowly crawled onto the train cursing and shoving each other, when they jumped up, grunting and screaming, into the half-closed train car windows. [. . .]

They drank tea and kept talking about thefts—present ones, past ones, Moscow ones, Kharkov ones, and others. Then a lady's little silver spoon disappeared, and everyone began to eye one another angrily and suspiciously. It seemed to me that an old speculator in leather goods had stolen it, while its owner stared most intensely at the vast pockets of my coat. [. . .]

In Kursk they caught [a thief]. This time it seems it was "a real one." They dragged him out of the next train car. He was dressed in a heavy military outer coat. Militiamen seized him, but the soldiers on board and the people in the train station roared:

"Give him up! No need! Give him to us!"

The militiamen resisted reluctantly, for the sake of pure formality, and were obviously afraid. A well-dressed gentleman of about sixty with a clean, pink bald spot ran out of our train car and yelled:

"Beat him, the S. O. B.!"

I saw the eyes of the man who was caught: at first they searched the crowd looking for a way out, then they begged, finally they stopped, glazed over, and dimmed. Someone hit him and blood appeared on his face, under his nose. Then the crowd overshadowed him and carried him away.

"Their [the thieves'] eyes should be poked out," said a lady, who then cuddled up and began to eat some chicken.

REVOLUTION AND THE VILLAGE

30. Setting up Local Soviets in Tambov Province
[86, pp. 372, 374–7]

The author, F. D. Sorokin, was a Socialist-Revolutionary sailor eager to share the news of the February Revolution with the peasants of his native Tambov province. In the document below he describes the peasant understanding of self-government.

The February Revolution found me in Petersburg or, to be more precise, in the vicinity of Petersburg.

Preferring to work in the province, especially among the peasants, I was very pleased when the Main Naval Headquarters decided to send sailors of Guard units called up from the reserves to defense-related factories. I took an assignment at the Novopokrovskii Sugar Plant. . . . The plant is located 14 versts from the village of Borisovka, my home town. I arrived in Tambov province on March 25. The peasantry at that time had only a vague idea of what happened in Petersburg. They knew that Nicholas was no longer on the throne but had absolutely no idea about who was ruling Russia in his place. [. . .]

Upon completion of the spring labors, the peasants began to devote more time to political and social issues. [. . .]

[. . .] I was visited every day by the peasants from different villages asking me to attend their assemblies. There were so many such requests that I could not satisfy them all. Peasants themselves took me from village to village. At the assemblies, they listened so attentively that I had to speak for many hours in a row. For example, in early May 1917, in the village of Bolshaia Danilovka in Karpel'skaia volost, peasants from all over the village—including many women—gathered to listen despite nasty and cold weather with rain and snow. A roomy peasant cabin and no less roomy entryway could not accommodate all the listeners, and many of them stood outside the open windows under the wet, sticky snow, which turned into rain by the end of the day. At that assembly, I spoke for exactly 7 hours, from 2 to 9 p.m. with a 10-minute break. At the assemblies, aside from attentive listening to the speeches, the peasants posed many questions. Their questions were quite diverse and substantial. Generally, they went like this: what if we elect a person to the Constituent Assembly who fails to defend our interests there? [. . .] The peasants also took great interest in the question of the courts, the organs of local self-government, the way these issues would be resolved by the Constituent Assembly. They wanted to know this ahead of time. As to their own ideas, they did not delineate any specific organizational forms of the organs of local self-government and simply kept saying that this is how it should be: everything belongs to the people and the people should decide everything. In God's eyes, all people are the same, but the important thing is for people to act together in unity. I emphasize the immense desire of the peasants for unity of action: that the people all across Russia should work together and that all institutions of local self-government should be united [. . .]

Thus, at all the rural assemblies I had to resolve and respond not only to issues of a state, political, economic, and public nature, but also private matters: to help reconcile a peasant with a son or a daughter-in-law, a neighbor with a neighbor, a peasant with the community, and the community with a peasant; there were even requests to deal with a divorce case, with damage claims, with expense compensation, and so on and so forth. The peasants were greatly dissatisfied with their priests, and not a single peasant assembly proceeded without mentioning the priests in some way. In most villages, peasant rural communities and parishes usually set the rates for what the priests could charge for their services both in money and in kind, while the communal lands that the priests used were confiscated first or reduced to the same size as the peasant plots in the commune. [. . .]

31. Finance Minister Andrei Shingarev[37] on the Food Crisis, May 21, 1917   [8 ,vol. 2, pp. 632–3]

The Russian economy remained relatively backward compared to the economies of the other major world powers. Its yearly increase in national income per head in the decades before World War I of roughly 1 percent, while similar to the European average, lagged in comparison with that of Japan (3 percent), the United States (2.5 percent), and Germany (2 percent). Still,

37. Andrei Ivanovich Shingarev (1869–1918) was a physician, scholar-activist in public health, journalist, expert on agricultural matters, and Kadet Duma deputy. He served in the first Provisional Government first as minister of agriculture and then as minister of finance. Imprisoned in Petrograd when the Bolsheviks came to power, he fell ill and was transferred to a hospital where a mob of Baltic sailors, with the collusion of Bolshevik Red Guards, brutally murdered him.

Its annual rate of growth of industrial output per head was perhaps the highest in the world at 2.5 percent. What held the country back, then, was the agricultural sector, which grew at an anemic quarter percent per year. As the industrial economy produced goods during the war largely for military purposes, peasants found few manufactured goods to buy and therefore often refused to sell their grain, preferring to consume it locally or to hold out for higher prices. This trend only became more pronounced after the February Revolution, as this alarming report by Finance Minister Shingarev pointed out.

On May 21, the All-Russian Congress on Food opened in the Moscow Commercial Institute. Over 1,000 delegates attended. Among the participants in the Congress were Ministers A. I. Shingarev and A. V. Peshekhonov. The Chairman of the [Moscow] Soviet of Workers' Deputies, L. M. Khinchuk, was elected presiding officer of the meeting.

Minister of Finance A. I. Shingarev addressed the following speech to the meeting:

"Comrades, permit me to welcome the Congress which has convened at a trying and difficult time [to discuss] a complex question of vital importance to the present existence of the State. Beginning with the first day of the revolution, and continuing until now, I have concerned myself with the question of food supply. I spent the past few days in one of the richest wheatgrowing areas, and I tried to find out why the problem of food supply was still not adjusted. I was in Voronezh, Rostov-on-the-Don, Novocherkassk. I attended many gatherings and meetings and [I was present] at the big Peasants' Congress in the Don oblast. Citizens, the question of food supply is not some kind of isolated aspect of our [national economy] as a whole in which disorganization has come about. It is, rather, that the entire nation is in an extremely difficult, I would say, critical situation. The country is beginning to fall apart. Our economy is nearing a dangerous [state of] disorganization. In many places [this disorganization] has become rampant and widespread. The State coffers are empty. The people do not pay taxes. [. . .] The cause of freedom can be lost in the economic chaos, complete anarchy, financial disorder, and starvation. The absence of a united organization, an organized power, is the root of all evils at the present moment. There is grain in all the provinces. In the Voronezh province and the Don oblast, in the northern Caucasus, the grain reserves are much larger than we had expected. But not enough grain has been delivered, and not enough is being delivered, because the local organizations are not efficient. [. . .] I am bound to state that we are experiencing a grave shortage not only of food, but of material [goods] as well. At the same time, the country is swelling with paper currency, claims against the Treasury are mounting, and I can foresee the terrible day

when the Treasury will say to the people: 'There is no more [money].' [. . .]
All that I have said, comrades, does not amount to despair and hopelessness.
And it is not for this purpose that I am speaking. But we must look squarely
at the truth and understand the seriousness of the danger. If the people become aware of this danger, this will serve a medicinal purpose in the present
situation. But the dose of this medicine must be very large—otherwise we
will experience the greatest disaster.

"I do not doubt that the people will extricate themselves from this misfortune. I believe that they will emerge without a fratricidal war, without bankruptcy, without bloodshed. This is the task before you. To this end we must
direct all the strength of our reason. Then will we be able to say that we are capable of performing the duty that has fallen upon us." *(Prolonged applause.)*

32. Recollections of a Peasant, Nizhegorod Province, 1850s–1917   [30, pp. 72–8]

*In 1861, following Russia's disastrous defeat in the Crimean War (1853–
1856), Emperor Alexander II, against the wishes of most of the country's
landowning nobles, freed Russia's 40 million serfs from bondage. Alexander
commanded the transfer to them of roughly half the land they had tilled for
their masters until then. In turn, the dispossessed landlords were to receive
monetary compensation at the going rate in the form of government bonds. Yet
the peasants were not off the hook. They were required to repay the cost of their
land over the course of 50 years. Moreover, the landlords managed to gain
hold, on average, of the best farmland and to keep for themselves forest and
pasture land, which previously they had allowed their serfs to use, according to
ancient custom. Finally, the peasants did not own the land they now called
their own; it belonged to peasant communes, which the government charged
with possessing the land thus distributed to the emancipated serfs. The peasant
recollections below underscore peasants' enduring hunger for the land they felt
they were entitled to and elucidates the roots of the peasant unrest that became
a serious problem for the Provisional Government by the summer of 1917.*

Poletaev, the lord of Spukha, was a cruel man. The peasants always spoke
of him thus: "Insatiable beast. Never it seems will he have drunk enough of
our blood." As soon as someone caused him displeasure or simply when
he was in a bad mood, he would send a person to the stables for whipping
and caning. And out of the stables people emerged either crippled or dead.
[. . .]

Girls and young women also could not escape him. [. . .] He would have his fun with a serf girl and then would give her to his dog trainers to be shamed or send her to a remote farm for hard labor until death.

Peasants were waiting for "Volia."[38] "Then he won't act like a cannibal anymore. They will cut his arms short. And we will be able to breathe freely."

But "Volia" did not bring them a reprieve.[39] It happened that the *mirovye posredniki*[40] registered all the good lands, along with the forests and meadows, to the lord, and the peasants only got sand and rocky soil.

And the peasants found themselves again under the lord's foot: "If you need wood for construction, go to the lord and bow down, and if you cut a pole without permission, court and prison will await you. [. . .]"

The peasants started waiting for his death. "He is childless, he will die, then his estate will go to the treasury. [. . .] Then perhaps we will have some *voliushka*."[41]

But their expectations were dashed again. The lord's conscience, which had so much peasant blood and torment on it, thought to propitiate them by bells and pound candles, which he offered to churches and monasteries. And before dying the lord, in order to take a good spot in heaven, summoned a priest and two witnesses and ordered them: "Write a testament. I leave my entire estate to the Poletaev convent. [. . .] Let them pray for my soul day and night. [. . .]"

Soon after the lord's funeral new heiresses arrived: a whole horde of nuns headed by a prioress. And everything was back as it was: the nuns turned out to be like lords and perhaps in some ways even worse. [. . .] The Spukha residents became so fearful that they would start running and hiding if they only heard the bell of an approaching police sergeant (*stanovoi pristav*). [. . .]

The February revolution reached Spukha as a faint echo, and at first it was not believed: perhaps it was just a temporary dysfunction. But a week later it turned out that the tsar was in fact gone, and so was the police sergeant. The Spukha residents got together and the first question that they raised was: "What should be done with the devil's monastic nest?" They decided unanimously to go all together to the nuns and run them out of there. [. . .]

"No way," admonished [the district militia chief, Socialist-Revolutionary] Kobylianskii. "Revolution was not forged so that the peasants could plunder without punishment. [. . .]"

---

38. "Volia" resonated deeply for the Russian common people as a state of absolute autonomy and freedom.

39. The reference is to the Emancipation of 1861.

40. Peace mediators worked out the details of land distribution following the abolition of serfdom in 1861.

41. The diminutive form of "volia."

The problem dragged on until soldiers from the front arrived. They immediately took the issue head on and started shaming the peasants: "You are girlie men," they taunted; "you got afraid of the black-tailed women." "But the authorities support them. What can we do?" replied the peasants. Around midday peasants gathered near the monastery gates; some of them had hunting rifles, and two or three had military-issue weapons.

Kobylianskii, looking official, came out on the porch and greeted them. Nobody responded. [. . .] The crowd kept pressing in on him. Kobylianskii jumped from the porch and began to retreat into the courtyard, walking backwards. "Get him!" yelled someone from the crowd. Kobylianskii pulled out a revolver and fired. The mob roared. Kobylianskii dashed to the gates and clobbered an old man with a gun who had tried to stop him. "Let's get the landlord's lackey!" people in the crowd were yelling. Kobylianskii ran to the church fence, firing as he ran. One of the former soldiers from the front took a rifle, a shot was fired, and Kobylianskii fell to the ground as if he had been cut down. Upon seeing that he was killed, the crowd began to disperse.

33. A Female Peasant on the Revolution in Voronezh Province, 1917   [30, pp. 66–8]

Even though the redemption payments were abolished in 1906, no redistribution of land occurred. The Russian peasantry believed deeply that all the land they worked belonged to them and that absentee landlords had no right to possess any land at all. When the Tsar abdicated in March 1917, for the peasants the most pressing matter was to distribute all the arable land among the communes. Yet the Provisional Government procrastinated about land reform.

Thus, many peasants gradually took matters into their own hands, beginning in Tula, Riazan, and Tambov provinces in central Russian and then across the country. They established their own authority in the countryside; harassed and expelled landowners (many of whom were women, since most men were away at war); destroyed land-ownership records; and seized crops, livestock, tools, and land. By late summer 1917, the peasants were in nearly total control of the countryside. The document below describes several instances of direct peasant action.

In our area, Makarov and Arkhangelsk volosts, there were six landlords. The spiders lived carefree, not thinking about anything. But then the February revolution broke out, and the spiders became agitated and started to weave their thick web. Night and day they rode on horses from one estate to another, their faces anxious. Only one landlord, Zhuravlev, immediately sold his estate and left nobody knows where.

The most prominent of landlords was Torzheskovskii—he had 6,000 desiatinas[42] of land and 500 desiatinas of forest. He was a real god of that area. He had 300 hired peasant laborers and 200 POWs whom he exploited at his tile factory. Part of his land he rented out and part of it he had cultivated by hired peasant laborers. This spider sat firmly in his nest until the very October days. But as soon as rumor spread to our remotest corners that [Prime Minister Aleksandr] Kerensky had been toppled—it was in the evening— the very next morning peasants from the nearby villages went with banners to "congratulate" the landlord, but he was no longer in his estate.

Then the peasants seized the lord's riches. Everyone took what he could: horses, ploughs, reapers, etc. They even laid their hands on the roofs and took sheet-iron from the shacks and hay from the haystacks. And in the spring [of 1918] they divided the land among themselves. [. . .]

And in the village of Novo-Markovo [in summer 1917] the situation was as follows. The peasant laborers got organized and started attacking the landlords. [. . .] Once they broke into an old woman's estate. They knocked at the door and were fired at. Still, some of them broke into the house. It turned out that the old landlady was not at home; it was a young girl who was shooting at them. She jumped out of the window, but there were people outside and they butchered her with axes. Then they left to prepare to attack other estates, but failed. The next day a unit of Kerensky's soldiers arrived. The search began, but they couldn't find anyone. [. . .]

Then as soon as the soldiers left, the peasant laborers again crawled out of their holes and continued their business. Then the landlord lost patience and paid their underlings to intercept them.

One dark, terrible night six peasant laborers were caught and locked in landlord Aleksandrov's basement, where they were humiliated with all kinds of torture; for example, their hair was rolled around nails and torn out. They were facing certain death, but less than three hours later a crowd approached the landlord's house and set them free, while the landlord managed to disappear, and nobody knew where he went. [. . .]

But then the great coup—the October revolution—burst forth. Our peasant laborers became Bolsheviks and started to preach the ideas of communism. [. . .][43]

42. A desiatina was a land measure equal to 2.7 acres.

43. This sentence, typical of many accounts published in the Soviet times, was meant to affirm the storyteller's credentials as a Bolshevik supporter and should be taken with a grain of salt.

REVOLUTION AND RELIGION

34. Russian Orthodox Parishioners Request Institutional Autonomy, May 1917   [3]

The people's revolution in 1917 reached into nearly every institution and organization of the country, including one considered by many to be ultraconservative: the church. Congresses of clergy and laypeople meeting in the months after the fall of the Tsar adopted resolutions overwhelmingly in support of the Provisional Government, the promised Constituent Assembly, and the opportunity for the church to free itself from state tutelage. In the following letter, sent to the Chairman of the Council of Ministers of the Provisional Government, representatives of the clergy and parishioners of the Boris and Gleb Church in Petrograd were requesting institutional and legal autonomy from the ecclesiastical structures of the church. Such requests were quite frequent in 1917, at least in Petrograd. The Russian Orthodox Church before 1917 was strictly hierarchical, allowing for very little parish autonomy.

The Parish of the Boris and Gleb Church located on the Kalashnikova Quay in Petrograd has convened a Parish Assembly composed of one elected representative for every one hundred parishioners. Expressing the collective will of its many thousand parishioners, on this present day of May 4 the assembly has prayerfully welcomed the dawn of the new free life of the church, which has begun to shine upon Russia.

Inspired by an unshakeable faith that the sun of the church's freedom and happiness will itself soon rise over Russia, which has been liberated and resurrected for a new life, the Boris and Gleb Parish expresses through its Parish Council its sincere confidence in the Provisional Government as the embodiment of the popular will of the whole Russian state.

Aware of the immense and noble burden and the great responsibility for the fate of Russia, which the Provisional Government bears, the Boris and Gleb Parish prays to the Lord God to strengthen and unify governmental power in the hands of the Provisional Government for the purpose of restoring order and legality to the state, of destroying all instigators of sedition, and of overcoming the internal and external enemies of the state.

Believing that the revival of the state is only possible when the soul is enlightened by the light of Christ's Truth, the Boris and Gleb Parish Assembly acknowledges that, since Christ's Church holds within itself the radiant source of new life and seeks to morally transform people's souls, the state cannot be truly reformed without the regenerative influence of the Church.

Therefore the Boris and Gleb Parish Assembly unanimously beseeches the Provisional Government to grant freedom of self-determination to the Russian Church and the rights of a legal person to every parish.

35. Resolutions of the First All-Russian Muslim Congress, May 1–11, 1917   [8, vol. 1, pp. 409–11]

There were 14 million Muslims, divided into roughly three dozen ethnic minorities, living in the Russian Empire in 1897, or 11 percent of the total population. Concentrated mostly in Central Asia, the Caucasus region, and the territory around Kazan on the Volga River, they had been incorporated into the empire through a series of conquests, beginning in 1552. Most spoke Turkic languages; a minority, Persian. After the February Revolution, peoples of Muslim faith disagreed about what organizations could best represent their interest. Some favored ethnic-based representation. Others supported a broader organization based on shared religious identity. The First All-Russian Muslim Congress sought to become such an organization. It drew on several years' experience and activism of the Union of Muslims of Russia, a liberal political organization that emerged from congresses of Russian Muslims convened in 1905–1906 and represented Muslim interests in the State Duma. The Congress's resolutions below express the views of many, but not all, Muslims on issues ranging from the form of government and the organization of the army to education and religion.

The Form Of Government

The All-Russian Moslem Congress, having discussed the question about the form of government in Russia, resolved: (a) to recognize that the form of government in Russia that guards best the interests of the Moslem peoples is a democratic republic on national territorial-federal principles; moreover, the nationalities that do not possess definite territory enjoy national cultural autonomy; (b) to regulate the general spiritual-cultural questions of the Moslem peoples of Russia and their common affairs by organizing a central general Moslem organ for all Russia, with legislative functions in this sphere.

The form, composition, and function of this organ are to be defined by the first constituent congress of representatives from all autonomous units.

On Military Organizations

Military conscription must be abolished. In the event, however, that the need should arise for the existence of a regular army, because of a struggle with any kind of militarism, the army must be national.

Should the need for a regular army be recognized after the close of the war, separate Moslem units should be created.

Cultural and Educational Matters

Control over educational and cultural matters must be in the hands of individual nationalities, who exercise their right through specially elected organs of each nationality.

Teaching in elementary schools must be conducted in the mother tongue of each group of the Turkic peoples. Teaching of the general Turkic language must be compulsory in the secondary schools. Teaching in higher schools is in the general Turkic language.

Universal, compulsory, and free elementary education must be introduced.

All elementary schools must be of one type without division into secular and ecclesiastical.

The system of schools must permit the free passing from the lower to the higher schools without examinations. The Russian language must be taught in schools as a separate subject.

Teachers and students of all nationalities in Russia should enjoy equal rights in every respect. [. . .]

Depending on local conditions, it is desirable that boys and girls be taught together.

In the event that the number of Moslem boys reaches three in schools of other nationalities, they must be taught their mother tongue and religion at the expense of the state. [. . .]

In order to prepare a teaching personnel for secondary schools, special Turkic departments must be introduced in Russian higher schools and in [teacher-training] courses.

With the opening of the 1917–18 academic year, teachers of national schools must be granted equal rights with the teachers of Russian schools and the same compensation.

Persons educated abroad should not be prohibited from teaching in Moslem schools.

The Temporary Religious Organization of the Moslems

Having discussed in several sessions the question of the religious organization of the Moslems, and having taken into consideration that the question of separation of the church from the state must be resolved at a special conference, the section on religious matters came to the following decisions:

1. It is necessary to organize a temporary religious administration to satisfy the spiritual needs of the Moslem population subject to the jurisdiction of the Orenburg Religious Council, and for the Kirghiz population should they express the wish to recognize the spiritual leadership of this administration.

Note: Delegates from the Turgai, Ural, Akmolinsk, and Semipalatinsk oblasts, present at the Congress, declared that the Kirghiz of these oblasts are ready to join the Orenburg Mufti.[44]

2. Irrespective of the question of separation or nonseparation of the church from the state, it is nevertheless necessary to outline the form and location of religious organizations.

---

44. Experts in Islamic law (Sharia).

Revolution and the War

36. Fraternization on the Western Front, April 1917
[74, pp. 61–3]

F. Zakharin joined the Bolshevik Party in 1912 and during World War I served in the Kara regiment. His unit took part in a small but growing movement of fraternization with German and Austrian soldiers that seriously undermined Russia's battle readiness, especially beginning in early 1917.

[. . .] I will discuss how fraternization started on the Western front, in Belorussia [. . .]

It went like this. We began by closely watching the German trenches without firing a single shot. The Germans watched us in turn and did not shoot either. In two or three days we would begin walking out over the top, individually and in groups. Again, no one fired on either side.

A peculiar stillness would then set in. You could read joy and hope in the soldiers' eyes. If any of the officers had given orders to attack at that time, he would have been torn into pieces [. . .]

I remember particularly well our first two meetings with German soldiers. Everyone felt tense and hesitant, since only recently we had been shooting at each other, killing each other, pouring lead into the trenches. And now we were approaching each other without weapons.

A dozen of our grenadiers walked through secret passages in the barbed-wire fencing and entered the neutral zone. A few minutes later, ten German soldiers appeared on the trench's breastwork. They came right to us and stopped. Then we stared each other in the eyes. Since we did not know the language, we all tried to read each other's eyes. They told us a lot. We saw tears of joy in the eyes of the German soldiers. Then everybody took their hats off and bowed and the handshakes began. The Germans took out their cigarettes; we took out pouches of Makhorka[45] and rolled our "goat legs." General smoking began. We tried the cigarettes—they were weak, just like grass. We decided to treat our recent enemies to our tobacco and rolled them some. For that we used newspapers with appeals from the Provisional Government: "War to the victorious end!"

---

45. A dark, pungent, strong tobacco smoked by the lower classes in Russia.

The German soldiers who remained in the trenches took a few pictures of our fraternization and gave them to us when we met again. The same pictures were printed in a German soldier newspaper.

The second fraternization was not as tense and was more organized. Both we and the Germans had interpreters. We even wrote a treaty in German and Russian, which had several paragraphs: not to fire on live targets on the surface or in the trenches; use fire only in extreme cases, when either side goes on the offensive or when scouts attempt to cut the barbed-wire fencing; to hold fraternizations once a week. This treaty was supposed to be passed to new units during rotations on this sector of the front. [. . .]

37. Proceedings of the Soldiers' Section of the Petrograd Soviet, May 10, 1917   [23, vol. 3, pp. 26–7]

The following document is excerpted from the newspaper Golos soldata *(Soldier's Voice). It shows that as Russian soldiers proceeded to organize themselves, their representatives in the soviets had to take on a variety of issues, from soldiers' rights to the conditions of POWs.*

The session of the Soldiers' section began at 2 p.m. in the Semicircular Hall of the Tauride Palace, Comrade Zavadie presiding. Secretary, Comrade Vatenin.

After the order of the day was announced, Comrade Pavlovskii delivered a brief report concerning national regiments,[46] and the resolution of the Executive Commission was read.

Next, Comrade Pal'tsman spoke in favor of the formation of national regiments, pointing out that these regiments could improve the combat readiness of the army and solidify the front. Comrades Volkov and Engel'gardt speak against the immediate formation of national regiments.

The debates are interrupted in order to hear an unscheduled statement by the Deputy War Minister Colonel Iakubovich.

Transporting soldiers from various fronts for the purpose of forming national regiments would to a great degree worsen the conditions on the railroads, which even now struggle to carry out their tasks.

[. . .] Colonel Iakubovich reported to the assembly that [War Minister] A. F. Kerensky had signed the Declaration of Soldiers' Rights, which the

46. Various nationalist organizations and institutions, including the Ukrainian Rada, requested the right to form military units along ethnic and national lines. Beginning in September 1917 Ukrainian regiments and divisions, Polish corps, and other such units were created.

former [war] minister, Guchkov, had failed to act upon since its delivery to him on March 6. On behalf of A. F. Kerensky, Colonel Iakubovich asked the assembly to help him explain to the soldiers outside of Petrograd the question of saluting. According to the signed Declaration, saluting is abolished, but a footnote states that saluting is retained as a voluntary mutual greeting. The Soviet welcomes Colonel Iakubovich's announcement with loud applause and asks him to send greetings to Minister Kerensky in the name of the section. [. . .]

Concerning POWs. One after another, soldiers who have escaped from German captivity or have been released as disabled speak of all the horrors and the difficult conditions our POWs face in Germany. The situation is terrible. The mortality rate is enormous. Twenty-five percent have died. And everyone unanimously points out that the former government was not at all interested in the fate of [our] POWs, while showing every leniency to the German and Austrian POWs. All the speakers pointed out that only by means of open threats to the German government to start treating [their] POWs the way they treat ours in Germany can any progress be made. And it was only because the governments of France and England made just such a categorical announcement that the French and English POWs enjoy completely different conditions than do the Russians. [. . .]

The session of the Soldiers' section ended close to 7 p.m.

38. Bolsheviks and Mensheviks Clash over an Alleged Insurrection, June 1917   [23, vol. 3, pp. 299–305]

By the summer of 1917, the Bolsheviks began to flex their muscles, not yet fully certain how much support they could count on. The Bolshevik Central Committee scheduled a protest rally for June 10, 1917, in the hope of bypassing and then prevailing over the Petrograd Soviet majority, which at that point still supported the Provisional Government. When the news of the planned rally reached the Petrograd Soviet, they cancelled the rally and then had to explain themselves, on June 11, to skeptical leaders of the Executive Committee of the Petrograd Soviet and of the Presidium of the All-Russian Congress of Workers' and Peasants' Deputies.

Chkheidze presiding.

[. . .] Kamenev.[47] We enter the ranks of the demonstrators only as a class-based and internationalist party. [. . .] The events in Petrograd are rooted in

---

47. Lev Kamenev (1883–1936) was a leading Bolshevik who had returned from Siberian exile in March 1917.

the government dragging its feet on the issues of the day. We had heard about the excitement of the masses. [. . .] A meeting was convened. The speakers revealed that the regiments and the workers were eager to act. Some comrades argued that this mood could only be actualized by means of protest rallies. Others opposed calling a rally. It was decided to call another meeting. That meeting was purely organizational. A huge majority voted in favor of calling a protest rally. That was the result. The majority supported calling a rally but only under specific slogans. There was no "Seizure of power" slogan. The only affirmative slogan was "All power to the Soviets." When news about this decision reached the Congress, it was argued that counterrevolutionaries wanted to hijack the rally. [. . .] So, we cancelled it at 12 a.m. [The newspaper] *Soldtatskaia Pravda* received our telephone message with suspicion. [. . .]

Tsereteli.[48] The main question has already been answered. The main question is: "Was there a conspiracy or not?" (Shouts: "Yes there was.") If there was no conspiracy then we made a mistake. Why was this concealed from the Congress? They wanted to catch the Congress off guard, offer it a fait accompli. It is not surprising that they then took steps, when the conspiracy was revealed. Their only choice was to quell it. We prohibited not the rally, but the possibility of a repetition of conspiracies. We have reached a brink, beyond which bloodshed begins. Counterrevolution did not raise its head. Anarchy is the only source of counterrevolution now. By striking anarchy we will kill counterrevolution. We must take decisive measures. Physical force is on the side of the majority of the masses. We must use all our authority to confiscate weapons [from the Bolsheviks].

Kamenev declares that the accusation that has been made must be substantiated in court. The Bolsheviks walk out in protest.

39. The Pavlovskii Guard Regiment Appeal to the First Turkestan Army Corps, June 1917   [85, pp. 24–5]

Russia's general staff and other senior officers adamantly insisted that Russia needed to take pressure off France and Great Britain to enable them to launch a successful offensive against Germany. They deeply feared that if Russia left the war, then Prussian militarism would triumph and Germany could dictate Draconian terms of defeat to Russia. The military leadership also hoped that the offensive would raise morale and halt the corrosive effects of democratization in the military. They were sorely mistaken, in part because the

---

48. Iraklii Tsereteli (1881–1959) was a leading Menshevik of Georgian nationality. At this time, he was minister of the postal and telegraphic service of the Provisional Government.

soldiers continued to meet in soldiers' committees, forums for challenging the government's entire war effort. This document reflects soldiers' growing anger about the military offensive that was just beginning.

Not earlier than June 16, 1917
    Greetings, dear comrades from the Turkestan [Army Corps],
    We are sending you our opinions as soldiers of the guard. Dear comrades, they use the guards to scare you and they use [regular] army men to scare us from refusing to go on the offensive. But do not fear: nothing will happen. Thanks to our organization, we soldiers of the guard told War Minister [Alexander] Kerensky to his face, when he came to visit us on June 16, that we will not go on the offensive and that we do not recognize him as minister. We want power to pass immediately into the hands of the peoples [of the Russian Empire], that is, to the soviets of soldiers', workers', and peasants' deputies. And he replied: Why do you not trust me, a socialist minister? But we said that we do not trust you and that if you are a socialist then you know that we are all citizens now, yet why have you issued orders so that an officer has the right to shoot his subordinate for not carrying out orders and that if a subordinate refuses to carry out his superior's orders then his wife or mother will be deprived of her food ration. Then he explained that these orders were developed by [Aleksandr] Guchkov together with the Polivanov Commission. When Guchkov left, [Kerensky] was given them to sign and signed them without reading them, and that's how this mistake happened, and so it was not his fault. And we said: What kind of a minister are you and how can you be trusted if you sign orders without reading them, and he said not a word to that. Then we all yelled: "Down with the Provisional Government, and power should pass to the people!" Comrades, all the warring states have already rejected [the idea of] annexations and contributions,[49] so that the people can decide the peace [terms]. But these ministers-capitalists and ministers-socialists, the burzhoois,[50] want to exterminate us and send us on the offensive. But we know what is going on and do not advise you either, comrades, to join in the offensive. By waging an offensive, we would only prolong the war, lose our freedom, and prevent Germany from completing their revolution. Revolution is now taking place in Germany. We asked Kerensky, why he had forbidden going on leave, and he said the soldiers' committees had recommended this step, because the soldiers

49. None of the belligerent states, contrary to the document's assertion, rejected the principle of "annexations and contributions," meaning the right of the victors to dispose of territory of the conquered and to demand reparations from them.
50. "Burzhooi" was a popular, and highly derogatory, form of "bourgeois."

travel home, become upset, and then lower morale in the ranks upon their return, so he suspended granting leaves until August 13. But we held our ground, so probably quite soon he will restore our right to go one leave. We greeted the War Minister with hooting and shouting and sent him off with hooting as well. He is surely sorry he visited the 1st Guard Corps. So long, comrades.

40. Alexander Kerensky at the Front, July 7, 1917
[8, vol. 3, pp. 962–6]

After initial success against Austria, the Russian offensive began to slow. As the Provisional Government was becoming a target of growing criticism from the left, Alexander Kerensky, as the minister of war, struggled valiantly to raise the troops' morale. The report below is excerpted from Izvestiia, *the newspaper of the Executive Committee of the Petrograd Soviet. It shows how committed Kerensky was to the offensive's success, a commitment that was not shared by everyone. In fact, by this time the offensive was already collapsing, in large part due to poor coordination among the several fronts. The resulting debacle not only further depressed morale and further split soldiers and officers but also put out of action some of the most reliable military units in the army. Overall, the offensive diminished the Russian army's prestige in the eyes of its allies. It also sparked the July Days, an attempted uprising in Petrograd.*

At a time when certain army units in Petrograd were demanding the removal and even the arrest of the Minister of War, A. F. Kerensky, and were shouting, "Down with the offensive!" A. F. Kerensky was touring the regiments of the revolutionary army of the Western Front, calling upon them to fulfill their duty to the country and the revolution.

Rumors about events in Petrograd had already reached the front, and the soldiers, as if in response to the demand of the Petrograd regiments, met the Minister with particular warmth and enthusiasm. The Minister did not receive such an enthusiastic welcome in the regiments of the Southwestern Front. There was complete unison between the Minister and the regiments of the Western Front which had thrown out all the cowardly and worthless elements from their midst. This was the unity of the will of the majority of the Russian democracy about which the Minister spoke before committees of the Petrograd Garrison units on June 13, on the eve of [his] departure to the Southwestern Front. At that time he expressed assurance that the entire Petrograd Garrison would submit to the will of the majority and would not inflict blows on the back of its Minister of War, who was placed on the front—and, moreover, by the revolutionary army—to perform his duty.

The Minister's hopes were not justified. Some Petrograd units, protesting against the war and the offensive, raised their armed hands . . . against their own brothers and stabbed them in the back. [. . .]

[. . .] On the morning of July 5 the Minister left Mogilev for Molodechno, where he arrived at 7:00 p.m.

Here the Minister was given an enthusiastic welcome by a crowd of many thousands of soldiers, expressing their sincere joy at the return of the popular Minister to the front. [. . .]

When the regiments gathered around the automobile and arranged themselves in an amphitheater [formation], A. F. Kerensky addressed the following words to them:

"I greet you on behalf of the free revolutionary people. I am happy and proud to have the honor to be among you and to endure with you all the anxieties of these great days. Having thrown off the chains of slavery of the tsarist power, the Russian people have become the freest people in the world. The people are now fighting for the happiness and freedom of the broad, working masses, for land and freedom, for the honor, independence, and dignity of the great free Russian people. Fighting in the name of the right to live freely, you are carrying, on the points of your bayonets, a message of the brotherhood of all peoples, of the triumph of the great principles of freedom, equality, and fraternity. The Russian people have many enemies. [. . .] If we are unable to defend freedom, it will perish, the red banners will fall, and the great day of celebration for the working masses will disappear. New generations will live in suffering and will curse the names of those who were unable to stand in the defense of freedom."

"We will not let this happen" was heard from all sides. [. . .]

With strong, prolonged shouts of "Hurrah" from the crowds of many thousands of soldiers, the Minister, escorted by a mounted reconnoitering detachment, drove off to the next regiments, situated considerably closer to the front lines. On the way there, rumblings of artillery fire were heard constantly, ever closer and closer. [. . .]

The Minister, met by the Marseillaise and strong prolonged shouts of "Hurrah," [. . .] spoke before a crowd of ten thousand soldiers. [. . .]

"Whatever happens to you tomorrow," continued the Minister, "today, calmly and bravely, with chests bared, we will go forward in the name of freedom, equality, and fraternity. Think, comrades; before us awaits a completely free, happy life. . . . Can one really be sorry to suffer and to give up one's life for such a life? Can there really be even a single coward and traitor who could forget his duty? [. . .]"

When the shouts of "Hurrah" quieted down, the commander of the army corps declared:

"Comrades, let us swear an oath that as soon as there is an order to advance, we will go, as one man, loyal to duty and to the appeal of the revolutionary leader, Minister Kerensky. From the bottom of our hearts—hurrah to Comrade Kerensky!"

A member of the Executive Committee spoke: "It was not only the Minister of War who spoke to us, but Comrade Kerensky, who has dedicated his whole life to the fight for land and freedom. As a revolutionary fighter, he has the right to demand that we execute his will. Then let us give him our word that at his order we will advance without fear or doubt!"

"We give [our word], we give [our word]" was heard from all sides. "Comrade, Minister, lead us; we are ready to advance!" [. . .]

41. Russian Message to the Allies Following the July Days, July 19 [8, vol. 2, pp. 1123–4]

A vast political gulf over the question of war divided the educated segments of society and the broader population. By mid-1917, most Russians desperately craved peace and an end to the struggle and their suffering, yet the letter below, written by Foreign Minister of the Provisional Government Mikhail Tereshchenko,[51] reflected the view that fighting alongside the democratic western Allies was fully consistent with the spirit of the Revolution, as well as a matter of honor for Russia.

At the moment, when new and grave misfortunes are threatening Russia, we consider it our duty to give our allies, who have shared with us the burden of the trials of the past, a firm and definite explanation of our point of view as to the conduct of the war.

The great tasks of the Russian revolution correspond to the magnitude of the upheaval it has caused in the life of the state. Reorganization of the entire governmental system in the face of the enemy could not be effected without serious disorders. Nevertheless, Russia, convinced that there existed no other means of safety, has continued common action at the front in accord with her allies. Fully conscious of the difficulties of her task, Russia has

51. Mikhail Ivanovich Tereshchenko (1886–1956) was a deputy in the Fourth Duma and a financier and owner of sugar factories and large landholdings.

taken up the burden of conducting active military operations during the reconstruction of the army and of the Government. The offensive by our armies that was made necessary by the strategical situation encountered insurmountable obstacles, as much at the front as in the interior of the country. The criminal propaganda of irresponsible elements was made use of by enemy agents and provoked a revolt in Petrograd. At the same time, part of the troops at the front, seduced by the same propaganda, forgot their duty to the country, and made it easy for the enemy to pierce our front. The Russian people, stirred by these events, showed, by their Government created by the revolution, an unshakable will, and the revolt was crushed, and its instigators brought to justice. All the necessary steps have been taken at the front for restoring the combat strength of the armies. The Government intends to bring to a successful end the task of establishing an administration capable of meeting all dangers and of guiding the country on the path of revolutionary regeneration.

Russia will not suffer herself to be deterred by any difficulty from carrying out her irrevocable decision to continue the war to the final triumph of the principles proclaimed by the Russian revolution. In the presence of the enemy menace, the country and the army will continue, with renewed courage, their great work of restoration as well as of the preparation on the threshold of the fourth year of war, for the coming campaign. We firmly believe that Russian citizens will combine all their efforts for the fulfillment of the sacred task of defending their beloved fatherland, and that the enthusiasm which lighted in their breasts the flame of faith in the triumph of liberty will direct the whole invincible force of the revolution against the enemy who threatens the country. We know that our liberty, as well as that of all humanity, depends on the issue of this struggle. The fresh trials imposed on it by the crimes of traitors can only strengthen still more the consciousness felt by the Russian people of the necessity of concentrating all its forces and all its possessions on one supreme effort for the salvation of the fatherland.

Strong in this consciousness, we are convinced that the retreat of our armies will be only temporary, and that it will not prevent them, reorganized and regenerated, from resuming at the appointed hour their onward march in the name of the defense of the fatherland and of liberty, and that they will victoriously finish the great work for which they have been compelled to take up arms.

[Foreign Minister Mikhail] Tereshchenko

The Provisional Government in Decline

42. Bolshevik Activism in Ivanovo-Voznesensk, June 1917
[32, pp. 2–3]

An important center of the textile industry employing 156,000 workers in 1914, the Ivanovo-Voznesensk economic district, which was divided between Vladimir and Kostroma provinces, lay 180 miles northeast of Moscow. The city itself was home to several thousand businesses with 30,000 employees. As such, it was a leader in revolutionary activism in the revolutions of 1905 and 1917. The author of the following document, F. N. Samoilov, was a textile worker, trade-union leader, and Social Democratic Party activist elected to the Fourth Duma in 1912. He chaired Ivanovo-Voznesensk's Soviet of Workers' and Soldiers' Deputies, which as his recollections indicate, openly challenged the laws and orders of the Provisional Government.

The second episode when the Ivanovo-Voznesensk Soviet of Worker and Soldier Deputies acted authoritatively by refusing to obey the laws issued and enforced by the Provisional Government took place in the middle of June. Since the premises of the Ivanovo-Voznesensk Executive Committee on Napalkovskaia Street were highly inadequate, it was decided to seek more suitable premises. For that purpose, a special commission composed of N. A. Zhidelev, V. S. Bubnov (then head of the city militia), and D. I. Shorokhov was elected. The commission was empowered to requisition to property, in case of necessity.

Very soon the commission designated the house of I. N. Polushin, a factory owner, on Aleksandrovskaia Street. At that time, he was serving in the military as an officer of the former army, and his house was rented out to the factory owner Derbenev. Old lady Derbeneva was then living there. The members of the above-mentioned commission learned from Kuchin, the manager of Derbenev's factory that Derbenev's lease of Polushin's house would soon expire.

When the commission arrived in the above-mentioned house and told old lady Derbeneva that she must be so kind as to vacate the house, since it was going to be occupied by the Soviet, she responded that it was not her house, that she was simply a tenant, and that they had to speak with the owner of the house. When she was reminded that her lease would soon expire, she became very agitated and screamed that nobody had the right to evict her, that they have no right to use violence against her, and that the house was private property. Therefore, if evicted, she would complain to the English, the French, etc.

After that, the members of the commission went to see the factory owner S. N. Polushin, the brother of the owner of the house. He greeted them very politely and in response to his question "How may I be of service to you?" V. S. Bubnov responded in a similarly polite fashion. Polushin then stated that it was not his house, but his brother's and that therefore his brother had to be contacted, not him. Then in a more decisive way Zhidelev asserted that, since the Soviet was in need of a house, the owners of the house should cooperate, since the Soviet was the de facto authority in the city. Polushin kept saying stubbornly that the house was the private property of his brother and that there was nothing he could do. Then D. I Shorokhov spoke in an even more decisive fashion. He demanded from Polushin a note stating that he knew his brother to be unopposed to the revolution and that he vouched that he would not resist should the Soviet occupy his house. Polushin prepared such a note, and very soon the house was occupied by the Soviet. The city duma, the majority of whose members were Bolsheviks, sanctioned this act of requisitioning immovable private property.

S. I. Polushin, despite his note, sent a complaint to Petrograd about the illegal seizure of the house by the Ivanovo-Voznesensk Soviet and then disappeared. As a result, some investigator arrived from the capital. But when he had just barely begun the investigation of this case, he was shown Polushin's above-mentioned note and was told to take a hike, which he did.

43. Alexander Kerensky on the Kornilov Affair, August 1917 [35, pp. xiii–xxiii]

A decorated military officer of Cossack origin, Lavr Kornilov (1870–1918) took part in expeditions in Central Asia and served as military attaché in China. Captured by the Austrians in 1915, he escaped a year later, much to popular acclaim. A harsh critic of the Imperial Russian regime, his Eighth Army was one of the few to distinguish itself during the June 1917 offensive. Consequently, he was appointed supreme commander on July 18. In this post, he urged the abrogation of Order No. 1 and the establishment of harsh discipline throughout the military and in the defense industries. He also deeply distrusted the Soviet and the Bolsheviks and definitely wished to launch a military operation against them.

As Russia's military fortunes worsened and the population grew more radical, Kerensky wavered between working with the military leadership to reduce the power of the Soviet and seeking mass support. At the same time he tried to draw reliable troops to Petrograd, ostensibly to protect the city but in reality to detach them from Kornilov. The following account is meant to justify Kerensky's role in what remains a murky set of events. The consequences of the Kornilov affair, however, were clear. It undermined the support of conservatives, especially in the military, for the Provisional Government; weakened the faith of ordinary people in Kerensky; strengthened the Red Guards[52] to whom Kerensky gave weapons for thwarting the alleged coup; and greatly increased the Bolsheviks' popularity.

[. . .] The regeneration of the fighting capacity of the army was the task of the Prime Minister, Kerensky, from the very first moment when he took over office from Gutchkov. It was necessary to liquidate the tendency of army reforms which had been carried out during the first two months of the Revolution, but in striving with this object the War Minister, Kerensky, could not permit the too harsh and premature steps which were demanded by the irresponsible partisans of "strong power." [. . .]

But all the danger from the activities of too hasty "reformers" was nothing in comparison with the terrible consequences of the secret intrigue which was carried on at the same time at Headquarters and in other places with the object of making a forcible coup d'état, and which already by the time of the Moscow Conference had attempted to accustom Russia and Kornilov himself to the idea of the military dictatorship of the latter. Information about conspiracies began to reach the Provisional Government as early as July, 1917; the breakthrough near Tarnopol deeply touched the feeling of national pride; moreover, after the abortive Bolshevik rising many thought that a courageous and well-organized assault on the Government was sure to succeed. Parallel with the open propaganda of the idea of a military dictatorship, secret work was going on. At the first stage separate conspirative circles were organized in which some military elements took an active part, among them a part of the members of the Main Committee of the old Russian Officers' League. [. . .] At one time the partisans of "strong power" sent out feelers to Kerensky; not meeting with any sympathy there, they directed their attention to Kornilov. "Kerensky does not want to be a dictator; then we will give him one," said V. Lvov. At the moment of the All-Russian Conference in Moscow on the 12th–25th of August, the idea of Kornilov's dictatorship

52. Red Guards were armed factory workers who played a significant role during the Revolution of 1905 and most of the events of 1917. Supporters of the Bolsheviks from summer of 1917, they were a key instrument of the government in dealing with food shortages in spring and summer 1918.

was already quite ripe, and the preparation of the coup d'état, anticipating the sympathy of the Conference, was in full swing. [. . .]

It is difficult to determine exactly when Kornilov became a conscious participant in the conspiracy and the head of the movement directed against the Government. In the first information about the conspiracies his name was not mentioned, but already on the 3rd of August, in a conversation with Kerensky, Kornilov spoke about a military dictatorship as about a possibility which might become a necessity. At the Moscow Conference the behavior of Kornilov towards the Provisional Government was very provocative. On the 23rd of August, at Headquarters, Kornilov spoke harshly to Savinkov about the Provisional Government; he found the continuation of Kerensky's power to be obnoxious and unnecessary and so on. But on the following day, on the 24th of August (6th of September, N.S.), before Savinkov's departure to Petrograd, Kornilov told him that he was going loyally to support the Provisional Government; he asked him to inform Kerensky of this, and Savinkov went away reassured. Now on this day the work of the conspirators was already in full swing.

The presence at Headquarters of the Deputy-Minister of War, Savinkov, from the 22nd to the 24th of August was called for, amongst other reasons, by the necessity for clearing up the conditions for the transference of the army of the Petrograd Military District to the Commander in Chief, also the conditions for sending a military detachment from the front at the disposal of the Provisional Government in connection with the proclamation of martial law in Petrograd. The proclamation of martial law in Petrograd was necessitated by the military situation created after the fall of Riga, [. . .] and by the possibility of riots and various attempts from the Left and from the Right.

All these considerations compelled the Government to demand for its own use a well disciplined army force. Savinkov, in transmitting this order of the Provisional Government to the Commander in Chief, pointed out that the strict conditions for sending troops for the use of the Provisional Government were that the detachment to be dispatched should not include the Caucasian "Savage Division" which was not reliable from the Government's standpoint, and that General Krymov should not be appointed to command it. General Kornilov definitely promised Savinkov on the 21st of August to fulfill exactly the proposal of the Provisional Government and not to send to Petrograd either Krymov or the "Savage Division"; but on the following day the 3rd Cavalry Corps was already moving towards Petrograd, with the "Savage Division" at its head, and the whole under the command of General Krymov, who had received definite instructions from Kornilov. [. . .]

While General Krymov's detachment was approaching the capital, the conspirators attempted to get hold of power "legally" by terrorizing the Government. On the 26th of August (8th of September, N.S.) Lvov, who had arrived in Petrograd from Headquarters, presented an ultimatum to the Prime Minister in the name of Kornilov. The Provisional Government must give up its power the same evening, transferring it to General Kornilov, who would form a new Government. Kerensky and Savinkov must immediately, during the night of the 26th–27th of August, depart for Headquarters, as Kornilov proposed to offer them posts as ministers in his Cabinet and would not take the responsibility for their lives if they remained in Petrograd. At the request of Kerensky, Lvov on the spot put in writing Kornilov's demands; then Kerensky asked Kornilov to come to the direct telegraphic wire, and Kornilov himself repeated to him the proposal to come immediately, confirmed Lvov's authority, and indirectly confirmed all that had been said by the latter. [. . .] [O]n the following day, the 27th of August, a wire was received from the Prime Minister[53] ordering Kornilov to surrender his office immediately and to come to Petrograd. Kornilov did not obey this order, but confirmed to Savinkov by the direct wire his refusal to submit to the Government. On the same day appeared Kerensky's appeal to the population about the Kornilov rebellion and Kornilov's appeal saying that he was "provoked" to make the rebellion and that he was acting against the Government, which was submitting to the "Bolshevik majority of the Soviets" and "working in agreement with the plans of the German General Staff."

Thus the armed revolt against the Government began [. . .] already on the 29th of August it became evident that the whole of the real force of the country was against Kornilov, and, as had been predicted to him by Kerensky himself some time before, Kornilov found himself in splendid isolation. [. . .]

---

53. This wire was actually sent by Nikolai Nekrasov, the transportation minister, without the permission of Kerensky, who tried unsuccessfully to halt its transmission.

CHAPTER 3

The Bolsheviks' Revolution and the Road to a New World

When the Bolsheviks came to power, it seems that they themselves were unsure about what to do next. They hated the old institutions and the old order—that much was clear. Among their pressing tasks was to abolish the landed estates, to nationalize the factories and banks, to end the war, to publish all secret treaties, to disband the traditional courts and replace them with people's courts, and to shut down opposition periodicals. But what exactly should emerge in their place? How could one build socialism in a country populated mostly by peasants? And who exactly should build it? The Bolsheviks did not always know the answers to such questions. Finally, they never thought of themselves as simply Russian revolutionaries and firmly believed that their seizure of power would serve as an inspiration for working people everywhere who would overthrow their governments, proceed to build socialism, and stretch out a helping hand to their Russian comrades. But when exactly would this happen? In a matter of weeks? Months? And what if the world revolution failed to come any time soon? Would not the first successful socialist revolution in world history risk being "strangled in its cradle" by the hostile forces of international capitalism?

The first set of documents, "Soviet Power Is Born" (Documents 44–49), indicates that by fall 1917 the leading Bolsheviks were in agreement with the majority of workers and soldiers in Petrograd that the Provisional Government was worthless, that capitalist exploitation should be ended, that Russia should leave the war, and that all the land should be tilled by the laboring peasants themselves. After more than 3 years of war and steadily increasing economic hardship, it was no wonder that millions of ordinary people had grown tired of the daily grind and privations, and now longed for liberation, for equality, and for a path toward a bright future. It seemed that Lenin,

Trotsky,[1] and other Bolshevik leaders offered just such a vision when they seized power in Petrograd and proclaimed that their regime was in fact based on "Soviet power"—the power of the worker's, soldier's, and peasants' soviets to finally implement broadly desired radical reforms.

In the course of the next few months the Bolsheviks and their supporters expanded their control. As the next section, "Soviet Power Spreads to the Provinces" (Documents 50–53), indicates, change of government was experienced in various ways. Regions, provinces, or cities with a staunch revolutionary tradition, like Saratov, quickly embraced the new regime. Places with a more deeply entrenched civil society and middle class, like Viatka, resisted longer. Localities dominated by the agricultural economy, like Perm, also resisted but in favor of the traditional pro-peasant party, the Socialist-Revolutionaries. Over the next several months, support for the Bolsheviks often waned. As Document 53 shows, new elections to local soviets often returned non-Bolshevik majorities. This represented a huge problem for the government, one often resolved by use of violence, intimidation, and electoral fraud.

It seems that the Bolsheviks were quick to demonize anybody who challenged their claims to power and resisted their policies. As this resistance grew, so did the list of their enemies. The Bolsheviks proclaimed that they were fighting the "class enemy," in particular the industrial bourgeoisie, but they applied this Marxist term very loosely. They also never hesitated to cultivate and foment populist hatred for the elites and in doing so referred to diverse groups of people and parties as "enemies of the people," a designation they borrowed from the French Revolution. The section under that title (Documents 54–62) focuses on those who could be targeted, including officers, intellectuals, the well-to-do, and anyone with glasses or soft hands, all of whom were often dehumanized with the derogatory term *burzhooi.*

Bolshevik revolutionary idealism is on full display in the section entitled "Socialist Dreams" (Documents 63–67), starting with Lenin's important work *The State and Revolution,* which he wrote during a lull in his fight to seize power and at the precise moment of the event that sealed the Provisional Government's fate in late summer 1917: the Kornilov Uprising. The Bolsheviks

---

1. Leon Trotsky was born Lev Davidovich Bronshtein (1879–1940) and grew up in a village in Kherson province, the son of a prosperous Jewish farmer. A leading Social Democratic activist and theorist, he was a prolific writer, a brilliant orator, and a superb organizer. After 4 years in prison and Siberian exile, he fled Russia in 1902 and spent most of the years before the 1917 revolution abroad. A Social Democrat unaffiliated with either the Bolsheviks or the Mensheviks since 1904, he joined the Bolshevik fraction in June 1917 because of his substantial agreement with Lenin's program at that time.

sought to reach as many people as possible with their Declaration of the Rights of the Working and Exploited People in January 1918 (Document 64), which was incorporated in large part as a bill of rights into the first Soviet Constitution in July. Its key element, the only one fully realized, was the nationalization of all private property. The next two documents are probably the most idealistic and hopeful. In the first, Anatolii Lunacharskii, the commissar for culture and education, lauds the new government's celebration of the traditional working-class holiday, May 1 (Document 65). Next, Aleksandra Kollontai, a Bolshevik feminist, envisions the many ways in which the lives of women were being transformed by the Communist revolution in Russia (Document 66). Finally, H. G. Wells, the British novelist, describes a frank encounter with the Bolshevik leader Lenin, whom he found wedded to Marxist dogmas and utopian in outlook but also capable of thinking freely and practically (Document 67).

However inspiring were their revolutionary dreams, the Bolsheviks experienced a number of rude awakenings in the course of the next several years. The following section, entitled "The Bolsheviks Go to the Village" (Documents 68–74), is devoted to Bolshevik policies and attitudes toward the countryside and agricultural production. The peasants, whom Marx considered the most backward and ignorant elements in society, nevertheless constituted an important part in the worker and peasant revolutionary coalition. By the spring of 1918 that coalition began to collapse. Bolshevik propaganda and official rhetoric divided the rural population into three social categories: the poor, the middle peasants, and the rich "kulaks." The overall purpose was to turn the former against the latter and to win support for the government's confiscation of grain surpluses from the villages. In most cases, however, the peasants themselves felt greater solidarity toward each other than to any outsiders preaching class strife in their midst. Many peasants (see Document 72) retained a deep attachment to their faith and religious institutions throughout the revolutionary period, confirming their benighted nature in the eyes of the country's new rulers. All the same, the government relentlessly sought to establish control over agricultural production and other economic activities, which it deemed to be an essential prerequisite for socialism. As Document 73 demonstrates, merely running an oil press for small-scale commercial purposes could land one in forced labor for a term of 5 years. Government inspectors were fully aware of official abuses of power (see Document 74), but while efforts were frequently made to punish wrongdoers, most rural inhabitants remained at the cruel mercy of commissars and other government agents.

"Matters of Survival" (Documents 75–82) catalogues in great detail, but also with pathos and drama, the harsh material circumstances into which most

Peasants View an Exhibit on the Lenin Agitation Train during One of Its Stops, 1920. RGAKFD. The Bolshevik government used every technological means at their disposal in order to raise the cultural and political level of the masses and to mobilize them for building socialism.

people were plunged during the first years of the Bolshevik regime. From workers and soldiers to intellectuals and civil servants, millions of people were driven back to the land, forced to engage in illegal trading, and reduced to pleading for help from senior government officials, as for instance when a handicapped worker asked Mikhail Kalinin, the government's figurehead, to enable him to acquire a cow and a horse (see Document 81). For many people in these times, making a living was beyond their ability; bare survival was the most they could hope for. Among the documents in this section are an eyewitness description by a schoolboy of citizens dismantling fences and houses in Moscow for firewood (Document 79) and a major Russian philosopher eking out an existence on an agricultural commune (Document 78). Even administrators of important institutions, like the University of Saratov, had to wheel and deal just to keep their doors open and the rooms more or less heated in wintertime (Document 77).

For the supporters of the Bolshevik vision, this only reinforced their commitment to "Building Socialism" without delay (Documents 83–91). This section begins with some definitions. Grigorii Zinoviev argues in Document 83 that socialism for the Bolsheviks did not include indiscriminate freedom of speech or assembly when that could strengthen the bourgeoisie. In regard to the economy, Lenin claimed that the central activity of the new state should consist in "accounting and control" of the production, distribution, and use of goods, resources, and services (Document 84). Voices in support of the new regime ranged from a feminist eager to implement the ideals of Aleksandra Kollontai to a Russian Orthodox priest renouncing his calling (Documents 86 and 87). Yet it was becoming increasingly clear that in pursuing their vision, the Bolsheviks relied more and more not on people's enthusiasm, but on the machinery of the new state. The system of government

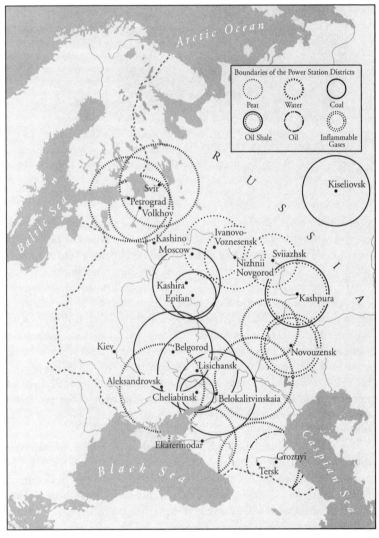

The Electrification of Soviet Russia, 1922.

that emerged by fall 1918, as revealed by Document 85, was parallel. The state and the party institutions overlapped, competed, and reinforced each other, but the party was always to have the last and decisive word. This arrangement worked far from smoothly. The governmental apparatus was often rather petty and inefficient as Documents 89 and 90 demonstrate clearly. Yet the officials running it were sometimes animated by an almost fervent faith in the power of government policies to transform both Russia and eventually the entire world (Document 91).

The last section, "Soviet Russia and the World" (Documents 92–94), thus serves as an important reminder of the global revolutionary implications of the Bolshevik vision. Starting with the lament by General Mikhail Tukhachevskii that the fledgling Soviet state failed to win its offensive against Poland at the end of the Civil War (Document 92), one sees clearly just how much the success of the Russian Revolution hinged in the Bolsheviks' minds on the eruption of revolution in Western Europe. A report on the activities of the Communist International in that area in 1921 (Document 93) indicates the care, efforts, and financial resources the weak and impoverished Soviet state lavished on trying to bring just such an eventuality to fruition. Probably the most important foreign policy venture of the first years of the Bolshevik regime is related in a description of steps taken by the Soviet state in regard to the multicountry international conference held in Genoa, Italy, in spring 1922 (Document 94).

Soviet Power Is Born

44. Vladimir Lenin Urges Seizure of Power, September 12–14, 1917   [44, vol. 26, pp. 19–21]

The Democratic Conference, convened by the Kerensky government on September 14–25, gathered together a broad spectrum of liberal and socialist political parties, including the Bolsheviks, for the purpose of resolving the growing political, military, and economic crises. On August 9, the Provisional Government finally set elections to the oft-delayed Constituent Assembly for November 12. The body was to meet on November 28. But for Lenin this was not revolutionary enough.

The Central Committee of the Bolshevik Party met on September 15 to discuss his letter (first published in 1921). A slim majority voted to preserve only one copy of it. A motion advanced by Kamenev to reject Lenin's proposal to seize power was defeated.

The Bolsheviks, having obtained a majority in the Soviets of Workers' and Soldiers' Deputies of both capitals, can and must take state power into their own hands.

They can because the active majority of revolutionary elements in the two chief cities is large enough to carry the people with it, to overcome the opponent's resistance, to smash him, and to gain and retain power. For the Bolsheviks, by immediately proposing a democratic peace, by immediately giving the land to the peasants and by reestablishing the democratic institutions and liberties which have been mangled and shattered by Kerensky, will form a government which nobody will be able to overthrow. [. . .]

The Democratic Conference represents not a majority of the revolutionary people, but only the compromising upper strata of the petty bourgeoisie. We must not be deceived by the election figures: elections prove nothing. [. . .]

The Democratic Conference is deceiving the peasants; it is giving them neither peace nor land.

A Bolshevik government alone will satisfy the demands of the peasants.

* * *

Why must the Bolsheviks assume power at this very moment?

Because the impending surrender of Petrograd will make our chances a hundred times less favorable.

And it is not in our power to prevent the surrender of Petrograd while the army is headed by Kerensky and Co.

Nor can we "wait" for the Constituent Assembly, for by surrendering Petrograd Kerensky and Co. can always frustrate its convocation. Our Party alone, on taking power, can secure the Constituent Assembly's convocation; it will then accuse the other parties of procrastination and will be able to substantiate its accusations. [. . .]

* * *

It would be naive to wait for a "formal" majority for the Bolsheviks. No revolution ever waits for that. [. . .] History will not forgive us if we do not assume power now. [. . .]

By taking power both in Moscow and in Petrograd at once (it doesn't matter which comes first, Moscow may possibly begin), we shall win absolutely and unquestionably.

45. Vladimir Lenin Urges Immediate Seizure of Power, October 1, 1917   [44, vol. 26, pp. 140–1]

Lenin continued to press on. The following letter, sent on October 1 to the Central Committee, the Moscow and Petrograd Party Committees, and the Bolshevik Members of the Petrograd and Moscow Soviets yet first published in 1921, prompted the two leading skeptical Bolsheviks, Lev Kamenev and Grigorii Zinoviev, to denounce Lenin's calls for an insurrection in the Menshevik-leaning newspaper Novaia zhizn *two weeks later.*

Dear Comrades,

Events are prescribing our task so clearly for us that procrastination is becoming positively criminal.

The peasant movement is developing. The government is intensifying its severe repressive measures. Sympathy for us is growing in the army. [. . .]

In Germany the beginning of a revolution is obvious, especially since the sailors were shot.[2] The elections [to the Soviet] in Moscow—47 per cent

---

2. In early August 1917, some 400 German sailors in Wihelmshaven on the North Sea mutinied to protest the war. Military courts tried, convicted, and executed 75 alleged ringleaders.

Bolsheviks—are a tremendous victory. Together with the Left Socialist-Revolutionaries we have an obvious majority in the country. [. . .]

The Bolsheviks have no right to wait for the Congress of Soviets, they must take power at once. By so doing they will save the world revolution (for otherwise there is danger of a deal between the imperialists of all countries, who, after the shootings in Germany, will be more accommodating to each other and will unite against us), the Russian revolution (otherwise a wave of real anarchy may become stronger than we are), and the lives of hundreds of thousands of people at the front.

Delay is criminal. To wait for the Congress of Soviets would be a childish game of formalities, a disgraceful game of formalities, and a betrayal of the revolution.

If power cannot be achieved without insurrection, we must resort to insurrection at once. It may very well be that right now power can be achieved without insurrection, for example, if the Moscow Soviet were to take power at once, immediately, and proclaim itself (together with the Petrograd Soviet) the government. Victory in Moscow is guaranteed, and there is no need to fight. Petrograd can wait. [. . .]

[. . .] Victory is certain, and the chances are ten to one that it will be a bloodless victory.

To wait would be a crime to the revolution.

Greetings, N. Lenin

46. Putilov Workers on Creating a Military Revolutionary Committee, October 24, 1917   [14, vol. 1, p. 103]

Week by week and even day by day the strength of the Bolsheviks had increased in Petrograd, especially after the Kornilov Affair. By September 25, the Petrograd Soviet elected a radical new leadership, composed of four Bolsheviks, two Socialist-Revolutionaries, and one Menshevik, with Trotsky as chair. The Putilov metalworking plant, the largest in Petrograd, employed over 10,000 workers and produced heavy weaponry for the state during World War I. Workers at the plant had been at the forefront of strikes and protests leading to the collapse of the monarchy in February 1917. When on October 16, 1917, the Petrograd Soviet voted to create a Military Revolutionary Committee, ostensibly for the defense of Petrograd,[3] many workers expressed their support

---

3. On October 9, the Plenum of the Petrograd Soviet voted to create a committee of defense to protect Petrograd against German invasion. The Bolsheviks at the meeting insisted that the proposed committee should assume all military power in the capital in order

for the committee in resolutions like the one provided below, even as the supporters of Mensheviks and Socialist-Revolutionaries worried that it would become a tool in the hands of Bolsheviks.

We, workers of the Putilov Wharf numbering 4,500, having reviewed a report concerning the creation of the Military Revolutionary Committee for the purpose of controlling the activities of the General Military Headquarters, whose members remain unchanged since they revealed themselves to be leading counterrevolutionaries during the Days of July 3 and 5, approve and will support in every way the resolution of the Petrograd Soviet of Workers' and Soldiers' Deputies. We also urge the Military Revolutionary Committee to take measures to disarm the officer training schools as soon as possible.[4]

Signed by the chairman and secretary of the assembly.

47. Speeches by Lenin and Trotsky to the Petrograd Soviet, October 25, 1917   [23, vol. 4, pp. 581–3]

After Lenin and Trotsky delivered the speeches excerpted below on October 25, the Winter Palace, formerly the residence of the Tsars and recently the seat of the Provisional Government, fell to Bolshevik supporters. The next day, October 26, Bolsheviks in Moscow seized the Kremlin. All the major Russian newspapers published reports from this session of the Petrograd Soviet, some more detailed than others. The document below is a rough, unedited record, which retains best the spirit of the session. While Trotsky reported on the logistics and reasons for the insurrection's success, Lenin's speech was more forward looking as he identified the key goals of the new "worker and peasant revolution."

That day and the next, the All-Russian Congress of Soviets adopted several Bolshevik decrees and formed a new government, the Council of People's Commissars (SNK), with Lenin as chairman. A new Central Executive Committee was also created, composed of 62 Bolsheviks and 29 Left Socialist-Revolutionaries, with Lev Kamenev as chairman.

---

to oppose potential counterrevolutionary actions. The plenum agreed. On October 12, the Executive Committee upheld the decision and changed the organ's name to the Petrograd Military Revolutionary Committee.

4. The students (cadets) in officer training schools were the military elements most loyal to the Provisional Government and most hostile to the Bolsheviks during this period.

Urgent session of the Petrograd Soviet
   Session of October 25, 1917. The session was called to order at 2:35 p.m.
Statement by Comrade Trotsky. "On behalf of the Military Revolutionary Committee, I proclaim that the Provisional Government exists no more."
(*Applause.*) "Several ministers have been arrested. Others will be arrested in
the next few days or hours." (*Applause.*)
   "The revolutionary garrison, which is at the disposal of the Military Revolutionary Committee, has dissolved the parliamentary session." (*Noisy applause. Shouting: "Long live the Military Revolutionary Committee."*)
   "We had been told that the uprising of the garrison at the present moment would elicit a pogrom and would drown the revolution in rivers of
blood. So far everything has occurred without bloodshed. We are not aware
of a single casualty. I do not know any examples in the history of the revolutionary movement, where such huge masses were involved with so little
bloodshed.
   "The power of the Provisional Government, headed by Kerensky, was
lifeless and awaited the broom of history to sweep it away.
   "We must mention the heroism and self-sacrifice of the Petrograd soldiers
and workers. We were awake here all night and, by telephone, monitored
how the units of revolutionary soldiers and worker-guards soundlessly went
about their business. The residents of Petrograd were sleeping and had no
idea that in the meantime one government was replacing another.
   "The train stations, the post office, the telegraph, the Petrograd telegraph
agency, the State Bank have been occupied." (*Noisy applause.*) "The Winter
Palace has not yet been taken. But its fate will be decided in the next few
minutes.
   "The Petrograd Soviet of W[orkers'] and S[oldiers'] D[eputies] can be
justly proud of the soldiers and workers, on whom it relies, whom it led into
battle and on to a glorious victory.
   "It is in the nature of bourgeois and petty bourgeois governments to de-
ceive the masses. At the present time, we, the Soviets of Sold[iers'], Work[ers']
and Peas[ants'] Deputies, stand before an unprecedented task: to create a government with no other goals but the needs of soldiers, workers, and peasants.
The state should be a tool by which the masses can fight for their liberation
from all slavery. This work cannot go forward without the involvement of
the soviets. The best elements of bourgeois science will understand that the
conditions created by the Soviets of W[orkers'], S[oldiers'] and P[easants']
D[eputies] will be the best conditions for their work.
   "Control over production must be established. Peasants, workers, and
soldiers must feel that the national economy is their economy. This is the
fundamental principle for establishing the government."

Presently, Comrade Trotsky mentions that next on the agenda are reports by the Military Revolutionary Committee and about the tasks of the power of the soviets. Comrade Lenin will speak on the second item. (*Unremitting applause.*) [. . .]

In response to a question about how the soldiers at the front view the events, Comrade Trotsky responds: "We have only had time to send telegrams. There is no response yet. But many times we heard representatives from the front reproach us that we had not yet undertaken decisive steps."

At this moment comrade Lenin appears in the hall. The audience begins a stormy ovation.

Comrade Trotsky continues: "We now have in our midst Vladimir Il'ich Lenin who, due to diverse circumstances, could not appear in our midst until this moment."

Comrade Trotsky describes Comrade Lenin's role in the history of the revolutionary movement in Russia and proclaims: "Long live comrade Lenin who has now returned to us." (*Again, stormy applause honoring Comrade Lenin.*)

Lenin's speech. "Comrades. The worker and peasant revolution, of whose necessity the Bolsheviks had always spoken, has occurred.

"What is the significance of this worker and peasant revolution? Above all, the significance of this coup is that we will now have a Soviet government, our own organ of rule without any participation of the bourgeoisie whatsoever. The oppressed masses will create a government themselves. The old state apparatus will be broken up at its core and the new apparatus of government will be created in the form of Soviet institutions.

"From now on a new phase of Russian history is beginning, and the present third Russian revolution will ultimately lead to the victory of socialism.

"One of your immediate tasks is an immediate end to the war. But it is clear to everybody that in order to stop this war, which is closely linked to the existing capitalist system, capital itself must be defeated.

"The worldwide labor movement, which is already beginning to develop in Italy, England, and Germany, will assist us in this task.

"A fair and immediate peace, which we have proposed to the international democracy, will find an enthusiastic response among the international proletarian masses everywhere. In order to strengthen this trust of the proletariat, we must immediately publicize all secret treaties.[5]

---

5. The Bolshevik Decree on Peace appealed to all the warring powers to cease fighting and negotiate a "democratic" peace. Appointed commissar for foreign affairs in the SNK, Trotsky immediately published the secret treaties signed by Russia and her allies relating to plans for redrawing state boundaries and allocating territory to the victors. Russia, for example, was to receive control over the Straits at Constantinople.

"Within Russia, a huge section of the peasantry has said: enough of playing with capitalists; we will join the workers. A single decree eliminating landed estates will gain for us trust.[6] The peasants will understand that the salvation of the peasantry lies only in a union with the workers. We will establish genuine worker control over production. We have now learned how to work in concert. The revolution that has just occurred testifies to that. We possess the power of mass organization that will prevail over everything and will lead the proletariat to world revolution.

"In Russia we must now begin building a proletarian socialist state.

"Long live the worldwide socialist revolution." (*Furious applause.*)

The meeting resolves not to open a debate on Comrade Lenin's speech. Since the members of the Military Revolutionary Committee are currently busy, their report is being postponed. Trotsky appears on the podium in order to make a statement.

Comrade Trotsky's statement. "One of the most pressing tasks of the Military Revolutionary Committee is to send a delegation to the front with information about the revolution that has taken place in Petrograd. The Petrograd Soviet should appoint commissars in order to dispatch them to the front. The Military Revolutionary Committee and its members cannot issue statements right now because they are constantly preoccupied with urgent work. I can report only that word has just been received that troops from the front are moving in the direction of Petrograd. It is essential to send commissars; it would be criminal on our part not to dispatch revolutionary commissars all over the country in order to inform the broad popular masses about what has happened." (*Voices from the audience: you are predetermining the will of the All-Russian Congress of Soviets.*)

"The will of the All-Russian Congress of Soviets has been predetermined by the enormous fact of the uprising of the Petrograd workers and soldiers, which occurred tonight. Now all that remains for us is to develop our victory."

---

6. The Decree on Land, taken in toto from the program of the Socialist-Revolutionaries, proclaimed the transfer of all large-scale landed property to township committees for eventual distribution to the peasants. By this means, the Bolshevik leaders, who in fact favored nationalization of all land, sought to win peasant support.

48. Joseph Stalin on the Nature of "Soviet Power," October 26, 1917   [71, pp. 39–42]

Born in Georgia to a cobbler and a washerwoman, Iosif Vissarionovich Dzhugashvili (pseudonym: Stalin, derived from the Russian word for "steel"; 1879–1953) graduated first in his class from the local church school and attended, but did not graduate from, the Georgian Orthodox seminary in Tiflis. He joined the Social Democratic Party in 1898 and the Bolshevik fraction,[7] for which he carried out armed robberies in 1906–1907. He escaped from arrest several times, but not in 1913, when he ended up in far Siberia until 1917. When Stalin wrote this article, he was still considered a junior member of the Bolshevik leadership, neither too intellectually sophisticated, nor very articulate. Yet his writing reveals an astute learner for whom the revolutionary experience of 1917 taught important lessons about how to secure power and how to deal with political rivals.

In the first days of the revolution the slogan "All Power to the Soviets" was a novelty. "Soviet power" was opposed to the power of the Provisional Government for the first time in April. The majority in the capital were as yet in favor of a Provisional Government without Milyukov-Guchkov. In June, this slogan obtained the demonstrative recognition of the overwhelming majority of the workers and soldiers. The Provisional Government was already isolated in the capital. In July, a struggle around the slogan "All Power to the Soviets" flared up between the revolutionary majority in the capital and the Lvov-Kerensky government. The compromising Central Executive Committee, relying on the backwardness of the provinces, went over to the side of the government. The struggle ended in favor of the government. The adherents of Soviet power were outlawed.

A dead season set in of "socialist" repressions and "republican" prisons, of Bonapartist[8] intrigues and military plots, of firing squads at the front and of "conferences" in the rear. This lasted until August. At the end of August the scene changed very radically. The Kornilov rebellion called forth the exertion of all the strength of the revolution. The Soviets in the rear and the

7. The Bolsheviks along with the Mensheviks constituted two leading fractions of the Russian Social Democratic Party. As the division (or divisions) between them grew, the term *fraction* began to signify a fully independent political organization.

8. The term *Bonapartist* referred to the seizure of power by Napoleon Bonaparte in 1799 and his hijacking of the French Revolution. All the political actors in 1917 were keen students of history and believed fervently that the greatest danger the fledgling revolution faced was a similar coup d'état at the hands of some charismatic leader.

Committees at the front, which were in a moribund state in July-August, "suddenly" revived and took power in their hands in Siberia and the Caucasus, in Finland and the Urals, in Odessa and Kharkov. Had they not done this, had they not taken power, the revolution would have been crushed. Thus, "Soviet power" proclaimed in April by a "small group of Bolsheviks in Petrograd" obtains the almost universal recognition of the revolutionary classes in Russia at the end of August.

It is now clear to all that "Soviet power" is not only a popular slogan, but the only sure weapon in the struggle for the victory of the revolution; it provides the only way out of the present situation.

The time has come for the slogan "All power to the Soviets" to be put into practice at last. But what is "Soviet power"; and how does it differ from every other power?

It is said that transferring power to the Soviets means forming a "homogeneous" democratic Ministry, organizing a new "Cabinet" consisting of "Socialist" Ministers, and, generally speaking, making "important changes" in the composition of the Provisional Government. But this is not true. Here, it is not a matter of substituting some persons for others in the Provisional Government. The thing is to make the new revolutionary classes the masters of the situation in the country. The thing is to transfer power to the hands of the proletariat and revolutionary peasantry. For this purpose a mere change in the composition of the government is inadequate. For this purpose it is first of all necessary thoroughly to purge all the government departments and offices, to expel the Kornilovites, and to place everywhere loyal members of the working class and the peasantry. Only then, and only in that case, will it be possible to speak of transferring power to the Soviets "at the center and in the districts."

What is the cause of the universally-known helplessness of the "Socialist" Ministers in the Provisional Government? What is the cause of the fact that these Ministers have proved to be miserable playthings in the hands of people outside the Provisional Government? [. . .] First of all the fact that instead of them directing their Departments, their Departments directed them. The fact, among others, that every Department is a fortress occupied by the bureaucrats of the tsarist period who transformed the good intentions of the Ministers into "hollow sounds," and who are ready to sabotage every revolutionary measure adopted by the government. [. . .]

Power to the Soviets means the thorough purging of every government office in the rear and at the front, from top to bottom.

Power to the Soviets means that every "Chief" in the rear and at the front must be elected and subject to recall.

All Power to the Soviets means that all "representatives of authority" in town and country, in the army and navy, in the "Departments" and "government-offices," on the railways and in the Post Office must be elected and subject to recall.

Power to the Soviets means the dictatorship of the proletariat and the revolutionary peasantry.

This dictatorship differs radically from the dictatorship of the imperialist bourgeoisie, the very dictatorship which Kornilov and Milyukov tried only very recently to establish with the benevolent participation of Kerensky and Tereshchenko.

The dictatorship of the proletariat and the revolutionary peasantry, i.e., the dictatorship of the toiling majority over the exploiting minority, over the landlords and capitalists, over the profiteers and bankers, for the sake of a democratic peace, for the sake of workers' control over production and distribution, for the sake of land for the peasants, for the sake of bread for the people.

The dictatorship of the proletariat and the revolutionary peasantry, i.e., open, mass dictatorship, exercised in the eyes of all, without plots and behind-the-scenes work; for such a dictatorship has no reason to hide the fact that no mercy will be shown to the lock-out capitalists who have intensified unemployment by means of various "unloadings," or to the profiteering bankers who have increased the price of food and caused starvation.

The dictatorship of the proletariat and the peasantry, i.e., a dictatorship without violence against the masses, a dictatorship which expresses the will of the masses, a dictatorship for the purpose of curbing the will of the enemies of these masses.

This is the class nature of the slogan "All Power to the Soviets." Events in home and foreign politics, the protracted war and the longing for peace, defeat at the front and defense of the capital, the rottenness of the Provisional Government and its "removal" to Moscow, chaos and famine, unemployment and exhaustion—all this is irresistibly drawing the revolutionary classes of Russia to power. This means that the country is already ripe for the dictatorship of the proletariat and the revolutionary peasantry.

The time has come for the revolutionary slogan "All Power to the Soviets" to be put into practice.

49. Revolutionary Demands of the 202nd Gori Infantry Regiment, November 4, 1917   [14, vol. 2, p. 106]

Even after the Bolshevik takeover, expressions of support for the Military Revolutionary Committee and its Bolshevik leaders continued to arrive in Petrograd from military units like the 202nd Gori Infantry Regiment, whose demands are listed in the document below.

The regimental committee of the 202nd Gori Infantry Regiment has resolved with all its might to support the Military Revolutionary Committee but also to demand of the Military Revolutionary Committee:

1) [To give] all power to the Soviets.
2) To immediately give all land to the working people by means of land committees.
3) To establish worker control over all factories, plants, private enterprises, and factories that work for the national defense.
4) Not to postpone the convocation of the Constituent Assembly.
5) To immediately conclude a truce on all fronts.
6) The speediest conclusion of a democratic peace.
7) To immediately supply all army organizations with instructions from the Military Revolutionary Committee.
8) To provide to all nationalities inhabiting the Russian state the right to genuine self-determination.
9) The regimental committee expresses the wish that the new government will be composed of representatives of all the socialist parties that have worked and are working for the good of the working people.

Soviet Power Spreads to the Provinces

50. The October Revolution in Saratov,[9] October 26–28
[32, pp. 44–5, 47, 49, 53, 58–62]

Mikhail Vasiliev-Iuzhin (1876–1937), the author, joined the Russian Social Democratic Party at its founding in 1898 and repeatedly suffered arrest and exile. Vasiliev-Iuzhin helped found the Soviet of Workers' and Soldiers' Deputies in Saratov in March 1917 and since the summer had been chairman of the Bolshevik Party Committee there. In his memoirs, he recalls how the Bolsheviks seized power in Saratov and expresses regrets about their leniency toward political adversaries. After the described events, Vasiliev-Iuzhin became a senior official of the All-Russian Cheka,[10] or secret police, and later a prosecutor and judge of the High Court of the USSR. He was executed during Stalin's terror.

In Saratov the October [1917] armed coup occurred in a rather peculiar way [. . . .] [I]n July of that rebellious year, we received only 7,182 votes in the elections to the City Duma—a bit more than the Kadets who obtained 6,654 votes. At the same time, the SRs, the Mensheviks, and the Bundists[11] who ran as a united front (in a single block) were supported by 36,476 votes, that is, five times more votes than the Bolsheviks!

The same thing happened in the elections to the Soviet of Workers' and Soldiers' Deputies. The elections to the second convocation of the Soviet took place in Saratov in June and produced an overwhelming majority of SR and Menshevik deputies.

Yet by August, on several occasions our Bolshevik resolutions won majority support in this SR-Menshevik-dominated Soviet. And when new elections to the Soviet were held in September, we got an overwhelming majority

---

9. A major center of heavy industry and commerce located on the Volga River 450 miles southeast of Moscow, Saratov had a population of 143,000 in 1900.

10. The All-Russian Extraordinary Commission for Combating Counterrevolution and Sabotage (All-Russian Cheka or Cheka) was established in December 1917. Over the next several months, local Chekas were set up at the provincial and district levels. These institutions were in principle subordinate to local soviets, but in practice they often acted autonomously and at best answered to the All-Russian Cheka.

11. The Bund was a Jewish socialist party founded in 1897.

of votes not only among workers but also among the soldiers of the 60,000-strong Saratov garrison. In the new Soviet, the Bolsheviks had 320 deputies (164 workers and 156 soldiers), the SRs had 103 (43 workers and 60 soldiers), and the Mensheviks had 76 deputies (72 workers and 4 soldiers). Both the workers and the soldiers had moved dramatically to the left.

That's why when a member of the Central Committee [V. P. Miliutin] came to Saratov in early October [1917] and asked me: "Would the Saratov workers and soldiers support Petrograd if an uprising against the Provisional Government broke out there?" I responded without hesitation: "I vouch for the majority of Saratov workers and soldiers of the Saratov garrison. Moreover, I cannot guarantee that the soldiers will not launch a spontaneous uprising independently of Petrograd in the nearest future. The soldiers' desire to return home, the prolongation of the war, the June offensive, and Kornilov's mutiny have turned them frightfully against Kerensky and the conciliatory parties. We are finding it difficult to keep them from premature action. If we oppose the outbreak of a spontaneous movement, which is likely to fail, then we must place ourselves at the head of any such movement." [. . .]

October 26 came. By then we already had more precise information about the events taking place in Petrograd. Undoubtedly, a successful coup took place there and a new, this time truly great revolution had begun. A proletarian revolution!

Now we also needed to act. The Soviet of Workers' and Soldiers' Deputies was to convene that night. But we had to assess our forces in advance, to put forth a plan of action, to find out about the enemy's plans and intent... [. . .]

It was about 3 a.m. The Soviet held a quick election to replace the Mensheviks and SRs who had left the Executive Committee [to protest the majority's decision to assume power]; all the deputies pledged to prepare their soldiers and workers for battle, and the session adjourned. We hurried to the Executive Committee building. [. . .]

The session of the Executive Committee lasted until morning. It was decided to proclaim immediately that all power had been transferred to the soviet, to depose the provincial commissar Topuridze replacing him with Lebedev, to disarm unreliable militia units replacing them with worker-members of the voluntary people's patrol, to capture the telegraph and telephone stations, and not to attack the [City] Duma yet, but to bring into combat readiness all the garrison units loyal to us and to arm as many workers as possible. [. . .]

Late in the evening [October 27], we were told that officer trainees from the [City] Duma led by [the Socialist-Revolutionary] Didenko had seized one of the small barracks and had taken several hundred rifles and much ammunition. The cadets had begun to build barricades and to dig trenches in the streets leading to the Duma. [. . .]

We decided to crush the Duma counterrevolutionaries the very next day. In the morning of October 28 the troops and armed workers were ordered to encircle the City Duma district. Our artillery led by Kuchin occupied its designated positions and targeted the building of the Duma with their weapons.

By noon the task set for our troops had been accomplished. The Duma "army" had also completed its preparations: it had set up some rather pitiful barricades, had installed machine guns, including in the bell tower of the church next to the Duma building. They had not a single cannon: all the artillery men were on our side.

We were certain of our victory. We could crush these miserable Duma counterrevolutionaries like flies. But at that time, since we were not yet hardened by the civil war, we thought it would be a shame to spill blood needlessly or to destroy buildings. [. . .]

[. . .] We gave the order to stop shelling the Duma, but to actually stop it was very difficult. The workers and especially the soldiers were terribly angered by the resistance, the systematic deceit, a sleepless night, and the casualties, albeit small, they had suffered. On our side two people had been killed and about ten lightly wounded.

Besides, the enemy continued to fire at us. Machine-gun fire from the church's bell tower was particularly intense; I observed it myself, and this circumstance particularly outraged the soldiers and workers.

Among our soldier Bolsheviks one person stood out: a good-natured bearded man Maksim Sukhov. I think he used to be a sacristan or a sexton and certainly retained some attachment to religion at that time. He in particular fired at the church with great vehemence.

"How did you, Comrade Sukhov, dare to shoot at your god?" I joked with him afterward.

"To god, I made the sign of the cross, and at the idols in the bell tower I swore! Anyway, no doubt god knew I was firing at the idols." [. . .]

I again made the soldiers give me their word to show their revolutionary self-control and not to harm the defeated and unarmed enemy, cautioning them that I was going to the Duma myself to lead them out. [. . .]

The procession lined up, I stood in the front, somebody raised the white flag, and we began to move down Moskovskaia Street toward our barricades. The enemy's barricade made of [bags of] quinces was already being dismantled and eaten.

Workers and soldiers poured out from the nearby streets and courtyards with rifles in their hands. [. . .]

"Hands up! Lift your hands up!" yelled dozens of voices.

"Stop! Stop!" an artilleryman screamed furiously from his gun-carriage, waving his revolver.

The procession stopped. The mass of soldiers were seized by anger and their agitation was growing. This was the most dangerous moment. Just one accidental or malicious shot and not a single prisoner would be left alive. They stood trembling with their hands up.

"Comrade, put away your revolver and step aside," I ordered the artilleryman forcefully. [. . .]

He could not speak because of his agitation and anger. But his screams, gestures, and countenance increased the agitation of the other soldiers. Pushing him aside, I quickly began to move forward. The prisoners rushed after me. Our movement seemed to moderate the agitation of the crowd. They cursed and threatened the prisoners and tore the epaulettes from several officers, but not a single serious violent act took place.

We approached the building of the Executive Committee. I ordered the immediate release of all women and little children. The school children were released later in the evening. [. . .]

Generally speaking, as in other places, as in Moscow and in Petrograd, we treated the first rebels against the proletarian revolution more than magnanimously and leniently. The enemies we released almost immediately went to the Don, to the Urals, to the Caucasus and Ukraine in order to set up regular counterrevolutionary armies against us. The instinct of the masses suggested a more correct tactic: the immediate and severe punishment of all enemies rising against the authority of the workers and peasants. Perhaps the period of the civil war would have been significantly shorter, perhaps much less of our own blood would have been shed later on, had we from the very beginning followed this keen instinct of the masses.

51. On Establishing Bolshevik Rule in Viatka Province, December 1917   [14, vol. 3, pp. 584–8]

The Bolsheviks often lacked established local leaders able to assume power. In such cases, the Bolshevik leadership sent trusted officials called commissars to impose Bolshevik control. Such an official, F. G. Luparev, was dispatched by the Military Revolutionary Committee to Viatka in the Ural Mountains on November 23, 1917. In the report below he describes the Bolshevik reliance on workers and soldiers from the local garrison and the initial opposition to their efforts, which often took the form of strikes by other workers and civil servants. They struck for various reasons. Factory workers sometimes disagreed with the Bolshevik commissars and demanded a coalition government of all socialist parties; civil servants viewed the Bolshevik government as illegal; and printers were angered by the closing down of presses, banning of newspapers, and abolition of press freedom.

[. . .] [H]aving arrived in the city of Viatka on 29 November, I was informed by the local executive committee about the situation in the province, which was as follows: supreme authority in the province was still in the hands of the provincial commissar of the Provisional Government and its Supreme Council for provincial administration, which consisted entirely of Kadets and right so-called socialists.

The Soviet of Workers' and Peasants' Deputies had just been elected, but even though all members of the Soviet share the VTsIK's[12] platform, there is no one to carry out any work, whether organizational or conceptual, which makes everything very complicated and difficult. The Bolshevik Party organization had always subsisted in the political underground and therefore has in its ranks insufficient party workers; there are no Left Socialist-Revolutionaries at all. Nevertheless, I decided first and foremost to liquidate the counterrevolutionary nest and to transfer power to the soviet. With these goals in mind, I proposed a series of measures consisting of the following: to secure the trust and support of the local garrison and workers. For that purpose I organized a joint meeting of the regimental and squadron committees of the whole garrison and of the military section of the Soviet.

At that meeting, a plan of action to destroy counterrevolutionary elements was worked out. We decided to proceed immediately with the election of leaders, and the next day a meeting of the 106th Infantry Reserve Regiment was held for that purpose. Afterwards, we made the rounds of the city and effected a changing of the guards at the governor's mansion. Guards were posted at the following premises and institutions: the electric station, the water works, the telephone switching station, and the provincial administration of the Commissar of the Provisional Government.

The Supreme Council did not react adversely in response to these steps, since it has no armed forces behind it; the whole garrison is on our side. But all these, so to speak, do-gooders found a different way to fight us; they formed a central strike committee of state employees, proclaimed a general strike, and all such governmental agencies as the State Bank, the Provincial Treasury, the Provincial Food Agency, etc., went on strike.

The situation was very serious, since we do not have enough people at our disposal to assign to all of these agencies commissars able to direct their activities. Threats and appeals cannot bring the same result as in Petrograd, because on the orders of the Supreme Council all state employees had been given one month's salary in advance. However bleak the picture, the Central Committee and I resolved to continue our work to strengthen the positions

12. The All-Russian Central Executive Committee of Soviets.

we occupied. Just today the order was issued to shut down the local [Kadet] newspaper *Viatskaia rech,* and the latest issue of *Viatskaia mysl* has been seized and confiscated; however, the latter's editorial board has signed a written pledge not to publish orders of the Supreme Council.

It has been as of yet impossible to arrest the Supreme Council, since all its members are in hiding.

I must also report that we are completely cut off from the outside world and have positively no idea what is going on with you. [. . .]

Since the orders and decrees of the central government do not reach us, it is very difficult to govern the province and to execute any measures in a timely fashion. Therefore I am asking Comrade People's Commissar of the Interior to send me urgently all information concerning governing the province and also [Comrade People's Commissar] for Military Affairs [to send me] decrees and orders on the demobilization of the army. Next I am forced to submit to you the following request: since all agencies have announced a strike and I cannot obtain a credit from the Provincial Treasury to support the Commissariat's employees, I am asking you, comrades, to help me by sending by courier one thousand rubles (1,000 rubles) at least for our most urgent initial needs. In the coffers of the local Soviet of Soldiers' and Workers' Deputies there is not a kopek, since the former Executive Committee handed no funds over to us, there are very few workers in Viatka, and taxing the propertied classes yields nothing since our position is still weak.

We will not cease the struggle, whatever obstacles the bourgeoisie may set before us, and I can say with confidence that the disobedient Viatka province will, in the end, be governed by the Soviets of Workers' and Soldiers' Deputies.

With comradely greetings,

The Viatka Provincial Commissar

52. A Bolshevik Agitator in Perm Province, December 1917   [14, vol. 3, pp. 615–6]

One of the key Bolshevik charges against the Provisional Government was that it kept postponing the elections to the Constituent Assembly. On arresting the Provisional Government, the Bolsheviks promised a speedy convocation of the Constituent Assembly and in deference to it even called their government, "a Provisional Revolutionary Government." Some leading Bolsheviks, including Lenin, thought that convening the assembly would be a political mistake but decided to go ahead with the electoral campaign. As the report from a Bolshevik agitator below demonstrates, during that campaign Bolshevik agitators often had to face a skeptical peasantry.

I, a soldier of the 2nd Machine Gun Regiment, was dispatched on November 19 as an agitator to Perm province, Verkhotuskii uezd. [. . .]

The purpose of my trip was that every step of the way I had to defend the party of the Bolsheviks, that is the People's provisional government. [. . .]

On November 27, I was in the village of Otradnovo. After the liturgy, I gathered a small group of people, stood on an elevated spot, and began to tell them about what had happened since the revolution of February 27, but mostly I was telling them about what happened between October 23 and 25: the transfer of power, Kerensky's offensive, Dukhonin's General Headquarters,[13] and the fact that the old government wanted to abandon Petrograd and move to Moscow. Very many things that were going on in Petrograd.

The peasants listened, but very occasionally voices from the crowd could be heard: we know you Bolsheviks! In our city you robbed the poorest of peasants!

I finished. After me a former teacher of that village, who was a Right Socialist-Revolutionary, stood up. He talked and the peasants approved of him as well. When he finished, I stood up and said: "Comrades, remember Kerensky? He was also an SR and dragged Russia around by its nose for eight months. He promised the peasants land and freedom yet was trying to carry on the war until its victorious end. Meanwhile the peasants were waiting for Kerensky to bring them peace on a platter, like a glass of tea, and to bring their sons, fathers, and brothers back from the trenches."

I furthermore talked about whether the people needed this war, who started it, and many other things, such as the number of wounded and killed, even approximately, in this bloody slaughter.

They wanted me to return as soon as possible and to ask the Petrograd Soviet to order the Verkhotuskii Soviet to establish order across the district. I promised to return.

Most of all I told them about the Constituent Assembly and what it was going to give to the people, what a monarchy is, and what a republic is. Then I asked them to vote for list number 6,[14] the party of the Bolsheviks in Perm province. But what most disoriented the peasants were the priests in whom the peasants believed quite strongly, even though the latter took money from the living and the dead. [. . .]

---

13. Nikolai Nikolaevich Dukhonin (1876–1917) was appointed supreme commander in chief by Kerensky on October 31, 1917. When he refused to negotiate a truce with Germany, the Bolshevik leadership dismissed and then arrested Dukhonin. Before he could leave for Petrograd, a mob of soldiers seized and brutally murdered him. Consequently, the Soviet expression "send someone to Dukhonin's General Headquarters" meant to murder that person.

14. The party list designations changed from province to province.

I said to the peasants: You will believe in us when your sons, fathers, and brothers come back from the front lines and when you drive across your own fields with a plough and a sowing-machine. Then you will say to us: "Forgive us, comrade." Now we ask for your trust, yet you refuse it. I returned to Piter.

Soldier M. Deriabin

53. Report on Establishing Soviet Power in Nizhegorod Province,[15] June 13, 1918   [40, vol. 1, pp. 44–7]

The following document was issued by the Nizhegorod Provincial Department of the Communist Party, whose purpose, as stated below, was to set up soviets throughout the province. Since this work had been completed by the time of the report, the Bolshevik leadership abolished the department soon thereafter. As the report indicates, popular support for the Bolsheviks had plummeted by early summer 1918.

After the October Revolution, the purpose of the Provincial Department was to organize Soviet power in the provinces.

It can be freely stated that until December 1917, for want of activists and proper organization, the department accomplished nothing. No more than fifteen soviets were registered, and of that number, upon inspection, a good half turned out to be fictitious. [. . .]

Beginning in December the staff of the Provincial Department expanded somewhat and more productive work began. It is true, however, that because of insufficient personnel it was not possible to service a given district in its entirety, and work proceeded only sporadically, without completion, now here and now there, shifting from one place to another, from one district to another.

At that time the department had already begun to deviate from its primary responsibility—organizing the soviets. Because of insufficient personnel in the Executive Committee, members of the Provincial Department had to go to the provinces in order to suppress disturbances, counterrevolutionary

15. An ancient Russian city situated at the confluence of the Oka and the Volga Rivers 270 miles east of Moscow and a key point of exchange between Europe and Asia, Nizhnii Novgorod [Nizhegorod] was one of the country's major industrial centers and the home of an immense trade fair, which was held each year in late summer. Its population in 1897 was 90,000 (1.6 million throughout the province), but the fair attracted some 400,000 people annually.

activities, etc. Nevertheless, in spite of this abnormal, unplanned, and incoherent work, in the course of one month (December 1917 to January 1918) approximately thirty soviets were set up and registered. During that period soviets were also organized in all [eleven] districts.

Beginning in January, the work of the Provincial Department made giant steps forward. [. . .]

Beginning in February and until recently, when famine began to be particularly strongly felt in the countryside, work in the province on strengthening Soviet power was making gigantic strides. At that time it could be boldly said that the entire countryside was supporting the soviets. Little kulaks, little priests, and counterrevolutionaries in the countryside concealed themselves in nooks and crannies. The authority of the central, provincial, and even uezd Soviet power was enormous. [. . .]

[. . .] The picture changed drastically when spring came. Pure and simple starvation shattered the foundations of Soviet power in the countryside. So-called "speculation on hunger" by rightist elements and counterrevolutionary agitation of priests helped pushed the masses rightward and fostered the development of animosity toward Soviet power. Mass attacks began against the soviets: either peacefully by means of reelections or, when the masses were more conscious and did not yield power easily to the kulaks and village exploiters, by means of armed rebellion.

The political conjuncture in the province has changed. According to a questionnaire prepared and distributed by the Provincial Department, the following situation has emerged: the following breakdown of political views has been registered across all the soviets in the province (at the present time soviets have been created in all townships):

Entirely leftist (Communists or Left SRs)	15%
Mostly leftist	4%
No party affiliation	58%
Mostly rightist	23%

The soviets we control in the province add up to 19%, and those of the right (since those with "no party affiliation" are also rightists but who fear to openly say so) constitute 81%. It is necessary to keep in mind that the percentage of left soviets continues shrinking every day, because the wave of reelections and dissolutions is rising and literally engulfing the whole province. In these circumstances, the work of the members of the Provincial Committee in the countryside is extremely difficult. Instead of the former respect and trust, the masses now express bitterness and suspiciousness. In order to avoid being lynched, our comrades must often travel by back roads, hiding their last names and party affiliation.

It is becoming risky to the highest degree to travel without armed protection. [. . .]

"ENEMIES OF THE PEOPLE"

54. Alexei Remizov, *The Lay of the Ruin of the Russian Land,* October 1917   [10, p. 76]

Alexei Remizov (1877–1957) was a Russian modernist writer. Involved in radical politics while at university, he spent 8 years in Siberian exile, where he avidly studied Russian folktales and calligraphy. Upon his return to European Russia, he devoted himself to writing in the ancient Russian style about saints' lives and heroic stories. The narrative excerpted below alludes to the Mongol conquest of ancient Rus in the 1200s. Remizov intended to express his anger and sorrow about what he thought was the Revolution's complete destruction of Russia's glory and soul, hinting, however, at its eventual regeneration.

[. . .] Blind leaders, what have you done!

The blood that soaked into our native soil has hardened the human heart. You have purged the soul from the Russian people.

Hark! The crazed monkey shrieks.

My Rus,[16] you are burning!

My Rus, you have fallen, and you cannot be lifted up. You will not rise again!

My Rus, my Russian land, defenseless motherland. The blood soaked into our native soil has left you pitiless; set on fire, you are burning! [. . .]

Many times I denied you in those bygone days and, with my forlorn and desperate heart, cursed you harshly for your offenses and falsehoods:

"I am not Russian! There is no truth in the Russian land!"

But now, no, I will not abandon you in your sin and in your tribulation, whether you are free or enslaved, loose or bound, holy or sinful, illumined by light or covered in darkness.

And how could I leave you? I am Russian, son of a Russian, from the very bowels of your soil. [. . .]

Oh, Russian people, what have you done?

---

16. The term *Rus* refers to the East Slav lands in the time before national consciousness and their division into the modern countries of Russia, Ukraine, and Byelorussia. It also, in common parlance, evokes the ancient culture and folkways of Russia.

You sought your happiness and lost everything. Rudely deceived, like a pig you have plunged into filth.

You believed.

Whom did you believe? Well, you have no one to blame but yourself, and no one to pay your debt but you.

Your fantasy land has vanished.

Where is your Russia?

It is now empty space.

This is your sin, oh, Russian people, your unforgivable sin.

And where is your conscience, your wisdom, your cross? [. . .]

Oh, Russian people, the Bright Day will dawn.

Hear you a horse's snorting?

A demented horseman, who emerged from the yellow fog and yearns to master the sea, shattered the old Rus and he will raise up a new one, new and free from doom.

I hear feathers quivering above my head.

This is the new Rus, beautiful and free, my princess.

Have faith, oh, Russian people: a Bright Day will dawn. [. . .]

55. Diary of an Anonymous Russian Official, Late 1917
[50, pp. 15, 17–8]

The diary, from which the excerpt below is taken, covers the period from October 1917 to September 1918 and is reflective of the mood of many civil servants who moved from trying initially to resist the Bolsheviks to passive acquiescence. Soon after writing the final entry, the author, an unknown midlevel employee of the Credit Chancellery of the Ministry of Finance and almost certainly a nobleman with impressive personal connections, entrusted it to an employee of the British Embassy in Petrograd. In the next several weeks, when nearly all the foreign embassies closed their doors, the employee who had received the text gave it to a Norwegian, Christian Christiansen, who took it with him back to Norway. There it was all but forgotten for many decades.

October 26, 1917, Thursday

Last night the Provisional Government breathed its last! Kerensky had already ditched the Winter Palace for the front yesterday morning. The other ministers were arrested last night in the Winter Palace, and people say they have been beaten badly. It serves them right; they have committed enough stupidities. Now let them pay. Pity that Kerensky ran away and was not hanged. [. . .]

October 27, 1917, Friday

The whole day was devoted to a meeting of the employees of the Credit Chancellery and then of representatives from all the agencies of the Finance Ministry. The meeting began at 2 in the afternoon and ended at 10 at night. We voted to launch a general strike and to mention in the [strike] resolution that, protesting against the seizure of state power, we, the employees of the Finance Ministry proclaim:

1. We do not find it possible to obey orders coming from those who have seized power;
2. We refuse to enter into business relations with them; and
3. until the creation of an authority enjoying universal popular recognition, we terminate our official activity, laying the responsibility for the consequences on those who have seized power. [. . .]

October 28, 1917

Yesterday *Novoe vremia* and *Rech* were published for the last time.[17] Today the "bourgeois" press is not seen, but even the newspapers of the Socialist-Revolutionaries sometimes are subjected to violence and destroyed by the Bolsheviks. The People's Commissar for Finance [Viacheslav] Menzhinskii[18] came to the [Finance] Ministry this morning, but finding only guards and couriers, he chose to leave quickly. [. . .]

October 31, 1917, Tuesday

[. . .] The Labor Commission of the Worker and Peasant Government, the former Labor Ministry, is mobilizing new employees, loyal to the revolution, inviting them to occupy positions in all agencies of the new people's government. The purpose is to replace those officials of the former Provisional Government who "due to their blindness sabotage their duties, without consideration of the consequences of their actions." [. . .]

An order has been issued to carry out work at the usual times from this day forward. If the strike in any agencies of the Finance Ministry continues, the heads of these agencies will be immediately arrested. [. . .]

17. A decree of October 27 banned "counterrevolutionary" periodicals. As the decree stated, "Liberty exists behind a screen only for the propertied classes who seek to confuse the minds of the masses." The press, in the hands of the bourgeoisie, it stated, "is no less dangerous than machine guns and bombs."

18. Viacheslav Rudolfovich Menzhinskii (1874–1934) was a learned Polish nobleman who joined the Russian Social Democratic Labor Party in 1902 and the Bolshevik fraction in 1903. An official of the Commissariat of Finance in 1917, he served in the All-Russian Cheka from 1919 and headed the secret police, the OGPU, from 1926 to 1934, when he died of natural causes.

November 1, 1917, Wednesday
   The strikes continue in our ministry [. . .]
   Because of Menzhinskii's threats, the private banks are again on strike.
The same goes for the State Bank. Savings banks will only be open for two
hours.

November 2, 1917
   [. . .] Power is now on the Bolsheviks' side, but their promises cannot be
fulfilled. They will not keep them and will find themselves utterly alone.
Peace there will not be; this is quite clear. Neither will there be bread. There
will be no kerosene or coal; complete deprivation will set in. As for freedom,
not a trace is left. The railroad workers are divided. So are the civil servants.
Thus, tomorrow in our ministry partial operations will begin, under the belief that we have already sufficiently expressed our political protest against
the usurpers of power. [. . .]

November 7, 1917
   [. . .] Menzhinskii has announced that if the Council of People's Commissars will not receive 10 million rubles, this amount will be taken by force
from the cashier's vault. The Council of the State Bank has resolved: The
Council does not consider itself authorized to satisfy this demand, since it is
not based on law. An account in the name of the Council of People's Commissars cannot be opened, since the Council [of People's Commissars] does
constitute a legal person. [. . .]

November 9, 1917
   The Bolsheviks have seized the Moscow office of the State Bank, which
had notes of credit for 100 million rubles. [. . .]

56. A Soldier Rails against Officers and Elites, November 14, 1917   [14, vol. 2, pp. 549–50]

*The following letter to the Military Revolutionary Committee reflects the deep
level of anger and hatred many soldiers felt for their commanding officers, as
well as rich people and the elites in general, anyone who in their view did not
sacrifice as much as they did in the course of the excruciating war years. Such
soldiers believed that the Bolshevik revolution meant that payback time had
finally arrived.*

Comrade members [of the Military Revolutionary Committee], together with the commissars of the popular masses, discuss my proposal.

Because of the difficulty of the current situation in the country, more specifically hunger and so that this no longer happens, I propose to check all the residents of Petrograd to see who is doing what, since I am confident that in the city of Piter you will find a half or a third living like birds, not doing anything, yet requiring food. For example, the thing that is most noticeable to me is prostitutes: here are so many of them that there is not a single house without them. You should take the strictest measures to exile them from Petrograd to the provinces so that they can work there for the hungry.

2. Then there are many hooligans who don't work, yet they need to buy denatured alcohol somehow and so in front of my own eyes they robbed the store on Malaia Okhta Street on November 11 at twelve midnight, and also if they meet anybody weak they will not pass him by. So, you should issue strict [rules] for alcohol sales and for denatured alcohol drinkers.

3. Then my most important proposal is well known to you and you haven't done anything about it. [. . .]

Only one percent of the officers [supported the October uprising]. Like in our First Reserve Regiment only two officers did and only one of them acted for the good of the people, the working and hungry masses, while the other one was a provocateur, and all our soldiers are running around and saying that if the Military Revolutionary Committee does not take action, then the soldiers themselves will deal with them, and all of the vile and repulsive officers will end up in the Neva [River]. And here is what I propose to do with them: demote them all to privates and give them the rights of soldiers, and their families should receive the same ration rights as soldiers' wives, not a kopek more, and revoke all their pensions. [. . .]

[. . .] At the present moment many officers are being elected from the ranks at squadron meetings. They will defend the soldiers and will go together with them wherever the people's government and all the working masses demand. Please do not delay for a single minute, before it is too late, allowing the election of officers from the ranks, because such officers will hesitate to act against neither military cadets, nor officer-Kornilovites, nor the Cossacks, nor the bourgeoisie with a fat belly like a spring mattress. [. . .]

57. The Murder of the Imperial Russian Family
[1, pp. 133–42]

On the night of June 12–13, 1918, Grand Duke Mikhail Aleksandrovich, who had refused the throne in March 1917, was murdered by agents of the

Cheka in Perm in the northern Ural Mountains. Nicholas II and his immediate family were next. They had been placed under house arrest in early March 1917 and were sent to Tobolsk in western Siberia by the Kerensky government in July 1917 in order to prevent their being used as a monarchist banner by counterrevolutionaries. In April 1918, the Bolsheviks transferred them again, this time to Ekaterinburg, 800 miles east of Moscow in the Ural Mountains. As Czechoslovak troops began to approach that city, on the night of July 16– 17, 1918, Yakov Mikhailovich Yurovskii (1878–1938), the head of the Ekaterinburg Cheka, orchestrated the murder of the Russian emperor and empress, along with their five children, as well as four servants. The next day, in Alapaevsk, 75 miles north-northeast, five more grand dukes and duchesses, along with a prince and a servant, were murdered and thrown down a mine shaft.

Yurovskii prepared the account excerpted below in early 1934. There are actually three versions of Yurovskii's account, each of them probably edited by others; leading scholars consider all of them generally accurate. The original 1918 report is missing, probably destroyed. Oddly, the Central Committee minutes for 2 months before and after these events are also missing. The government officially announced the execution of the emperor on July 19, claiming that the decision had been made locally, endorsing it, and noting that the emperor's wife and children had simply been evacuated.

On the 16th in the morning [. . .] I prepared 12 revolvers and designated who would shoot whom. Comrade Filipp [Goloshchekin][19] told me that a truck would arrive at midnight; the people coming would say a password; we would let them pass and hand over the corpses to them to carry away and bury. [. . .]

The truck did not arrive until half past one. The extra wait caused some anxiety—waiting in general, and the short night especially. Only when the truck had arrived (or after telephone calls that it was on the way) did I go to wake the prisoners. Botkin slept in the room nearest to the entrance. He came out and asked me what the matter was. I told him to wake everybody, because there was unrest in the town and it was dangerous for them to remain on the top floor. I said I would move them to another place. Gathering everybody consumed a lot of time, about 40 minutes. When the family had dressed, I led them to the room in the basement that had been designated earlier. [. . .] Although I told [the victims] through Botkin that they

19. Filip Isaevich Goloshchekin (1876–1941) was the military commissar of the Ural region, secretary of the Urals regional party committee, and a personal friend of Iakov Sverdlov. In early July 1918, he stayed in Sverdlov's apartment in Moscow and met with Lenin.

did not have to take anything with them they collected various small things—pillows, bags, and so on and, it seems to me, a small dog.

Having gone down to the room (at the entrance to the room, on the right there was a very wide window), I ordered them to stand along the wall. [. . .] Nicholas had put Alexei on the chair and stood in such a way, that he shielded him. Alexei sat in the left corner from the entrance, and so far as I can remember, I said to Nicholas approximately this: His royal and close relatives inside the country and abroad were trying to save him, but the Soviet of Workers' Deputies resolved to shoot them. He asked "What?" and turned toward Alexei. At that moment I shot him and killed him outright. [. . .] Bullets began to ricochet because the wall was brick. [. . .]

[. . .] When the firing stopped, it turned out that the daughters, Alexandra Feodrovna, and, it seems, Demidova and Alexei too, were alive. I think they had fallen from fear or maybe intentionally, and so they were alive. Then we proceeded to finish the shooting. (Previously I had suggested shooting at the heart to avoid a lot of blood). Alexei remained sitting petrified. I killed him. They shot the daughters but did not kill them. Then Yermakov resorted to a bayonet, but that did not work either. Finally they killed them by shooting them in the head. Only in the forest did I finally discover the reason why it had been so hard to kill the daughters and Alexandra Feodrovna.

After the shooting it was necessary to carry away the corpses [. . .] Having confirmed they were dead, we began to carry them out. It was discovered that traces of blood would be everywhere. I said to get some smooth woolen military cloth immediately and put some of it onto the stretchers and then line the truck with it. [. . .]

After instructions were given to wash and clean everything, at about three o'clock or even a little later, we left. I took several men from the internal guards. I did not know where the corpses were supposed to be buried, as I have said. Filipp Goloshchekin had assigned that to Comrade Yermakov. [. . .] At about two-three versts (or maybe more) from the Verkh-Isetskii Works, a whole escort of people on horseback or in carriages met us. [. . .]

The truck was stuck and could not move. I asked Yermakov, "Is it still far to the chosen place?" He said "Not far, beyond the railroad beds." And there behind the trees was a marsh. Bogs were everywhere. I wondered, "Why had he herded in so many people and horses? If only there had been carts instead of carriages." But there was nothing we could do. [. . .] I found out we had gone about 15–16 versts from the city and had driven to the village of Koptyaki, two or three versts from there. We had to cordon the place off at some distance, and we did it. Besides that, I sent an order to the village to keep everybody out, explaining that the Czech Legion was not far away, that our units had assembled here and that it was dangerous to be here. I ordered

the men to turn back anybody to the village and to shoot any stubborn, disobedient persons if that did not work. Another group of men was sent to the
town because they were not needed. Having done all of this, I ordered [the
men] to load the corpses and to take off the clothes for burning, that is, to
destroy absolutely everything they had, to remove any additional incrimi-
nating evidence if the corpses were somehow discovered. I ordered bonfires.
When we began to undress the bodies, we discovered something on the
daughters and on Alexandra Feodrovna. I do not remember exactly what she
had on, the same as on the daughters or simply things that had been sewed
on. But the daughters had on bodices almost entirely of diamonds and
[other] precious stones. Those were not only places for valuables but protective armor at the same time. That is why neither bullets nor bayonets got
results. [. . .] The valuables had been collected, the things had been burned,
and the completely naked corpses had been thrown into the mine. From that
very moment new problems began. The water just barely covered the bodies. What should we do? We had the idea of blowing up the mines with
bombs to cover them, but nothing came of it. I saw that the funeral had
achieved nothing and that it was impossible to leave things that way. It was
necessary to begin all over again. But what should we do? Where should we
put the corpses? [. . .]

I went to the town executive committee, to Sergei Yergerovich Chutskaiev
who was its chairman at the time to ask for advice. Maybe he knew of a place.
He proposed a very deep abandoned mine on the Moscow high road. I got
a car, took someone from the regional Cheka with me, Polushin, it seems,
and someone else and we left. [. . .] We looked over the place and decided it
was good. The only problem was to avoid onlookers. Some people lived near
the place and we decided to come and take them away to the town and after the project let them come back. [. . .]

[. . .] I drove to Voikov, head of supply in the Urals, to get petrol or
kerosene, sulphuric acid too (to disfigure the faces) and, besides that, spades.
I commandeered ten carts without drivers from the prison. Everything was
loaded on and we drove off. [. . .] I decided to bury some corpses on the
road. We began to dig a pit. At dawn it was almost ready, but a comrade
came to me and said that despite the order not to let anybody come near, a
man acquainted with Yermakov had appeared from somewhere and had
been allowed to stay at a distance. [. . .]

So that plan was ruined too. We decided to fill in the pit. Waiting for
evening, we piled into the cart. [. . .] We headed for the Siberian high road.
Having crossed the railroad, we transferred two corpses to the truck, but it
soon got stuck again. We struggled for about two hours. It was almost midnight. Then I decided that we should do the burying somewhere around

there, because at that late hour nobody actually could see us. [. . .] A fire was made and while the graves where being prepared we burned two corpses: Alexei and Demidova. The pit was dug near the fire. The bones were buried, the land was leveled. A big fire was made again and all the traces were covered with ashes. Before putting the other corpses into the pit we poured sulpheric acid over them. The pit was filled up and covered with the [railroad] ties. The empty truck drove over the ties several times and rolled them flat. At 5–6 o'clock in the morning, I assembled everybody and stated the importance of the work completed. I warned everybody to forget the things they saw and never speak about them with anybody. [. . .]

In the evening of the 19th I went to Moscow with my report.

58. Private Letters from a Bolshevik Activist, July 17–18, 1918   [91]

At the time of writing the document below, Yakov Semyonovich Sheikman was the chair of the Bolshevik fraction and of the provincial soviet in Kazan, an industrial center of 206,000 with a large Muslim population on the Volga River. An active participant in the October coup, he was a delegate to the Fifth Congress of Soviets, which met in July 1918. As such, he participated in quashing the Left Socialist-Revolutionary uprising that broke out at the same time. His wife wanted him to write of his convictions to their son after he nearly died in an armed attack. He was executed a few weeks later when Kazan fell to the Czechoslovaks. He was 27.

[. . .] [Y]our mother has asked me to write you a letter. If I am killed, you will have detailed advice from your father who loves you and your mother endlessly. I am more than happy to fulfill your mother's wish. [. . .]

When I was elected Chairman of the Kazan Soviet, I threw myself into my work. The work was enormous. A succession of meetings sometimes went on for days without a break. You can imagine how difficult it all was, since we had simultaneously to build up, to tear down, and to defend ourselves against enemies who had no shortage of furious hatred toward us.

The whole country was engulfed in the flame of the Civil War.

Having suffered defeat in open battle, the bourgeoisie and its underlings set about laying ambushes. Sabotage acquired incredible forms and reached colossal proportions. The intelligentsia, which had without complaint supported the bourgeoisie, did not want to serve the working class. As if that were not enough, it joined an alliance with the bourgeoisie directed against the working class. [. . .]

Counterrevolution struck Soviet Russia painfully. Yet Soviet power courageously repulsed the blows falling on it from all sides and soon went on the offensive.

Where our enemies were prevailing, there was no mercy for us. But we also showed no mercy. Here it is necessary to tell the truth: our enemies were more brutal than us. They were senselessly brutal. Often, if not always, their cruelty resulted from cowardice. [. . .]

So, dear Emi, we are surrounded. Perhaps I will have to die. Every moment danger awaits us. That's why I decided to write to you. Of course I haven't been writing for print. No time for that. But perhaps this will be interesting to you.

I always think of you when I am exposed to danger.

I want you to have a photograph or some other memento of me.

Do not be upset if I am killed. Believe me, it is not terrible.

I want you, too, to be selflessly brave. Never fear death. Be faithful to yourself. Banish fright. I would hope that you will never side with the oppressors and will always stand with the oppressed, not fearing to lose your life.

Work should become the foundation of your life. Do not waste time. Work. Work will give you joy. Beware of debauchery. It destroys all the best in a human being, destroys nature. Material well-being should never be your life's goal. Forgive me that I am speaking in such a didactic manner, but I want to express my thoughts to you briefly. Treat women beautifully and nobly. Remember that I measured men by how they treated women.

Honesty and straightforwardness have always appealed to me.

I hate lies. I despise deceptive people.

Sweet Emi, it is so funny: I am speaking with you so seriously, and your mama writes that you have just learned how to sit up. While eating porridge, you smear it all over your little face. And I am giving you advice. It is funny, isn't it? [. . .]

Sverdlov told me that [former Tsar] N. A. Romanov was killed. His family was transferred to Alapaevsk. I was sorry the whole family was not destroyed. This is not bloodthirstiness speaking, but a sense of precaution. Ekaterinburg is threatened. They must be destroyed before the Czechoslovaks take them under their protection. [. . .]

We talked about Lenin. The Bolsheviks are incredibly fond of Vladimir Il'ich. Il'ich is a god. Truly, what a powerful figure. I know not a single person who can be compared to Lenin. His will is indomitable. His sagacity is prophetic. I was recently browsing through his articles "Against the current."

Two years before the revolution he dared to express the thought that in Russia power would be in the hands of the working class. To say nothing of his political enemies, his political friends considered it a fantasy. It is not for nothing that one bourgeois said to me of Lenin: "Lenin must be the happiest person. He is the only person who has seen his fantasy become reality." Of course, Lenin is happy to see the theory he has devoted his whole life to develop into reality. Lenin cannot be afraid of death. He is already immortal. [. . .]

It is pleasant to think about Lenin. When you follow him, your strength multiplies tenfold. [. . .]

I am going to bed. Good night, my dear boy. I borrowed a nickname for you from the drugstore. When you used to take cod liver oil, I thought I should call you "gold fish." [. . .]

The Mensheviks and the Right SRs (actually, there are no Left SRs any more [. . .]) are still wailing. I want to tell them: "Don't cry little child, don't cry in vain, your tear will not fall on a voiceless corpse as a drop of living dew." Their tears are crocodile tears. Shakespeare writes: "If that the earth could teem with your tears, each drop would prove a crocodile."[20] I cannot stand these animals with soft flesh and wet eyes.

Hiding behind revolutionary phrases they do their vile business. The best thing is to fight an enemy who confronts you directly and openly. At least there is honesty there. As to the Mensheviks and the Right SRs (the latter especially), they constantly act furtively, seeking to employ Trojan methods for combating the government. [. . .]

There is a lot of wretchedness in Soviet officials (not all, of course, are like that, but many). Careerism, sycophancy toward highly placed comrades, toadyism, subservience, etc., etc., have always provoked in me aversion. And these qualities in Soviet activists make me want to shoot such gentlemen on the spot—they serve not ideals but individuals for financial gain.

Emil', when you grow up, despise such people. Such people are traitors and scoundrels. Show them no mercy.

I am speaking with you as with a big boy. But you are still such a little one. You are probably sleeping and don't care a whit that daddy is speaking to you of revolution. Good night, my baby. I want to kiss you.

---

20. Sheikman is paraphrasing Shakespeare, who has Othello say: "If that the earth could teem with woman's tears/Each drop she falls would prove a crocodile." *Othello*, Act 4, Scene 1.

59. A Local Misunderstanding about the Role of Muslim Clergy, September 1918   [40, vol. 1, p. 107]

Generally hostile to religion, the Bolshevik leadership treated the Muslim community more leniently than it did either Christians or Jews because it sought to project an anticolonialist attitude in order to appeal to peoples in the Middle East and did not want to appear to be the heir to Imperial Russian colonialism. Thus, mullahs, unlike priests and rabbis, enjoyed full civil rights; some Muslim religious schools continued to function; and Islamic courts preserved judicial authority until the late 1920s. However, as the following document suggests, this relative leniency did not alter the fundamental Bolshevik view that Islam like other religions had no place in the future Communist world and that the Muslim clergy posed an ideological threat to Soviet power. The following document was sent as a directive from the head of the Nationalities Section of the Communist Party Committee of Nizhegorod province to the Nationalities Section of the Sergach District Party Committee, which was severely rebuked for its decision to organize a congress of Muslim clergy.

We are extremely surprised by your intention to convene a congress of Muslim clergy in order, as you stated in your minutes, to explain to the masses the goals and tasks of the Soviet Republic.

Through whom do you want to conduct this agitation among the masses? Through the clergy, those died-in-the-wool reactionaries, our convinced ideological opponents? Can you really imagine these clerical individuals, who are shot through and through with a religious worldview, going out from your congress and propagating our ideas about the dictatorship of the proletariat and our consequently mercilessly harsh attitude toward the bourgeois class, our sworn enemy? Have you ever seen any organization of the Russian Communist Party convene a congress of the Russian clergy? It should be clear to everyone that a party organization, by simply inviting members of the clergy to a congress, would endow them with even greater strength and weight in the eyes of the non-party masses, who would clearly see that by inviting the clergy to the congress and by exchanging opinions with them we ourselves would be recognizing the huge influence the clergy has over the masses as their leaders.

The idea of convening such a congress reveals only a lack of political sense and of a clear understanding of the methods and means of our agitation and propaganda, which is why we found it necessary to explain to you our outlook in detail.

In light of the above, the Nationalities Section of the Provincial Committee has resolved to suspend the convocation of your congress, which we urgently telegraphed you about the day we received your minutes. Instead of such congresses, use *our* agitators to conduct a series of lectures and talks in order to inculcate into the masses a correct understanding in regard to religion in general and the clergy in particular. Organize more frequent conferences for non-Communists to discuss issues of vital concern. Point out to the masses the extraordinary nature of the current situation, including the struggle against hunger and against our military enemies. Recruit volunteers, call for the maximum assistance to the front with food and supplies.

Those are our immediate tasks, which must be carried out at all costs.

60. Correspondence of Maxim Gorky and V. I. Lenin, September 6 and 15, 1919   [33, pp. 146, 148]

A prolific and celebrated author, Maxim Gorky, pseudonym of Aleksei Maksimovich Peshkov (1868–1936), focused his literary work on ordinary people and the downtrodden. Arrested and persecuted frequently as an enemy of the Imperial Russian regime, he was close to the Bolsheviks and a personal friend of V. I. Lenin from 1902 on. Yet from the moment the Bolsheviks seized power, Gorky consistently denounced their repressive measures and failure to respect human rights. He intervened with the Soviet leadership repeatedly, and often successfully, on behalf of political prisoners and intellectuals suffering from persecution and material deprivation. As the exchange below indicates, Lenin was not pleased with his efforts.[21]

Vladimir Il'ich!

[. . .] Several dozen leading Russian scholars have been arrested. [. . .]

For me the riches of a country, the strength of a people are expressed in the quantity and the quality of its intellectual forces. A revolution makes sense only when it fosters the growth and development of these forces.

[. . .] I know you will say the usual things: "this is a political struggle," "who is not with us is against us," "neutral people are dangerous," and the like.

[. . .] The vast majority of the representatives of the hard sciences are neutral and objective, like science itself; these people are apolitical.

Among them the majority is old and sick; prison will kill them; they are already weakened by hunger.

Vladimir Il'ich! I am joining these people and would prefer arrest and imprisonment (even if only by my silence) in the destruction

---

21. Gorky left Bolshevik Russia in October 1921 but returned, at Stalin's request, in 1929.

of the best, most valuable forces of the Russian people. For me it has become entirely clear that the "Reds" are just as much enemies of the people as are the "Whites."

Letter of V. I. Lenin to Maxim Gorky, September 15, 1919.

What a misfortune, you say! What an injustice! Intellectuals having to spend a few days or perhaps even weeks in prison in order to avert the massacre of tens of thousands of workers and peasants! [. . .]

The intellectual forces of the workers and peasants are growing and strengthening in the struggle for the overthrow of the bourgeoisie and of their accomplices, little intellectuals, the lackeys of capital, who think they are the brains of the nation. In reality, they are not the brains, but the s[hit].

61. Parishioners Demand to Teach the Catechism, December 1919   [11, p. 50]

The parish of the Aleksandro-Nevskaia Church, located at the south end of Petrograd near the Moscow Gates, adopted the following resolution, on December 21, 1919, in defense of their right to teach their children the Catechism. The reason for its adoption was the gradually stricter enforcement of orders and decrees banning religious instruction to children.

Agenda
    1. Teaching the Catechism to children of the parishioners of this church
    2. Where to teach the Catechism
The meeting unanimously elected citizen A. I. Nikolaev as chairman of the general meeting and citizen F. I. Bunakov as secretary of the general meeting.

In regard to item 1 of the agenda, on teaching the Catechism to children of the parishioners of this church, the general meeting of parishioners unanimously resolved that the church council of the parish should immediately begin organizing the teaching of the Catechism and that a request for the appropriate permission be submitted to the proper governmental departments.

In regard to item 2 of the agenda, on where the teaching of the Catechism should take place, the general meeting of parishioners also unanimously resolved: to conduct the teaching of the Catechism in the church building until private accommodation is found and to direct the church council to find resources for heating and outfitting a part of the church for the instruction of parishioners' children, to obtain the necessary textbooks, to develop a curriculum for teaching the Catechism, and to commission the parish priest, N. P. Frolovskii, to teach it.

Chairman of the general meeting A. Nikolaev

Sekretary F. Bunakov

62. Appeal to Lenin Denouncing the *Burzhoois* in Kazan, November 1920   [45, pp. 217–28]

When the Bolsheviks expanded the definition of the term burzhooi *to refer to virtually any representative of the traditional elites, including intellectuals, they were building on and encouraging the broad popular distrust, envy, and even hatred for such people. While not everybody bought into the rhetoric of class hatred, it resonated among some, as is clear from the following anonymous letter from Kazan.*

Dear Comrade Lenin! I cannot avoid pointing out an outrageous phenomenon that can still be observed in our Soviet Russia. Even though it has been more than two years since power in Russia has been in the hands of the Soviets of Workers', Peasants' and Red Armymen's Deputies, in all major industrial cities of Soviet Russia certain phenomena can be observed that do not at all indicate the existence of the dictatorship of proletariat. I want to point out the most insulting one.

In a city (Kazan in this case, but, as I pointed out, it happens in all major cities) there live many former prominent factory owners and *burzhoois* and when you enter their apartments you would think that "the good old times" are back again. These gentlemen do not know that the Civil War is raging and that power is in the hands of the workers. As in the past, they reside in luxurious, spacious, and warm apartments with luxurious furniture. In their kitchens you can still see a fat cook with a white cap who boils and fries. [There is] a large variety of servants. Again [you] hear the words "lord" and "lady," and in the summer, as formerly, they go to "relax" in their country homes. And this is happening at a time when we have a dictatorship of the proletariat and the workers are almost starving and freezing and still live in tiny, damp kennels. When I see this, I become ashamed for the proletarian revolution. Why has no attention been paid to this yet? Why are workers not moved into bourgeois apartments and the *burzhoois* into worker's cellars? Why is their furniture not being requisitioned for workers' clubs? And why anyway has this gang of *burzhoois* not yet been destroyed?

I am turning to you, Comrade Lenin, as to our leader and the most loyal friend of the proletariat, and I am waiting so that this issue, which concerns me and many other honest communists, can be resolved by an appropriate decree.

In the meantime, farewell, dear Comrade Il'ich; be healthy and live to instill fear among the enemies of the proletariat. [. . .]

Socialist Dreams

63. V. I. Lenin, *The State and Revolution*, August 1917
[44, vol. 25, pp. 459–70, 472–4]

Lenin composed this important lengthy pamphlet in August and September 1917, when he was hiding in Finland from the Provisional Government. The work expounded his views of the nature of the state and its relationship to capitalism and replacement by a new Communist order. Published only in 1918, though preceded in print by the preface and the first two sections of chapter 1 in December 1917, The State and Revolution *was considered a masterpiece of Marxist theorizing by subsequent Soviet authorities who published 7 million copies in 47 languages of the USSR. The sections below discuss the contours of a future Communist society and argue that transition to such a society would require dictatorial methods and a different kind of a state.*

Chapter V. The Economic Basis of the Withering Away of the State
2. The Transition from Capitalism to Communism
   Marx continued:

> Between capitalist and communist society lies the period of the revolutionary transformation of the one into the other. Corresponding to this is also a political transition period in which the state can be nothing but the revolutionary dictatorship of the proletariat.

Marx bases this conclusion on an analysis of the role played by the proletariat in modern capitalist society, on the data concerning the development of this society, and on the irreconcilability of the antagonistic interests of the proletariat and the bourgeoisie. [. . .]

In capitalist society, providing it develops under the most favorable conditions, we have a more or less complete democracy in the democratic republic. But this democracy is always hemmed in by the narrow limits set by capitalist exploitation, and consequently always remains, in effect, a democracy for the minority, only for the propertied classes, only for the rich. [. . .]

[. . .] [F]rom this capitalist democracy—that is inevitably narrow and stealthily pushes aside the poor, and is therefore hypocritical and false through and through—forward development does not proceed simply, directly and moodily, towards greater and greater democracy, as the liberal professors and petty-bourgeois opportunists would have us believe. No, forward development, i.e., development towards communism, proceeds through the dictatorship of the proletariat, and cannot do otherwise, for the resistance of the capitalist exploiters cannot be broken by anyone else or in any other way.

And the dictatorship of the proletariat, i.e., the organization of the vanguard of the oppressed as the ruling class for the purpose of suppressing the oppressors, cannot result merely in an expansion of democracy. Simultaneously with an immense expansion of democracy, which for the first time becomes democracy for the poor, democracy for the people, and not democracy for the money-bags, the dictatorship of the proletariat imposes a series of restrictions on the freedom of the oppressors, the exploiters, the capitalists. We must suppress them in order to free humanity from wage slavery, their resistance must be crushed by force; it is clear that there is no freedom and no democracy where there is suppression and where there is violence. [. . .]

Only in communist society, when the resistance of the capitalists have [*sic*] disappeared, when there are no classes (i.e., when there is no distinction between the members of society as regards their relation to the social means of production), only then the state . . . ceases to exist, and it becomes possible to speak of freedom. [. . .]

In other words, under capitalism we have the state in the proper sense of the word, that is, a special machine for the suppression of one class by another, and, what is more, of the majority by the minority. Naturally, to be successful, such an undertaking as the systematic suppression of the exploited majority by the exploiting minority calls for the utmost ferocity and savagery in the matter of suppressing, it calls for seas of blood, through which mankind is actually wading its way in slavery, serfdom, and wage labor.

Furthermore, during the transition from capitalism to communism suppression is still necessary, but it is now the suppression of the exploiting minority by the exploited majority. A special apparatus, a special machine for suppression, the state, is still necessary, but this is now a transitional state. It is no longer a state in the proper sense of the word; for the suppression of the minority of exploiters by the majority of the wage slaves of yesterday is comparatively so easy, simple, and natural a task that it will entail far less bloodshed than the suppression of the risings of slaves, serfs, or wage-laborers, and it will cost mankind far less. And it is compatible with the extension of democracy to such an overwhelming majority of the population that the need for a special machine of suppression will begin to disappear. [. . .]

Lastly, only communism makes the state absolutely unnecessary, for there is nobody to be suppressed—nobody in the sense of a class, of a systematic struggle against a definite section of the population. We are not utopians, and do not in the least deny the possibility and inevitability of excesses on the part of individual persons, or the need to stop such excesses. In the first place, however, no special machine, no special apparatus of suppression, is needed for this: this will be done by the armed people themselves, as simply and as readily as any crowd of civilized people, even in modern society, interferes to put a stop to a scuffle or to prevent a woman from being assaulted. [. . .]

3. The First Phase of Communist Society

[. . .] It is this communist society, which has just emerged into the light of day out of the womb of capitalism and which is in every respect stamped with the birthmarks of the old society, that Marx terms the first, or lower, phase of communist society.

The means of production are no longer the private property of individuals. The means of production belong to the whole of society. Every member of society, performing a certain part of the socially-necessary work, receives a certificate from society to the effect that he has done a certain amount of work. And with this certificate he receives from the public store of consumer goods a corresponding quantity of products. After a deduction is made of the amount of labor which goes to the public fund, every worker, therefore, receives from society as much as he has given to it. [. . .]

But people are not alike: one is strong, another is weak; one is married, another is not; one has more children, another has less, and so on. [. . .]

The first phase of communism, therefore, cannot yet provide justice and equality; differences, and unjust differences, in wealth will still persist, but the exploitation of man by man will have become impossible because it will be impossible to seize the means of production—the factories, machines, land, etc.—and make them private property. [. . .]

[. . .] The socialist principle, He who does not work shall not eat, is already realized; the other socialist principle, An equal amount of products for an equal amount of labor, is also already realized. But this is not yet communism, and it does not yet abolish bourgeois law, which gives unequal individuals, in return for unequal (really unequal) amounts of labor, equal amounts of products. [. . .]

4. The Higher Phase of Communist Society
Marx continues:

[. . .] The state will be able to wither away completely when society adopts the rule: From each according to his ability, to each according to his needs, i.e., when people have become so accustomed to observing the fundamental rules of social intercourse and when their labor has become so productive that they will voluntarily work according to their ability. [. . .]

Until the higher phase of communism arrives, the socialists demand the strictest control by society and by the state over the measure of labor and the measure of consumption; but this control must start with the expropriation of the capitalists, with the establishment of workers' control over the capitalists, and must be exercised not by a state of bureaucrats, but by a state of armed workers. [. . .]

If really all take part in the administration of the state, capitalism cannot retain its hold. The development of capitalism, in turn, creates the preconditions that enable really all to take part in the administration of the state. Some of these preconditions are: universal literacy, which has already been achieved in a number of the most advanced capitalist countries, then the training and disciplining of millions of workers by the huge, complex, socialized apparatus of the postal service, railways, big factories, large-scale commerce, banking, etc., etc.

Given these economic preconditions, it is quite possible, after the overthrow of the capitalists and the bureaucrats, to proceed immediately, overnight, to replace them in the control over production and distribution, in the work of keeping account of labor and products, by the armed workers, by the whole of the armed population. [. . .]

Accounting and control—that is mainly what is needed for the smooth working, for the proper functioning, of the first phase of communist society. All citizens are transformed into hired employees of the state, which consists of the armed workers. All citizens become employees and workers of a single countrywide state syndicate. All that is required is that they should work equally, do their proper share of work, and get equal pay; the accounting and control necessary for this have been simplified by capitalism to the utmost and reduced to extraordinarily simple operations—which any literate person can perform. [. . .]

Then the door will be thrown wide open for the transition from the first phase of communist society to its higher phase, and with it to the complete withering away of the state.

64. Declaration of the Rights of the Working and Exploited People, January 1918   [44, vol. 26, pp. 423–5]

As with so many important official documents of the period, Vladimir Lenin (in this case with assistance from Nikolai Bukharin and Joseph Stalin) wrote this text, which the All-Russian Central Executive Committee adopted on January 3. The purpose of this declaration was to provoke an immediate confrontation between the Bolshevik-controlled government and the Constituent

Assembly, and indeed it stated categorically that the soviets, and not the Constituent Assembly, were the sole legitimate governing authority of the country. The Constituent Assembly, dominated by Socialist-Revolutionaries, rejected a motion to approve the text during its sole meeting on January 5. Approved by the Third All-Russian Congress of Soviets a week later, the declaration was largely coterminous with Article One of the Soviet Constitution, passed on July 10, 1918, by the Fifth All-Russian Congress of Soviets.

The Constituent Assembly resolves:

I. 1. Russia is hereby proclaimed a Republic of Soviets of Workers', Soldiers', and Peasants' Deputies. All power, centrally and locally, is vested in these Soviets.

2. The Russian Soviet Republic is established on the principle of a free union of free nations, as a federation of Soviet national republics.

II. Its fundamental aim being to abolish all exploitation of man by man, to completely eliminate the division of society into classes, to mercilessly crush the resistance of the exploiters, to establish a socialist organization of society, and to achieve the victory of socialism in all countries, the Constituent Assembly further resolves:

1. Private ownership of land is hereby abolished. All land together with all buildings, farm implements, and other appurtenances of agricultural production, is proclaimed the property of the entire working people.

2. The Soviet laws on workers' control and on the Supreme Economic Council are hereby confirmed for the purpose of guaranteeing the power of the working people over the exploiters and as a first step towards the complete conversion of the factories, mines, railways, and other means of production and transport into the property of the workers' and peasants' state.

3. The conversion of all banks into the property of the workers' and peasants' state is hereby confirmed as one of the conditions for the emancipation of the working people from the yoke of capital.

4. For the purpose of abolishing the parasitic sections of society, universal labor conscription is hereby instituted.

5. To ensure the sovereign power of the working people, and to eliminate all possibility of the restoration of the

power of the exploiters, the arming of the working people, the creation of a socialist Red Army of workers and peasants, and the complete disarming of the propertied classes are hereby decreed.

III.   1. Expressing its firm determination to wrest mankind from the clutches of finance capital and imperialism, which have in this most criminal of wars drenched the world in blood, the Constituent Assembly whole-heartedly endorses the policy pursued by Soviet power of denouncing secret treaties, organizing the most extensive fraternization with the workers and peasants of the armies in the war, and achieving at all costs, by revolutionary means, a democratic peace between the nations, without annexations and indemnities and on the basis of the free self-determination of nations.

   2. With the same end in view, the Constituent Assembly insists on a complete break with the barbarous policy of bourgeois civilization, which has built the prosperity of the exploiters belonging to a few chosen nations on the enslavement of hundreds of millions of working people in Asia, in the colonies in general, and in the small countries.

   The Constituent Assembly welcomes the policy of the Council of People's Commissars in proclaiming the complete independence of Finland, commencing the evacuation of troops from Persia, and proclaiming freedom of self-determination for Armenia.

   3. The Constituent Assembly regards the Soviet law on the cancellation of the loans contracted by the governments of the tsar, the landowners, and the bourgeoisie as a first blow struck at international banking, finance capital, and expresses the conviction that Soviet power will firmly pursue this path until the international workers' uprising against the yoke of capital has completely triumphed.

IV.   [...] Supporting Soviet power and the decrees of the Council of People's Commissars, the Constituent Assembly considers that its own task is confined to establishing the fundamental principles of the socialist reconstruction of society. [...]

65. Anatolii Lunacharskii's Description of the May Day Celebration, 1918 [79, p. 47]

Anatolii Vasil'evich Lunacharskii (1875–1933) became a Marxist in high school and joined the Social Democratic Party in 1895. A Bolshevik from 1903, he wrote and edited various publications for the party, mostly abroad, concentrating on philosophical and aesthetic works. His effort to elaborate the concept of "god-building," which conceived of socialism as the highest form of religion, led to personal and political tensions with Lenin. Yet he supported the Bolshevik seizure of power in October 1917, seeing it as the dawn of a new world, and was immediately put in charge of promoting culture and education as commissar for enlightenment, a post he held until 1929. His major achievements in this area were defending cultural treasures from popular violence, promoting literacy, developing cultural agitation and "monumental propaganda," and enabling artists and other cultural figures of the left to express themselves relatively freely. The excerpt from his sketchbook below conveys his enthusiastic belief that the Bolshevik Revolution not only liberated the working masses but also gave birth to an altogether new culture.

[. . .] Many squares and streets of the city are adorned. [. . .]

And with what delight the artistic youth have given themselves to their task! Many worked without straightening their backs for 14–15 hours in a row on huge canvasses. Having painted a giant peasant and a giant worker they then wrote in well-defined letters:

> "We will not surrender Red Petrograd" and "All Power to the Soviets."

[. . .] I went to the Neva [River] earlier and there was a real magic fairly tale!

Ships adorned with thousands of brightly colored flags made the Neva look so richly bedecked that my heart, weighed down by cares, could not but start beating joyfully.

I think anyone who saw this spectacle—and it was seen by half of Petrograd—will agree that it was unforgettably beautiful and touchingly joyful.

In the evening an amazing battle of light and darkness began. Dozens of spotlights cast shafts of light that glided through the air like white swords.

Their bright rays fell on the palaces, fortresses, ships, and bridges and snatched from the night one beauty of our captivating Northern Rome after another.

Rockets dashed to the sky; multicolored stars fell.

Fountains and clouds of smoke illuminated by these peculiar and pale dancing rays created a whole poem, a whole symphony of fire and darkness in a rich gamut of hues, leaving the impression of a kind of eerie grandeur. Cannon thundered from the Peter-and-Paul Fortress.

Yes, the celebration of the First of May was official.

The state celebrated it.

The power of the state was seen in many ways. But the idea that the state, which had been our bitterest enemy, and is now ours, was celebrating the First of May as its greatest holiday, is not this very idea exhilarating?

But believe me, if this celebration had been only official, nothing but cold and emptiness would have come from it.

No, the popular masses, the Red Navy, the Red Army—all the truly working folk poured their strength into it. That is why we can say: "Never before has this celebration of labor been molded into such beautiful forms."

66. Alexandra Kollontai, "Communism and the Family," 1920   [37, pp. 250–60]

A long-standing Social Democrat and feminist, Alexandra Kollontai (1872– 1952) joined the Bolshevik fraction in 1914. After the party's seizure of power in October 1917, she was named people's commissar for social welfare, the most senior position occupied by a woman until 1956. She quit the post in March 1918 to protest the Treaty of Brest-Litovsk,[22] but remained deeply involved in the Bolshevik socialism-building efforts. In November 1918, she organized the First All-Russian Congress of Working and Peasant Women, where she read the following report on the future of women and the family in a socialist society. Appointed the second director of the Central Committee's Zhenotdel or "Women's Department" in 1920, her activities as a leader of the Workers' Opposition caused her dismissal from that post in 1922.[23]

Women's role in production: its effect upon the family

Will the family continue to exist under communism? Will the family remain in the same form? These questions are troubling many women of the working class and worrying their menfolk as well. [. . .]

22. The Treat of Brest-Litovsk, ratified by the Congress of Soviets in mid-March 1918, ceded one-third of European Russia to Germany. See also the headnote to Document 109.

23. The following year, she was the first woman in the world to receive an ambassadorial post. She spent the rest of her life serving abroad.

There is no point in not facing up to the truth: the old family in which
the man was everything and the woman nothing, the typical family where
the woman had no will of her own, no time of her own, and no money of
her own, is changing before our very eyes. But there is no need for alarm. It
is only our ignorance that leads us to think that the things we are used to
can never change. [. . .]

Housework ceases to be necessary

[. . .] The individual household is dying. It is giving way in our society to
collective housekeeping. Instead of the working woman cleaning her flat, the
communist society can arrange for men and women whose job it is to go
round in the morning cleaning rooms. The wives of the rich have long since
been freed from these irritating and tiring domestic duties. Why should
working woman continue to be burdened with them? In Soviet Russia the
working woman should be surrounded by the same ease and light, hygiene
and beauty that previously only the very rich could afford. Instead of the
working woman having to struggle with the cooking and spend her last free
hours in the kitchen preparing dinner and supper, communist society will
organize public restaurants and communal kitchens.

[. . .] The working woman will not have to slave over the washtub any
longer, or ruin her eyes in darning her stockings and mending her linen; she
will simply take these things to the central laundries each week and collect the
washed and ironed garments later. That will be another job less to do. Special
clothes-mending centers will free the working woman from the hours spent
on mending and give her the opportunity to devote her evenings to reading,
attending meetings, and concerts. Thus the four categories of housework are
doomed to extinction with the victory of communism. And the working
woman will surely have no cause to regret this. Communism liberates woman
from her domestic slavery and makes her life richer and happier.

The state is responsible for the upbringing of children

But even if housework disappears, you may argue, there are still the children
to look after. But here too, the workers' state will come to replace the family; society will gradually take upon itself all the tasks that before the revolution fell to the individual parents. [. . .]

Just as housework withers away, so the obligations of parents to their children wither away gradually until finally society assumes the full responsibility. Under capitalism children were frequently, too frequently, a heavy and
unbearable burden on the proletarian family. Communist society will come
to the aid of the parents. In Soviet Russia the Commissariats of Public
Education and of Social Welfare are already doing much to assist the family.
We already have homes for very small babies, crèches, kindergartens, children's colonies and homes, hospitals and health resorts for sick children,

restaurants, free lunches at school, and free distribution of text books, warm clothing, and shoes to schoolchildren. All this goes to show that the responsibility for the child is passing from the family to the collective. [. . .]

Communist society considers the social education of the rising generation to be one of the fundamental aspects of the new life. The old family, narrow and petty, where the parents quarrel and are only interested in their own offspring, is not capable of educating the "new person." The playgrounds, gardens, homes, and other amenities where the child will spend the greater part of the day under the supervision of qualified educators will, on the other hand, offer an environment in which the child can grow up a conscious communist who recognizes the need for solidarity, comradeship, mutual help, and loyalty to the collective. What responsibilities are left to the parents, when they no longer have to take charge of upbringing and education? The very small baby, you might answer, while it is still learning to walk and clinging to its mother's skirt, still needs her attention. Here again the communist state hastens to the aid of the working mother. No longer will there be any women who are alone. The workers' state aims to support every mother, married or unmarried, while she is suckling her child, and to establish maternity homes, day nurseries, and other such facilities in every city and village, in order to give women the opportunity to combine work in society with maternity.

Working mothers have no need to be alarmed; communist society is not intending to take children away from their parents or to tear the baby from the breast of its mother, and neither is it planning to take violent measures to destroy the family. No such thing! The aims of communist society are quite different. Communist society sees that the old type of family is breaking up, and that all the old pillars which supported the family as a social unit are being removed: the domestic economy is dying, and working-class parents are unable to take care of their children or provide them with sustenance and education. Parents and children suffer equally from this situation. Communist society has this to say to the working woman and working man: "You are young, you love each other. Everyone has the right to happiness. Therefore live your life. Do not flee happiness. Do not fear marriage, even though under capitalism marriage was truly a chain of sorrow. Do not be afraid of having children. Society needs more workers and rejoices at the birth of every child. You do not have to worry about the future of your child; your child will know neither hunger nor cold." [. . .]

The woman who takes up the struggle for the liberation of the working class must learn to understand that there is no more room for the old proprietary attitude which says: "These are my children, I owe them all my maternal solicitude and affection; those are your children, they are no concern of mine and I don't care if they go hungry and cold—I have no time for other children." The worker-mother must learn not to differentiate between yours and mine; she must remember that there are only our children, the children of Russia's communist workers.

The workers' state needs new relations between the sexes; just as the narrow and exclusive affection of the mother for her own children must expand until it extends to all the children of the great, proletarian family, the indissoluble marriage based on the servitude of women is replaced by a free union of two equal members of the workers' state who are united by love and mutual respect. In place of the individual and egoistic family, a great universal family of workers will develop, in which all the workers, men and women, will above all be comrades. This is what relations between men and women in the communist society will be like. These new relations will ensure for humanity all the joys of a love unknown in the commercial society, of a love that is free and based on the true social equality of the partners.

Communist society wants bright healthy children and strong, happy young people, free in their feelings and affections. In the name of equality, liberty, and the comradely love of the new marriage, we call upon the working and peasant men and women to apply themselves courageously and with faith to the work of rebuilding human society, in order to render it more perfect, more just, and more capable of ensuring the individual the happiness which he or she deserves. The red flag of the social revolution which flies above Russia and is now being hoisted aloft in other countries of the world proclaims the approach of the heaven on earth to which humanity has been aspiring for centuries.

67. H. G. Wells Meets with Lenin, 1920
[88, pp. 123–4, 128–39]

Herbert George Wells (1866–1946) was a prolific English writer, most famously of science fiction, and a prominent socialist and advocate of a world state. He visited Soviet Russia for two weeks in September 1920. Wells was interested in meeting Lenin because of both the Russian leader's extreme internationalism and his visionary faith in technological modernization. In the course of their conversation, summarized below, Wells noted Lenin's particular interest in electrification, by which he hoped both to radically transform Russia and to usher in a communistic age across the world. "Communism," Lenin proclaimed dramatically in 1920, "is Soviet power plus the electrification of the whole country." In December, the Eighth Congress of Soviets unanimously approved a plan for the total electrification of Russia.

My chief purpose in going from Petersburg to Moscow was to see and talk to Lenin. I was very curious to see him, and I was disposed to be hostile to him. I encountered a personality entirely different from anything I had expected to meet.

Lenin is not a writer; his published work does not express him. The shrill little pamphlets and papers issued from Moscow in his name [. . .] do no more than rehearse the set ideas and phrases of doctrinaire Marxism. [. . .]

The arrangements leading up to my meeting with Lenin were tedious and irritating. [. . .] The Kremlin as I remembered it in 1914 was a very open place, open much as Windsor Castle is, with a thin trickle of pilgrims and tourists in groups and couples flowing through it. But now it is closed up and difficult of access. There was a great pother with passes and permits before we could get through even the outer gates. And we were filtered and inspected through five or six rooms of clerks and sentinels before we got into the presence. This may be necessary for the personal security of Lenin, but it puts him out of reach of Russia, and, what perhaps is more serious, if there is to be an effectual dictatorship, it puts Russia out of his reach. If things must filter up to him, they must also filter down, and they may undergo very considerable changes in the process.

We got to Lenin at last and found him, a little figure at a great desk in a well-lit room that looked out upon palatial spaces. I thought his desk was rather in a litter. I sat down on a chair at a corner of the desk, and the little man—his feet scarcely touch the ground as he sits on the edge of his chair—twisted round to talk to me, putting his arms round and over a pile of papers. He spoke excellent English. [. . .]

I had come expecting to struggle with a doctrinaire Marxist. I found nothing of the sort. I had been told that Lenin lectured people; he certainly did not do so on this occasion. [. . .] Lenin has a pleasant, quick-changing, brownish face, with a lively smile and a habit (due perhaps to some defect in focusing) of screwing up one eye as he pauses in his talk; he is not very like the photographs you see of him because he is one of those people whose change of expression is more important than their features; he gesticulated a little with his hands over the heaped papers as he talked, and he talked quickly, very keen on his subject, without any posing or pretenses or reservations, as a good type of scientific man will talk.

Our talk was threaded throughout and held together by two—what shall I call them?—motifs. One was from me to him: "What do you think you are making of Russia? What is the state you are trying to create?" The other was from him to me: "Why does not the social revolution begin in England? Why do you not work for the social revolution? Why are you not destroying Capitalism and establishing the Communist State?" [. . .]

In the days before 1918 all the Marxist world thought of the social revolution as an end. The workers of the world were to unite, overthrow Capitalism, and be happy ever afterwards. But in 1918 the Communists, to their own surprise, found themselves in control of Russia and challenged to produce their millennium [. . .] the commonplace Communist simply loses his temper if you venture to doubt whether everything is being done in precisely the best and most intelligent way under the new regime. [. . .] Lenin, on the other hand, whose frankness must at times leave his disciples breathless, has recently stripped off the last pretense that the Russian revolution is anything more than the inauguration of an age of limitless experiment. "Those who are engaged in the formidable task of overcoming capitalism," he has recently written, "must be prepared to try method after method until they find the one which answers their purpose best."

We opened our talk with a discussion of the future of the great towns under Communism. I wanted to see how far Lenin contemplated the dying out of the towns in Russia. The desolation of Petersburg had brought home to me a point I had never realized before, that the whole form and arrangement of a town is determined by shopping and marketing, and that the abolition of these things renders nine-tenths of the buildings in an ordinary town directly or indirectly unmeaning and useless. "The towns will get very much smaller," he admitted. "They will be different. Yes, quite different." [. . .]

Did I realize what was already in hand with Russia? The electrification of Russia?

For Lenin, who like a good orthodox Marxist denounces all "Utopians," has succumbed at last to a Utopia, the Utopia of the electricians. He is throwing all his weight into a scheme for the development of great power stations in Russia to serve whole provinces with light, with transport, and industrial power. [. . .] Projects for such an electrification are in process of development in Holland and they have been discussed in England, and in those densely-populated and industrially highly-developed centers one can imagine them as successful, economical, and altogether beneficial. But their application to Russia is an altogether greater strain upon the constructive imagination. I cannot see anything of the sort happening in this dark crystal of Russia, but this little man at the Kremlin can; he sees the decaying railways replaced by a new electric transport, sees new roadways spreading throughout the land, sees a new and happier Communist industrialism arising again. While I talked to him he almost persuaded me to share his vision.

"And you will go on to these things with the peasants rooted in your soil?" [. . .]

"Even now," said Lenin, "all the agricultural production of Russia is not peasant production. We have, in places, large scale agriculture. The Government is already running big estates with workers instead of peasants, where conditions are favorable. That can spread. It can be extended first to one province, then another. The peasants in the other provinces, selfish and illiterate, will not know what is happening until their turn comes. . . ." [. . .]

In him I realized that Communism could after all, in spite of Marx, be enormously creative. After the tiresome class-war fanatics I had been encountering among the Communists, men of formulae sterile as flints, after numerous experiences of the trained and empty conceit of the common Marxist devotee, this amazing little man, with his frank admission of the immensity and complication of the project of Communism and his simple concentration upon its realization, was very refreshing. He at least has a vision of a world changed over and planned and built afresh.

He wanted more of my Russian impressions. I told him that I thought that in many directions, and more particularly in the Petersburg Commune, Communism was pressing too hard and too fast, and destroying before it was ready to rebuild. They had broken down trading before they were ready to ration; the co-operative organization had been smashed up instead of being utilized, and so on.[24] That brought us to our essential difference, the difference of the Evolutionary Collectivist and Marxist. [. . .] I believe that through a vast sustained educational campaign the existing Capitalist system can be civilized into a Collectivist world system; Lenin on the other hand tied himself years ago to the Marxist dogmas. [. . .] He had to argue, therefore, that modern Capitalism is incurably predatory, wasteful, and un-teachable, and that until it is destroyed it will continue to exploit the human heritage stupidly and aimlessly, that it will fight against and prevent any administration of natural resources for the general good, and that, because essentially it is a scramble, it will inevitably make wars. [. . .]

24. Before 1917, consumer, credit, and producer cooperatives in Russia were very strong, having emerged in part from ordinary people's experiences with trades associations (*arteli,* in Russian) and the peasant commune (*mir*). The economic chaos visited upon Russia by the World War dramatically stimulated the movement's development. This trend continued after the Bolsheviks' seizure of power thanks to the nationalization and shutting down of private enterprise, the cooperatives' natural competitors. By January 1920, however, the cooperatives were merely a cog in the machinery of the Communist state.

THE BOLSHEVIKS GO TO THE VILLAGE

68. "The Well Fed and the Hungry," a Newspaper Commentary, April 1918   [78]

Urban dwellers in the major cities suffered from inadequate supplies of food from as early as 1916, but the situation deteriorated acutely in January 1918. The harvest of 1917 was small, and during the spring peasants plowed much of their surplus grain into new fields confiscated from big landowners. The peasantry, now largely in charge of the countryside, gradually refused to sell their grain for devalued paper rubles, while industrial output in the cities plummeted, leaving fewer goods the cities could exchange for grain. A crisis was brewing. In response, one of the government's tactics was to unleash a propaganda campaign that castigated the kulaks (well-to-do peasants) and urged the local poor to help requisition grain. The article below from the government run newspaper Bednota *(The Poor) is an example of such propaganda.*

Russia is facing difficult, hungry times before the new harvest comes. One has to get ready for harsh deprivations. [. . .]

In many provinces the rich peasants and, bluntly, kulaks still have grain but don't wish to sell it either to people in their village or to others. Moreover, when grain is brought to a public store for the needy, these people without conscience want to grab a share first with their greedy hands. And they are given it, even though in the village everybody knows how much grain he [*sic*] already has.

So where can the hungry villages and cities get grain, if the rich keep sitting by their granaries like dogs on a chain?

Until the village poor organized themselves into soviets and Bolshevik committees, the kulaks did what they wanted and taunted hungry Russia.

Then resolutions were passed everywhere demanding that grain surpluses beyond one's personal need be confiscated at a fixed price.

It is easy to pass a just resolution, but how easy to carry it out?

The kulaks went into a frenzy and refused to give up their grain. They all are waiting for prices to go up to 200 rubles and more per pood.[25]

---

25. A unit of measure equal to 36 pounds.

"We will die by our granaries but will not give even a crumb to you ragamuffins."

That's what the kulaks were shouting in one of the villages of Novgorod province, when the poor began to requisition grain for public use.

Indeed, the kulaks are ready, if not to die for their provisions, then to starve others to death or tear them into pieces. [. . .]

In Bogoroditskii district [. . .] real battles are taking place between the peasant bourgeoisie and the Red Guards who are supported by the village poor and primarily by soldiers from the front.

A unit from Bogorodskii district that arrived at Uzlovaia [station] was not allowed to requisition and was surrounded by bourgeois gone savage. Thirteen Red Guards were killed. They grabbed the commander of the unit and smashed his head in against the rails.

That's how the village bourgeoisie operates.

If the village soviets and above all the rural poor fail to launch a merciless struggle with the rural burzhois who have the grain, then all of Soviet Russia will suffer.

No mercy to the well-fed village oppressors! Wage the most brutal struggle against them, including executions, if they dare to take up arms against the hungry.

We sympathize with the peasant youths of the village of Smirnovo, Riazan' district, who resolved to use terror against the kulaks. Twelve of the most ferocious village oppressors who refused to give grain to the starving were shot on the spot. After that, the rest of them agreed to concessions and began to surrender grain to the food commissar. [. . .]

69. Notes of a Grain-Confiscation Worker, October 1918
[59, pp. 16–8]

The breakdown of the food supply system beginning in early 1918 led the Bolshevik leadership gradually to expand the powers of local officials in this area and culminated with a decree establishing a "food dictatorship" on May 13, 1918. According to this ruling, anyone who failed to surrender "surplus grain" or who used grain reserves to produce moonshine was to be considered an "enemy of the people" and punishable with "imprisonment for not less than ten years, confiscation of property, and banishment forever from their communities." Food detachments (prodotriady) were set up immediately to confiscate "surplus" grain throughout the countryside. To assist with implementing the food dictatorship, Committees of the Poor (Kombedy) were instituted on June 11, 1918. They were also intended to win support for the government in the

countryside, to create a counterweight to the village soviets, which were often
hard to control, and to drive a wedge between rich and poor peasants. In
August, a series of decrees urged trade unions, factory committees,[26] *and urban*
and rural soviets to send their own detachments into the countryside in order
to requisition grain. In the document below, a member of one such detachment
describes his first encounters with the countryside.

The evening came. We began to get ready for bed, laughing and joking.

My neighbors [Nikolai Petrovich] Makarov and Sobolev were already snoring, but I could not sleep. I could not forget Krasnov's stern warning: "You are not going for a visit to your mother-in-law but into the depths of a brutal class struggle."

He called on us to be vigilant and not to tarnish the honor of communists.

I was worried not about the danger but whether I would handle the task. I have never lived in the countryside and did not have any idea about the peasant lifestyle. Theoretically, I had a notion of kulaks, middle peasants, and poor peasants, but what are they in real life? To be sure, the kulaks don't walk around in tails and stove-pipe hats. [. . .] I should read Lenin's works on the peasant issue carefully again.

A new morning came, bright and calm. We sat by the open door of the train car, our feet hanging out and with delight breathed in the clean, fragrant air, so unusual, so unlike the city's.

Groves, hillsides, rivers passed by us, and the silent horizon appeared in the remote bluish haze. So good! [. . .]

Like a mockery of nature's grandeur, there also stood close to the railroad tracks villages with plain wretched huts. Little windows, thatched roofs, half-dilapidated yard benches, wicker fences bent to the ground. In the dirt, practically naked children, dressed in rags, were swarming around together with chickens and pigs.

In the centers of the villages, well-built brick houses with iron roofs stood out like islands. These houses, as well as solid wooden barns and churches behind the brick fences, were drowning in gardens. These were the possessions of the village rich: the priests and the kulaks with whom we were going to have a merciless struggle. I wanted to pour the sea of poverty over the islands of wealth and flood them, sweep them away without a trace.

---

26. Factory committees first emerged in spring 1917 to promote workers' interests, to keep management in check, to help manage factories, and, in cases where the factory administration had fled, to run the entire industrial operation. Within months, assemblies of representatives of these committees met periodically to coordinate a broad range of activities.

Windmills were a great curiosity to us. This was the first time most of us had seen one. The seasoned Makarov explained the unsophisticated structure of these devices not forgetting to stress that the local rich controlled them and derived from them substantial profits. We listened to him with interest, asking many questions. Our acquaintance with the village had begun.

The train went fast, not stopping at small stations. We were given priority passage.

In Tambov, the commander of our Food Unit went to the Provincial Party Committee and, during his absence, allowed us to go into the city and especially recommended we visit the market.

Sobolev and I stayed behind in the train car, and, when the others had returned carrying bread or boiled potatoes, we went to the market together, where we lost track of each other.

Walking down the rows of stalls, I could not believe my eyes. After only two days, it was as if we had appeared in a different world: in the stalls were genuine flavorful bread, pots of milk, eggs, bacon, and vegetables, while potatoes were steaming away in kettles. Carts filled with bags were standing aside, presumably flour. Sheep were huddling together, piglets were squealing, and lots of chicken—fried, boiled, and live. Purchasers paid for the food with "kerenkis,"[27] but the vendors more eagerly accepted currency from the era of Nicholas II.

I walked around the market in astonishment: so much for the grain monopoly, so much for fixed prices! It seemed that they still lived by their own laws here.

But who were these people trading in the market? These were not the poor who have not enough to eat themselves. Nor do the middle peasants have adequate surplus for trading. So these traders were kulaks, their underlings, and speculators, enriching themselves from starvation. [. . .]

Watermelons! Where else will I have a chance to try this rare delicacy! I picked the largest one and asked: "How much for a watermelon?"

When the woman received her forty million in "kerenkis," she looked at me cunningly but said nothing.

I grabbed my heavy purchase and quickly walked toward the station. The boys will be glad!

"Hey, come and get your watermelon," I said joyfully, while climbing into the train car.

Makarov looked at my burden and said something to the boys.

---

27. As inflation continued to increase after the February Revolution, the Provisional Government was forced to issue ever-larger quantities of paper currency, including 20- and 40-ruble banknotes, popularly called *kerenki*.

An explosion of laughter followed. I was confused. Then Makarov said through laughter:

"There has been a mistake, commander. What you brought is not a watermelon, but a very real pumpkin."

Everyone laughed again in a kindly manner. [. . .]

After lunch, Makarov came to me, laid his hand on my shoulder, and said: "Don't take offense that we had a little laugh. It was without spite, in a friendly way. But if you think about it, what happened today is an example of how little some of us know about the land and how much we still have to learn."

Nikolai Petrovich was absolutely right, and in my soul I thanked him for his kind words.

70. Vladimir Mayakovsky Mocks an Avaricious Peasant Woman, 1920   [47]

Vladimir Mayakovsky (1893–1930) was a major Russian poet and playwright. He joined the Bolshevik fraction of the Social Democratic Party in 1908. He was jailed three times for political activity. In 1911, he joined the Moscow Art School where he became a leading member of the Russian Futurist movement. He celebrated the Bolsheviks' coming to power and the new regime in many works of poetry, plays, and screenplays, as well as posters and comic strips for propaganda and agitation purposes, many of which appeared as the so-called windows of satire of the Russian Telegraph Agency (ROSTA). Like many Russian intellectuals, Mayakovsky was hostile to materialism, commerce, and "petty bourgeois" values. In the verses below, he attacks the greed, selfishness, and political ignorance of a peasant woman who refuses to offer a bagel to a Red Army soldier.

Proletarians of All Countries, Unite!

1
This story happened
In a certain republic.
A peasant woman floated to market,
Floated with bagels.

2
Then she heard music
Of stamping in the air.

That was Red Army men
Rushing to crush the *pany*.[28]

3
One of them wants a bagel,
Saying to her: "Dearie!
Give a bagel to the hungry one!
You go not to the front yourself!

4
If my mouth has nothing in it,
I will be weak like a holy relic.

5
A *pan* will eat the republic
If we lose our might."

6
Quoth she, not in my lifetime
Will I give you my bagels!
Get thee gone, soldier.
What's the republic to me?

7
Our unit marched, thin and gaunt,
Against the *pany*, giants all,
Who, in their might, swept us away
In the very first battle.

8
The *pan* is running, cruel and furious,
Bringing death to the workers.
Among other things, he reached
The stupid peasant woman in the market.

9
The *pan* sees her, plump and fair,
Sitting among her bagels.

---

28. *Pan* (plural *pany*) means Polish nobleman in Russia. In Soviet times, the term was
pejorative.

In a second she is eaten,
She and her bagels.

10
Now go to the square and look!
Neither peasant nor bread in sight.
Surely the lesson is clear:
Feed the red defender aright.

11
So feed the army of the reds!
Bring them bread without howling,
so that you won't lose your bread
Along with your head!

71. A Letter to Lenin from Peasants of Vologda Province,[29] 1920   [42, pp. 7–9]

Drawing on Marxist theory, the Bolsheviks conceptually divided the peasants into poor, middle, and rich in order to incite the former two against the latter and thus sow discord in the countryside, the better to dominate it. Yet, traditionally Russian peasant villages were governed by majority rule, with heads of all the households enjoying voting rights in village assemblies. Therefore it was often difficult to divide villagers along class lines. This failure often translated into political failure as well. The document below shows that many peasants opposed Bolshevik efforts to define them in class terms and spoke proudly of themselves as honest laborers.

To Commissar Lenin, Chairman of the RSFS Republic.

Complaint of middle-peasant and poor-peasant laborers of the Kurbanskaia volost, Kadnikovskii district, Vologda province.

We middle- and poor-peasant laborers have never been either *burzhooi,* or speculator-profiteers, or drunkards, or pick-pockets, or lazybones-parasites of either the upper or lower class. [. . .] The rich sneakily avoided the burden of state and public taxes, and there is nothing you can take from these lazybones who because of their laziness abandoned their lands and businesses and failed to learn anything good and therefore engaged in extortion, theft, and card playing and relied entirely on our labor in their life. And these are the people you have given trust and power to. Being in charge in the provinces, they have not tried and are not trying to raise and improve the working level of the people. All they do is extort, rob, and take away what has been amassed by hard and persistent labor and thrift. [. . .]Why are you standing up for lazybones and scoundrels and through them attacking us laborers? [. . .]

We are asking you to force and compel them to work, since it is useless to apply moral persuasion to them (as in the fable about the cook and the cat). [. . .] Let's take for example 4 families in the village of Nekrasovo: the first one is Kulikhin's, which has three plots of land and seven healthy, strong men; they abandoned their land and house and wander around and beg. Another family is the Kostiunenoks, which have 2 family members (51 years old), didn't have land and a house, but took the land abandoned by the first

---

29. Located some 300 miles north of Moscow, Vologda province had a population of nearly 1.4 million in 1897. A habitual place of political exile, the province was also home to numerous textile, metalworking, and wood-processing factories. The region was and remains famous for its butter and cheese.

family, added manure to it, and produced grain. The third family (the Solovievs) have 7 strong laborers for three plots of land, live an idle life at home playing cards and have neither cattle, nor grain. The fourth family (Obraztsovs) is a woman who has young children and old folks to care for; she ploughs the land herself and takes care of everything else. And so it turns out that Kulikhin and the Solovievs think of themselves as poor, while the Kostinenkos and Obraztsovas are considered *burzhooi:* grain and livestock were taken away from them and then the authorities imposed on them contributions[30] and heavy taxes (the state tax).

There are as many such examples as there are people. And to look more closely, to examine people's lives in more detail, these poor lazybones are richer than us a thousand times. The wealth of the peasant is accumulated through thrift. So where is justice? There is no such thing.

Representatives of poor- and middle-laborers of the village of Nakrasovo: Nikolai Molchanov, A. Obraztsov signed in lieu of Vasilii Soloviev because of his illiteracy, Pelageiia Obraztsova, Aleksandr Kachanov.

Representatives of poor- and middle-laborers of the village of Shchekotovo: signatures follow.

Representatives of poor- and middle-laborers of the village of Bol'shaia (signatures).

Village Nelitovo (signatures)
Village Sukmanitsy (signatures)
Village Kopylovo (signatures), etc.

72. Citizens in Kostroma Denounce the Closing of Their Church, February 1920   [45, pp. 153–4]

An ancient Russian city dating to the 12th century, Kostroma was a place of exile for Mikhail Romanov, the founder of the Romanov dynasty, and boasted many architectural monuments, both civil and religious. By 1918, closures of churches were becoming more and more frequent, affecting a number of parishes, like the one whose members submitted the complaint below. It is not clear whether any action was taken on the basis of this complaint, but church closings continued. Furthermore, numerous churches, including two cathedrals in the Kostroma kremlin (ancient fortress), were dynamited in the 1920s and 1930s.

---

30. "Contributions" were special monetary and property assessments imposed on the well-to-do.

On February 9 of this year, the director of the local Civil Registration Department sealed the Smolensk Church in our commune. This church houses an icon-fresco of Our Lady of Smolensk that is deeply venerated by the environing urban and rural population. Consequently, the church had constantly been open to worshippers, hundreds of whom visited daily. The purpose of closing our temple remains unknown to us, since the school commission found it to be unsuitable for use as a school. It can moreover scarcely possess substantial value for accommodating any other agency because of its extremely small space and its internal layout. Yet this causes great anxiety both in the local population, especially among the members of our commune, most of whom work in local factories, and in the surrounding peasant population, who are mostly simple people very strongly affected by the loss of the sacred objects, which they revere. We must say that such forced closing of churches without any obvious need exerts a very negative effect on the relatively educated people who consider churches and icons[31] only one aspect of their faith, weakens the support for Soviet power of those positively disposed toward it, and decisively drives the simple people into the ranks of its opponents. At the very least, the fact of terrible dissatisfaction with this measure among the local factory population is undeniable. Our commune numbers over 700 people. We are religious people. We will not give up our religion, and in the present difficult days find our sole consolation in the House of the Lord. We neither bother nor harm anyone with our religion. We honestly fulfill our civic duty. Our religion not only does not hinder this but substantially helps by calling upon us to carry out the tasks we are charged with honestly and in good conscience. We do not force anybody to join us, we do not ask for any subsidies from anybody to help maintain our churches, and therefore we are completely at a loss about the restrictions imposed on the fulfillment of our religious needs and about the hatred toward us religious people on the part of certain irreligious people in power. It is finally time for those heading the agencies in charge of separating the Church from the State to understand that physical restrictions in the religious sphere leads not forward, not to a new life, but backward, to the savage past. It is time to appoint to these positions more cultivated people,

---

31. Icons play a significant role in Eastern Orthodox religious practice. Typically painted on wood though also sometimes on plaster (fresco), icons are believed to provide a symbolic window onto a holy reality. Orthodox believers pray to the holy person through the icon. Russian Orthodox icons, which derived from but expanded beyond Byzantine styles and practices, depicted Mary, the Mother of God, far more than any other religious figure. (Russian Orthodox believers emphasize Mary's status as mother rather than as a virgin.) The most venerated icons in Russia were images of Mary believed to have miraculously appeared in specific places, including Kazan, Vladimir, and Smolensk.

ones capable of being guided in their work not only by personal feelings and considerations, but above all by what will benefit the state. In light of the above considerations, we ask the Council of People's Commissars to issue an order to reinstate our use of the Smolensk Church and to pay serious attention to the activities of the head of the local Civil Registration Department, Nikolai Pavlovich Orlanskii. [. . .]³²

73. Peasants Sentenced for Petty Commerce, January 1921
[16, p. 626]

The abolition of markets was fundamentally important to the Bolshevik vision of socialism, and they went to great lengths to punish those who pursued private entrepreneurial activity. Many such people, whom the Bolsheviks viewed as selfish, greedy, and counterrevolutionary, successfully evaded the Bolsheviks' wrath. Those who did not were prosecuted by a number of official bodies, including Revolutionary Tribunals, as was the case with the peasants described in the document below. The Revolutionary Tribunals followed only rudimentary procedural norms and were not bound by a specific code of law until the adoption of the 1922 Criminal Code, relying instead on "revolutionary consciousness." Thus the severity of a particular sentence was hard to predict, although people generally preferred to be handled by the Revolutionary Tribunals rather than by the Cheka.

January 17, 1921. In the name of the Russian Socialist Federative Soviet Republic, the Penza³³ Provincial Revolutionary Tribunal (chairman Mikalov, members Bogomolov and Trofimov), in open session in the village of Macha, heard the case against citizens of the village of Bugrovka of the Machinsk township, Chembarsk district, Penza province, Grigorii Vasiliievich Kechin, 47 years of age; Ivan Vasiliievich Kechin, 47 years of age, and Dmitrii Vasiliievich Kechin, 50 years of age. The charges were that these citizens had without authorization opened the oil press belonging to them in the village of Bugrovka and had used it to process oil seeds to make oil for private citizens. From the circumstances of the case the Tribunal has determined that the owners of the oil press, the brothers Kechin—Grigorii, Ivan, and Dmitrii

---

32. Twenty pages of signatures of members of the Bogoiavlenskaia religious commune in Kostroma were attached to the document.

33. Penza province is located in the Volga uplands, 300 miles southeast of Moscow. A hub for three railroad lines and the site of more than 150 small factories, including two iron foundries, the province was largely rural.

Kechin—indeed carried out the processing of oil seeds to make oil without the authorization of the food regulatory agencies. All three defendants confessed their guilt. The Penza Provincial Revolutionary Tribunal for Food Matters has found the citizens Grigorii, Ivan, and Dmitrii Kechin guilty of opening the oil press without authorization and of illegally pressing oil seeds in order to make oil for private citizens and therefore sentence Grigorii Vasiliievich, Ivan Vasiliievich, and Dmitrii Vasiliievich Kechin to the deprivation of freedom and to forced public works for a period of 5 (five) years each. The defendants shall be detained in custody to prevent flight.

Chairman (signature illegible)
Members (signatures illegible)

74. Economic Conditions and Abuses in Rural Russia, January 1921   [45, pp. 241–3, 246–9]

The Red Army became one of the strongest pillars of the Soviet regime through fighting successfully against the anti-Bolshevik forces and peasant insurrections. The Bolshevik leadership had high hopes for the new generation of Red Army officers and commanders and set up a variety of schools and courses to train them for new revolutionary battles ahead. But the Red cadets were not isolated from the rest of Russian society. Many had relatives in various provinces and during their leaves of absence learned firsthand about abuses of local government officials and general conditions in the countryside, as did cadets Morozov and Bobrikov in the documents below.

Impressions by Cadet Morozov during his leave in the village of Pesin of Pershinskaia volost, Shadrinksii district, Ekaterinburg province:

1. Railroads. Most stations are filled to the limit with Red Army men traveling on unlimited or short-term leaves. The station halls for the public are dirty and cold. [. . .]

2. The food issue and requisitions.

For fulfilling its requisition [of grains] on time, the district received [a medal of the Order of] the Red Banner. But at what cost did the peasants get this Red Banner? The district's oats have been taken entirely; not a seed was left even for sowing. The rye crop failed utterly. The wheat harvest was confiscated from many people; enough seeds were left for sowing one to one and one-half desiatina of land, a negligible quantity, given the size of the district. They promise to furnish more seeds for sowing, but the peasants view this promise as laughable, since last year seed grain was provided too late, almost a month after planting time. [. . .]

Last year just our village alone left 3,000 desiatins of good land unsown. And what can be expected in the current year? [. . .]

Only one-half a pood of potatoes per person remains, with nothing left for planting; all the rest was taken, and all of that rotted. [. . .] They gathered the potatoes when it was cold out and, while they were still frozen, dumped them into warm storage rooms, which spoiled them.

Meat requisitioning did not go any better. Some of the cattle taken from the peasants by requisition quotas died because of poor care and feeding. The rest of the cattle was slaughtered with negligence, skins not being collected. [. . .] Many cows were slaughtered two-three weeks before giving birth to calves. Such handling is extremely criminal, especially since you cannot plant cattle and it cannot grow in a year. Last year was even worse. In addition, most of the meat was allowed to go bad. [. . .]

The population is terribly intimidated and a spark would be sufficient to ignite a great fire of rebellion.

The prisons are filled with imagined saboteurs. Never in the past, even in the times of tsarist rule, were the prisons so overflowing as at the present time. I will cite one case as an example: a totally illiterate and uneducated 70-year-old man was imprisoned. When asked what he was put in prison for, he responded: "Well, children, I am some sort of shapoteur [i.e., saboteur]." [. . .]

3. Animal-drawn transport. Peasants with horses are forced to work 100–250 versts from home, where no fodder whatsoever is given to their horses, while the peasants have nothing but straw, and even that cannot be taken from home in large quantities. For this reason, many horses die. There is not a household in the village that has not lost horses. Besides, it often happens that peasants who arrive at the designated places of work receive no assignments and live there idly. [. . .]

All peasants have now developed the same view: that the communists' rule is coming to an end, which is why they are trying to destroy the agriculture economy so quickly. Simply opening one's eyes leads to such a conclusion.

Our district was always a flourishing land, and now one sees only ruins. [. . .]

Report by Cadet F. M. Bobrikov on observations during his leave in Orel province:

For three years the Red Army has been fighting the bandits of counter-revolution, bearing all hardships and deprivations for the sake of Soviet power, for the bright future, for truth. But there is yet no truth. According to the decrees and decisions of the center, authority in the provinces is independent. [. . .][34] To prevent the unnecessary shedding of blood, the most urgent and decisive measures need to be taken [to fight] against bureaucratism and the internal enemies of Soviet power.

I was home on leave in Orel province, Maloarkhangels'kii district, Gubkinskaia volost, in the village of Orliaki, where I witnessed many irregularities. Based on what I was told about the actions of the district authorities, I was extremely shocked to learn that some people want an end to Soviet power. The peasant is deprived of all freedom. Whatever he says, he is considered a saboteur and is arrested for trifles. [Officials] resort to the lash, guns, and the like. Those who should be punished get off. [. . .] Some agents do such vile things that they should be wiped off the face of the earth, but they are still alive. One agent nicknamed "Ivan the Lord" committed such dark deeds that it is unbearable. He took as much requisitioned food as he wanted. He took good things and stashed them in his home. And now he has been transferred from our volost to Netrubitskaia volost. There is no control over such persons. They do whatever they want to the peasants. They charge for milling as much as they want and allow milling in exchange for bribes, since the mills and creameries are [officially] closed. [. . .]

Lumber is given out arbitrarily. One person, the forest warden Ivan Iegorushkin, a citizen of the village of Peresukhi, takes the lumber himself but gives it out to peasants only in exchange for bribes. If some manufactured goods or salt are supplied, then almost nothing is left by the time they reach the citizens. And still you have to bring eggs [to exchange]; otherwise they give you nothing. Whatever agency you go to, you find white-legged people sitting. They drink tea with butter and milk, but if a peasant asks them about business matters he is told: "Stand outside the door." The red tape is terrible. No sense can be made of it. Drunkenness is universal. [. . .]

They come to some village, drink all the hooch they want and demand a good set of horses. If there is no good horse, they threaten the citizens with weapons. [. . .]

---

34. Local government officials in early Communist Russia enjoyed great independence from central control. Following the principle of revolutionary consciousness, whereby supporters of the revolutionary cause were thought to be endowed with proper judgment from a class viewpoint, the All-Russian Central Executive Committee and All-Russian Congress of Soviets devolved enormous power to local institutions. For example, the Eighth Congress of Soviets in 1920 declared that "Decrees of local congresses can be rescinded only by the highest Congress," meaning the All-Russian Congress of Soviets. Party and secret police inspections revealed widespread corruption and abuse, which sometimes resulted in stiff sanctions, and even capital punishment. Such actions failed to root out the abuse of power.

MATTERS OF SURVIVAL

75. A Soldier's Petition for Assistance, January 4, 1918
[45, pp. 35–6]

Russians had traditionally pleaded for help and bureaucratic intercessions from powerful officials, as a means to cut through red tape and to seek justice. Such petitions multiplied manyfold during the revolutionary era. The document below was sent to the All-Russian Central Executive Committee of Soviets (VTsIK).

PETITION

I ask the VTsIK of the SRK and SD[35] to pay attention to the following: I served in the ranks of the active army for more than three years and presently am on a three-month leave issued by the Illness Commission. I arrived at my birthplace, the city of Petrograd, where I have neither home nor land and where I found my mother starving and sick; all of our belongings were sold for the sake of her survival. So, is there a solution to this situation? After all we both are serving our MOTHERLAND.

On the basis of the above, I ask the VTsIK of the SRK and SD for any kind of work or employment in order to provide for my old mother a more or less bearable life and not the life of a pauper, since after three years of suffering, should not I and do not I have a right to something more than the life of a pauper?

Private Nikolai Viktorov
Member of the Executive Committee of the 166th Infantry Division
Petrograd, January 4, 1918

76. Letter by an Unknown Soldier to Lenin, February 20, 1918   [45, pp. 54–5]

In March 1917, the Provisional Government began a process of state control over the grain trade, yet the unimpeded activity of producer and consumer

---

35. Abbreviation for the Soviet of Workers', Peasants', and Soldiers' Deputies.

cooperatives ensured a steady supply. Tens of thousands of independent peddlers, mostly women, also met consumer demand. After the government decreed the confiscation of grain by force of arms in May and June and outlawed the transportation by train of all private cargo in the summer, the activity of "bagmen," or illegal traders, mushroomed. By fall 1918, even Lenin admitted that half of all grain in the country was distributed by the bagmen. The actual figure was probably higher. Thus, millions of petty entrepreneurs, constantly harassed by the Cheka, kept millions of consumers from starvation. It is not clear whether the author of the following angry complaint to Lenin was a bagman himself, but he clearly rejected government policies as harmful to the people.

Hungry Moscow
February 7/20,1918
   Comrade Lenin-Ulianov!
   I would like to ask you as the leader of the proletariat: what is going to happen next? There is no bread, no flour, no potatoes, nothing to eat, and by the way new mouths keep coming and coming. But, comrade Lenin, I am asking you: what is going to happen next? According to your order no flour or grain can be bought outside of Moscow or, to put it differently, they can be bought but cannot be transported, even as hunger forces people to take most desperate measures. You go to a train station hoping to buy something, and they meet you with firearms. I demand your response: why have you outlawed buying flour or bread in other provinces? I think that whoever is able would travel south and buy [them] even at an expensive price, but your order does not allow this, and therefore one has to go and act not in accordance with your directions, but simply with rifles in hand and seize flour and grain. As the leader of the government you do not take care of the railroad system, yet nobody else is in a position to do so. We are hungry and will not be repairing train cars and locomotives for you, since we are already disheartened, while you are turning a blind eye to all this, yet is there really no grain in our country? Take the south, take Siberia: granaries there overflow with grain, but perhaps you don't even want to think about us, the hungry ones, since it seems to me that you as the Chairman of the Commissars are allotted not one-eighth pound of bread, but more. Consequently, someone who is well fed will not understand a hungry one and therefore you don't want to think about it. . . .
   [. . .] Comrade Lenin! Come to your senses and legalize transporting flour from other provinces. That way you will save the populace from death. I am telling you as a comrade, everybody is strongly complaining about you because of the order forbidding the transportation of flour. Perhaps you are thinking that I am writing to you as a SPECULATOR, but no, I am a soldier who

returned from the front and saw his family in such conditions that it is quite understandable that anger has flared up, since, having suffered at the front, I now have to witness little children starving. [. . .]

77. Travails of a Provincial University, 1918
[93, pp. 217–9, 221]

One of the founders of the Imperial Saratov University (1909), Vladimir Ziornov was serving as professor of physics and rector of the university when he had to deal with a growing economic crisis and the Bolsheviks' attempts to reorganize the system of higher education. In September 1919, the government formally decreed that "worker departments" should be established in all universities to provide remedial training for factory workers to enable them to complete courses of higher learning quickly, generally part-time. In the memoir below, written in 1944 as a private recollection for his grandson, Ziornov describes how he dealt with the challenges facing the university. In March 1921, he was arrested and imprisoned by the provincial Cheka for having presented three lectures before the parish of the Cathedral of Saratov, in which he argued that science does not contradict faith. He was released but banished from Saratov.

[. . .] These were quite peculiar and sometimes difficult times, since the rector had to take care of all financial matters, while the country's economy was in a very bad state. I think it was during the very first year of my rectorship [1918], when it turned out that Saratov had no oil reserves, yet all the furnaces in the new buildings were designed to burn heating oil. There were no reserves of firewood. The University Council was very much concerned about this and ordered the immediate conversion of all furnaces to burn wood. When I reported that there was no firewood in the city either, the members of the Council said that they would go into the forest themselves and that it would be possible to mobilize all the students and that firewood could therefore be procured without outside assistance.

I had to submit to the decision of the Council, even though I knew that nothing would come of it. We obtained authorization to spend one million rubles for furnace conversion (that was still a lot of money in 1918) and remodeled all the heating systems. Some professors indeed went into the forest in the mountains near Saratov to collect firewood, but these procurements did not evolve into a large-scale effort. [. . .]

The following winter, the situation was entirely different. In the course of the summer, a lot of oil was brought to Saratov in tankers, but it could not be transported further by railroad, because the railroad system was in complete disarray. All the tanks on the bank of the River Volga were full, but it turned out to be difficult to bring the oil from the bank to the university. The carters either refused to work for money or demanded sums we were unable to pay. [. . .] We received a lot of alcohol from the district alcohol agency (Raispirt). So we decided to pay the drivers with alcohol instead of or in addition to money. I personally observed the transactions: a carter would immediately drink half a bottle of alcohol and everyone ended up happy. [. . .]

At the end of the heating season it turned out that we had become so preoccupied with raising the temperature in the buildings that we had exhausted all the oil we were entitled to too quickly. We needed roughly 90 more tons. A lengthy correspondence with the district oil agency (Raineft) loomed. Then I remembered that I had once met the head of Raineft (or its deputy), who, it turned out, was a violinist. He had asked me to lend him the score of Borodin's Second String Quartet. Naturally, I did not want to part with it and said that I did not have it. But now I decided to sacrifice it.

[. . .] At Raineft I sought out the director and acted as though I had come exclusively to give him the score.

"Can you imagine," I said to him right away, "that I was digging through my sheet music and came upon a copy of the quartet you wanted." We talked about music in the most friendly way and then I said. "Well, I actually have another matter. We are running out of heating oil."

"Are you kidding?" he exclaimed. "Do you really have to waste time on such trivia? We'll give you as much as you need." [. . .]

There were also difficulties like this: money transfers from Moscow were very irregular. Sometimes a whole bunch of sovznaks [Soviet rubles] was brought and then there would be nothing for a long time. We wrote and cabled to Moscow repeatedly. Supposedly, Lenin himself was briefed on this and replied that "people who are clever can survive without money." Indeed, we lived without money. Alcohol became the favored medium of exchange. All the departments, including philology and law, resorted to all kinds of pretexts so as to order alcohol. For example, this pretext: alcohol is required for cleaning book covers, as one division of the department of philology claimed. It is true that at the time many private libraries were being brought in from large landed estates and that a small amount of alcohol was used for cleaning moldy old book covers. Yet most of the alcohol served greater purposes.

[. . .] The entire request was for approximately 60 buckets of alcohol. [. . .] Raispirt took a cut of four buckets: we pretended to receive sixty buckets but in fact got only fifty-six. Raispirt also had to survive! I did not complain about such trifles. [. . .]

Despite deteriorating living conditions, all courses of study at the university continued. In 1918 it was announced that the doors of the university would open to all working people.

When I entered to begin my first lecture, the lecture hall was filled with all kinds of individuals, who, of course, neither could nor thought seriously about studying in a university. I literally could not move in the huge lecture hall. Not only all the seats and galleries but all the aisles were packed with people. The auditors stood right in front of the podium and almost sat on the stage itself. No experiments with my lectures were conceivable under such circumstances. But the size of the audience quickly began to ebb, and by wintertime, as I already mentioned, the lecture halls became extremely cold, and I ended up meeting with two to three dozen genuine students in my office. [. . .]

78. Intellectuals in Late 1918 and Early 1919
[73, pp. 488–90, 495–6, 499]

Fiodor Avgustovich Stepun (1884–1965) completed a doctorate in philosophy at the University of Heidelberg in 1909. Back in Russia he edited a philosophy journal and lectured across Russia. He fought in World War I and was gravely wounded in Galicia. Having served in the Provisional Government, Stepun was arrested but quickly released after the Bolsheviks came to power. He settled in Moscow where he worked as literary and artistic director of the Demonstration Theater of the Revolution in 1919, but after staging two plays he was fired "for lack of understanding of proletarian culture." In the excerpt from his memoirs reprinted below, he recalls the daily hardships, but also the artistic thrill and excitement of the first revolutionary years.

The winter of 1918–19 was horrible. All kinds of unknown tenants moved into our apartment on a variety of orders. [. . .]

[. . .] In the back room a German woman, who came from nobody knew where, was coughing strenuously. [. . .]

Her Spanish flu is exacerbated by pneumonia. [My wife] Natasha catches a mild form of the same flu and Aunt Lida a grave form. While herself ill, Natasha cares for the two afflicted women. The doctor prescribes medicine, but to obtain it is absolutely impossible. Finally, after endless efforts, friends of friends manage to get something from the Kremlin drugstore. But more important than medicine is heat. We have no firewood, since our storage shack has been requisitioned. We have to warily break into our own shack at night and steal our own firewood in order to save the dying. They could not be saved: first the German woman died, then a few weeks later Aunt Lida.

Then it turns out that it is more difficult to be buried in Soviet Russia than to be shot.

In order to bury a German woman without relatives, we had to obtain her death certificate from the chairman of the tenants' committee who was never home.[36] Then we had to take that certificate to various agencies and stand there for hours in order to obtain a permit for purchasing a coffin and permission to dig a grave. But who will dig it? A former janitor demands either half a bottle of vodka or five pounds of bread. We cannot get bread, but a bacteriologist we know in charge of a laboratory helps us get alcohol. This goes on for several days. At last we put the dead woman into the coffin; her cheeks have been eaten hollow by rats, her feet gnawed down to the bone.

When Aunt Lida died, coffins were no longer available. We fashioned a coffin ourselves from a few boards torn from the hallway partition and ourselves carried the dead woman on tiny sledges over bare stone pavement covered with autumn mud to the remote Vagan'kovskoe cemetery. [. . .]

What is the most surprising is that we not only continued to work with great dedication at the theater but had noisy and careless fun organizing literary-musical soirees, like the famous actors' parties of the Khudozhestvennyi Theater,[37] which sometimes ended with dancing. [. . .]

[. . .] After I quit the State Demonstration Theater, for some time I continued to teach in theater schools and studios: at Korsh's, the Lebedev Studio, and the Studio of Young Trainees. Of the latter I have the fondest recollection [. . .] rare classes by [Konstantin] Stanislavskii were real holidays amidst the daily grind.[38]

[. . .] Stanislavskii taught what no one but he could teach: the ability to listen within oneself and to distinguish true artistic creativity from its superficial imitation. In doing so, he used his own methods developed through long practice.

---

36. Tenants' committees (*domovye komitety* or *domkomy* for short) were created at the beginning of World War I. Usually dominated by property owners, they were intended to manage food distribution. They were used by the Communist government to manage apartment buildings, to instill communitarian spirit, and to maintain surveillance over residents.

37. The Moscow Artistic Theater was founded in 1898 by Konstantin Stanislavskii and Vladimir Namirovich-Danchenko.

38. Konstantin Stanislavskii (1863–1938), an actor and director, was one of the greatest theatrical innovators of the twentieth century.

"Here is a sofa," he spoke smiling with his charming smile and with his sunny agate-color eyes. "Imagine it has pins stuck in it; examine it by touch and try to take them out without getting pricked. [. . .]"

Male and female students in turn approached the sofa and pretending to fear to prick themselves, felt about on the sofa as if with care.

"It does not seem, my friends, that you believe in the pin," he would say to the young trainees, pulling a few pins from the flap of his jacket and sticking them into the sofa. The students then again began to explore the sofa, but now their hands moved differently. [. . .]

In Moscow, people were being shot; in the countryside they were starving and dying from typhus. All people thought about was [getting] a piece of bread and how to survive, yet I was tormenting Natasha, myself, and our horse the whole night long in order to lecture twenty young women and men about Eleusinian Mysteries[39] and the false principles of the French eighteenth-century theater. Who needed it? Was that not complete insanity?

79. Ordinary Life in Moscow, as Seen by a Schoolboy, November 1919   [34, pp. 370–1]

Food and fuel were the main concerns for most urban dwellers, including Muscovites. By fall 1919, a fuel crisis forced them to search desperately for wood and other means of heating and cooking. On November 22, Lenin warned in a circular letter to all party organizations that "[t]he fuel problem has become the central problem. The fuel crisis must be overcome at all costs, otherwise it will be impossible to solve the food problem, or the war problem, or the general economic problem." Lenin's main solution to these problems was to insist that "Labor conscription for the whole population must be carried out."[40]

The author of the document below, S. Mikhailov, age 16, was one of several high-school students taking external college-preparatory classes in fall 1919 at Moscow's Shaniaev People's University[41] who each turned in a similar

39. The Eleusinian Mysteries were initiation ceremonies for the cult of Demeter and Persephone in ancient Greece. Stepun was facetiously indicating just how passionately he and his students engaged in the theater.

40. V. I. Lenin, *Collected Works,* 47 vols. (Moscow: Progress Publishers, Moscow, 1965), 30: 139–42.

41. Founded in 1908 under the auspices of the Moscow City Duma, the Shaniaev University trained students, in separate programs, at the university and the high-school level but without issuing diplomas. These two programs were taken over by central state institutions, respectively, in 1919 and 1920.

assignment on the topic "Moscow in November 1919." While his composition mainly depicted the city's main woes, Mikhailov nevertheless proclaimed his faith in a bright future.

I am a Muscovite in the full sense of the word. Not only was I born in Moscow, but throughout my, in truth still comparatively brief life, I have not traveled from the "heart of Russia" farther than sixty miles. [. . .] This year snow fell early, and Moscow was dressed early in its brocaded winter garb. And this attire, I must confess, much becomes the face of our Mother-Moscow. Under the white shroud many not entirely attractive corners of the city have become less visible and take on a decent look. But winter has brought with it a phenomenon, which began in the summer and now has grown to epidemic proportions. I mean the dismantling of fences, barns, and even homes for firewood. Prompted by the cold, Muscovites are obliged to destroy homes that probably would serve for several more years. Should you walk the streets, you will see such a picture. A group of people, armed with makeshift iron crowbars, swarms around the ruins of a house trying, among the collapsed plaster and broken bricks, to find some splinters or pieces of wood. I apologize in advance before my kindly compatriots for the unflattering comparison, but these people, honestly, to an extraordinary degree resemble [. . .] hyenas or jackals in the desert. The impression made by a stove[42] just standing there is especially grim and increases the ugliness of the scene. All this destruction makes poor Moscow similar to a city that has suffered a huge fire or a powerful bombardment. Another exceptionally characteristic phenomenon for these days is that the majority of passers-by carry some load. One, contentedly glancing around, carries a bag of potatoes on his back. Another stumbles under the weight of a sack-full of cabbage. A third, looking behind him, like "a thief in the night," hides under his arm a little bag of flour or a carefully wrapped hunk of bread. These two episodes fully convey the moods and aspirations reigning among the inhabitants of Moscow. Hunger and cold—these are the two main enemies of the Muscovites. They force many people to shunt aside spiritual needs, and they transform the lives of many people into the struggle for a piece of bread. Yet I am far from giving in to depression and melancholy. I firmly believe that this difficult time will pass and that there will come a better one, a kingdom of Labor, Knowledge, and Art. And in order to achieve this, it is necessary to work, work, and work, and not give in to depression or sadness.

42. Russian stoves were huge brick structures that doubled as furnaces.

80. Commerce and Money in Civil War Moscow
[52, vol. 2, pp. 49–50]

The author of the diary excerpts below, Nikita Okunev, was a 50-something Tolstoyan. The well-paid Moscow agent of a riverboat company during World War I, he had voted for the Kadets, loved the theater, and read many newspapers. His two-volume diary was first published via samizdat *(typed underground copies) in the late 1970s. After describing economic hardships that he and his family experienced, Okunev then mentions that his economic condition suddenly improved because he was a "spets," which was short for* spetsialist *(expert). This happened as the Bolsheviks began to recognize their dependence on (bourgeois) specialists and experts in order to build socialism, until the rising proletariat could acquire adequate technical skills. Still, depending on the sensitivity of their work, specialists were oftentimes paired with political commissars to ensure their hewing to the party line.*

June 25 1920

Today I earned another 4,500 rubles with my [streetcar] "number 11."[43] I also got 2,058 rubles in "bonuses" for the period of May 16–June 1, but these contributions to the family treasury make no impression whatsoever. My wife and daughter feel utter contempt for my earnings. They would like me to engage in some kind of speculation, as supposedly do "all smart people." And in order to prove me wrong, they throw themselves into trading at Sukharevka [Market]. What they trade is quite petty, some sweets, and their entire store is in their hand baskets, but the results, of course, put my wages to shame. What I earn in one month, they sometimes can get in one or two days. It does not come easy though. You have to rush somewhere in the morning "to get the goods" and then stand for hours under the burning sun or under the rain on Sukharevskaia Square, while running the risk of being "seized" and taken to the Cheka (my wife has already spent one night there). Generally this is not a pretty situation for both them and me. And both sides seem to be right. Perhaps I am more to blame than they, but what can I do?! When I say that I don't need this or that, they say that they need it and that I, as a husband and father, should provide the means for the family's existence. They also give hundreds of examples in which husbands and fathers do not permit their loved ones such a "downfall." Nor is it "a downfall," in their opinion, but work for a real man. My daughter is partic-

---

43. By taking "streetcar number 11," which in early Soviet parlance meant going on foot, a Soviet employee could claim transportation expenses and then pocket the reimbursed sums.

ularly firm in this view. She is so carried away with trading that she went and quit her office job, unconcerned about bearing the status and lack of rights of a person without occupation. So what is going on in the final analysis? Precisely this: that I have only two children; one is a communist, the other a speculator. [. . .]

Raspberries have become available: 900 rubles per pound; strawberries can be bought for 400 rubles, wild strawberries for 500 rubles a pound, black currants for 300 rubles. [. . .]

July 6 1920

[. . .] I am getting tons of money: bonuses, 4,200 in overtime pay, and finally, as of May 16, 12,000 rubles per month as "an expert" (or "spets," as is customary to say in the contemporary abbreviated jargon) instead of my former salary of 3,500 rubles. [. . .]

81. A Letter from a Worker to Mikhail Kalinin, 1919
[45, pp. 124–5]

The son of a peasant, Mikhail Ivanovich Kalinin (1875–1946) joined the Social Democratic Party at its founding in 1898, organized workers in the Revolution of 1905, and took part in the October seizure of power. Elected chairman of the All-Russian Central Executive Committee of Soviets following Iakov Sverdlov's death in 1919, he was the folksy figurehead of the Soviet state for more than 3 decades. Many ordinary people addressed complaints like the one below to Kalinin, hoping he could understand their needs better than the party bosses could.

Worker Arkadii Sergeevich Ivanov to the Chairman of the All-Russian Central Executive Committee, Comrade Kalinin

Request

I have the honor to ask Comrade Kalinin not to refuse the request of a handicapped worker to buy, at a reasonable price in any province, a cow and a horse necessary for the feeding of his family of six. I reside in the village of Susanino of [St.] Petersburg[44] province, where we have timber facilities that

---

44. For many years after the city was renamed Petrograd in 1914, people still used the former name.

provide firewood for the city of [St.] Petersburg. More than 50,000 cubic sazhens[45] of firewood have already been prepared, but, given the insufficient number of horses available, only a scant amount of the wood has been transported from the woods. Had I a horse, I would help with transporting the firewood, according to my abilities, and in the spring I need a horse for field work. It is totally impossible for me to buy a cow and a horse within the limits of this and the nearby provinces because of terribly inflated prices. Therefore I am asking you, comrade Kalinin, as an old metal-industry worker yourself, hoping that you will not refuse the request of an old worker, who worked for twenty-two years in various factories and lost his health, and will grant permission to buy and bring home a cow and a horse and by doing so will give me the opportunity to survive and to provide for my family without resorting to monetary assistance from the republic.

Metal worker of the former Armament plant
Arkadii Sergeevich Ivanov

82. The Tragedy of Abandoned Children in Civil War Russia [92, pp. 9–25]

By 1916 there were perhaps 50,000 homeless children in Russia. Private voluntary organizations, principally the Unions of Zemstvos and Towns, rushed to succor them, generally without impediment from the Imperial Russian government. Due both to the breakdown of the traditional family and to war-induced social and economic dislocation, there were some 7 million orphaned children by 1921. Strenuous official promises to the contrary, few orphanages existed to care for them. The account below, written by the Socialist-Revolutionary Vladimir Zenzinov, describes civil society's efforts to address this problem.[46]

45. A *sazhen* was equal to 2.13 meters.

46. After university study in several European cities, the author, Vladimir Mikhailovich Zenzinov (1880–1953), joined the Socialist-Revolutionary Party. He spent 4 years in Siberian exile before World War I and was a member of the SR Party's Central Committee and of the Executive Committee of the Petrograd Soviet in 1917. He opposed the Bolshevik seizure of power, joined the Ufa Directory in 1918, and emigrated to France in 1920. He died in New York.

[. . .] "The League of Rescue for Children," writes Mme. E. D. Kuskova,[47] "dates from the autumn of 1918, when two fronts of battle were already formed in the interior, and Moscow was cut off from the South. At the end of September, I received from Poltava a letter written by V. G. Korolenko,[48] the Russian author who has since died. This letter had been brought by a man who had passed through the lines of the Reds.

Korolenko wrote that an age of terror was about to begin, that the whole country would be divided into Reds and Whites and that it would mean mutual extermination. The children must be saved, and an organization started on the lines of the Red Cross. [. . .]

"After receiving this letter," adds Mme. Kouskova, "I rapidly organized a big meeting, for it was still possible to do so at that date. [. . .] The heads of the organization were people known for their activity in social works, and co-operatives; from the political point of view, they were cadets, socialists, and neutrals, without party; none of them were Bolshevists."

The League's activities were fertile of results.

"In one year," writes Mme. Kuskova, "fourteen colonies for children had been started near Moscow [. . .] They learned to read and write and to work at some trade, under the supervision of excellent and disinterested teachers.

"After even one year in a colony these children, uncouth and covered with vermin when found, became unrecognizable, and in some of the colonies they succeeded in interesting the children in the management and good up-keep of the place, awakening in them a sense of responsibility. They estab-lished their own system of disciplinary punishment." [. . .]

About 3,500 children—orphans or orphaned on one side—received the attention of the League, whose resources were furnished by the co-opera-tives, who had not been nationalized at that date. Valuable convoys—whole wagon-loads of produce—were sent by the wealthy co-operatives in the south, arriving from Poltava, Kiev, and Kursk. These southern regions were cut off from Moscow by the line of battle, but wagons bearing this inscrip-tion: "League of Rescue for Children under the patronage of the Danish Red Cross" were allowed to pass, and one may remark that during this time of famine the League often shared its provisions with the Bolshevists, and sent food, too, to the Children's Rescue Homes organized by the Soviet government. [. . .]

47. Ekaterina Dmitrievna Kuskova (1869–1958) was a leading public activist. In a work of 1899, dubbed "Credo" by her orthodox Marxist opponents, she advocated seeking to raise workers' standard of living instead of focusing on political revolution. In 1921, she joined Gorky in appealing abroad for famine relief and was expelled from Russia in 1922. She died in Geneva.

48. For biographical information on Korolenko, see Document 107.

"For us, children are neither White nor Red, but merely Russian, and it is our duty to protect them against the miseries of civil war." [. . .]
Until the spring of 1920 the activity of the League was normal, without obstacle from the Soviet authorities. [. . .]
"[Gradually there] came direct attacks against the League." [. . .]
"We cannot permit these Kishkins[49] and Kuskovas to educate the children of our proletarians, even if they have been deserted."
The League kept coming up against obstacles of all kinds, and at last came to an end as an independent social organization [on January 1st, 1921].

A similar fate befell the Council for the Defense of Children which, although a Soviet institution, in which it differed from the League, and connected with several commissariats, was nevertheless an organization endowed with a certain autonomy. [. . .]

49. Nikolai Kishkin (1864–1930) was a medical doctor, the director of a Moscow clinic, and a leading Kadet. He also joined the All-Russian Committee for Famine Relief.

Building Socialism

83. Grigorii Zinoviev[50] at the All-Russian Congress of Trade Unions, January 7–14, 1918   [12, p. 81n2]

Although the Bolsheviks came to power in Russia under the banner of industrial labor and with rhetoric and an ideology that placed its interests above all others, trade unions in Soviet Russia quickly lost independence from the government authority. In the speech below, Zinoviev explains why such independence could not possibly be tolerated by the Bolshevik state.

Of course, we also in a certain sense stand for the independence of the trade union movement, its independence from the bourgeoisie. We have overthrown the power of the bourgeoisie, and at the moment when the working class together with the poorest peasantry has achieved the transfer of power to the working class, when your unions have become an element of government, what is the substantive meaning of their independence right now? According to the representatives of the right wing, the substantive meaning of their independence constitutes independence from the Soviets of Workers' and Peasants' Deputies for the purpose of supporting saboteurs and supporting those who are fighting against the worker-peasant government, for the purpose of supporting those who are organizing strikes against the working class "in the name of" the sacred right to strike and the freedom of association. [. . .] We have never used the name of the revolution to propose granting the freedom to strike and the freedom to sabotage to those gentlemen who support the bourgeoisie.

---

50. Grigorii Yevseevich Zinoviev (1883–1936) joined the Social Democratic Party in 1901 and the Bolshevik fraction in 1903 and for years was among Lenin's closest associates, though in October and November 1917 he wavered and objected to the Bolshevik seizure of power. He was Communist Party boss in Petrograd from March 1918 and chairman of the Comintern from March 1919. A contestant in the struggle to succeed Lenin after his death in 1924, he lost out to Stalin and was executed following a sham "show trial."

84. V. I. Lenin, "The Immediate Tasks of the Soviet Government," April 1918   [44, vol. 27, pp. 241–4, 251, 257, 259–61, 264, 271]

A party that for over a decade had focused its rhetorical and organizational efforts on the overthrow of the old order now had to shift its focus from destruction to construction. Lenin wrote the following article in order to explain how he envisioned a transition from capitalism to socialism and to inspire fellow party members in the face of a daunting task. On April 26, the Central Committee unanimously approved the basic outline of the following work, whose full version ran through over ten editions in Soviet Russia in 1918.

[. . .] In every socialist revolution [. . .] the principal task of the proletariat, and of the poor peasants which it leads, is the positive or constructive work of setting up an extremely intricate and delicate system of new organizational relationships extending to the planned production and distribution of the goods required for the existence of tens of millions of people. Such a revolution can be successfully carried out only if the majority of the population, and primarily the majority of the working people, engage in independent creative work as makers of history. Only if the proletariat and the poor peasants display sufficient class-consciousness, devotion to principle, self-sacrifice, and perseverance, will the victory of the socialist revolution be assured. By creating a new, Soviet type of state, which gives the working and oppressed people the chance to take an active part in the independent building up of a new society, we solved only a small part of this difficult problem. The principal difficulty lies in the economic sphere, namely, the introduction of the strictest and universal accounting and control of the production and distribution of goods, raising the productivity of labor and socializing production in practice. [. . .]

Keep regular and honest accounts of money, manage economically, do not be lazy, do not steal, observe the strictest labor discipline—it is these slogans, justly scorned by the revolutionary proletariat when the bourgeoisie used them to conceal its rule as an exploiting class, that are now, since the overthrow of the bourgeoisie, becoming the immediate and the principal slogans of the moment. [. . .]

The bourgeoisie in our country has been conquered, but it has not yet been uprooted, not yet destroyed, and not even utterly broken. That is why we are faced with a new and higher form of struggle against the bourgeoisie, the transition from the very simple task of further expropriating the capitalists to the much more complicated and difficult task of creating conditions in which it will be impossible for the bourgeoisie to exist, or for a new bourgeoisie to arise. Clearly, this task is immeasurably more significant than the previous one; and until it is fulfilled there will be no socialism. [. . .]

Our work of organizing country-wide accounting and control of production and distribution under the supervision of the proletariat has lagged very much behind our work of directly expropriating the expropriators. This proposition is of fundamental importance for understanding the specific features of the present situation and the tasks of the Soviet government that follow from it. The center of gravity of our struggle against the bourgeoisie is shifting to the organization of such accounting and control. Only with this as our starting-point will it be possible to determine correctly the immediate tasks of economic and financial policy in the sphere of nationalization of the banks, monopolization of foreign trade, the state control of money circulation, the introduction of a property and income tax satisfactory from the proletarian point of view, and the introduction of compulsory labor service. [. . .]

The raising of the productivity of labor first of all requires that the material basis of large-scale industry shall be assured, namely, the development of the production of fuel, iron, the engineering and chemical industries. [. . .]

Another condition for raising the productivity of labor is, firstly, the raising of the educational and cultural level of the mass of the population. This is now taking place extremely rapidly, a fact which those who are blinded by bourgeois routine are unable to see; they are unable to understand what an urge towards enlightenment and initiative is now developing among the "lower ranks" of the people thanks to the Soviet form of organization. Secondly, a condition for economic revival is the raising of the working people's discipline, their skill, the effectiveness, the intensity of labor, and its better organization. [. . .]

The Russian is a bad worker compared with people in advanced countries. It could not be otherwise under the tsarist regime and in view of the persistence of the hangover from serfdom. The task that the Soviet government must set the people in all its scope is: learn to work. [. . .] The possibility of building socialism depends exactly upon our success in combining the Soviet power and the Soviet organization of administration with the up-to-date achievements of capitalism. We must organize in Russia the study and teaching of the Taylor system[51] and systematically try it out and adapt it to our own ends. At the same time, in working to raise the productivity of labor, we must take into account the specific features of the transition period

---

51. Frederick Winslow Taylor (1856–1915), an American mechanical engineer and management consultant, used time and motion studies to improve labor efficiency.

from capitalism to socialism, which, on the one hand, require that the foundations be laid of the socialist organization of competition, and, on the other hand, require the use of compulsion, so that the slogan of the dictatorship of the proletariat shall not be desecrated by the practice of a lily-livered proletarian government.

Among the absurdities which the bourgeoisie are fond of spreading about socialism is the allegation that socialists deny the importance of competition. In fact, it is only socialism which, by abolishing classes, and, consequently, by abolishing the enslavement of the people, for the first time opens the way for competition on a really mass scale. [. . .]

We have scarcely yet started on the enormous, difficult but rewarding task of organizing competition between communes, of introducing accounting and publicity in the process of the production of grain, clothes, and other things, of transforming dry, dead, bureaucratic accounts into living examples, some repulsive, others attractive. [. . .] Model communes must and will serve as educators, teachers, helping to raise the backward communes. The press must serve as an instrument of socialist construction, give publicity to the successes achieved by the model communes in all their details, must study the causes of these successes, the methods of management these communes employ, and, on the other hand, must put on the "black list" those communes which persist in the "traditions of capitalism," i.e., anarchy, laziness, disorder, and profiteering. [. . .]

[. . .] [I]t is not difficult to see that during every transition from capitalism to socialism, dictatorship is necessary for two main reasons, or along two main channels. Firstly, capitalism cannot be defeated and eradicated without the ruthless suppression of the resistance of the exploiters, who cannot at once be deprived of their wealth, of their advantages of organization and knowledge, and consequently for a fairly long period will inevitably try to overthrow the hated rule of the poor; secondly, every great revolution, and a socialist revolution in particular, even if there is no external war, is inconceivable without internal war, i.e., civil war, which is even more devastating than external war, and involves thousands and millions of cases of wavering and desertion from one side to another, implies a state of extreme indefiniteness, lack of equilibrium, and chaos. And of course, all the elements of disintegration of the old society, which are inevitably very numerous and connected mainly with the petty bourgeoisie (because it is the petty bourgeoisie that every war and every crisis ruins and destroys first), are bound to "reveal themselves" during such a profound revolution. And these elements of disintegration *cannot* "reveal themselves" otherwise than in an increase of crime, hooliganism, corruption, profiteering, and outrages of every kind. To put these down requires time and *requires an iron hand.* [. . .]

[.] Wc must consolidate what we ourselves have won, what we ourselves have decreed, made law, discussed, planned; consolidate all this in stable forms of *everyday labor discipline*. This is the most difficult, but the most gratifying task, because only its fulfillment will give us a socialist system. We must learn to combine the "public meeting" democracy of the working people—turbulent, surging, overflowing its banks like a spring flood—with iron discipline while at work, with *unquestioning obedience* to the will of a single person, the Soviet leader, while at work. [. . .]

85. Party-State Relations in Nizhegorod Province, October 1918   [40, vol. 1, pp. 56–7]

From its inception, the Soviet leadership developed two parallel structures of governance. The state apparatus descended from the Council of People's Commissars and the All-Russian Congress of Soviets to the local soviets and agencies and commissariats ostensibly controlled by them. But this entire edifice in reality received orders from the party apparatus, which maintained its control by ensuring the appointment of utterly loyal party members to positions of responsibility within the state hierarchy. This system emerged gradually as the Bolsheviks established their control over the soviets, and even in late 1918 many party members in the provinces remained confused about exactly how the distribution of power between the soviets and the party organs worked. Central Committee officials, like Kaganovich, the main figure in the document below, were often dispatched to the provinces to communicate and clarify party strategy.

Komolov: Comrade [M. S.] Sergushev[52] explained that the party may not do anything, neither arrest nor confiscate. Is this just? If I come across a counterrevolutionary or a saboteur, I must arrest him.

[L. M.] Kaganovich:[53] Comrade Sergushev said: the duty of the party is to watch over everything, but [. . .] if the provincial [party] committee orders the execution of ten people and adopts such a resolution, it is not we who carry it out; to execute and to arrest is not the business of the provin-

---

52. M. S. Sergushev was the secretary of the Nizhegorod Communist Party committee.

53. Lazar Moiseevich Kaganovich (1893–1991), a factory worker of poor Jewish background, joined the Bolshevik Party in 1911. Drafted during World War I, he secretly agitated against the war while in uniform. He became one of Joseph Stalin's closest associates, beginning in 1922. He was sent to Nizhegorod province in May 1918.

cial committee. The provincial committee gives an order to the chair of the Cheka, who is a member of our party, and he carries it out. You yourself must strive to ensure that members of the committees of the poor, chairs of these committees, chairs of the soviets, the military commissars—are Bolsheviks-Communists; you as the party give them orders as members of your party, and they are obligated to obey you in the localities. If the party as a whole, gathered in plenary session or in committee, gives the order to arrest someone, then it has the right to order the military commissar as a member of the party to carry it out, but not officially (no one must know about this; you will not see in the press an announcement of the provincial party committee). The provincial committee gives the order, but officially it is made public by government authorities—the military commissariat or the Cheka.

86. A Feminist Agitator on Her Work in 1918–1919
[36, pp. 220–7]

In the Origin of the Family *(1884), Friedrich Engels argued that women could gain civil equality only through economic independence and through society assuming responsibility for housekeeping and child rearing. Thus, liberated women could enter relationships with men purely for love. Inspired by this argument, the Bolsheviks issued a decree of December 16, 1917, creating a system of no-fault divorce based on incompatibility. Furthermore, in 1919 a Woman's Department (Zhenotdel) of the Central Committee was established to "refashion women" for the building of socialism. Local zhenotdely sprang up across the country also for this purpose. Yet the funding for communal dining rooms, boarding schools, day-care centers, and other means of liberating women generally failed to materialize. Despite the early idealism of some activists, neither most women nor the government wished to give up the traditional family.*

[. . .] In December 1917, a department for the Protection of Motherhood and Infancy was established under the auspices of the Commissariat of State Welfare (social security), which was headed by A. M. Kollontai. [. . .] A physician and Bolshevik party member since 1907, Vera Pavlovna Lebedeva, was put in charge of this agency. The Department for the Protection of Motherhood and Infancy was intended to conduct clinical observation of children and pregnant women by means of a wide network of support centers, nurseries, kindergartens, and other institutions designed for pregnant women, mothers, and infants. This task could be carried out only with the active support of worker and peasant women themselves.

In the summer of 1918, I was working in the district town of Aleksin in Tula[54] province. The executive committee of the district soviet charged me, a young woman worker, with conducting a meeting of women in Streletsk township. The purpose of the meeting was to read and discuss the governmental decree on the creation of the state agency for the protection of motherhood and infancy. The director of the department of social welfare, I. V. Stepanov, told me:

"Read the decree at the meeting of women, clarify its meaning to them, stressing especially that nothing like this existed before the revolution and that this is only the beginning. A party member, Comrade Liapin, will accompany you to the meeting."

So I went with Liapin to the meeting. The peasant women listened carefully as I read the decree to them:

"The spark of life of two million infants was snuffed out in Russia every year because of the ignorance and the lack of consciousness of the oppressed people, because of the inertia and indifference of the class-based state. [. . .]

"You, working women, laboring citizen-mothers with your sensitive hearts, you, courageous builders of the new public life, idealistic teachers, pediatricians, midwives—all of you are being called upon by the new Russia to fuse your minds and feelings in the construction of a great edifice of social protection of the coming generations." As I read these lines of the decree, my voice trembled from the deeply stirring words.

The women were silent, but our proposal to open a nursery and a kindergarten in Streletsk township sparked a furious protest:

"We need neither nurseries nor kindergartens. We reared our children without them!"

"First a kindergarten, then a cart load of taxes. No!"

"They will remove our children's crosses and deliver them to the treasury. We will not give up our children!"

They really kicked up a din and would not listen to our pleadings. Then, having settled down, they expressed their views:

"Soviet power is our power. It gave land to the peasants—a great thank you for that. We bow deeply for that. Thank you for caring about us, mothers and children. It is also good for us to have equal rights. But we will give our children to neither nurseries nor kindergartens!" [. . .]

In the summer of 1918, local soviets received an order to send to Moscow women to attend a nine-month course for motherhood- and infancy-

54. Known as a major center for weapon manufacturing and the capital of samovar production, Tula province lies 100 miles south of Moscow and had a population of 1.5 million in 1897.

protection workers. The Aleksin district Executive Committee sent me. As I recall, about fifty women attended this course from cities around the country. Our studies began on September 1, 1918, at 12 Solianka Street.

In January 1919, a six-week course for agitators and organizers of the Commissariat of State Welfare's departments for the Protection of Motherhood and Infancy met in the same building. [. . .]

The lecture halls were cold. We studied in our coats, but we bore the cold stoically and learned with enthusiasm. We stayed in a dormitory set up for us in the former Nicholas Institute for Well-born Girls.

[. . .] Our practical studies were held in the best medical institutions of the capital. In the course of nine months, even in the extraordinarily difficult conditions of those times, not a single class was cancelled. As a result, the program trained us very well.

A lot of attention was paid to the political education of students. Political literacy was taught by A. M. Kollontai, one of the best propagandists of our party. Alexandra Mikhailovna spared no efforts on our behalf: she not only educated us, but also nurtured us and cultivated in us loyalty to the ideals of socialism and Bolshevik convictions and also drew us students into the public life of Moscow. A. M. Kollontai well understood that, having finished the course, we would return to our hometowns, sometimes in the most obscure corners of the country, and would face difficult work among the local women. She did everything possible to give us a multifaceted training to confront this task. We students were grateful to her for taking the initiative to enable us to see and hear Vladimir Il'ich Lenin. [. . .]

Upon my return to Aleksin, I enthusiastically engaged in my work as director of the sub-department for the Protection of Motherhood and Infancy. Later I became instructor of the women's department of the district party committee. In December of 1919, I joined the Communist party, and in 1920 I became the director of the district women's department.

87. An Orthodox Clergyman Renounces His Priesthood, December 26, 1918   [11, p. 39]

While the Orthodox Church rejected the Bolshevik government's efforts to curb its influence, some members of the clergy, especially those alienated from the church hierarchy, embraced the vision of a society based on equality and collective labor, as the document below indicates.

I, the undersigned priest of the Nikol'skaia church of the Talabinsk district of Pskov province and uezd, Leonid Nilov Kolosov, in the presence of the administrator of the Commissariat of Internal Affairs of the Union of the Communes of the Northern Oblast, Comrade Kaplun, and the secretary of the Commissariat, Comrade Pedder, declare by this renunciation that I renounce my priesthood and my spiritual status in general, acknowledging that what I was teaching was a lie and that the path down which I led laypeople was a sham, based on the backwardness and ignorance of the people for the sake of personal self-interest. The sole religion of the peoples and of our Russian people in particular is honest and free labor, which will bring the working people of the whole world to a bright and free celebration of the triumph of the ideas of socialism.

Leonid Nilov Kolosov

88. Repressive Measures for Failure to Remove Snow, February 15, 1919   [57, p. 123]

The document below is an order by the Council of Workers' and Peasants' Defense. Created on December 13, 1917, the council was empowered to mobilize all the resources of the country for national defense. Its mandates were to be implemented unconditionally. The Defense Council exercised strict military discipline over all workers in the transport, food supply, and war-industries sectors, which the Bolsheviks considered vitally important for victory, once the Civil War gained steam.

The Council of Worker-Peasant Defense at its session of February 15 of this year, having considered the issue of exemptions granted to various people residing within 20 versts of railroad lines, resolved:

To order [Efraim] Sklianskii,[55] Markov, [Grigorii] Petrovskii,[56] and [Feliks] Dzerzhinskii[57] to immediately arrest several members of the executive committees and committees of the poor in those localities where snow is not being cleared entirely satisfactorily from the railroad tracks; in these same

---

55. From April 1918 to March 1924, Efraim Sklianskii (1892–1925) was deputy chair of the revolutionary military council and as such Trotsky's most trusted assistant.

56. Grigorii Petrovskii (1878–1958) was commissar of the interior from November 1917 to March 1919 and then head of the Ukrainian Soviet government until 1939.

57. Born into a Polish noble family, Feliks Dzerzhinskii (1877–1926) was a Social Democrat beginning in 1895. He joined the Bolshevik Party in 1917 and headed the Cheka from its creation in December 1917.

localities, to take hostages from among the peasants, so that they can be shot if the snow is not being cleared away; to schedule, within one week, a compliance report indicating the number of people arrested.

89. Red Tape in Communist Russia, September 1919
[7, pp. 356–7]

During the last years of his life, Lenin was increasingly preoccupied with what he considered the extreme "bureaucratization" of the Soviet government and was furious over the cases of bureaucratic inefficiency like the one recounted below by Vladimir Bonch-Bruevich.[58] In response, Lenin proposed a number of measures from harsher criminal punishment for bureaucratic ineptness to some form of "worker control" over state agencies, but with little success.

Even a few months of the new life had not passed as Petrograd and Moscow, and after them all the towns and villages of vast Russia, were filled to brimming with new bureaucrats. It seems that from the very creation of the world until our days there was never under the sun such a colossal, scandalous quantity of bureaucrats as in the days after the October Revolution.

The course of the revolutionary events [. . .] moved our social relations in such a way that it was considered the summum bonum to decisively nationalize everything, from the biggest factories and plants, right down to barbershops with one barber, one electric trimmer, and two razors, along with the last carrot in alimentary matters. Everywhere there were patrols so that no one could pass with any foodstuffs; everyone was put on rations, receivable from Narkomprod.[59] Footwear, utensils, clothing—everything was given out by ration cards, and to accomplish this there were not enough buildings in which to house the institutions and fill them with civil servants.

In order to receive any little trifle, it was necessary to travel many miles, from office to office, signing, cosigning, countersigning, re-signing, and registering ill-fated little documents, which flowed in a torrent and literally

58. A historian, ethnographer, publisher, editor, and Social Democratic activist from 1895, Vladimir Dmitrievich Bonch-Bruevich (1873–1955) joined the Bolshevik fraction in 1903 after the second party congress. Close to Lenin, he was the leading Bolshevik publisher of legal and illegal periodicals, both in Russia and abroad before 1917. Following the October Revolution, Bonch-Bruevich became a secretary of the Council of Peoples' Commissars, a position that led to his deep involvement in the day-to-day matters of government and put him in close proximity to the top leaders of the Bolshevik Party.

59. The Commissariat for Foodstuffs provided peasants with goods in exchange for grain.

flooded all of the channels for the distribution of consumer goods. Some comrades attempted to quantify all these ordeals and "goings through Soviet purgatory." Thus, for example, M. S. Ol'minskii,[60] who suffered in the explosion in the Moscow [party] committee[61] and whose jacket was reduced to rags, was granted by the Moscow Soviet an order for a jacket. In order to receive it, he, having recovered from a concussion, patiently went from institution to institution and, as befit a highly experienced statistician, pedantically calculated all the signatures he needed to amass before obtaining the right to a jacket, which he had lost in such an extraordinary circumstance. It turned out that our honored comrade had to visit fourteen premises before he received the final document granting him the right to obtain the most ordinary jacket. I recall very well how Ol'minskii with the epic serenity of a historian recounted this "actual case" to Vladimir Il'ich [Lenin] and how Vladimir Il'ich literally boiled with indignation about this way of doing business, which we ourselves had established.

"Chinoiserie, bureaucratism, red-tape," he roared. "It is easier to make a revolution than to establish a revolutionary way of life. We'll have to battle seriously and for a long time against this."

90. The Supreme Council of the National Economy in Action, February 1920   [69, pp. 38–40]

As the Bolsheviks proceeded to nationalize key Russian industries, they had to come up with ways to manage the ever-expanding economic assets of the Soviet state and to replace what they took to be the chaos of the markets with socialist order and efficiency. Following the creation of the Council of Workers' and Peasants' Defense on December 13, 1917 (see Document 88), the Supreme Council of the National Economy (VSNKh) was established on December 14, 1917. Subordinated directly and solely to the Council of People's Commissars, it was intended to coordinate and unify the totality of activities and finances of the national economy. Empowered to seize and amalgamate all branches of industry and commerce, as well as any factories and other enterprises, no aspect of economic life, from factory committees and trade unions to regulating organs of the People's Commissariats and the All-Russian Council of Workers' Control,

60. Mikhail Stepanovich Aleksandrov (pseud. Ol'minskii), 1863–1933, was a revolutionary activist and literary scholar. In 1919 he was an editor of *Pravda*.

61. On September 25, 1919, anti-Bolshevik terrorists detonated a bomb in the building of the Moscow Bolshevik Party committee on Leont'ev Lane where some 100 party members were meeting, wounding several.

escaped its purview. Local branches (SNKhs) managed economic affairs in the provinces. The following document is excerpted from the minutes of the Presidium of the Supreme Council of the National Economy from its meeting on February 7, 1920, and reveals an unprecedented level of micromanaging the national economy.

Item 1299. In re: The Main Committee on Structural Materials

Resolved: (1) The management of the production of construction materials of mineral origin should remain under the purview of the Chemical Department of the VSNKh; (2) acknowledge that the tasks of the section of construction materials, which is being formed for that purpose in the Chemical Department, include: the merger of brick and lime plants into a group under the management of a head agency, the formulation of specific production tasks for provincial SNKhs, the timely financing of provincial SNKhs, and arranging the provision of the finished products to the state.

Item 1300. In re: Firewood Transportation Plan for February of this Year (report by comrade Ksandrov)

Resolved: (1) Communicate to the Supreme Transportation Council that its bureaucratic delays in considering and approving the plans on firewood transportation for February of this year are having a harmful effect on the work of the Main Fuel Committee; ask the Supreme Transportation Council to consider and approve the above-mentioned plans no later than February 10 of this year; (2) approve the February plan for firewood transportation; (3) under penalty of legal responsibility, forbid the local organs of the Main Forest Committee to submit firewood without duly completed paperwork and the local organs of the Main Fuel Committee to receive firewood without such paperwork.

Item 1303. In re: Supplying Rags to the Main Directorate for State Enterprises in the Paper Industry. [. . .]

Item 1304. In re: Transferring the Oranienbaum [electric power] Station to the Urals region. [. . .]

Item 1297. Transfer engineer N. N. Vashkov from the Kol'chugin Plant to the Department of the Electrotechnical Industry [of the Supreme Council of the National Economy] as Assistant Director of the Department. [. . .]

Items 1302, 1306. Request that the Council of Defense carry out urgent special deliveries of fuel to sugar-beet plants to avoid the imminent loss of improved raw material and that it urgently furnish banknotes to local timber production facilities, appointing Comrades Lomov and Syromolotov to report on this issue to the Council of Defense. [. . .]

Item 1308. Order all head agencies and centers to provide the metal-weaving factory in Moscow with the necessary metals and materials as a matter of extraordinary priority.

Items 1309, 1310. Nationalize and subordinate to the Main Directorate for Textile Enterprises: the Polar Boot Factory in Kazan; [and the following nine] textile factories [. . .]

91. The Electrification of Russia
[39, pp. 121–8, 134–5, 137–8]

On November 14, 1920, a small electric power station, constructed by the local agricultural cooperative, came online in the village of Kashino, Volokolamsk district, in the northwest of Moscow province. Since this was one of Russia's first village power stations, Vladimir Lenin and his wife Nadezhda Krupskaia attended the opening ceremony. The author of the account describing their visit, Stepan Kruglov, formerly the chairman of the district Executive Committee, was head of the district Communist Party committee at the time of the ceremony.

[. . .] The chairman of the [power station] association, Rodionov, stood up and delivered a short speech. He said: "Dear guests and fellow villagers! I congratulate you on the great and festive celebration for the peasants of Kashino: the launching of the electric power station. New life is beginning in our village, in our life, and in our economy; a life, which is bright, joyful, and prosperous. Electricity is a great resource for our village. And this day is particularly great and dear for us, and it will always remain in the memory of the peasants of Kashino, because it has been made joyful by the visit of our dear leader, the head of the Soviet government, Vladimir Il'ich Lenin and his wife Nadezhda Konstantinovna Krupskaia."

Everyone rose for a lengthy standing ovation. Rodionov went on: "Only thanks to Comrade Lenin and the party of Bolsheviks, which he founded and leads, were we able to free ourselves from the landlords and to build our own power station, and, as you see, to talk freely here with the representatives of the district authorities and the head of the Soviet government."

Then he raised a glass of beer and proposed a toast:

"Let's drink to our new life, to the head of the Soviet government, Comrade Lenin, to his spouse Comrade Krupskaia!" [. . .]

Rodionov offered Vladimir Il'ich a snack and said: "Enjoy your meal, Vladimir Il'ich, and do not fault us for our poverty. Our little wealth we are happy to share from the bottom of our heart."[62]

Lenin, smiling, expressed his thanks, and replied: "This is not poverty at all. On the table are bites of meat, good bread, and even something to drink. What more could be desired in these difficult transitional times! We will defeat our enemy at the front, will undertake peaceful construction, will rebuild our industry and agriculture, and then we will have a better life. But for now this is very, very good! A plentiful table like this can be permitted only to celebrate the launching of an electric power plant."

Il'ich was eating little, and to the peasants' entreaties, he replied: "Thank you, I had a good meal before leaving Moscow and am not hungry yet." [. . .]

The peasants told Vladimir Il'ich how difficult life was in 1918–1919: there was no bread; they ate oil cake [solid residue from oily seeds] and various food substitutes. Now the food situation has improved. If only there were some finished goods, like cotton prints and so on, then life would be entirely good. And it would also be great to change the arrangement with grain requisitioning, so that the peasant would not be afraid to plant anymore. We do understand, said the peasants, that the state cannot exist without taxes, but the peasant needs to feel confident in his work, to know what he must surrender and what he will have left, so that he can plan ahead for his livelihood.

Vladimir Il'ich listened to everybody very carefully, sometimes interrupting the speaker in order to ask clarifying questions.

Having listened to the peasants' complaints about the issues that mattered most to them, Lenin clearly and simply explained the reasons for the shortage of industrial goods and food in the country. He dwelled longer on grain requisitioning, explaining its causes and importance for feeding the workers and the army during the civil war period.

Vladimir Il'ich said that the civil war was nearing its end. The Soviet government was stronger, and soon a new system of taxation would be instituted. [. . .]

The peasants spoke with Lenin completely freely. As we say, they opened their souls to him. They expressed their discontent about certain actions of the Soviet government with such candor as they would probably have feared to show even when speaking among themselves.

---

62. This is a Russian saying.

The women, who stood not far from the table listening to this conversation, were very worried, fearing that something bad might result. One woman could not bear it and called her husband to the kitchen. There he was surrounded by other women who tried to convince him that the men should speak more carefully, otherwise Comrade Lenin might think that our peasants were against the Soviet government.

But the candid discussion, which Lenin himself invited, continued on. The peasants felt themselves uncoerced, and Vladimir Il'ich conducted the chat with such sincerity that the peasants spoke with him as with a good friend come to visit, with the difference that he better understood what was happening in the country and knew better than they the path necessary for the further development of the country. [. . .]

[Later], Rodionov opened the assembly and read a prepared speech. He said:

"Comrade fellow-villagers, on behalf of all of you, I express gratitude to Comrade Lenin and Comrade Krupskaia for the attention that they have paid to us by visiting our village and participating in our celebrations. Only thanks to Soviet power, which is headed by Comrade Lenin, we, the peasants of Kashino, were able to build our electric power plant and obtain 'the unnatural light,' which will illuminate our peasant darkness, our simple huts. This light will not only cut through the nightly darkness of the village but will also enlighten our minds and consciousness. It will illumine the path that we peasants must tread harmoniously with the workers in order to build a new, free life, our Soviet state. Earlier, under the tsarist government, the peasants could not even imagine having such a light; it seemed completely inconceivable. The revolution freed up science and confined the darkness into this 'little bubble,'" and he pointed to the electric light bulb hanging next to the podium on a pole. "A wide road for the free expression of labor has now opened before the peasant and every working person. Our joy of liberation is great. A huge laboring flood of peasants has set out toward the building of a new life." [. . .]

Lenin's speech was many times interrupted by vigorous applause. [. . .]

"Comrade peasants! I will talk about the significance of electricity at the end, but first of all let me share some joyful news.

"I just received information that things are going quite well at the front.

"Wrangel[63] will be no more in a week.

"We know this for certain.

"There will be peace with Poland. We will achieve it.

---

63. A career military officer, Piotr Nikolayevich Wrangel (1878–1928) commanded a cavalry unit in World War I and was military commander of all the anti-Bolshevik forces in the south at the end of the Civil War, replacing Anton Denikin.

"What is good for the landlords is not good for the peasants, and this we know too. We need peace in order to heal our wounds and to begin the organization of the peasant economy.

"We cannot achieve this until we do away with all our enemies.

"You see that your village Kashino is turning on the electricity. This is only one village. But it is important for us that the whole country be filled with light.

"The Soviet government is currently developing an electrification project. Electricity will cultivate and fertilize the land for us and will carry us forward.

"Electricity is a great power, but in the hands of the working people it is the greatest power.

"There will be a time when Soviet power will grow strong, the economy will be set right, and the factories and plants will be up and running!

"But in order for this to happen, above all the worker-peasant union must be strong, strong in deeds, not in words."

At the end of Lenin's speech a furious ovation erupted again.

SOVIET RUSSIA AND THE WORLD

92. The Polish-Soviet War, 1920   [82, pp. 60–3]

The Polish-Soviet War began in April 1920 when Polish forces invaded Ukraine, quickly occupying Kiev. Within weeks the Red Army counterattacked and, following a string of military successes, launched an offensive against Poland in early July. By August, however, the offensive stalled and was reversed. The author of this document, Mikhail Tukhachevskii (1893–1937), was a Polish aristocrat who won medals for bravery in battle during World War I. He rose quickly in the Red Army during the Civil War and commanded the Bolshevik forces in the Polish-Soviet War as well as in suppressing the Kronstadt rebellion (see Documents 131–134) and Tambov peasant uprising in 1921 (see Document 127). The Soviet failure to push into Poland dashed the Bolsheviks' hopes of turning the Russian Revolution into a European one. Tukhachevskii explains just how real this opportunity seemed at the time.

[. . .] Even before our offensive, all of Belorussia, which was under the oppression of the Polish landlords and White Polish armies, was boiling and seething with peasant uprisings. [. . .]

The situation in Poland in just the same way appeared favorable to the revolution. A strong proletarian movement and a no less threatening movement of agricultural workers were putting the Polish bourgeoisie in a very difficult position. Many Polish communists believed that we only had to reach the ethnographic Polish boundary and the proletarian revolution in Poland would be inevitable and guaranteed. Indeed, when we occupied the Belostok district, we received the most enthusiastic sympathy and support there from the worker population. Mass rallies passed resolutions about joining the Red Army. The peasantry at first viewed us with suspicion because of the agitation of the Polish priests and nobles, but very soon they grew familiar with us and calmed down. The agricultural worker population definitely sympathized with us. Thus what we encountered in the part of Poland we occupied was undoubtedly sympathetic to the socialist offensive and ready to accept it. [. . .]

Discussions of the awakened national sentiment within the Polish working class, following our offensive, naturally result from our having lost the campaign. Fear, of course has big eyes [a Russian saying]. Let's not forget that as we approached Warsaw the worker population of Prague, Lodz, and other industrial centers grew extremely agitated but was repressed by bourgeois Polish volunteer units. [. . .]

Could Europe have responded to this socialist movement with an explosion of revolution in the West? The events suggest that it could have. Our sweeping victorious offensive shook up and caused a stir in all of Europe, hypnotized everyone and everything, and drew all eyes toward the East. Both working-class and bourgeois newspapers were preoccupied with only one question: the Bolshevik offensive. [. . .]

Thus, Germany was seething with revolution and needed only to connect with the militant stream of the revolution in order to achieve the final conflagration.

In England the working class was in the same way engulfed by the liveliest revolutionary movement. The operations committee engaged in an open struggle with the English government. The position of the latter was definitely unstable. The situation was reminiscent of the state of the tsarist government during the days of the Soviet of Workers' Deputies in 1905.

In Italy a genuine proletarian revolution broke out. The workers were seizing factories and plants and set up their own government. And if not for the vile actions of the Social Democrats, then the revolution could have easily assumed huge proportions.

In all the countries of Europe, the fortress of capital faltered. The working class raised its head and took up arms. There is no doubt that had we won a victory on the Vistula[64] then revolution would have engulfed the whole of the European continent with its fiery flame.

Of course, when a war is lost, it is very easy to find political mistakes, political missteps. But the situation just outlined above speaks for itself. Revolution from without was feasible. Capitalist Europe was shaken to its foundations, and if not for our strategic errors, if not for our military defeat, then perhaps the Polish campaign would have become the missing link between the October revolution and the Western European revolution.

---

64. The longest river in Poland, the Vistula runs from the Carpathian Mountains in southern Poland, through Krakow and Warsaw and up to the Baltic Sea in the north.

93. Report on Activities of the Comintern, March 1921
[48]

The Communist International (Comintern), or Third International, was founded in Moscow in early March 1919 at the height of efforts by Communists to seize power in Central Europe. In late March a Hungarian Soviet Republic was established under the leadership of Bela Kun (1886–1938), a close ally of the Bolsheviks, and in early April a Bavarian Socialist Republic, which imitated the Russian example, was proclaimed. The purpose of the Comintern was to coordinate efforts of Communist parties around the world to foment and achieve the overthrow of "bourgeois" governments by revolutionary means. Some thirty Communist parties and organizations, including several from former provinces of the Russian Empire, sent fifty-two delegates to take part in the founding. The Bolshevik leadership genuinely and enthusiastically believed in the imminent spread of revolution across Europe. In summer 1919, Zinoviev, the chairman of the Comintern, declared that "in a year all Europe shall be Communist. And the struggle for Communism shall be transferred to America, and perhaps also to Asia and other parts of the world." The Second Congress of the Comintern, held in July–August 1920, imposed twenty-one conditions for membership, including the obligation "to give unconditional support to every soviet republic in its struggle against the forces of counterrevolution." The Bolshevik leaders subsidized and controlled the Comintern throughout its existence. They used it to promote the development of Communist parties and to encourage their efforts to bring about revolution throughout Europe, as this report by a senior Comintern official indicates.

To the Chairman of the Executive Committee of the Comintern (IKKI), Comrade Zinoviev
Copy to the General Secretary

During my trip I visited the following countries: POLAND, CZECHO-SLOVAKIA, AUSTRIA, ITALY, GERMANY, LITHUANIA, and LATVIA. I will present my proposals about these countries in that order.

I. POLAND

The Polish Communist Party is the only large illegal party closely linked to the masses. It has a strong influence on the working class. [. . .] It has almost no income and is forced to live entirely at the expense of the IKKI. The needs of the party are many. Until October 15, 1921, they received from us 1,000,000 German marks per month, and after that date, because of a change in the exchange rate, nearly double that amount. [. . .]

II. CZECHOSLOVAKIA

[. . .] Here is my proposal in terms of financing the Czech Communist Party: provide substantial assistance as a loan for organizational expenses and for newspapers to prevent their press from collapsing; also this year allocate a certain amount for waging their electoral campaign for parliament; they will need a large amount, since the bourgeois parties will be fighting hard against them. [. . .]

III. AUSTRIA

[. . .] [T]he Austrian Communist Party does not constitute a revolutionary base, nor does it stand up to the military cliques seeking to attack Russia. [. . .] [Y]et cutting off subsidies threatens the closure of [their] newspaper. [. . .]

My proposal is to purchase a printing press for publishing *Die Rote Fane* [. . .] under the condition that it would not be given to the party but would remain a private enterprise under the control of the IKKI. [. . .]

IV. ITALY

[. . .] I think it is a mistake that the party does not allow its members to join pan-proletarian organizations that combat the fascists. The working masses are much angered by fascism, and this mood could be used for Communist propaganda and for unifying workers in the struggle against the fascists. [. . .]

The party lives entirely at the expense of Comintern and has no hopes for independent existence. Their only available revenue is 50,000 party cards at 5 lira each per year for a total of 250,000 lira. By contrast, the expenses for the central apparatus and subsidies to local organizations alone add up to 733,200 lira per year. If one adds to this 240,000 lira for illegal work and 100,000 for relations with other parties, then, together with expenses for their newspapers and publishing operations, the grand total reaches 4,306,000 lira, which under the current circumstances we are absolutely unable to provide. [. . .]

V. GERMANY

[. . .] Concerning the financing of the Communist Party of Germany, the party itself seeks to receive less assistance from Comintern but cannot do without it entirely. Still, it is possible to reduce this assistance without damaging the work of the Communist Party. They can reduce the central apparatus and terminate newspaper subsidies for local organizations. [. . .]

Director of the Department of International Relations of the IKKI

94 Soviet Policy in Regard to the Genoa Conference, May 1922   [85, pp. 233–5]

In April–May 1922, diplomats from 34 countries met in Genoa, Italy, to for-mulate policies for rebuilding central and eastern Europe, for resolving an eco-nomic crisis that resulted in, among other problems, extremely high inflation in Germany, and for working out relations between the capitalist west and the Communist east. During the conference, representatives of Germany and So-viet Russia met in the small town of Rapallo, 15 miles to the east, and signed their own treaty of cooperation and diplomatic recognition of each other's bor-ders and territorial integrity. A secret covenant, adopted in July, authorized the German military to train on Soviet territory, contravening a key provision of the Treaty of Versailles. The Central Executive Committee resolution below ar-ticulates the Soviet view of the socioeconomic conditions of the capitalist world and explains the necessity of the Rapallo Treaty.

Having heard the report by Comrade [Adolf] Ioffe on the Genoa Confer-ence, the VTsIK has reached the following conclusion:

[. . .] The international political and economic situation is marked by the extreme instability of the capitalist system in its entirety.

Politically, this situation is manifested in the absence of genuine peace, in an arms race, in increased antagonism among the great powers, in the dan-ger of colossal new imperialist wars, etc.

The Genoa Conference has brought fully to light deep contradictions between England and France, Japan and the United States, the victor coun-tries, and Germany, Italy, and France, etc. The conference has totally exposed the fictitiousness not only of the League of Nations but also of the so-called Entente.

On the other hand, the civil war in Ireland; the civil wars in China, India, and Egypt; the war of national liberation in Turkey against its enslavement by foreign capital; and the ubiquitous aggravation of social-class conflicts (English strikes, labor uprisings in South Africa, a lockout in Denmark, strikes in Germany, etc.)—all taken together objectively demonstrate the continuing disintegration of the socio-political system of capitalism.

Economically, this disintegration finds its screaming expression in the fact that the mighty "victor" countries, which enriched themselves in the war by means of undisguised and cynical plunder, cannot restore even the pre-viously existing capitalist relations three-and-a-half years after the war's end. The Versailles Treaty is bankrupt both in reality and in the minds even of the bourgeois circles: the severe global crisis, the chaos in world currencies, the impossibility of settling on a capitalist basis the issue of mutual financial

claims and debts, the fundamentally disrupted economic balance between
Europe and America, the profound decline of certain countries of Europe,
the impossibility even in the eyes of bourgeois scholars and politicians of
achieving economic recovery without involving Russia in the economic
process—these are the symptoms of economic disintegration. [. . .]

Regardless of the immediate outcome of the Genoa conference, all the recent dynamics of international relations bear witness to the inevitability of
a temporary coexistence of the Communist and bourgeois systems of property during this stage of historical development and force even the most irreconcilable enemies of Soviet Russia to seek ways to accept the communist
system of property, now that their four-year-long efforts to destroy this system have collapsed.

Therefore, the VTsIK welcomes the Russo-German Treaty concluded at
Rapallo as the only correct solution to the difficulties, chaos, and danger of
war. [. . .]

CHAPTER 4
Popular Opposition and Civil Wars

Initial resistance to the Bolshevik seizure of power was minor. For many of their staunch opponents, the Bolsheviks' vision of building socialism in an underdeveloped country appeared to be so absurd that they thought it was only a matter of weeks before the regime would collapse under the burden of its own incompetence. Also, it took a while for the news from Petrograd to reach Russia's many distant provinces. Nor did most people seem to care about the fate of the Provisional Government. The fate of the Constituent Assembly was a different story.

The Bolsheviks allowed elections to a Constituent Assembly to proceed according to plan in November and December 1917, though not without some harassment of candidates and political parties to their right. The results were dismal from the Bolsheviks' point of view: only one-quarter of the electorate voted for them, along with another tiny sliver for the Left Socialist-Revolutionaries. They argued, plausibly, that the results would have been different had the latter party actually appeared on the ballot. Yet even then it seems unlikely that the main pro-peasant Socialist-Revolutionary Party would not have remained the biggest winner. "The Fate of the Constituent Assembly" (Documents 95–98) shows how ordinary people viewed the body that was supposed to give Russia a constitution, how the voting process functioned, and how the assembly, whose convocation liberal and radical Russian intellectuals had dreamed of for two decades, was shut down at gunpoint after its first meeting.

The dissolution of the Constituent Assembly angered the Socialist-Revolutionaries, but it was arguably the deterioration in living conditions, not politics, that led to a growing dissatisfaction with the Bolshevik government even among the groups whose interests they claimed to represent first and foremost: the industrial workers. For one thing, food was scarce in the cities during the winter of 1917–1918, and the Bolsheviks lacked nonviolent means to improve the situation. For another, factory production often

Soviet Russia's First Coat of Arms, 1918.

declined rapidly after workers gained control of their workplaces. In many cases, hostility toward the Bolsheviks was articulated and channeled by socialist activists of the Socialist-Revolutionary and Menshevik Parties. As "Worker Unrest" (Documents 99–104) suggests, disgruntled factory workers responded in the spring and summer of 1918 with critical resolutions and work stoppages. The new authorities issued appeals urging calm and asking for support, arrested radical activists, and sometimes fired all the employees of a given factory.

As tensions in the country deepened, the government increased the severity with which it struck at opponents to its rule. The section entitled "Red Terror" (Documents 105–107) gives a sense of both the violence and the heated rhetoric provoked by the attempted assassination of Lenin on August 30, 1918. Although the official Red Terror is generally dated from that moment, relatively large-scale political violence had been applied during the summer (and continued during the Civil War period).

The heart of Chapter 4 is the section "Reds versus Whites and Those in Between" (Documents 108–120). Lenin himself argued soon after coming to power that socialism could not be brought to Russia without massive violence, and that the capitalist forces of the world would fight tooth and nail to thwart such designs (Document 108). Yet as one Socialist-Revolutionary activist later claimed, the opponents of Bolshevism never managed to summon all their strength (Document 109). In fact, the Russian Civil War was far more complicated than the old-fashioned view of Reds versus Whites.

Ultimately, the Bolsheviks won the Civil War for several reasons. First, although the anti-Bolshevik cause enjoyed some support from Russia's wartime Allies, including military landings in the north and Far East, this assistance was halfhearted. Having just fought a desperate and devastating war, the peoples of Western Europe and America were not eager to embark on another. Moreover, many in those countries were at least cautiously hopeful

The Russian Civil War, 1918.

about the Bolshevik experiment. Second, while vast numbers of ordinary people in Russia opposed the Bolsheviks, the latter used ruthless methods to quell the opposition. When Mensheviks and Socialist-Revolutionaries won heavily in the elections to many provincial and city soviets in European Russia in the spring and summer of 1918, the Bolsheviks simply disbanded the soviets and devolved power to various executive authorities, including the executive committees, the Bolshevik-dominated revolutionary committees

Citizens Dismantling a House in Moscow. Hoover Institution, Boris Sokolov
Collection, Envelope fA. Ordinary urban dwellers systematically dismantled
houses, fences—anything made of wood—in order to heat their homes and
cook during the Civil War period.

(of which there were hundreds by summer 1918 and thousands by 1920),
the Cheka, the Communist Party, and various representatives sent from
Moscow on an ad hoc basis. Third, socialist activists who had spent their
lives fighting for revolution had enormous difficulty bringing themselves to
fight vehemently against a government that loudly and continuously proclaimed itself "revolutionary." Basically, the Bolsheviks successfully denied
all their opponents the right to carry the banner of revolution. Finally, the
enemies of Bolshevism never managed to unite effectively around a single
leader, ideology, platform, or organization.

Ordinary people were often caught in the middle of the two sides and
suffered accordingly. Jews were disproportionately victimized in this context
(see Document 118). Throughout the Civil War, Russia's peasants engaged
in episodic "partisan warfare" against both Reds and Whites. They were concerned—not without reason—about a restoration of landlords' rights should
the anti-Bolshevik coalition triumph. Once its fortunes began to dim, after
its high point in mid-1919, however, the peasantry across Russia more and
more let loose their anger at government policies of grain confiscation, interference in village life, and the mass draft into the army, as detailed in "Peasants in Revolt" (Documents 121–127). Peasant rebels resorted to a variety
of means, from legal arguments appealing to established laws (Document
121) to armed resistance. The government responded with the argument
that only they could prevent the return of the landlords and with massive

repression, including the seizure of thousands of hostages and massacres with artillery shells and poison gas.

Meanwhile, the Russian Empire had begun to collapse, with dozens of former provinces and regions breaking away and forming (often weakly) independent countries. "The Birth of New Nations" (Documents 128–130) speaks to the struggles of three of them. The Kazakh people of Turkestan, who had never had their own country, tried to secede after the Revolution but were forcibly reincorporated into Soviet Russia. Georgia had been an independent kingdom for centuries before its conquest by Russia in the first half of the 1800s. For nearly 5 years the Georgians managed to establish an autonomous state dominated by Mensheviks. They sought help from Western governments but received little. Finally, even relatively small ethnic groups, like the Buddhist Kalmyks, who also had never existed as a separate country, sought not independence but a defense and recognition of their civil rights.

"The Kronstadt Rebellion" (Documents 131–134) was the most jarring incident of popular rebelliousness for the Bolsheviks because it involved many sailors who had been among the staunchest supporters of the new regime. The rebellion was prefigured by, and linked to, worker unrest in Petrograd in January and February 1921 (see Document 131), as well as profound discontent throughout the countryside and across the entire Baltic Fleet. The Kronstadt rebels, in a manifesto released in early March (Document 132), pointed to this broad discontent and denounced the oppressive Communist regime. The rebels expressed their discontent in diverse media, including newspapers, resolutions, and even satirical verses (see Document 133). The government, for its part, denounced the rebels as stooges of reactionary forces, foreign powers, and international capitalism (Document 134). They then crushed the rebellion mercilessly, in an act of brutality that many observers considered the death knell of the noble socialist experiment in Russia.

The Fate of the Constituent Assembly

95. A Peasant Recalls the Elections to the Constituent Assembly, November 1917   [30, pp. 42–4]

The election to the Constituent Assembly, which took place on November 12, 1917, used the party list system, whereby voters chose not individual representatives but from among numerous political parties, which were designated by number. The new Bolshevik government banned nonsocialist newspapers and harassed the Kadets but allowed the elections to go forward. Never before had Russians participated in elections based on universal, equal, secret, and direct voting by both sexes, as established by the Provisional Government. (Soldiers had the right to vote at age 18, civilians at age 20.) The following document relates to a village in Tula province and describes how peasants weighed their electoral choices. How peasants voted varied from province to province, but overall most seem to have voted less for a specific political platform than for a political actor or party they considered "one of us."

I was only thirteen, but I remember very well that night when my father came back from a village meeting and brought some sheets of paper with him. Each sheet was divided into nine numbered sections. It was 1917.

"What is this for, Daddy?" I asked.

"Tomorrow at the village meeting all people from 18 to 60 years old will vote for whichever party they like. Here there are nine numbers on each sheet. It means that there are nine parties, and each has its own number. Under each number there is the party's name and its program concerning the peasants. Each man or woman who has the right to vote will have to tear off the number of the party he chooses and put it in a box."

I read all numbers in order, and I remember very well that the party of the Bolsheviks was number 5 and the Mensheviks were number 1.

"Which party, which number to vote for? Which party will lead us where—who knows?" My father spoke worriedly. He was already an old man: 57 years of age and illiterate. "All right," he concluded, "we will see tomorrow at the meeting. I will do like the others. Those soldiers who have returned from the war know what to do. I will do like them. Like Vasilii Fateev and Semen Maksimov. I will do like them."

"Do you remember, Daddy, when my cousin Andrei sent us a letter from the Baltic Sea? It said which number to vote for, but I don't remember which one."

"Yes, it is good you reminded me, but that letter is now in the village of Sychevka. The Apollonovs have it. Go get it tomorrow; let someone read it at the meeting."

The next day, as soon as the sun rose, I went to Sychevka for the letter, which said which party was precious and useful for the peasant population. When I returned, the meeting had already begun. The peasants were sitting in a school and discussing which number to vote for. Some were saying one thing, others were saying something else, gathering around soldiers back from the front. About a dozen people were holding the sheets with clearly printed numbers on them.

The teacher was asked to read aloud one of the campaign posters displaying the number 5. The peasants liked it very much. Then number 1 was read. This one also seemed suitable, but it was different because it offered land with redemption payments, while the former offered land without redemption payments. Again, loud debates followed.

I looked for my father. He was standing with a soldier whom I had never seen before and was listening to what that solider was saying about the origins of the parties and their attitudes toward the peasantry. I gave the letter to my father, and he gave it to that soldier saying: "Here, read what he wrote from the navy." The soldier read quietly and then returned the letter.

"Nonsense," he said. "Here it says that you should vote for the Bolsheviks and talks in a glowing way about the future rule of the soviets."

Then he read the letter again, aloud.

"Still he is mistaken," said the soldier having finished reading. "Even though your nephew is a sailor, he does not understand party matters well. Do what you want, but I would advise you to vote for number 1. It would be better and correct."

"But what does the letter say about the number?" asked my father.

"Here it says the Bolsheviks; therefore it is number 5."

"I am for the Bolsheviks, for number 5, too," said my father and went over to vote.

96. Peasant Letters to the Constituent Assembly, December 1917–January 1918   [83, pp. 187, 188–9]

Although the Bolsheviks won only 25 percent of the vote countrywide, they won a plurality in Petrograd (45.2 percent of the total vote), and in some provinces, such as Smolensk, they commanded a majority of the electorate. In most cases, this result was probably caused by the belief of a growing number of people that the Bolsheviks would quickly end the war and grant them full control over the land. Still, the peasantry gave more than half of the entire electorate to the Socialist-Revolutionaries, whom they viewed as more tested and consistent advocates of their interests. As the documents below show, the peasantry placed diverse and often urgent hopes in the assembly.

No later than December 30, 1917

I have the honor to most humbly request that the gentlemen-members of the high assembly, the chosen ones of the great people of the Russian land, not refuse to protect me, since from the very cradle and until the present time I have been suffering the torment and torture of evil people who have sought to wipe me and my relatives off the face of the earth. They assault me greatly with hypnosis, try to intoxicate me, etc.

F. S. Zinchenka, Petrovka, Gadiachskii district, Poltava province
Presented in an open letter for general knowledge

January 1, 1918

Resolution

We, the undersigned thirteen peasant heads of household of Yaroslavskii province, Poshekhonskii district, Ermakovskaia volost, village of Pervoe Izmailovo, having gathered today for a community assembly, all unanimously have resolved to categorically and unconditionally demand from the people's delegates that the Constituent Assembly be convened, that all power be given to the Constituent Assembly, on which we peasants have laid all our hopes, and that we peasants are waiting for the Constituent Assembly as for the bright day of the Resurrection of Christ, since without [a central] authority all our affairs are suspended. For this we sign, peasants. [Ten signatures follow.] [Community Seal.]

January 3, 1918

We, the citizens of the village Iermakovo of the Ermakovskaia volost, Poshekhonskii district, Yaroslavskii province, signed below, have passed the present resolution as to follows:

1. Since the deputies we have elected to the Constituent Assembly still cannot open the Assembly, and since all order has broken down, we are asking to open the Constituent Assembly as soon as possible, upon the convocation of which, order and the laws will hopefully be restored. 2. The Constituent Assembly should be responsible only to the people and give account

to the people and not to some other presently existing organizations. We sign the resolution [26 signatures follow].

Rural elder of the First Ermakovskaia Community
Aleksandr Nikolaevich Strelkov
[Community Seal.]

97. Viktor Chernov,[1] "Russia's One-Day Parliament," January 5, 1918   [87, pp. 68–72]

The traditionally pro-peasant party of Socialist-Revolutionaries, which won more than 50 percent of the votes to the Constituent Assembly, along with some moderate Bolsheviks and most Mensheviks, who had received only a tiny fraction of the vote, advocated allowing the assembly to fulfill its mission of hammering out a constitution for Russia. Lenin and other hard-line Bolsheviks, by contrast, insisted on shutting it down as quickly as possible. Confrontation was inevitable. In 1931, the Socialist-Revolutionary Chernov wrote the following account of the Russian Constituent Assembly's one and only session, over which he presided.

When we, the newly elected members of the Constituent Assembly, entered the Tauride Palace, the seat of the Assembly in Petrograd, on January 18, 1918, we found that the corridors were full of armed guards. They were masters of the building, crude and brazen. At first they did not address us directly, and only exchanged casual observations to the effect that "this guy should get a bayonet between his ribs" or "it wouldn't be bad to put some lead into this one." When we entered the large hall, it was still empty. The Bolshevik deputies had not yet appeared.

A tank division billeted in Petrograd remained faithful to the Assembly. It intended to demonstrate this faithfulness by participating in the march to the Palace which was to pass on its way the barracks of the Preobrazhenskii and Semenovskii Regiments, the two best units of the Petrograd garrison. At the meetings held by these regiments, resolutions were invariably adopted demanding the transfer of state power to the Constituent Assembly. Thus a prospect was open for the consolidation of democratic forces.

---

1. Viktor Chernov (1873–1952) was a founder and the major theoretician of the Socialist-Revolutionary Party. A leader of the party's fraction in the Second Duma and editor of its Paris-based theoretical newspaper *Revoliutsionnaia Rossiia*, he was named minister of agriculture in the Provisional Government. He emigrated in 1920 and died in New York City.

But the Bolsheviks were not caught off guard. They attacked the columns of demonstrators converging on the Tauride Palace from various parts of Petrograd. Whenever the unarmed crowd could not be dispersed immediately, the street was blocked by troops or Bolshevik units would shoot into the crowd. The demonstrators threw themselves on the pavement and waited until the rattle of machine guns quieted down; then they would jump up and continue their march, leaving behind the dead and wounded until they were stopped by a new volley. Or the crowd would be bayoneted by enraged Bolshevik outfits, which would get hold of the banners and placards carried by the demonstrators and tear them into scraps.

The Assembly hall was gradually filled by the deputies. Near the dais were placed armed guards. The public gallery was crowded to overflowing. Here and there glittered rifle muzzles. Admission tickets for the public were distributed by the notorious [Moisei] Uritskii.[2] He did his job well.

At last all the deputies had gathered in a tense atmosphere. The left sector was evidently waiting for something. From our benches rose Deputy [Grigol] Lordkipanidze, who said in a calm, businesslike voice that, according to an old parliamentary custom, the first sitting should be presided over by the senior deputy. The senior was S. P. Shvetsov,[3] an old Socialist Revolutionary (SR).

As soon as Shvetsov's imposing figure appeared on the dais, somebody gave a signal, and a deafening uproar broke out. The stamping of feet, hammering on the desks, and howling made an infernal noise. The public in the gallery and the Bolshevik allies, the Left Socialist-Revolutionaries, joined in the tumult. The guards clapped their rifle butts on the floor. From various sides guns were trained on Shvetsov. He took the President's bell, but the tinkling was drowned in the noise. He put it back on the table, and somebody immediately grabbed it and handed it over, like a trophy, to the representative of the Sovnarkom (Soviet of Commissars), [Iakov] Sverdlov. Taking advantage of a moment of comparative silence, Shvetsov managed to pronounce the sacramental phrase: "The session of the Constituent Assembly is open." These words evoked a new din of protest. Shvetsov slowly left the

2. Moisei Uritskii (1873–1918) was a long-time Social Democratic activist who joined the Bolshevik Party a few months before the October Revolution, in which he played an active role. The head of the Petrograd Cheka at the time of the events recounted here, he was assassinated on August 30, 1918, by a Socialist-Revolutionary terrorist.

3. Sergei Porfirievich Shvetsov (1858–1930) took part in the "Going-to-the-People" movement in the early 1870s. He joined the People's Will in 1880 and the Socialist-Revolutionary Party in 1900. He was elected to the Constituent Assembly as a leader of the Socialist-Revolutionaries in the Don region.

dais and joined us. He was replaced by Sverdlov, who opened the session for the second time, but now in the name of the Soviets, and presented its "platform." This was an ultimatum: we had just to vote Aye or No.

In the election of the Assembly's President, the Bolsheviks presented no candidate of their own. They voted for Maria Spiridonova, nominated by the Left SRs. Later they threw Spiridonova into jail and tormented her until she was on the verge of insanity. But at this moment they wanted to take full advantage of her popularity and reputation as a martyr in the struggle against Tsarism. My nomination as candidate for the Presidency received even greater support than had been expected. Some leftist peasants evidently could not bring themselves to oppose their own "muzhik minister." I obtained 244 votes against 150.

I delivered my inauguration address, making vigorous efforts to keep self-control. Every sentence of my speech was met with outcries, some ironical, others spiteful, often buttressed by the brandishing of guns. Bolshevik deputies surged forward to the dais. Conscious that the stronger nerves would win, I was determined not to yield to provocation. I said that the nation had made its choice, that the composition of the Assembly was a living testimony to the people's yearning for Socialism, and that its convention marked the end of the hazy transition period. Land reform, I went on, was a foregone conclusion: the land would be equally accessible to all who wished to till it. The Assembly, I said, would inaugurate an era of active foreign policy directed toward peace.

I finished my speech amidst a cross-fire of interruptions and cries. It was now the turn of the Bolshevik speakers—[Ivan] Skvortsov[-Stepanov] and [Nikolai] Bukharin. During their delivery, our sector was a model of restraint and self-discipline. We maintained a cold, dignified silence. The Bolshevik speeches, as usual, were shrill, clamorous, provocative, and rude, but they could not break the icy silence of our majority. As President, I was bound in duty to call them to order for abusive statements. But I know that this was precisely what they expected. Since the armed guards were under their orders, they wanted clashes, incidents, and perhaps a brawl. So I remained silent.

The Social Democrat [Iraklii] Tsereteli rose to answer the Bolsheviks. They tried to "scare" him by leveling at him a rifle from the gallery and brandishing a gun in front of his face. I had to restore order—but how? Appeals to maintain the dignity of the Constituent Assembly evoked an even greater noise, at times turning into a raving fury. [Pavel] Dybenko and other demagogues called for more and more assaults. Lenin, in the government box, demonstrated his contempt for the Assembly by lounging in his chair and putting on the air of a man who was bored to death. I threatened to clear the gallery of the yelling public. Though this was an empty threat, since the guards were only waiting for the order to "clear" us out of the hall, it proved temporarily effective. Tsereteli's calm and dignified manner helped to restore peace.

There was a grim significance in the outburst that broke loose when a middle-of-the-road deputy, Severtsov-Odoievskii, started to speak Ukrainian. In the Assembly the Bolsheviks did not want to hear any language except Russian. I was compelled to state emphatically that in the new Russia, each nationality had the right to use its own language whenever it pleased.

When it appeared that we refused to vote the Soviet "platform" without discussion, the Bolsheviks walked out of the sitting in a body. They returned to read a declaration charging us with counterrevolution and stating that our fate would be decided by organs which were in charge of such things. Soon after that the Left SRs also made up their minds. Just before the discussion of the land reform started, their representative, I. Z. Steinberg, declared that they were in disagreement with the majority, and left the Assembly.

We knew that the Bolsheviks were in conference, discussing what to do next. I felt sure that we would be arrested. But it was of utmost importance for us to have a chance to say the last word. I declared that the next point on the agenda was the land reform. At this moment somebody pulled at my sleeve.

"You have to finish now. There are orders from the People's Commissar."

Behind me stood a stocky sailor, accompanied by his armed comrades.

"What People's Commissar?"

"We have orders. Anyway, you cannot stay here any longer. The lights will be turned out in a minute. And the guards are tired."

"The members of the Assembly are also tired but cannot rest until they have fulfilled the task entrusted to them by the people—to decide on the land reform and the future form of government."

And leaving the guards no time to collect themselves, I proceeded to read the main paragraphs of the Land Bill, which our party had prepared long ago. But time was running short. Reports and debates had to be omitted. Upon my proposal, the Assembly voted six basic points of the bill. It provided that all land was to be turned into common property, with every tiller possessing equal rights to use it. Amidst incessant shouts: "That's enough! Stop it now! Clear the hall!" the other points of the bill were voted.

Fearing that the lights would be extinguished, somebody managed to procure candles. It was essential that the future form of government be voted upon immediately. Otherwise the Bolsheviks would not fail to charge the Assembly with having left the door open for the restoration of the monarchy. The motion for a republican form of government was carried unanimously.

In the dawn of a foggy and murky morning I declared a recess until noon.

At the exit a pale-faced man pushed his way to me and beseeched me in a trembling voice not to use my official car. A bunch of murderers, he said, was waiting for me. He admitted that he was a Bolshevik, but his conscience revolted against this plot.

I left the building, surrounded by a few friends. We saw several men in sailor's uniforms loitering near my car. We decided to walk. We had a long distance to go, and when I arrived home I learned that rumors were in circulation that the Constituent Assembly had dispersed, and that Chernov and Tsereteli had been shot.

At noon several members of the Assembly were sent on reconnaissance. They reported that the door of the Tauride Palace was sealed and guarded by a patrol with machine guns and two pieces of field artillery. Later in the day a decree of the Sovnarkom was published by which the Constituent Assembly was "dissolved."

Thus ended Russia's first and last democratic parliament.

98. A Bolshevik Account of the Constituent Assembly   [61, pp. 1–20]

Dissolving the Constituent Assembly was an outrage for liberals and Socialist-Revolutionaries. For the Bolsheviks, however, it was a historic milestone, a departure from what they viewed as formal democracy in favor of a new system of power based, at least in name, on the network of Soviets of Workers', Soldiers', and Peasants' Deputies. The account of Fiodor Raskolnikov,[4] who was a member of the Bolshevik fraction of the Constituent Assembly, sheds light on Bolshevik deliberations about how to handle the assembly and hails what many of them thought was a new era in revolutionary Russia's politics.

In one of the large rooms [of the Tauride Palace] the Bolshevik fraction were assembling. Here I met the Central Committee members and the Party's best organizers, Stalin and Sverdlov. [. . .]

---

4. Fiodor Raskolnikov was the pseudonym of Fyodor Il'in (1892–1939). He joined the Bolshevik fraction in 1910. As a midshipman, he helped organize the rebellion at the Kronstadt naval fortress in early July 1917 and on July 4 led some 5,000 sailors in a march to the Tauride Palace. Commissar of the Baltic Fleet from late 1918, he was promoted to commander the next year. After the Kronstadt rebellion of early 1921, he was made ambassador to Afghanistan. Other diplomatic posts followed. He rejected a summons to return to Moscow in 1939 and issued an open letter denouncing Stalin. Some months later, he died in mysterious circumstances in Nice, France. Rehabilitated posthumously in 1961, he was again banned from public mention in 1964. He wrote the excerpt below in 1918.

Discussion of the agenda began. Someone set forth a plan for how we should work if the Constituent Assembly were to enjoy a protracted existence. Bukharin stirred impatiently on his chair and lifted his finger to ask permission to speak. "Comrades," he said, in an angry and sarcastic tone, "do you really think we are going to waste an entire week here? We'll be here for three days at the most." A quizzical smile played on Vladimir Il'ich's pale lips. Comrade Sverdlov, holding in both hands a typewritten sheet of paper, slowly read out the declaration of the rights of the working people. [. . .]

After a brief debate, the Bolshevik fraction voted that, if the Constituent Assembly should fail to accept the declaration that day, we must immediately walk out of it. [. . .]

Suddenly we learnt that the SRs had organized a demonstration which was advancing on the Tauride Palace with anti-Soviet slogans. Soon afterwards the news was brought that this demonstration had been dispersed, at the corner of Kirochnaya Street and Liteiny Avenue, by Red troops who fired in the air. On the bronze dial of the clock the hand was approaching four. [. . .]

The immense amphitheater, with its glass ceiling and stout white columns, was full of people. [. . .]

The SRs were evidently prepared for a triumph and had distributed the roles among themselves. As though at a signal, a decrepit old man, all overgrown with hair and with a long grey beard, clambered awkwardly and short of breath on to the high tribune. It was the Zemstvo worker and former member of Narodnaia Volia,[5] Shvetsov. Comrade Sverdlov, who was supposed to open the proceedings, had lingered somewhere and was late.

With an old man's trembling hand Shvetsov picked up the chairman's bell and shook it hesitantly: its dear tinkling sound rang through the hall.

The SRs intended to open the Constituent Assembly independently of the Soviet power. To us, on the contrary, it was important to emphasize that the Constituent Assembly was being opened not on its own initiative but by the will of the All-Union Central Executive Committee of the Soviets, which had no intention of handing over to this Assembly its rights as master of the Soviet land.

When we saw that Shvetsov was seriously going to open the proceedings, we started frenzied interruptions. We shouted, whistled, stamped our feet, and banged our fists on the thin wooden lids of the desks. When all that failed to do the trick, we leapt to our feet and rushed towards the tribune

---

5. Narodnaia Volia (People's Will) was a revolutionary organization founded in 1879 that planned and carried out politically motivated assassinations, including that of Tsar Alexander II in March 1881.

with shouts of "Get down!" The Right SRs hurled themselves forward to defend their doyen. A certain exchange of fisticuffs took place on the parapet-covered steps of the tribune.

Shvetsov rang his bell in dismay and soundlessly, helplessly moved his pale, quivering lips. We drowned with our uproar his feeble old man's voice. One of us grabbed Shvetsov by the sleeve of his jacket and tried to drag him from the tribune. Then, suddenly, beside the portly, podgy Shvetsov, there appeared, up there on the tribune, the lean, narrow-shouldered figure of [Iakov] Sverdlov, in his black leather jacket. In a masterfully confident manner he took the bright nickel-plated bell from the dumbfounded old man and with a careful but firm gesture moved Shvetsov out of his way.

A furious din, with shouts, protests and banging of fists on desks, arose from the benches of the indignant SRs and Mensheviks. But Sverdlov stood firm on the tribune, like a marble monument, calm and unmoved, looking around at his adversaries, with an expression of provocative mockery, through the large, oval lenses of his pince-nez. Coolly he rang the bell, and with a sweeping, authoritative gesture of his thin, hairy hand he silently called the Assembly to order. When the noise gradually subsided, Sverdlov addressed the entire hall, with unusual dignity, in his loud, distinct bass voice. "The Executive Committee of the Soviets of Workers' and Peasants' Deputies has authorized me to open the proceedings of the Constituent Assembly."

"There's blood on your hands! There's been enough bloodshed!" the Mensheviks and SRs squealed hysterically, like dogs whose tails had been trodden on. Loud applause from our benches drowned these hysterical lamentations. [. . .]

"We do not doubt that sparks from our conflagration will fly all over the world, and that the day is not far distant when the working classes of all countries will rise up against their exploiters just as in October the Russian working class rose up, followed by the Russian peasantry."

Triumphant applause broke from us like a migrant flock of white swans suddenly taking off into the sky.

"We do not doubt," went on the chairman of the Central Executive Committee, still more boldly and confidently, as though catching fire from the gunpowder of his own words, "that the true representatives of the working people who are sitting here in the Constituent Assembly are bound to help the Soviets to put an end to class privileges. The representatives of the workers and peasants have acknowledged the right of the working people to the means and instruments of production, ownership of which has hitherto enabled the ruling classes to exploit the working people in every way. Just as, in their day, the French bourgeoisie, at the time of the great revolution of

1789, proclaimed a declaration of rights for freedom to exploit the people, who were deprived of the instruments and means of production, so our Russian Socialist revolution must make its own declaration."

Again, all the members of our fraction applauded warmly. The other fractions, suspicious, maintained a hostile silence.

"The Central Executive Committee expresses the hope that the Constituent Assembly, in so far as it correctly expresses the interests of the people, will associate itself with the declaration which I am now to have the honor to read to you," said Comrade Sverdlov. Calmly and solemnly, without haste, he then read the declaration, ending his address with these words: "By authority of the All-Russian Central Executive Committee of the Soviet of Workers', Soldiers', and Peasants' Deputies, I declare the Constituent Assembly open."

We rose to our feet and sang the *International*. All the members of the Constituent Assembly also got up. [. . .]

The Right SR Lordkipanidze raised a point of order. When he reached the tribune he spoke hastily and excitedly, as though afraid that he was about to be deprived of the right to speak. Angrily he said: "The SR fraction would have thought that the Constituent Assembly should have begun its work long before this. We consider that the Constituent Assembly can itself open its own proceedings: there is no other authority but that of the Constituent Assembly empowered to open them."

The indignation that filled us burst forth. Whistling, uproar, shouts of "Get down!" rattling and banging of desks drowned the speaker's words. Behind him, on the high-placed chairman's seat, Sverdlov remained unmoved. To observe the proprieties he rang his nickel-plated bell and, turning towards us his cheerful, merrily smiling eyes, offhandedly let fall, with assumed impartiality: "I must ask you to be quiet." [. . .]

Ivan Ivanovich Skvortsov-Stepanov slowly mounted the tribune. Turning his whole body towards the right-wing benches and nervously jerking his close-cropped grey head, he spoke with great feeling, rising to passion, to expose the hypocrisy of the Right SRs.

"Comrades and citizens!" boomed Skvortsov-Stepanov, loudly and clearly, emphasizing his words with vigorous gestures of his long, thin hand, "I must first express my astonishment that the citizen who spoke before me threatened to break with us if we took certain steps. Citizens sitting on the right! The break between us has been consummated long since. You were on one side of the barricades, with the White Guards and the military cadets, and we were on the other, with the soldiers, workers, and peasants."

In passing, Ivan Ivanovich, being a theoretician, gave his opponents a lesson in elementary politics: "How can you," he wondered, "appeal to such a concept as the will of the whole people? For a Marxist 'the people' is an inconceivable motion. the people does not act as a single unit. The people as a unit is a mere fiction, and this fiction is needed by the ruling classes. It is all over between us," he summed up, "You belong to one world, with the cadets and the bourgeoisie, and we to the other, with the peasants and the workers." [. . .]

"The very fact that the first session of the Constituent Assembly has opened proclaims the end of civil war among the peoples who inhabit Russia," declaimed Viktor Chernov mellifluously as he cast his wide-open eyes in triumph around the hall. The audience was not particularly attentive: even the SRs chattered among themselves, yawned, or left the hall. Our people continually interrupted him with scornful laughter, ironical remarks, and mockery.

The public who filled the galleries were also bored by Chernov's empty and tedious verbiage, and kept answering him back from up there. He lost patience, invited the interrupters to go away, and at last threatened "to raise the question whether some persons here are in a condition to conduct themselves as befits members of the Constituent Assembly."

Chernov's impotent threats eventually caused us to lose control of ourselves, and the resulting uproar smothered his voice, like a drowning man clutching at a life belt he snatched up the chairman's bell and tinkled it—then helplessly sank back into the broad and massive armchair, so that only his shaggy grey head was visible. [. . .]

We were summoned to a meeting of our fraction. On Lenin's initiative we resolved to quit the Constituent Assembly on the grounds that it had rejected the declaration of the rights of the working and exploited people. Lomov and I were entrusted with the task of announcing our departure. Somebody proposed that we all return to the meeting hall, but Vladimir Il'ich stopped us from doing that.

"Don't you realize," he said, "that if we go back in there, and then, after reading our statement, walk out of the hall, the sailors on guard, electrified by our action, will at once, on the spot, shoot down everybody who stays behind? We must not do that, on any account," said Vladimir Il'ich in a categorical tone. [. . .]

The empty benches on the left side of the hall, where the Bolsheviks had been sitting not long before, yawned like a black abyss. In his sailor's cap, worn at a jaunty angle and with a thick tuft of jet-black hair sticking rakishly out from under it, and with his chest swathed in machine-gun belts, the cheerful commander of the guard, Zheleznyakov, stood by the door. Beside him were clustered in the doorway several Bolshevik deputies, tensely observing what was happening in the hall. [. . .]

Suddenly into our room came, with quick, firm tread, Dybenko—a strapping, broad-shouldered figure with thick black hair and a short, neatly-clipped beard, and wearing a new, grey winter overcoat gathered at the waist.

Choking with laughter he told us, in his booming bass voice, that the sailor Zheleznyakov had just gone up to the chairman of the Assembly, placed his broad hand on the shoulder of a Chernov numb with astonishment, and said to him in a peremptory tone: "The guard are tired, I propose that you close the meeting and let everybody go home." [. . .]

In England there was once a "Long Parliament." The Constituent Assembly of the RSFSR was the shortest parliament in the entire history of the world. It ended its inglorious and joyless life after 12 hours and 40 minutes.

When, in the morning, Dybenko and I told Vladimir Il'ich of the miserable way the Constituent Assembly had ended, he screwed up his dark eyes and at once grew cheerful.

"Did Viktor Chernov really submit unquestioningly to the guard-commander's demand, without making the slightest attempt to resist?" Lenin asked, in amazement. And, leaning right back in his chair, he laughed long and infectiously.

Worker Unrest

99. Worker Complaints about Difficult Material Conditions, April 1918   [54, pp. 206–8]

For many months after seizing power, the Bolsheviks' domination of the soviets was neither certain nor complete. The nationalization of industry and banking, coming on the heels of several war-related crises, caused a dramatic collapse of economic output. With fewer goods available for trade to peasants for grain, urban dwellers began to suffer from hunger. In spring 1918, benefiting from a widespread change in people's moods, Mensheviks and Socialist-Revolutionaries repeatedly won seats on local soviets, with the support of disillusioned workers. Bolshevik officials in turn often disbanded these soviets and used coercion to achieve more favorable results in subsequent elections. Many other workers rejected all party affiliation and hoped that the entire working class could simply strive together to achieve participatory democracy. In one instance of grassroots organization, there emerged in Petrograd an Emergency Assembly of Representatives of Factories and Plants of Petrograd, which issued the following appeal.

May Day is approaching. On that day workers of all countries celebrate their labor holiday. The May banners talk about the brotherly solidarity of all workers, about the struggle against the slavery of hired labor, against class domination, against militarism. [. . .]

This year we have to approach the worker holiday not in a holiday fashion. The external war broke the international union of workers; the internal war has broken our own ranks. Life is getting harder and the working class has it the hardest.

With every day unemployment is growing; more and more plants are closed; thousands and thousands more workers are thrown out on the street; starvation, want, and impoverishment keep growing.

The four years of war caused a lot of destruction in the national economy. The tsarist regime left a hard legacy to the revolution. But there was never a time when the collapse was so great and so hopeless as now.

The terms of the Treaty of Brest[-Litovsk] fundamentally undermine Russian industry. Russia has neither coal, nor bread, nor harbors, nor money. It is broken, torn into pieces, with new borders ripping through and across the flesh of our land; the civil war is still raging and the enemy's offensive is continuing—what kind of industry can there be? [. . .]

Unemployment is growing.

But the authorities fight it in the way of the old officialdom. They throw millions into cafeterias—but one can't feed all the hungry and it is not what the workers need.

What is needed is work, restoration of enterprises, opening of factories and plants. [. . .]

Most of all what is needed is a cessation of the civil war. [. . .]

[The current trade unions] have ceased being class organs and have become organs of government. [. . .]

The working class is incapable of protecting its interests; the whole country has no rights, is broken, enslaved, and is torn apart by fratricidal hostilities.

This year May the First is not a celebration, but a day of struggle. [. . .]

The working class should make this day a day of struggle for the restoration and the unification of Russia, for the democratic organs that have been crushed in its name, for the cessation of civil war, for independence and the revival of its class organizations, for the right to work.

Comrade unemployed, you don't have your own separate interests!

Those who work today can become unemployed tomorrow. [. . .]

The whole working class has the same task and the same interests!

So comrades, do prepare for a united celebration of May the First!

Tell yourselves about your needs!

Join the common ranks!

Go under common banners!

Struggle together for:

The opening of factories and plants,

Bread and work,

The restoration of democratic organs,

The independence of worker organizations,

For the cessation of civil war,

For universal peace!

100. An Eyewitness Account of the Obukhov Plant Strike, June 1918 [12, pp. 118–22]

Founded in 1863, the Obukhov Plant in St. Petersburg produced heavy machinery and armaments. In early June 1918, the majority of workers at the factory were highly disgruntled with economic and political conditions and had slowed their work almost to a halt. At a general assembly on June 16 they expressed their intention, at the upcoming elections to the Petrograd Soviet, to "clean out and renovate the Soviet" so that it would cease to be "a tool for the establishment of an antidemocratic dictatorship." Four days later a well-known Bolshevik leader, V. Volodarskii, was assassinated. It was in this context that the events recounted below took place. The day following these events, on June 23, a detachment of 300 sailors arrived from Kronstadt, along with a cavalry unit and several companies of infantry. They cordoned off the entire Nevskii ward and began searching and arresting workers. An armored train also arrived, and two artillery batteries took up positions on either bank of the Neva River. Later in the evening, the Kronstadt sailors disarmed sailors of the Naval Mine Division on several destroyers and other vessels.

[. . .] Volodarskii[6] was killed at about 7 p.m., approximately the same time when his enemies at the Obukhov plant were proposing a resolution in support of the Constituent Assembly. [. . .]

On the night of June 20, 1918, most of the active SRs in the Nevskii ward were arrested, including, and foremost, Mr. [Grigorii] Eremeev.[7]

When news of his arrest became known, his supporters stirred up a terrible noise, and the plant on that [next] day never commenced its operations. They demanded Eremeev's release.

In the morning, as Iliia Petrovich [Ivanov, the Bolshevik commissar of the plant,] was on his way to work, his friends stopped him and urged him not to go.

"Comrade Ivanov, there is unrest at the plant; nobody is working. They threaten to drown the Bolsheviks in the Neva. Trouble may occur."

When Ivanov reached the plant, he learned [. . .] that the workers protesting Eremeev's arrest were on strike and were threatening all the Bolsheviks and especially the commissar and the chairman of the plant's administration. [. . .]

At the Smolnyi[8] the commissar and the chairman of the plant's administration asserted that the way things were going necessitated closing the plant

---

6. Born Moisei Goldshtein (1891–1918), V. Volodarskii was a member of the Jewish and Ukrainian Social Democratic Parties before World War I. A gifted orator, he became the Bolshevik commissar for propaganda and agitation in Petrograd. An unknown assailant (who later turned out to have been a Socialist-Revolutionary) killed him on June 20, 1918.

7. The formal term of address "Mr." (*gospodin*), formerly expressing great respect and deference, under the Communist regime implied contempt. Even the more democratic term "citizen" (*grazhdanin*) was considered passé. "Comrade" (*tovarishch*) was reserved for Communists and supporters of Soviet power.

8. The Smolnyi Institute, formerly a school for well-born girls, became the Bolshevik headquarters during the Revolution.

and imposing martial law in the ward. Zinoviev hesitated to do that. It was decided that Ivanov would go to the Putilov plant in order to ascertain whether the workers would go on strike, if the Obukhov plant were shut down.

The secretary of the factory committee of the Putilov factory [and Bolshevik leader Ivan] Ogorodnikov told Ivanov that Obukhov workers had gone to the Putilov power plant and asked for support should the Obukhov plant decide to act. According to Ogorodnikov, some at the power plant were in favor of action, but most were on the side of Soviet power.

"So if we close the [Obukhov] factory, you will prevent the workers from acting?" asked Ivanov.

"Yes, we will; you can count on it,"—replied Ogorodnikov.

When Ivanov returned to his ward, he told the local Bolshevik leaders about [his] conversations at the Putilov plant, and they decided to close the plant without notifying Smolnyi, should the situation at the plant fail to improve within 24 hours.

The situation did not improve.

On the morning of June 22, the plant gathered again for a rally. They summoned Ivanov by telephone to discuss matters with him. Ivanov's speech consisted in warning that their failure to return to work would result in the plant's closing.

After the commissar stepped down from the podium, a sailor began to shout: so this is how the commissars speak to us! [. . .]

Bold voices spoke of rebellion at the rally that day.

Ivanov was told that it had been decided to use the factory whistle to call for a cross-ward rally where firearms would be distributed.

"There should be no whistle; extinguish the boilers," ordered the plant commissar.

Soon an announcement was ready also:

"June 22, 1918
"COMRADE WORKERS!!!

"We have repeatedly pointed out that rallies during working time are inadmissible and that poor work habits undoubtedly damage productivity, whose reestablishment has been achieved at enormous cost. At the present time, we are forced to announce in the most decisive fashion that such an attitude toward work will not be allowed and that you will be paid neither for June 21 nor for any other idle days.

"If you do not return to work today, June 22, the plant will be closed starting on June 25.

"Chairman of the Plant Administration Antonov
"Plant Commissar Ivanov."

Work began neither on June 22 nor on the following day. Antonov and Ivanov went to Smolnyi to report on what had happened. There they found [Mikhail] Lashevich.[9]

"How is everything?" he asked.

"Actually, an uprising is being prepared in the ward and the [Navy's] Mine Division is planning to fire on the plant and perhaps on Smolnyi as well."

"What needs to be done?" asked Lashevich.

"We need help, Comrade Lashevich."

Lashevich instantly picked up the phone and ordered that a unit of 300 reliable sailors be sent immediately from Kronstadt.

As soon as Lashevich had given the order, [Pyotr] Zalutskii[10] approached. Lashevich turned to him: "So, Zalutskii, prepare a decree. The Obukhov plant has been closed."

Just then Zinoviev came in.

"What's up," he asked, seeing the delegates from the unruly plant.

"The plant has been closed. We demand your sanction. There is no other way!"

"Okay, then," said Zinoviev and then added patting his neck with his palm: "Here is where your plant is sitting."

Three hours later a unit of Kronstadt sailors was already disembarking on the bank of the Neva. [. . .]

Soon the order was ready: "Given the recent sharp decline in productivity at the Obukhov plant caused by the employees' obvious, steady violation of the necessary labor discipline; given the convening of meetings during work time; and given the unproductive use of the people's money and fuel allocated to the plant, the Obukhov plant is closed as of June 25 this year.

"1. All workers, clerks, and technical staff are fired.

"2. The plant and floor committees are liquidated concurrently with the closing of the plant. Committee members are fired on the same basis as other workers.

"3. The accounts are settled as of the day of the work stoppage."

9. Mikhail Lashevich (1884–1928) joined the Bolshevik fraction in 1906 and was made a member of the Petrograd party committee in 1918. A supporter of Zinoviev, he was expelled from the party in 1927 and, despite his readmission, apparently killed himself the following year.

10. A Bolshevik from 1907, Piotr Zalutskii (1888–1937) worked closely with Zinoviev and was purged from the party in 1927, reinstated in 1928, and shot 9 years later.

101. Demands of Workers of the Yaroslavl[11] Junction of the Northern Railroad, June 18, 1918   [54, p. 421]

The meeting, whose resolution is printed below, was attended, according to the minutes, by "more than 3,000" people. Three days later, a similar general meeting of railroad workers, this time in Vspole, also in Yaroslavl province, adopted the same resolution with only seven negative votes. Both events took place following government decrees on fighting the "peasant bourgeoisie," on creating food detachments tasked with seizing grain from the peasantry, and on forming committees of village poor (kombedy) whose purpose was to divide the villagers by social class and to foment tension among them. Railroad workers, like most nonagricultural employees in Russia, were often closely tied to village life through family members living in the countryside, which made many of them critical of Bolshevik policies, as is shown in the resolution.

Having heard numerous speakers address the food problem and given that not only our junction but the whole country is suffering from the cruel oppression of hunger, we, the railroad associates, clerks, mechanics, and workers of Yaroslavl have resolved: in light of the current government's inability to organize food matters, we demand:

1) The immediate abolition of the People's Commissars, who are capable only of issuing decrees and not of making things work, and the immediate convocation of an All-Russian Constituent Assembly.

2) To introduce free trade immediately, without further delays, since the shortage of foodstuffs will not only hinder the improvement of railroad operations but will lead to their total collapse.

3) That our comrades, the printers, print and send copies of this resolution to all the corners of Russia. Let this be a warning: if free trade is not legalized within 10 days, we reserve for ourselves the right to resort to any and all measures.

The present resolution was adopted by all in attendance with seven nays and eight abstentions.

---

11. Yaroslavl was a provincial capital located 140 miles northeast of Moscow.

102. Petrograd Factory Workers Call for a Strike, June 1918 [54, pp. 354–5]

On June 26, 1918, an Emergency Assembly of Representatives of Factories and Plants of Petrograd met and passed the following appeal. Because of arrests, raids, plant closings, threats of fines and firings, and around-the-clock armed patrols, only a few factories and printing plants went on strike.

Appeal to strike on July 2

Workers! Hunger is strangling us. Unemployment is tormenting us. Our children drop to the ground because of malnutrition. Our press has been crushed. Our organizations are being destroyed. The freedom to strike has been abolished. And when we raise the voice of protest, they shoot at us and throw us out of the gates, as with the comrades from the Obukhov plant.

Russia is again turned into a tsarist dungeon. Our country has been handed over to enemies to be divided up and plundered. We cannot go on living like this.

Workers from Nizhnii Novgorod, Tula, Vladimir, and many other areas have already declared their protest against the crimes of the Soviet government. We call upon you to do likewise.

We, the representatives of Petrograd workers, are calling upon you to hold a one-day political strike of protest. We are scheduling this strike for Tuesday, July 2.[12]

On Tuesday, July 2, let life stop in factories and plants, electric power stations, printing presses, trade enterprises. Let the streetcars and railroads stop also.

The water works and hospitals can work on this day.

Only food cargo should be carried on railroads on that day.

The strike of July 2 will show that the Soviet regime is hostile to the working class. The strike of July 2 will show that just like in the old days under tsarism, workers are fighting for the power of the people, for civil liberties, for a united and independent Russian Republic.

Down with the death penalty!

Down with executions and the Civil war!

Down with lockouts!

Long live the Constituent Assembly!

Long live the freedom of speech and assembly!

Long live the freedom to strike!

Long live the strike of July 2!

---

12. In bold in the original.

103. Instructions on Disrupting a Strike Planned
for July 2, 1918   [46, p. 141]

*As workers in opposition to Bolshevik policies (often led by Mensheviks) began
to organize "extraordinary" worker assemblies in the hope that they would
constitute a parallel political structure alongside the soviets, they increasingly
attracted the attention of the security police (Cheka).*

June 28, 1918

From the Commissariat for the Revolutionary Protection of the City of
Petrograd and from the Extraordinary Commission on Fighting Counterrevolution and Speculation.[13]

Because of the one-day political strike planned by the [Extraordinary] Assembly of Representatives [of Factories and Plants of Petrograd] for July 2,
the Extraordinary Commission on Fighting Counterrevolution and Speculation of Petrograd recommends that the ward soviets, by means of their subordinate agencies, undertake every necessary measure to prevent the strike
from occurring.

These measures should not be of an exceptional nature, should not exceed the limits of normal activity. It is allowable to capture and arrest individuals conducting agitation for the strike, to investigate and arrest strike
committees members, etc.

All those arrested should be directed to 2 Gorokhovaia Street.[14]

Factory whistles should be under the control of our people; street rallies
should be prevented to the extent possible.

For this purpose, it is necessary from time to time to send out patrols to
prevent the accumulation of groups of people in city squares and [other]
open places.

Chairman: Uritskii
Secretary: Ioshilov

13. I.e., the Cheka.
14. At this address was headquartered the Petrograd Cheka and formerly various agencies of the Imperial Russian security police.

104. Putilov Plant Workers Denounce Bolshevik Policies, August 1918 [46, pp. 156–7]

The Fifth All-Russian Congress of Soviets opened in Moscow on July 6, the very day when Iakov Bliumkin, a Left Socialist-Revolutionary, assassinated Wilhelm Count von Mirbach-Harff (1871–1918), the German ambassador to Russia and previously the key negotiator of the Treaty of Brest-Litovsk. Thus began an ill-starred and short-lived rebellion of Left Socialist-Revolutionaries, whose leaders hoped the assassination would provoke a war between Russia and Germany, a war they expected to lead to victory by reenergizing the revolution and freeing it from Bolshevik authoritarianism. The document below indicates that contrary to the government efforts to portray the Left Socialist-Revolutionaries as an isolated handful of ultraradicals, their goals did have an appeal at least among some workers and peasants.

Resolution adopted at the general meeting of the Putilov plant and wharf on August 6, 1918, with 16,000 present, with nine voting against and twenty abstaining.

(1) We demand the immediate re-legalization of all socialist newspapers; (2) the immediate release of all arrested socialists, including Comrade [N. N.] Glebov; (3) the unrestricted purchase of any food items by both cooperatives and worker organizations and [their] unrestricted conveyance to Petrograd; (4) the immediate abolition of the death penalty and executions by firing squad; (5) the immediate disarmament of all armed bands[15] operating on railroads under the cover of the Red Army flag, wreaking havoc and executions on workers and peasants. (6) We, the workers, assert that the Red Army was created from the proletariat and laboring peasantry not for executing workers and peasants but to lead the struggle against imperialists and global predators who want to suppress and devour the Russian revolution. (7) We denounce the arrest of half the Fifth All-Russian Congress of workers' and laboring peasants' delegates. (8) We denounce the way in which delegates at the Fifth All-Russian Congress of Soviets were represented. (9) We demand an end to making distinctions between the working peasantry and the proletariat and dividing them into privileged and underprivileged. (10) We protest the forced disbandment of peasant soviets, such as those in Novgorod, Pskov, Viatka, and elsewhere. (11) We denounce the presence, at the

---

15. The "armed bands" referred to in the document were in fact officially sanctioned units (*zagraditel'nye otriady*) posted at railway, waterway, and highway junctions and stations with the express purpose of forbidding the transport of foodstuffs exceeding 20 pounds per person.

Fifth All-Russian Congress of Soviets, of representatives of Austro-German and Anglo-French capital headed by the executioner Mirbach. (12) We denounce the implementation of the Treaty of Brest[-Litovsk], which is inviting more and more demands from the Austro-German bourgeoisie and is thereby leading to the plunder of workers and peasants and thus is threatening to destroy the Russian and worldwide revolution.

Long live the Soviets of Worker, Red Armymen, and Peasant Deputies.
Long live the dictatorship of the working people.
Down with the dictatorship of individuals.
Down with the predatory Treaty of Brest[-Litovsk].
Help Ukraine continue its rise.
Long live the Red Army.

Red Terror

105. Zinoviev's Hysterical Reaction to the Assassination of Uritskii, August 30, 1918   [72, pp. 154–5]

From February 1917, Elena Stasova (1873–1966), served in numerous re-sponsible posts within the Bolshevik hierarchy, including as a secretary of the Petrograd party committee and in the Presidium of the Petrograd Cheka. On August 30, a terrorist killed Moisei Uritskii, the head of the Petrograd Cheka. In the memoir excerpted below, which was published in 1957, Stasova describes Zinoviev's call for unleashing mass terror (see also Docu-ment 106) in Petrograd in response to that assassination. Stasova seemed to suggest that Zinoviev had acted on his own initiative. In reality, however, he had a powerful backer in Moscow, Vladimir Lenin. Following the assassi-nation of Volodarskii on June 20, 1918, workers in Petrograd had wanted to avenge the death of this popular figure with mass terror. When Lenin learned that Zinoviev had thwarted such actions, he was furious, and wrote immediately to him that "we are discrediting ourselves; we are putting the brakes on a revolutionary initiative of the masses—fully justified. This is un-ac-cept-able!"

Generally, I did not like to speak at meetings of the Petrograd [Party] Com-mittee or the Central Committee, because I considered myself insufficiently competent in regard to political issues. I spoke only when the issue was not mentioned by other comrades or was framed incorrectly.

Uritskii was killed on August 30, 1918, at 10 a.m., and at 2 p.m. all the active functionaries of the Petrograd committee convened at the Astoria [Hotel]. Zinoviev delivered a speech. He pointed out that counterrevolu-tion had raised its head, that this was the second murder of a senior party worker (Volodarskii had been the first). He asserted that "appropriate meas-ures" had to be taken. Among such measures, he proposed to allow all work-ers to punish the intelligentsia in any way they saw fit, right on the street. The comrades remained silent in embarrassment. Then I took the floor and said that in my opinion Zinoviev's proposal had been caused by panic. My words outraged Zinoviev; he ran out of the room screaming that my rude-ness was totally out of bounds. I turned to the chairman of the meeting

[Boris] Pozern[16] and said that if Zinoviev believed that he could not remain at the meeting because of my presence then it was better for me to leave. Pozern remarked that just because Zinoviev was nervous was no reason for me to be nervous and asked me to continue. I said that I considered Zinoviev's proposal wrong, because we would be the first to suffer from it. The Black Hundreds would pretend to be workers and would slaughter our leaders. [. . .]

Apparently my words unzipped people's lips: the comrades who spoke after me supported my position. Ultimately, it was decided to create special district troikas[17] to track down counterrevolutionary elements.

106. Official Demand of "Blood for Blood," August 31, 1918   [38]

The editorial below was published in Krasnaia gazeta, *a mass circulation daily and an official organ of the Petrograd Soviet of Workers' and Soldiers' Deputies, in response to terrorist attacks against Bolshevik leaders launched by Socialist-Revolutionary activists. The evening of the same day, August 30, when a terrorist killed Moisei Uritskii, the head of the Petrograd Cheka, Fanni Kaplan, shot and wounded Lenin. The Red Terror formally began in the next few days. Yet the rhetoric of violence and dehumanization of the enemy had begun weeks earlier, as peasant unrest gathered strength across the country. For example, on August 4 the party daily* Pravda *proclaimed: "The domination of capital can be ended only when the last capitalist, landlord, priest, and officer stops breathing." Bolshevik leaders viewed their struggle as implacable.*

We will make our hearts into steel. We will temper them in the fire of suffering, in the blood of [our] fighters.

We will make them hard, steadfast, and unbending.

So that no pity will enter into them; so that they will not falter at the sight of an ocean of enemy blood.

16. Boris Pozern was a member of the fraction of Unified Social Democrats (or Mezhraiontsy) during World War I and joined the Bolsheviks, along with the rest of the fraction, in July 1917.

17. Troikas were three-person teams often associated in early Soviet history with political repression. At this time they mostly consisted of representatives from the Cheka, the party, and the Commissariat of Justice.

For we will unleash this ocean.

Without mercy, without compassion, we will slaughter enemies by dozens and hundreds.

Let there be thousands.

Let them drown in their own blood!

No more painting our banners scarlet with the blood of fighters for the people's cause! No more mercy for executioners and their inspirers!

We will not arrange for them a spontaneous mass slaughter—oh, no!

In such a slaughter, people with little to do with the bourgeoisie might perish, while true enemies of the people might slip away.

Systematically and purposively we will ferret out the real *burzhoois* with fat purses and their underlings.

The murderer of comrade Uritskii was an SR. The SRs and the Mensheviks everywhere carry out the bloody orders of their masters.

In Yaroslavl, Samara, Baku, Petrograd—everywhere—these Cains, the Menshevik-SR leaders, on orders from the bourgeoisie, slaughter the sturdy fighters of the revolution.

There will be no mercy for them either.

For the blood of Comrade Uritskii, for the wounding of Comrade Lenin, for the attempt on Comrade Zinoviev, for the unavenged blood of Comrades Volodarskii and Nakhimson,[18] of the Latvians, of the sailors—let the blood of the bourgeoisie and its servants flow—let there be more blood!

107. Letter of V. G. Korolenko to A. V. Lunacharskii, June 19, 1920   [49, pp. 385–7, 389]

Vladimir Galaktionovich Korolenko (1853–1921), a writer, journalist, editor, and human-rights activist, had devoted his life before 1917 to fighting against injustice, repression, and capital punishment. A socialist staunchly opposed to the Imperial Russian regime, he spent 5 years in Siberian exile from 1879 to 1884. When revolution broke out and the monarchy fell in 1917, he rejoiced. Yet he rejected the Bolshevik policies of repression and despaired of the violence on both sides of the Civil War. Living in Poltava, Ukraine, Korolenko

18. Semyon Nakhimson (1885–1918) was a Bolshevik activist from 1912. After the Bolshevik coup, he served as political commissar of the Latvian military units, the Bolsheviks' most loyal military force. He was killed while trying to crush the Right Socialist-Revolutionary rebellion in Yaroslavl in early July 1918.

pleaded tirelessly with Commissar for Enlightenment Anatolii Lunacharskii and other moderate Bolshevik leaders to spare the lives of people he considered wrongfully convicted. One such letter is excerpted below.

Anatolii Vasil'evich,

Of course, I have not forgotten my promise to write a detailed letter, especially since I deeply wished to do so. To express one's candid views about the most important aspects of public life has long been for me, as well as for many sincere writers, the most essential need. Due to the presently established "freedom of speech," this need cannot be satisfied. We, the dissenters, have to write not articles, but memoranda. [. . .]

[. . .] During tsarist times I wrote a lot about capital punishment [. . .] Sometimes I managed even to save people condemned by military tribunals, and there were instances when after the suspension of a sentence there emerged evidence of innocence and the accused were freed. [. . .]

But execution without a trial, execution by administrative process was exceedingly rare even back then. [. . .]

[. . .] Once, a senior member of the All-Ukrainian Cheka, upon meeting me at the Poltava Cheka, where I often went in those days with various requests, asked me for my impressions. I answered that if under the tsarist government district gendarme stations had been granted the right not only to exile people to Siberia but also to execute them, that would be the same situation as we see today.

He replied to me, "But this is for the good of the people."

I do not believe that just any means can truly be used for the good of the people. Administrative executions, established systematically and continuing for over two years can certainly never serve such an end. Once, last year, I described in a letter to Kh. G. Rakovskii [Chair of the Council of People's Commissars of Soviet Ukraine] one instance when in the street *chekisty*[19] shot several so-called "counterrevolutionaries." They were in the process of being escorted in the dark of night to a cemetery where it was customary to stand people in front of an open grave and shoot them in the head without further ado. [. . .] People in the morning going to market saw pools of blood, which dogs were licking, and listened to tales of local people about what had occurred the night before. I asked Rakovskii whether he thought that those few [executed] people, even had they been the most active agitators, could have told the crowd anything more striking and provocative than that sight.

19. Officials of the Cheka, the Bolshevik secret police.

[. . .] It is bitter for me to think that you, too, Anatolii Vasil'evich, instead of calling for sobriety and reaffirming the need for justice and a concerned attitude toward human life, which has now become so cheap, in your speeches appear to be expressing solidarity with these "administrative executions." This is exactly what it sounds like in the local press. From my very soul I wish that in your heart you could hear echoes of the mood that once united us on the most important questions, when we believed that the movement toward socialism must be founded upon the best aspects of human nature, meaning the courage to fight openly and to show humaneness even toward one's enemy.

Reds versus Whites and Those in Between

108. Lenin on the Inevitability of Civil War, December 1917   [44, vol. 26, pp. 400–3]

How much resistance did the Bolsheviks think they would encounter after coming to power? On a number of occasions, Lenin stressed that the Bolsheviks were acting in the interests of an overwhelming majority of the working people, implying that little violence on their part would be needed. Yet his article written on December 24–27, 1917, but published only after his death in 1926, reveals a much more militant, albeit realistic, view. Similarly, Martin Latsis (1888–1938), a senior Cheka leader, wrote in a book published in 1920 that "Civil war is a war to the death, a war in which no prisoners are taken and no agreements take place, while the enemy is finished off."

[. . .] Those tyrannized by capitalist routine, shocked by the thundering crash of the old world, and the blast, rumble, and "chaos" (apparent chaos) as the age-old structures of tsarism and the bourgeoisie break up and cave in cannot see the historical prospects; nor can those who are scared by the class struggle at its highest pitch when it turns into civil war, the only war that is legitimate, just, and sacred—not in the clerical but in the human sense— the sacred war of the oppressed to overthrow the oppressors and liberate the working people from all oppression. [. . .]

[. . .] We have always known, said, and emphasized that socialism cannot be "introduced," that it takes shape in the course of the most intense, the most acute class struggle—which reaches heights of frenzy and desperation—and civil war; we have always said that a long period of "birth-pangs" lies between capitalism and socialism; that violence is always the midwife of the old society; that a special state (that is, a special system of organized coercion of a definite class) corresponds to the transitional period between the bourgeois and the socialist society, namely, the dictatorship of the proletariat. What dictatorship implies and means is a state of simmering war, a state of military measures of struggle against the enemies of the proletarian power. [. . .]

The drooping intellectuals are terrified when the bourgeoisie and the civil servants, employees, doctors, engineers, etc., who have grown accustomed to serving the bourgeoisie, go to extremes in their resistance. They tremble and utter even shriller cries about the need for a return to "conciliation." Like all true friends of the oppressed class, we can only derive satisfaction from the exploiters' extreme measures of resistance, because we do not expect the proletariat to mature for power in an atmosphere of cajoling and persuasion, in a school of mealy sermons or didactic declamations, but in the school of life and struggle. To become the ruling class and defeat the bourgeoisie for good the proletariat must be schooled, because the skill this implies does not come ready-made. The proletariat must do its learning in the struggle, and stubborn, desperate struggle in earnest is the only real teacher. The greater the extremes of the exploiters' resistance, the more vigorously, firmly, ruthlessly, and successfully will they be suppressed by the exploited. The more varied the exploiters' attempts to uphold the old, the sooner will the proletariat learn to ferret out its enemies from their last nook and corner, to pull up the roots of their domination, and cut the very ground which could (and had to) breed wage-slavery, mass poverty, and the profiteering and effrontery of the money-bags. [. . .]

109. The Early Anti-Bolshevik Resistance and Why It Failed, Spring 1918   [81, pp. 11–26]

Like most anti-Bolshevik activists, the author of this document, Vladimir Zenzinov, abhorred the March 3, 1918, Peace Treaty of Brest-Litovsk more than any other government policy. Yet Lenin, who had carefully questioned senior military commanders, believed that the army was incapable of fighting and that therefore the Revolution could only be saved by agreeing to any terms imposed by the Central Powers, including signing a treaty that ceded one-third of European Russia to Germany. Lenin prevailed over his doubting comrades. But political activists like Zenzinov viewed the act as treasonous and therefore believed that seeking the help of Russia's wartime Allies (France, Britain, and the United States) in their struggle against the Bolshevik government was entirely patriotic. In this document Zenzinov discusses the efforts to forge a broad anti-Bolshevik coalition and the reasons why these efforts ultimately failed.

[. . .] Not for one minute did the Party of Socialists Revolutionaries give up the thought of crushing the Bolsheviks with the armed forces. On the one hand, the party had always kept alive its combat traditions. Following these traditions the party was accustomed to respond to violence with force. On the other hand, among its members the belief reigned that only by means of the armed force of the people was it both possible and necessary to confront the Bolsheviks, that any other attempt would only lead either to the further strengthening of the Bolshevik power or to the complete restoration of the regime smashed by the revolution.

[. . .] I found a special combat group affiliated with the Moscow [Socialist-Revolutionary] party organization, which pursued the task of overthrowing Soviet power by armed force. Each district (Moscow was divided into districts following the old party practice) had such special military-combat organizations.[20] The military commission of the Moscow Committee tried to form such organizations predominantly from the most democratic proletarian elements—these were mainly workers and demobilized soldiers—and tried scrupulously to avoid the elements called "White Guardist" in the Bolshevik jargon. I must admit that this work was very difficult. It was impeded, on the one hand, by the fact that, even though the anti-Bolshevik mood was quite strong among Moscow's workers (this became quite pronounced in the spring during the elections to the Moscow Soviet of Workers' Deputies, when the only reason why the Bolsheviks' opponents did not receive an overwhelming majority was that during the elections the Bolsheviks set in motion their entire system of terror), they nevertheless could not resolve to act against the Bolsheviks with armed force: still quite a few workers continued to side with the Bolsheviks, and the prospect of a civil war within the working class itself scared even the most ardent opponents of Soviet power among the workers. On the other hand, this work was particularly complicated because of the political circumstances created by Soviet power. It should not be forgotten that the preparation of an armed uprising against the Bolsheviks was invariably punished by Soviet power with execution by shooting and at that time such executions were taking place in Moscow every night. Even the revolutionary elements most tested in the struggle against the autocracy retreated in the face of such a prospect. In addition, the system of security policing and internal spying blossomed under Soviet power more than it ever did in the times of the autocracy. [. . .]

Not wanting to restrict ourselves within the party framework, we wanted nevertheless to find out on whom else we could rely in our armed struggle against the Bolsheviks. Exploring these issues we discovered several conspiratorial organizations. In the spring of 1918, Moscow was of great interest in that regard, and the Bolsheviks were right when they kept seeing conspiracies everywhere. One could say that Moscow was indeed seething with them. We found traces of the military organization of Savinkov, of General Brusilov,

---

20. Radical socialist parties, beginning in 1905, set up "combat organizations" for the purpose of orchestrating armed attacks against the government and its officials. In some cases, these practices continued into the early Bolshevik period.

of the National Center,[21] of the Union of Regeneration,[22] finally of monarchist organizations, some with German participation. It was necessary to sort all this out, to find out which organizations we could go along with. It goes without saying, of course, that some of them—the rightist, monarchist, and German ones—were openly hostile to us and our attitude toward them could be just as determined as toward the Bolsheviks. [. . .]

[Our relations with the Savinkov organization] did not go beyond providing information; soon that also ended because certain permanent aspects of Savinkov's work led to such coolness in relations between us that our meetings turned out to be undesirable for both sides. Besides, in May Savinkov's organization was much weakened by extensive arrests of its members, and subsequently in June and July Savinkov evacuated it from Moscow, as he recounted to me personally.

Aside from the Savinkov organization, the work of the Union of Regeneration was of interest to us. The Union of Regeneration as an organization emerged and was formed in March–April 1918. In essence, it was not so much an organization as a personal association of several people joined by a unity of common basic political tasks. These tasks can be summarized as follows: the need for an armed struggle against the Bolsheviks, the creation of a popular yet unaccountable coalition-based authority, the rejection of the Brest[-Litovsk] Peace [treaty], the continuation of a joint struggle with the allies against the Central Powers, a military intervention in Russia against Germano-Bolshevism. The founders and participants of the Union of Regeneration belonged to different political parties, but were joined in the Union of Regeneration as individuals without representing anybody—it was an association of individuals in the strict sense of that word, since its members were not even tied among themselves by [party] discipline and at that time did not have any branches in the provinces. [. . .]

Contacts between the SR party and the Union of Regeneration were constant, though they too were more of a personal rather than an organizational nature. [. . .]

All of us fighting with the Bolsheviks back then held to a particular position: we were ardent supporters of continuing the war with Germany

---

21. The National Center was a nonsocialist, anti-Bolshevik force dominated by Kadets and allied with the Volunteer Army in southern Russia and supportive of the Allied cause.

22. Established in spring 1918, the Union of Regeneration brought together political activists from the left and the center, mostly Right Socialist-Revolutionaries, Social Democrats, and Left Kadets, to create an underground organization opposed to the Bolsheviks. Their main goals were to relaunch a military offensive in cooperation with the Allies against Germany, to mount an insurrection in the Volga region against the Bolsheviks, to set up a provisional government, and to convene a constituent assembly.

together with the Allies and viewed the Bolsheviks, who had signed the Peace [Treaty] of Brest[-Litovsk], as people who had entered into an alliance with the enemies of our motherland. Therefore, there was no QUESTION about intervention for us: the military role of the Allies in Russia who were fighting against Germany and its allies, the Bolsheviks, in essence was no different for us than the role of those Russian troops that had been sent to France to fight Germany on the Western Front. [. . .]

Conversations with official representatives of the Allies in this regard took place several times, both in Petrograd and in Moscow. [. . .] It should be noted that the French conducted these negotiations on behalf of all the Allies.

The essence of these negotiations was simple: we all insisted on the need for military assistance to Russia and to those forces that were fighting against Germany and the Bolsheviks. Landings in Russia's North and in the Far East were discussed as was assistance to the military struggle against the Germans and the Bolsheviks inside Russia.

The Allies responded to our proposal with complete unanimity. They promised landings; they were developing a strategic action plan together with our military representatives (General V. G. Boldyrev had these conversations on behalf of the Union of Regeneration with the French General Lavergne), jointly with them we even produced the text of a solemn declaration, to be proclaimed at the landing, which announced the goals of providing military assistance to Russia and solemnly and unequivocally asserted that the Allies thereby did not seek any territorial conquest in Russian and did not infringe on the sovereignty of the Russian people. The landing question, while veiled in great secrecy, was always answered to us with absolute certainty: the representatives of the Allied missions had asserted to us many times that the landing question had been resolved by the Allies positively, that the expedition had already been put on ships and would land in Murmansk and in Vladivostok; sometimes even the approximate dates were given. ("Now, as we are talking, the expedition is probably landing on the shore. [. . .]") Thus, for example, at the beginning of July, [Joseph] Noulens [the French Ambassador,] was telling N. D. Avksentiev in Vologda that Vologda would be occupied by the Allies by July 15. As is known, the uprising of the Savinkov organization in Yaroslavl and Rybinsk was also based on those promises: the Savinkov organization, supported in Yaroslavl by Menshevik workers, took control of Yaroslavl and held it hoping that the Allies would arrive any day from Vologda, rumored already to have been occupied by the Allies. General V. G. Boldyrev, together with representatives of the French military mission, developed a plan for the creation by joint Russian and Allied efforts of a Volga-Ural-Northern Front.

Later on, more specifically in the fall of 1918, [French Prime Minister] Georges Clemenceau and [French Minister of Foreign Affaires Stéphane] Pichon categorically denied that the Allies, and the French government in particular, had adopted any such positions. [. . .] But we, the participants in these negotiations, assert categorically that these conversations, which were of an official nature, did take place. In time, history, one should hope, will clarify whether the Allied representatives in Russia acted on their own initiative or something else was going on. One thing has to be stated clearly now: at the time we fully trusted the promises of the Allies and upon these promises built our plans engaging many thousands of people. [. . .]

110. Launching the Volunteer Army, 1917–1918
[17, pp. 22–35]

The Bolsheviks worked hard to paint all their adversaries in the White movement with the same brush and frequently referred to them as "tsarist generals." In fact few of the leading White generals were monarchists. Certainly the author of the following document, Anton Ivanovich Denikin (1872–1947), was not. The son of a former serf who rose through the military ranks and of a Polish seamstress, he commanded various units in World War I and served as chief of staff to Lavr Kornilov in summer 1917. He led the anti-Bolshevik military forces in the south from April 1918 to April 1920. A man of personal charm and literary flair, he recounted the events of the Revolution and Civil War with impressive objectivity in many volumes. In the following document, Denikin[23] recounts the tentative first steps of the White Volunteer Army, which formed on Russia's southern frontier and consisted of a disproportionately high number of officers.

The idea of bolstering up the decaying army by Volunteer formations had already arisen in the spring of 1917, but failed to materialize because the various Soviets and committees were afraid that the Volunteers would become "the bulwark of counterrevolution." [. . .]

Nevertheless, the idea of Volunteer service was not abandoned. It was being propagated by the generals imprisoned at Bykhov[24] and by the former

23. After the Civil War, Denikin emigrated to France and, after World War II, to the United States, where he died.

24. Bykhov was a town in the Pinsk district of Mogilov province with a population of 6,536 in 1897. Here, in early September 1917, numerous senior officers were imprisoned following Kornilov's failed coup.

Commander in Chief, General [Mikhail] Alekseev,[25] with whom we kept in touch. [. . .]

If formerly, for political and moral reasons we did not avail ourselves of the opportunity to escape, now that power had passed to the Bolsheviks, there was nothing to keep us at Bykhov. [. . .]

Where to go next? Undoubtedly, to the Don Cossack territory.

The Cossacks, with their strong traditional social order, their army which held out longest against disintegration—the Cossacks, with their prosperity and large land holdings won in the past by their defense of the Russian borders, and in the present by universal military service—the Cossacks, a freedom-loving community which had not bowed to the Bolsheviks, and was restoring its self-government—were looked upon as the mainstay of law and order, and by their very nature as opposed to Communism. [. . .]

The way lay across fifteen hundred versts of a country aflame with Red Revolution. The frost was severe. The regiment advanced, tracked on all sides, falling into Bolshevist ambushes, fired upon at every river or railway crossing, suffering casualties. [. . .]

However, after covering more than four hundred and fifty kilometers, Kornilov saw that the march would claim too many victims. Not wishing to endanger the men still more by his presence, he resolved to push on by himself. He bade the regiment farewell, and, disguised as a peasant, boarded a train at a remote station. [. . .] The other generals left Bykhov by train, under disguise and with forged documents, traveling in trucks crowded with boisterous, mutinous troops, passing stations at which were posted the proclamations of revolutionary committees ordering the seizure and chastisement of "the fugitive Bykhov generals." To trace us amid the general chaos was difficult, and we all reached the Don territory safely. [. . .]

General Alekseev arrived in Novocherkassk, the capital of the Don territory on 15th November, before us, and immediately set about the formation of an armed force, which was destined to play such an important part in the history of the Russian Revolution. [. . .] Conditions in the Don area, however, as in other Cossack lands, proved to be both unfavorable and extremely complicated. [. . .]

Between the Cossacks proper and the peasants who leased small holdings on Cossack lands a fierce feud was raging, in which an active part was taken by the local Soviets, supported by riotous soldier rabble which, as reserve [. . .] troops, had overrun the territory. The Cossacks were powerless to resist them, as their own contingents were still at the front. When, however, the Cossack divisions began to trek homeward, they brought bitter disappoint-

25. See p. 19, n. 12.

ment. From the front they imported actual Bolshevism, divested, of course, of all idealism, but conspicuous by a repudiation of all authority, by mutinies, aggression, and chiefly by a refusal to fight against the Soviet Government, which had falsely pledged itself "to maintain the immunity of Cossack rights."

The Volunteer rally in these circumstances roused open apprehension and discontent in Cossack circles. The opinion prevailed that the Soviet Government's preparations for a military expedition against the Don were caused by the presence of these "uninvited guests," and that the Soviet's favor and personal safety could be purchased by submission.

In spite of the total lack of funds, General Alekseev, full of ardor, set about forming the Volunteer Army. Telegrams in cipher were sent everywhere summoning officers to Novocherkassk. One of the hospitals was converted into an officers' hostel, which became the cradle of the Volunteer Movement, and contributions for "Alekseev's organization" soon began to pour in. It was a touching—and to some, perhaps, a comic sight, to see the former Commander in Chief, who had ruled over armies millions strong and wielded a war budget of milliards, now fussing around to procure a dozen beds, a few poods of sugar, and, if possible, a paltry sum of money to house, warm, and feed the homeless, persecuted warriors.

And they came in their numbers—officers, cadets, military schoolboys, and a very few old soldiers—at first one by one, then in groups. Those who could, escaped from the prisons, others from disrupted army units. Some managed to get through the Bolshevist cordons easily, others were seized and flung into prison, held as hostages, or drafted into the Red Guard, often flung into the grave. [. . .] All trekked to the Don without the least knowledge of what awaited them there; they pushed blindly on through the close darkness of the Bolshevist night, to where the names of leaders whom popular legend linked with the Don shone as a beacon amid the surrounding gloom. Unfortunately these were but hundreds, while tens of thousands, at their wit's end what to do, compelled by circumstances to "wait and see," turned to peaceful occupations, became civilians or went submissively to register with the Bolshevist commissars, to be first tortured in the Cheka and later drafted into the Red Army. [. . .]

After many and prolonged hardships, part of the regiment, singly or in groups, dribbled to the Don Cossack territory, and in January 1918 reassembled in Novocherkassk. [. . .]

[. . .] By common consent of the senior generals and public men who took part in the movement, its leadership was entrusted to General Kornilov, recently arrived from Bykhov. General Alekseev, already suffering from a grave disease, took over the control of external relations and finance. [. . .]

111. Leon Trotsky's Armored Train   [80, pp. 351–60]

On March 13, 1918, Trotsky resigned as people's commissar for foreign affairs and assumed the positions of people's commissar of the army and navy and chairman of the Revolutionary Military Council, a body created on March 4, largely at his instigation. While many other Bolsheviks at this time favored relying only on committed revolutionaries and elected officers, Trotsky advocated using former Imperial Russian officers in senior posts. In order to keep them loyal, members of their families were taken hostage and "political commissars" were placed at their side. Trotsky proved himself, by all accounts, a brilliant and highly successful military organizer and commander. In the memoir excerpted below, he describes the challenges of building and commanding a new Red Army.

Now it is time to speak of "The train of the Chairman of the Revolutionary Military Council." During the most strenuous years of the revolution, my own personal life was bound up inseparably with the life of that train. The train, on the other hand, was inseparably bound up with the life of the Red Army. The train linked the front with the base, solved urgent problems on the spot, educated, appealed, supplied, rewarded, and punished.

An army cannot be built without reprisals. Masses of men cannot be led to death unless the army command has the death-penalty in its arsenal. So long as those malicious tailless apes that are so proud of their technical achievements—the animals that we call men—will build armies and wage wars, the command will always be obliged to place the soldiers between the possible death in the front and the inevitable one in the rear. And yet armies are not built on fear. The Tsar's army fell to pieces not because of any lack of reprisals. In his attempt to save it by restoring the death-penalty, Kerensky only finished it. Upon the ashes of the great war, the Bolsheviks created a new army. These facts demand no explanation for anyone who has even the slightest knowledge of the language of history. The strongest cement in the new army was the ideas of the October revolution, and the train supplied the front with this cement. [. . .]

Every regiment, every company, comprises men of different qualities. The intelligent and self-sacrificing are in the minority. At the opposite pole is an insignificant number of the completely demoralized, the skulkers, and the consciously hostile. Between these two minorities is a large middle group, the undecided, the vacillating. And when the better elements have been lost in fighting or shoved aside, and the skulkers and enemies gain the upper hand, the unit goes to pieces. In such cases, the large middle group do not know whom to follow and, in the moment of danger, succumb to panic.

On February 26, 1919, I said to the young commanders gathered in the Hall of Columns in Moscow: "Give me three thousand deserters, call them a regiment; I will give them a fighting commander, a good commissar, fit officers for battalions, companies and platoons—and these three thousand deserters in the course of four weeks in our revolutionary country will produce a splendid regiment..."

[. . .] For two and a half years, except for comparatively short intervals, I lived in a railway-coach that had formerly been used by one of the ministers of communication. The car was well fitted out from the point of view of ministerial comfort, but it was scarcely adapted to work. There I received those who brought reports, held conferences with local military and civil authorities, studied telegraphic dispatches, dictated orders and articles. From it I made long trips along the front in automobiles with my co-workers. In my spare time I dictated my book against Kautsky, and various other works. In those years I accustomed myself, seemingly forever, to writing and thinking to the accompaniment of Pullman wheels and springs. [. . .]

[. . .] I can only partially reconstruct the orbit of the train's movements from the place names under the leading articles in the train newspaper, *En Route:* Samara, Cheliabinsk, Viatka, Petrograd, Balashov, Smolensk, Samara again, Rostov-on-Don, Novocherkask, Kiev, Zhitomir, and so on, without end. [. . .]

What was the train of the Chairman of the Revolutionary Military Council seeking on the civil-war fronts? [. . .] Out of bands of irregulars, of refugees escaping from the Whites, of peasants mobilized in the neighboring districts, of detachments of workers sent by the industrial centers, of groups of communists and trades-unionists—out of these we formed at the front companies, battalions, new regiments, and sometimes even entire divisions. Even after defeats and retreats, the flabby, panicky mob would be transformed in two or three weeks into an efficient fighting force. What was needed for this? At once much and little. It needed good commanders, a few dozen experienced fighters, a dozen or so of communists ready to make any sacrifice, boots for the barefooted, a bath-house, an energetic propaganda campaign, food, underwear, tobacco, and matches. The train took care of all this. We always had in reserve a few zealous Communists to fill in the breaches, a hundred or so of good fighting men, a small stock of boots, leather jackets, medicaments, machine-guns, field-glasses, maps, watches, and all sorts of gifts. Of course, the actual material resources of the train were slight in comparison with the needs of the army, but they were constantly being replenished. [. . .]

The most important sacrifices came from institutions. A new group of Communists would be drawn from the institutions and put immediately into an unreliable regiment. Stuff would be found for shirts and for wrappings for the feet, leather for new soles, and an extra hundredweight of fat. But of course the local sources were not enough. After the conference, I would send orders to Moscow by direct wire, estimating our needs according to the resources of the center, and, as a result, the division would get what it desperately needed, and that in good time. [. . .]

The war unrolled on the periphery of the country, often in the most remote parts of a front that stretched for eight thousand kilometers. Regiments and divisions were cut off from the rest of the world for months at a time. Very often they had not enough telephone equipment even for their own intercommunication, and would then succumb to hopelessness. The train, for them, was a messenger from other worlds. We always had a stock of telephone apparatus and wires. A wireless aerial had been arranged over a particular car in our train, so that we could receive radio messages from the Eiffel Tower, from Nauen [Germany], and from other stations, thirteen in all, with Moscow, of course, foremost. The train was always informed of what was going on in the rest of the world. [. . .]

Part of the train was a huge garage holding several automobiles and a gasoline tank. This made it possible for us to travel away from the railway line for several hundred versts. A squad of picked sharpshooters and machine-gunners, amounting to from twenty to thirty men, occupied the trucks and light cars. A couple of hand machine-guns had also been placed in my car. A war of movement is full of surprises. On the steppes, we always ran the risk of running into some Cossack band. Automobiles with machine-guns insured one against this, at least when the steppe had not been transformed into a sea of mud. Once during the autumn of 1919, in the province of Voronezh, we could move at a speed of only three kilometers an hour. The automobiles sank deep into the black, rain-soaked earth. Thirty men had to keep jumping off their cars to push them along. [. . .]

Sometimes the train was cut off and shelled or bombed from the air. No wonder it was surrounded by a legend woven of victories both real and imagined. [. . .] The news of the arrival of the train would reach the enemy lines as well. There people imagined a mysterious train infinitely more awful than it really was. But that only served to increase its influence on morale. [. . .]

The train crew performed many other tasks besides their special duties. They lent their help in time of famine, during epidemics of disease, in propaganda campaigns, and at international congresses. The train was the honorary head of a rural district and of several children's homes. Its Communist local published its own paper, *On Guard*. Many an incident of adventure and battle is recorded in its pages, but unfortunately this, like many other records, is not in my present traveling archives. [. . .]

112. An Appeal to Join the Chinese Red Army Battalion
[90, p. 142]

Some 40,000 to 50,000 Chinese volunteers, in some cases forming entire regiments, fought in the Red Army during the Russian Civil War. Most had lived in Siberia for decades, having migrated north from their homeland. During World War I, a large number had been recruited by the Imperial Russian government to work in factories, road building, and the construction of fortifications and other defensive installations. The following appeal conveys their sense of solidarity with Soviet Russia.

To all revolutionary socialist-Chinese!

Comrades! All of you who left China, a bourgeois republic, where the coolies are suffering under indescribable oppression, you who are looking for shelter in Soviet Russia, you, who are revolutionaries in a revolutionary country, join us!

One thousand eight hundred of us have been fighting against the capitalist hordes of Romanians, Haidamaks,[26] and Germans, and we will not put our guns down until either we die or the units of the global counterrevolution are defeated.

Revolutionary Chinese brothers! Whoever stands for the liberation of the enslaved, join our ranks! Whoever is for the defense of the power of workers and peasants, march with us! All the obstacles and walls must be shattered, and the liberated coolies of China must unite with the victorious proletariat of the whole world.

Comrades! All of you join the ranks of the Red Army's Chinese battalion. Let us subordinate our will to revolutionary discipline so that, closely united, we can stand against the capitalist armies. [. . .]

113. An Imperial Russian General Fights for the Bolsheviks, February 1918   [7, pp. 243–9, 252–4, 283–5]

One of the remarkable features of the Red Army, which gave a great boost to its combat prowess, was the large number of old regime officers who joined it.

26. Originally, Haidamaks were armed bands of Ukrainian Cossacks and peasants who rebelled against the Polish nobility in the 18th century. During the Civil War, nationalist Ukrainian cavalry units often referred to themselves as "Haidamaks."

While some were coerced into providing their military expertise or thought they
had no other choice in order to feed themselves and their families, others were
moved by careerism, customary obedience to authority, or a genuine belief that
the Bolsheviks were now the new caretakers of the Russian state and therefore
had to be helped for the sake of the motherland. Among the most famous was
Mikhail Dmitrievich Bonch-Bruevich (1870–1956). He served as an intelli-
gence officer and a commander in World War I and was close to his brother,
Vladimir, a leading Bolshevik. After the dynasty fell, he joined the Pskov city
soviet and was one of the first Imperial Russian generals to join the Bolsheviks
after the October coup. In the excerpt from his memoir published in 1957
he provides a recollection of those days and explains his reasons for joining the
Bolsheviks.

Smolny, as we approached it, brilliantly lighted and bustling with activity,
was in violent contrast to the dark and silent and empty streets piled with
snowdrifts, through which we had driven from the station. The square in front
of the building was jammed with field kitchens, armored cars, caissons, and
teeming with Red Guards, some wearing sheepskins, some shabby overcoats
or trench-coats, still others had turned out in nondescript jackets. Here and
there bonfires burned and torches smoked, brought by the workers from factory and workshop. All told, the impression was that of an armed encamp-
ment, or, perhaps, a frenzied mob about to storm an enemy stronghold. [. . .]

Pushing vigorously, cursing for good measure, our guide worked his way
through the milling crowd. [. . .] Stepping inside I saw my brother joyfully
getting up to meet me.

"They are in a hurry to see you and your colleagues," he said as we embraced, and before we had a chance to catch our breath he had ushered us
into a smallish room empty but for a large plain deal table and a sorry sort
of stool by the door (probably used by the sentry). A large-scale map showing Petrograd, the Gulf of Finland, Narva, Lake Chudskoye and areas to the
south lay spread on the table. I took all this in when my brother stepped out
through another door, leaving me and my companions to ourselves.

A few minutes later that door flew open and a group of men came in, all
of them distinguished by that appearance which was characteristic of professional revolutionaries in the years before the Revolution: haggard faces,
carelessly worn clothes, and a simplicity and directness of address.

The first to enter was a sturdy individual, slightly below average height,
with a brow made all the wider by baldness, a reddish-brown beard and
moustache, and a keen and lively glance. His modest suit (it may have been
turned), the polka-dot tie that was to become familiar to millions and millions, and his nervous hands and his manner of sticking his thumbs in the

armholes of his waistcoat helped me recognize Lenin, such as he had often been described to me by my brother, such as I had remembered him from the few photographs in the latter's possession. [. . .]

We shook hands, Lenin and I, and I presented the generals.

Lenin was obviously pressed for time. [. . .] At the risk of appearing impolite (I was to learn later that he was exceptionally well-mannered and considerate), Lenin quickly stepped over to the map laid out on the table, and, speaking very rapidly and addressing me and the other ex-generals, informed us that the Germans were advancing on Narva and that some of their cavalry units had already been spotted near Gatchina.

"You and your friends," Lenin went on, "shall have to start figuring out immediately measures to defend Petrograd. We haven't any troops. None at all," raising his voice. "The workers of Petrograd shall have to serve as our armed force." [. . .]

[. . .] In the afternoon of February 23, I again went to see Lenin. He received me in his modestly furnished Smolny office, now familiar to millions.

I reported that the reconnaissance groups were setting off one after another, and so were the supporting detachments. [. . .]

I had occasion to convince myself later that Lenin had a good grasp of the fundamentals of military science and was especially well-informed on the nature and circumstances of Russia's participation in the First World War. It was easy and pleasant to work with him. He had an extraordinary gift for listening to one, and did so in such a way that I, for one, experienced a feeling of elation every time I got through reporting to him, regardless of whether or not my suggestions were accepted. He had a profound comprehension of the problem under discussion, as evidenced by his rejoinders; and there was an air about him peculiarly his, an indescribable air of simplicity, comradeship, and respect for those that worked with him—the first chairman of the Council of People's Commissars. [. . .]

The penchant for arguing hours on end over trifling points and talking merely in order not to appear worsted by another speaker—a trait characteristic of the Russian intelligentsia—assumed, after the downfall of the monarchy, the proportions of a major calamity. Never before over its many centuries of history had Russia heard so much pointless argument and rhetoric as after the February Revolution. The entire arsenal of oratorical subterfuge hitherto used by experienced parliamentarians became overnight the common property of virtually the whole multi-million population of the former Russian empire. Such a thing as a time-limit was utterly disregarded, and it became next to impossible to stop an overenthusiastic speaker. It became just as difficult to refuse the floor to any sufficiently persistent individual well versed in the art of countering the efforts of a chairman to restrain his oratorical itch.

It was to take the Great October Revolution some time to establish control over this endless flow of talk, so characteristic of the Kerensky epoch. [. . .]

To get back, however, to our description of the way we, the military leadership of the Supreme Military Council, went about achieving the difficult tasks set by Lenin and the Central Committee of the Bolshevik Party. [. . .]

It was now necessary to co-ordinate the activities of all these groups and detachments. Unfortunately there was not a single general or staff officer among my personnel who could be spared to handle this difficult work.

Luckily for us, as I was sitting in my private coach and wondering which one of the senior officers of my small staff could be released with the minimum detriment to our work and entrusted with the direction of operations on the Narva Front, in came ex-General Parskii,[27] whom I would have least of all expected to see.

"Mikhail Dmitrievich," he began, when barely over the threshold. "I have been deeply worried about my right to stand by idly while the Germans are threatening Petrograd. I have no interest, of course, in the socialism preached by your Bolsheviks; but I am ready to work loyally with them, or with the devil himself, for that matter, to save Russia from German domination. [. . .]"

He stammered, overcome with emotion, and stopped at a loss of words.

"You're a godsend, indeed, Dmitri Pavlovich," I cried enthusiastically. "How about taking command of the Narva Front?"

I had come to know General Parskii on the Northern Front. [. . .] He knew—and understood—the rank-and-file soldier. He was an expert in the direction of military operations; and he was endowed with that tenacity of purpose which would help him keep a level head in the extraordinary circumstances that would inevitably attend his service with the but recently created Red Army. [. . .]

I telephoned my brother, who had been busy forming detachments and getting them off to the front during the past few days, and told him how Parskii came to be the first battle-experienced general to offer us his services.

"I believe others will now follow suit," I said. [. . .]

Still another case comes to my mind. [. . .] General Arkhangel'skii.[28] [. . .]

Our two families were soon on friendly terms, we often exchanged calls, and often met each other at the homes of mutual friends. I had, by then, formed a rather good overall opinion of Arkhangel'skii, who had shown him-

---

27. Dmitrii Parskii (1874–1921) commanded the Northern Front in the early Civil War and signed an appeal to former officers to join the Red Army in 1920.

28. Aleksei Arkhangel'skii (1872–1957?) fought with the anti-Communist forces in the south until their evacuation from the Crimea in 1920. He settled in Paris and headed the Russian All-Military Union, an emigré anti-Communist political organization, from 1938 to 1957 after its previous chairman, Evgenii Miller, was abducted by Soviet agents.

self to be an excellent staff officer, a good friend, and a man of ready sympathy. [. . .]

"I see you are an important man now, Mikhail Dmitrievich," he said to me with a note of irony in his voice.

Comments of this order, coming from former colleagues of mine, were nothing new to me, and I had acquired the habit of taking the bull by the horns in such cases.

"Someone has to accept responsibility," I answered, "everyone is trying to avoid it, but there has to be somebody to take the helm and steer our military ship. There are no military experts among the members of the new government, but the state won't survive without any army. If we go on this way, without a trained army, we may live to see German policemen in the streets of Moscow using their night-sticks to hit Russians on the head, including you and me, my dear Aleksei Petrovich. I doubt whether you would like that. So far as I am concerned, I am against it; so I am doing what I can to prevent it."

Arkhangel'skii heard me out impatiently and when I had finished my lengthy argument began to complain that everything was going to the dogs and that it was impossible to go on working.

"I am going to the Crimea, to join my family," he said; and, pointing to the Bolshevik leaders of the Supreme Military Council who were just then entering the room, he added: "As to these people, I am completely fed up with them."

I tried to argue that it was impossible to re-create the atmosphere of the old General Staff, and that it was necessary to carry on regardless of prevailing conditions in order to keep things going.

But Arkhangel'skii went on grumbling and repeating in an undertone that he would throw everything up and go away.

And that is exactly what he did. He resigned there and then. [. . .]

114. An Appeal by Left SR Workers to Sailors and Red Army Men, March 19, 1919   [56]

Contrary to Bolshevik efforts to portray their struggle in "Reds versus Whites" terms, a growing number of revolutionaries felt that they represented an alternative to both sides. After the Left SRs failed to spark a countrywide uprising against the Bolsheviks in July 1918, most of them entered the anti-Bolshevik underground. During the Civil War, they refused to support either the Reds or the Whites, and instead tried to build up and base themselves on the soviets as a grassroots political force. They also organized or fomented labor unrest and strikes, mutinies in the armed forces, and peasant uprisings. The following appeal was approved all but unanimously by 4,000 railroad workers at a general meeting of the Aleksandrovskie Wagon and Locomotive Workshops on the Nikolaevskaia Line, which ran from Petrograd to Moscow. The appeal was then issued as a leaflet by the Petrograd Committee of the Left SR Party.

Comrade sailors and Red Army men!

We, the workers of the Aleksandrovskie Wagon and Locomotive Workshops of the Nikolaevskaia Railroad call upon you with a request for help.

Save the workers of Piter.

For over a week the Glorious Putilov factory has been fighting against the Bolshevik provocateurs, executioners, and murderers.

The Bolshevik authorities fired upon a general meeting of the Treugolnik Plant.[29]

The Bolshevik authorities fired upon a general meeting of the workers of the Rozhdestvenskii streetcar depot. Hundreds of arrested Putilovites, hundreds of arrested workers from all the Petrograd factories and plants are languishing in the Bolshevik dungeons.

Sailors and Red Army men do not shoot at workers. It is drunken Latvian and Chinese hirelings, as well as Bolsheviks, who spill proletarian blood.

A band of executioners from Gorokhovaia[30] disguised as sailors has been captured and delivered to the Putilov Plant, the heart of the world revolution.

They force people to work by threat of execution; those who don't work are dragged to Gorokhovaia.

Factories and plants are full of machine guns and armored vehicles.
Wives and children are moaning and weeping
Hundreds of workers are arrested and shot.

The Bolshevik authorities have betrayed the promises of Red October.
The Bolshevik authorities have betrayed the workers, peasants, sailors, and Red Army men.

TODAY Bolshevik executioners shoot and kill us workers.
TOMORROW Bolshevik executioners will be shooting and killing you sailors and Red Army men.

---

29. The Treugolnik Plant was a huge rubber-manufacturing concern in Petrograd.
30. The street where the Cheka was headquartered.

Th..... is only one response to the divide-and-conquer tactic of the Bolshevik tormentors.

Strength is in unity!

Comrade sailors and Red Army men, do not allow the spilling of the
blood of comrades.
LET'S ALL RISE UP AS ONE TO DEFEND THE PUTILOVITES!
Let's all rise as one to defend all Petrograd workers.
Down with commissarocracy.
All power to the freely elected worker and peasant soviets.
Comrade sailors and Red Army men!
Be prepared for the day of general protest—that day is near.

115. Winston Churchill Urges French Support for Anti-Bolshevik Forces, Late 1919   [77, pp. 77–82]

*The Bolsheviks repeatedly cited Allied intervention as proof that the whole
Old World was eagerly plotting to destroy Soviet Russia by any means possible.
On the other hand, many participants in the White movement were skeptical
and bitter, thinking that the Allies were not doing nearly enough to help them
defeat the Bolsheviks. Yet, as the letter below indicates, there were real disagreements in Britain and France about what role, if any, they should be
playing in Russian affairs, especially after the conclusion of World War I.
Some, like the letter's author, Winston Churchill, urged more involvement.
Even so, by the time he wrote these lines, the Whites had been effectively
defeated.*

Private and Confidential
War Office. White Hall. C.W.T.
21st November, 1919

[To Mr. Louis Loucheur][31]
    I write to you because I am becoming increasingly anxious about the
situation in Europe which, it seems to me, may develop in such a way as to
affect not only the victory but the safety of England and France; and because

---

31. Louis Loucheur (1872–1931) was a conservative politician in Third Republic France
who served as chief economic advisor to President Georges Clemenceau at the Paris Peace
Conference in 1919.

we have talked over so many aspects of Anglo-French interests together during our collaboration in the war.

I heard with great regret from Mr. Lloyd George that the French Government has absolutely decided to cut off all supplies and assistance to the anti-Bolshevik Russians. I must say quite frankly that this appears to me to be a suicidal policy for France. If the Russian National forces get the upper hand and overthrow the Bolshevik regime after France has abandoned them, they will undoubtedly be animated by sentiments of lasting resentment towards the Entente Powers, in whose cause they lost more than three million men. If, on the other hand, they are beaten, as is very likely, Europe will have to reckon with a mighty Jacobin[32] military Empire rallying the National Russian spirit to recover Russian lopped-off provinces, and dividing the populations of the Entente countries by revolutionary propaganda fed by the financial resources of a powerful State. In either event these hostile Russian forces will look to Germany, where alone she can get the instructors and organizers to develop their military life and to rebuild their economic power. In Germany, on the other hand, there can only be one policy—to unite with Russia, either Bolshevik or anti-Bolshevik whichever comes uppermost. Russia can give back Germany everything she has lost. Munitions, man-power, raw material, markets, expansion; all can be found by Germany in Russia.[33]

It was by the re-union of Russia and Germany that Napoleon was overthrown and Germany restarted on her career of world power in 1813. [. . .] Against a Russo-German combination, England and France could never indefinitely maintain a war on land. And what is America going to do? Can you really base your national safety, and expect us to base ours, on the chance that the United States will send two or three million men to Europe on the next occasion and will get them there in time? I think it would be madness to trust to a factor so inscrutable. Understand, my friend, that I am not thinking of any immediate danger, but only of the dangers of five or ten years hence. I fear more than I can express the re-union of Russia and Germany, both determined to get back what they have lost in the war, the one through being our ally, the other though being our foe, and both convinced that acting together they will be irresistible. [. . .]

I am young enough to have to look ahead so far as the future of my own country is concerned, and I am bound to say, speaking of the years which lie before us, that I should deeply regret to see England involved in such a hopeless situation. [. . .] I cannot believe that a policy of "strafing Germany into

32. The Jacobins were a political faction who came to dominate the French Revolution in 1793–1794.

33. It was indeed the case that the 1922 Rapallo treaty established Russia and Germany as military partners for nearly two decades.

the arms of Russia" and of leaving Russia "to stew in her own juice" is the last word which the political genius of France has to speak upon so terrible a matter. We ought, on the contrary, to do our utmost to make a success of the Socialist Government in Germany so that the German people will see that it is to their advantage to continue under such a Government; we ought to do our utmost to weave together and take the lead of all the anti-Bolshevik forces which now exist, and to give them the material and moral aid which they require and the political guidance of which they stand in such desperate need; we ought to try to bring about a good arrangement between the anti-Bolshevik Russian forces and the border States on a basis which will secure the greatest concentration against the Bolshevik tyranny; we ought to strengthen Poland in every way and promote a unity of action between Poland and the Russian National forces; we ought to direct our policy from a common point of view in these matters and be ready to make sacrifices and exertions in whatever directions are necessary. In this way alone shall we succeed in taking those steps best calculated to ward off the formidable dangers which gather in the East.

I understand that a new Inter-Allied Conference is to be held upon the subject of Russia. It is very likely that this will be the last opportunity of dealing in a coherent manner with this problem.

I do trust that you will let me know your views and what you think is possible, treating this letter, of course, not as an expression of ministerial opinion but as the private reflections of an English friend with whom you worked in the war.

116. America's Intervention in Siberia, 1918–1920
[28, pp. 71, 81–2, 92, 97]

General William Sidney Graves (1865–1940) was commander of the American forces in Siberia from September 1918 until they were repatriated in early 1920. Despite pressure from the French, British, and Japanese, he steadfastly refused to give support to the Whites or to work in any way against the Bolsheviks. First, he had clear orders from President Wilson who refused to take sides or to interfere in Russia's internal affairs. The purpose of the American intervention, in Wilson's mind, was solely to help the Czechoslovaks return home through Siberia. Bolshevism, he thought, was merely a sort of wayward liberalism, while reactionary conservatism was unregenerate. Second, Graves witnessed outrages perpetrated in eastern Siberia by such Cossack warlords as I. M. Kalmykov and Grigorii Semyonov, who were funded by Japan and thus almost entirely outside the control of Admiral Aleksandr Kolchak (1874–1920),

the supreme leader of the Siberian Regional Government following a coup that
ejected Socialist-Revolutionary politicians in November 1918.[34] *Graves, how-*
ever, seemed to think that they were in cahoots. In his memoir, excerpted below,
Graves elaborates on his view of the situation in Russia.

[. . .] As previously noted, I received my orders, written on July 17, on
August 3, which were given, not only to the United States Military, but were
in the form of a policy, applicable to all United States representatives, in
which there were definite, clear, and positive instructions that no United
States representative would intervene or take sides in Russian affairs. [. . .]

It soon became evident at these Allied meetings that I was an unknown
quantity, and their principal darts were fired at me, when any differences
arose. There were basic differences in our policies which could never be reconciled as long as my instructions remained. England, France, and Japan always had as their objective to do all the damage possible to the Bolsheviks,
while I was trying to keep out of trouble with any Russian party. The principle of non-intervention had been broadcast throughout the world and
everyone in Siberia, Russian and foreigner, knew of this promise before Allied troops entered Siberia. From my point of view, this policy was sound
and there isn't a nation on earth, that would not resent foreigners sending
troops into their country, for the purpose of putting this or that faction in
charge of their Government machinery. The result is not only an injury to
the prestige of the foreigner intervening, but is a great handicap to the faction the foreigner is trying to assist. [. . .]

On November 5, [1918,] an extract from a letter the War Department
had received from the State Department was cabled to me as it related directly to questions arising in Siberia. This letter stated that the Consul General was authorized, not only to keep in personal touch, if possible, with local
Governments, but to permit consular officers under him to give aid and advice to these Governments, in their effort to improve local conditions. This
communication also stated that the United States Government was not yet
prepared to recognize any new Government in Russia. At this time all towns
on the railroad in Siberia were in charge of the Whites and consular agents
were all located along the railroad. To give "aid and advice" to local and municipal officers, in practice, was giving aid and advice exclusively to the
Whites, which naturally caused the Bolsheviks to claim the United States
was helping the Tsarist adherents. [. . .]

34. In April 1919, forces under Kolchak's command had reached the Volga River. By
June, however, a Bolshevik counteroffensive pushed back to the Urals and continued advancing. Bolshevik officials executed Kolchak in Irkutsk in February 1920.

117. Activities of Nestor Makhno's Partisans, February–May 1920 [84]

Born into a poor Ukrainian peasant family, Nestor Makhno (1888–1934) was drawn early to anarchist political activism.[35] His charisma enabled him to lead various anarchist groups and ultimately an entire movement covering a huge territory from the Dniester River in the west to the Don River in the east. A brilliant military leader, Makhno joined forces variously with the Reds and the Whites, depending on political expediency. Lev Golik (?–1920) was the chief of counterintelligence of Makhno's Revolutionary Insurgents Army of Ukraine. His account provides a rare glimpse into the daily activities of the Makhnovites, in which the lines between ideological anarchism and banditry were often blurred. After the Bolshevik government crushed the Whites, it turned resolutely against Makhno, dispersing his followers and driving him into exile.

[. . .] February 11, 12, 13 [1920]. We crossed the railroad and derailed an empty freight train between Guliai-Pole[36] and Gaichur. In the village of Vozdvizhenka we hacked to death two Bolshevik agitators who had organized a Revolutionary Committee and departed for Rozhdestvenskaia, where we captured ten Red Army soldiers of a *prodotriad*. We stripped their clothes off but did not hurt them. [. . .]

February 20. The other day in Voskresensk the Reds shot twelve Makhnovites and burned down two huts. Dermenzhi escaped and met up with us today with fifteen fellows. They say there are many prisoners in Tsarekonstantinovka; it would be great to free them. But how can Daddy [i.e., Makhno] be convinced of that? He wants to capture Guliai-Pole and seize some money. We left Fedorovka for Shagarovo. The unit is growing: we now have seventy cavalrymen and ten *tachankas* [i.e., horse-drawn carts] with machine-guns.

February 21. We descended on Guliai-Pole and took 500 prisoners, two machine guns, and numerous shells! Red Army soldiers have been taking our side, but our leaders are afraid to accept them. Two million in cash were

---

35. Although the idea of anarchism grew out of socialist thought in England and France in the mid-19th century, Russian thinkers and activists, such as Mikhail Bakunin (1814–1876) and Peter Kropotkin (1842–1921), were the undisputed leaders of the worldwide anarchist movement beginning in the 1860s. Their goals were to tear down the political and economic structures of society and to establish instead cooperative, egalitarian communities.

36. A town in southeastern Ukraine, the birthplace of Makhno.

taken from the army treasury and divvied out to the rebels, 500 rubles each, and 1,000 rubles to each commander. We stayed for three or four hours. Suddenly, the Red Cavalry approached from Pologi and drove us out of Guliai-Pole. [Makhno's brother] Savva, M. Skoromnyi, and Vorobiev did not manage to escape; their fate is unknown. [. . .]

February 23. Last night we arrived in Gavrilovka, where we took one Red engineer and two Food Army men; we immediately slaughtered them. Zabud'ko came out of hiding with five fellows and joined our unit. M. Budanov and Popov organized rallies and pasted leaflets all around.

February 24. Several anarchists came from Guliai-Pole. They say that the Reds shot [Commander] Korostylev. We left for Komar by way of Andrianovka.

February 25. In the morning we left for Bolshaia Ianisol, where we killed one food commissar and two Red Army soldiers. We sounded the tocsin and held a rally. The Greeks don't want to fight. After lunch we moved to Maiorskoe, then on to Sviatogokhovka. We captured one Bolshevik, the organizer of the Revkom. Petrenko ran him through.

February 26. We held a rally in Sviatodukhovka. Then Makhno got drunk and like an idiot started throwing money at the peasants. At headquarters he got into a fight with Karetnikov. He wanted to shoot Popov because of his flirting with Galina. He was tied up and laid on a *tachanka*. [. . .]

March 1. We left for the village of Varvarovka at noon. On the way there, we stopped a train, on which we disarmed a Red company. We shot their commander and welcomed thirty volunteers. In the evening we raided Guliai-Pole and knocked out the 6th Soviet regiment. We took seventy-five Red Army soldiers together with the regimental commander Fediukhin, who was badly wounded in battle. He asked to be shot and Kalashnikov satisfied his request. Fifteen prisoners joined our unit. We approached Novoselovka.

March 3. In the morning we left for Fedorovka, where we hacked to pieces the Chairman of the Revolutionary Committee, a worker who was sent from Pologi, and left for Konskie Razdory. At the Magedovo junction we tore up the railroad tracks and [telegraph] wires, smashed a telegraph machine, and sent a steam locomotive on to Pologi. [. . .]

March 15. We left Gavrilovka for Komar. On the way there we burned down the German settlement of Mariental because the Germans had killed our scout. We killed thirty men and took their horses. In Komar the Greeks surrendered a German who had escaped from Mariental. He pleaded, but Makhno personally shot him. The 22nd Soviet Punitive Regiment was here a day earlier shooting former Makhnovites. For example, they shot seven people in Komar; in Bogatyr, ten and burned down two huts; in Konstantin, twelve and torched one hut.

March 16. We left for Andrianovka settlement and without warning captured the Third Company of the 22nd Punitive Regiment. Yesterday this
company had shot fifteen Makhnovites and burned down five homesteads.
The peasants were frightened. But when we came, they showed heroism by
massacring the captives. There were 120 of them, led by the Communists,
whom the peasants beat with sticks, stabbed with pitchforks, and shot individually and in groups. With machine guns, S. Karetnikov, Kalashnikov, and
Popov shot some of the captives, their hands tied behind their backs and
stripped naked. [. . .]

118. Violence and Daily Life in a Jewish Community during the Civil War   [26, pp. 74–8, 103–9]

*The author describes tragic events he witnessed as a child, aged 9, in Savran, a
small town, or shtetl, in Odessa province, in southwestern Ukraine. The town
had roughly 3,200 Jews in 1900. During the Civil War years the town, like
many other Jewish settlements, was subject to numerous raids and attacks by
various armed detachments interested in replenishing their food supplies. Such
encounters often degenerated into looting and killing.*

This invasion by a band of Petliura's[37] soldiery was to set the pattern for
the months that followed. A week might go by without an alarm, then the
cry would be heard: People running! Doors would be locked, shutters
latched, children and mother down into the shelter, father patrolling up-
stairs, watching the street through chinks in the shutters. Sometimes a troop
would ride through town, fire a few shots, and be gone. More often, they
would hunt down several Jews, present them with a list of demands, send
one to spread the word to the rest of the *shtetl,* and hold the others for ransom. The demanded *kontributsia* usually included so many pairs of boots,

---

37. A Ukrainian of Cossack extraction, Simon Petliura (1879–1926) was a revolutionary activist in his youth and prolific Social Democrat and Ukrainian nationalist journalist between the revolutions. Military forces under his command fought against Bolsheviks
to the north, anti-Communist Whites to the south, and Romania to the southwest. He
came to Paris in 1924 where a Jewish anarchist, possibly linked to the Soviet security
forces, assassinated him, allegedly in revenge for anti-Jewish pogroms. Historians are divided over Petliura's role in the slaughter of Jews in Ukraine during the Civil War, though
it seems that Petliura was personally not an anti-Semite and that the troops who engaged
in pogroms were never under his direct control.

so many blankets, so much silver and gold, vodka, greatcoats, food, grain for the horses—all to be delivered by a certain hour, or the hostages would be killed and the town sacked.

The desperate emissary would run from house to house, announce himself to the families cowering inside, enlist others to spread the word and help with the collection. Before long, a line of men, usually the elders, would be carrying loads to the soldiers encamped in the market square. What happened next depended on whether the soldiers were drunk or sober, on the mood of the moment, on their need to hurry on; on whether a degree of discipline still held the troops together as a soldierly unit, or the group was a random collection of stragglers joined together for looting and for mutual protection against other marauding bands. The bearers of the *kontributsia* might be let off with some casual blows, and the troop mount and move on. There were occasions when the raiders were not in a hurry. Some of the men delivering the loot would be kept as additional hostages, and the rest sent back for more. When one bearded patriarch protested mildly that there was nothing more left in the town after all the previous exactions, he was knocked down, kicked in the head, and killed. The others went back, gathered a little more of the ransom demanded, and made another delivery.

The two rabbis of the community, the red rabbi and the black rabbi (so named for the color of their beards), presided over the two synagogues, and were the natural leaders of the Jewish community. Their political differences were long forgotten in the time of troubles. Together they shaped the responses of the town to the unprecedented challenges we faced. During each assault it was necessary to gauge from the reports of the messengers the probable reactions of the raiders. Full compliance with demands, even if the goods were still available, might well lead to a full pogrom, in the expectation of rich booty. Too little might anger them and risk the loss of lives. Enough had to be held back to satisfy future requisitions. The two rabbis gauged the dwindling resources of the town, and attempted to balance the growing danger of starvation against the loss of lives by violence. They did not always decide correctly.

Between raids, a semblance of orderly life repeatedly asserted itself. The ancient organic relationship of town and country was never entirely extinguished. The *mujiks* [peasants] still needed the skills that the Jewish artisans could provide. Trade goods were no longer coming to the surviving stores in town. No one was safe on the roads, and the railways had long since become utterly disorganized. Paper money had less and less exchange value. But in basements and other hiding places there were still quantities of goods stored away, and these were grudgingly brought out, a little at a time, and bartered for the food the *mujiks* were able to bring to market. The farmers too were caught up in the chaos and disorganization of the shifting regimes. Grain, cattle, and horses were at the mercy of official foragers from the central government in the cities. [. . .]

We lived through a long summer on the slopes of a rumbling volcano. There were no picnics in the park, no rides through the countryside. The woods and the fields were there, the birds wheeled and soared as always, but this was not the same world. Families clung close together, there was constant inventory-taking by parents—is everyone here? Wait, where's Dave? He's just in the yard, picking pears from the tree. Tell him to get down this minute, I don't want to start looking for him if there's an alarm. There were no evening gatherings around the samovar. There were no bright and festive Sabbaths and holidays. There was no school to go to. Services at the synagogue were abbreviated, sparsely attended, and watchful. Men were fearful of leaving families at home and having to make their way back through streets occupied by raiders.

When neighbors met, there was talk of the good old days, so often complained of in the past, when Stepan and a few officials had to be propitiated with occasional gifts. The streets had been secure day and night, people had been unworried at their work, on Saturdays and holidays the synagogues had been filled and the streets safe for the leisurely return to home and family. It was possible to travel to Balta or Bershad or Odessa, by wagon or train. There was so little crime that the murder of my great-grandfather by highwaymen long before I was born was still a lively subject of conversation. Life had been difficult under the Tsar. For Jews, the countless restrictions, indignities and oppressions, both petty and harsh, were a heavy burden. But, with all its burdens, life had been mostly predictable, orderly. Now, the most unendurable element in our lives was the chaos, the absence of all restraint, all authority. In a period when no one any longer was answerable for his behavior, the powerless scattered Jewish settlements discovered themselves to be more vulnerable than ever. [. . .]

[. . .] Could these *mujiks* around us be the same people as the characters in the books I had been devouring in the town library? The answer that suggested itself offered a new hope that helped to sustain us in our time of troubles. The constricted lives of poverty and ignorance condemned these *mujiks* to a life of toil and bestiality. But now the revolution was beginning. Would not the next generation reach a stage of civilization in which savagery would be extinguished? We knew of no pogroms in the Western European countries where education was available to all—none in England or in Scandinavia, and certainly not in Germany, where there was said to be no illiteracy whatever. It seemed reasonable to hope—if only we managed to survive the present onslaughts, we might live to see the very savages around us transformed by the revolution into peaceful, tolerant, civilized neighbors. [. . .]

119. Intercepted Personal Correspondence, Samara
Province,[38] March 1920   [16, pp. 71–2, 468–9]

Following the practice of the Imperial Russian security police, the Bolshevik government, which had plenty of reasons to be worried about the popular mood in the provinces, continued to open private correspondence, but much more extensively. As in Imperial Russian times, most people had no idea their personal letters were being violated. Information from private letters was extracted and summarized in weekly secret police reports, like the one excerpted below. It could also lead to arrest and prosecution of the letters' authors.

[. . .] 2458. Staraia Maina, January 22: "The barracks are not heated, every day 20–30 people die from typhus.[39] There is dirt everywhere, tons of lice."

2459. Buguruslan, February 17: "They seized all the livestock and grain. The soldiers had our remaining grain made into flour, and we were left hungry. Life is very hard."

2460. Dermarino, January 18: "The livestock and grain are taken away; they leave 36 pounds of salt per person per month and 1 pound of kerosene; there is no sugar. They inventory everything. They say they are taking it to the front, but in fact they eat everything in the rear."

2461. Malaia Glushitsa, February 8: "Because of the typhus epidemic, school has been canceled, and all the female teachers have been mobilized into a newly created epidemic unit." [. . .]

2465. Buzuluk, January 9: "In Vodnaia Logachevka all female comrades have risen against the Communists and the Jews.[40] Everyone is crying in a single voice: 'Long live Soviet power, down with the commune and the Yids!' About 20 Communists were seized."

2466. Buzuluk, January 13: "The punitive expeditions seize grain. When they find what is hidden, they take it without paying."

---

38. Located in the middle of a huge expanse of steppe on the steep left bank of the Volga River 550 miles east-southeast of Moscow, Samara was an important grain-trading and commercial center in Imperial Russian times, but experienced significant devastation during the years of the Civil War, when it was a battleground between the Red Army and Bolshevik forces.

39. Spread among humans by lice, typhus caused 2–3 million deaths in Russia from 1918 to 1922.

40. Since a number of leading Bolsheviks were Jews, many people thought they were one and the same. In reality, all the Jewish Bolsheviks repudiated their ethnic and religious heritage and indeed execrated religion in general.

2467. Village of Milrulino, Buguruslanskii district, January 6: "We live very well; we have grain and livestock; nothing is being seized; and we receive assistance." [. . .]

2473. Melekes, January 10: "We have no newspapers and live as if in the woods. The trains don't run; There is no firewood. In school things are going well; we have covered a lot in the past half-year."

2474. Samara, February 17: "Red Army men, civil servants, and workers go every day to clear snow drifts from railroad and streetcar tracks. Steam engines are being repaired properly in the repair shop."

2475. Bugul'ma, February 3: "They take grain and livestock but don't give meat to the soldiers. People are dying from typhus." [. . .]

2542. Samara, January 18: "It's like a terrible nightmare—the decree of the central government on transforming the army into an army of labor.[41] Is serfdom being introduced or what? The free citizen's labor is being replaced by slave labor. They want to tear the entire army away from their families; they are turning free people into slaves. I think some people will oppose this not only in words."

2543. Ekaterinovka. February 8: "Soviet power also is trying to keep the people from dying of hunger and for that purpose is sending agitators to the countryside to give explanations." [. . .]

2855. Samara, February 20: "Not far from Samara the Reds were driven out from Bugul'ma, Buguruslan, and Melekes. There are unit mutinies, and something is expected to happen in Samara."

2856. Samara, February 6: "The mood in Samara is good; good news is coming from the fronts. We engage in Sunday volunteer work;[42] not only Communists and Red Army men are participating, but non-Party members as well. It seems that the epidemic has decreased, but another one could happen. All necessary preventative measures are being taken." [. . .]

2607. Krasnyi Iar, March 17: "All deserters have been driven out. In Makarievo they were driven out. Forty people were shot." [. . .]

2514. Buzuluk, December 15: "What do you mean you can't escape [from the army]? I traveled two thousand versts without any papers and you are afraid to travel 200."

41. A decree issued in fall 1918 established a universal labor obligation for people ages 16 to 50. In practice, the decree had few practical results. As the Civil War drew to a close, Trotsky advocated creating labor armies from demobilized Red Army conscripts, arguing that drastic measures were needed to rebuild the country. These armies were disbanded in late 1921.

42. "Voluntary" labor Saturdays and Sundays (*subbotniki* and *voskresniki*) began in 1919 and were launched with great fanfare on May 1, 1920. Conceived by Lenin as expressing the very essence of Communist labor, they gradually became a political obligation.

2515. Sorochinskoe, January 20: "I live at home; 45 deserters are hiding in our village."

2516. Buzuluk, January 22: "All your comrades are home; you should come home too."

120. What Went Wrong with Denikin's Volunteer Army, 1918–1920   [81, pp. 271–84]

The author of the letter excerpted below, General Aleksandr Sergeevich Lukom-skii (1868–1939), served as a senior military organizer for the supreme commanders of the Russian Army during the final months of the Imperial government, the first months of the Provisional Government, and most of the period when Denikin commanded the Volunteer Army. He also chaired the government of the territory controlled by Denikin in 1919 and early 1920. The letter, written to Denikin on March 7, 1920, and harshly critical of his policies and of the general condition of the White movement, was never sent, because Denikin resigned his post in early April.

Kind Sir, Anton Ivanovich!

Having disengaged myself from the Volunteer Army, I would like never-theless to write to you in full candor about everything that has disturbed me and continues to disturb me, as well as to share my doubts. [. . .]

Did you ever [. . .] allow anyone to express opposition to your actions? No, not at all!

One dared with confidence to contradict you only in private; otherwise each of us risked falling out of favor. [. . .]

You became absorbed with yourself, and naturally, as a consequence, both distrust and a certain alienation developed gradually between you and your closest associates. [. . .]

[. . .] [T]o a large degree under the influence of [General Ivan] Ro-manovskii,[43] while being yourself an enemy of any abuse and plunder, you

---

43. Ivan Pavlovich Romanovskii, the quartermaster general of the Russian armies under the Provisional Government, was Denikin's most trusted associate. "I can tell him things that I would not even tell my wife," he said. He was extremely brave and calm under fire, but his personality was icy, and few other White officers trusted or felt endeared to him. He was often called "the evil genius of the Volunteer Army."

turned a blind eye to the activities of such gentlemen as [General V. L.] Pokrovskii[44] and [General Andrei] Shkuro.[45]

"One must not forget," as Romanovskii often said, "that the incentive of plunder for a Cossack detachment is at the very same time an incentive for victory and an encouragement for moving forward."

We have experienced what such an "incentive" leads to.

All of this taken together gradually contributed to your being surrounded only by nonentities, and aside from Romanovskii there are no loyal people. Your policies, moreover, exacerbated these problems.

I divide these policies into external and domestic, the former towards "the newly formed entities" of Poland and Romania and the latter towards the areas liberated from the Bolsheviks.

External policy. You liked to say that you must act with integrity and in the interests of Russia's "great power" status. You believed that you could not make any promises that would have constrained the future Russian state or impinged upon the borders of the Russian state as of 1914.

To implement such a policy, *real* force was required, which you and Romanovskii nevertheless overrated.

You did not take into account that in the case of a final victory over the Bolsheviks and the reunification of a strong Russia, your promises would not have had any significance and a strong Russia would have implemented the policies it deemed necessary and was capable of.

Not only various Azerbaijans, Georgias, Latvias, [. . .] but also Poland and Romania would have bowed before a strong Russia. [. . .]

It seemed that in this struggle it was necessary to unite all the anti-Bolshevik forces and aspirations toward one goal: victory over the Bolsheviks. The rest would have fallen into place naturally. [. . .]

Domestic policy. Fundamental elements of your domestic policy were the following:

a) "The inviolability of property."

Correctly considering the land question crucial, you issued an order that "latifundias" be destroyed, that landlords be left with small estates, where advanced agriculture could be practiced (exceptions were allowed for estates with advanced agriculture), and that landlords receive compensation for the confiscated land. [. . .]

---

44. General V. L. Pokrovskii was a sadist who apparently delighted in executions.

45. General Andrei Grigorievich Shkuro (1887–1947), an audacious and brutal warrior, had been the leader of a special guerilla unit in World War I. In spring 1918, he organized an anti-Bolshevik Cossack unit in the Caucasus region and joined Denikin's forces as the commander of a Cossack brigade. By May 1919, he commanded an entire cavalry corps.

Even so, when the front began to collapse, Romanovskii told me: "Our failures at the front and the uprisings in the rear are explained above all by the fact that our policies were too far to the right, in particular, they favored landlords."

I categorically disagree and believe that your proposed resolution of the land question was generally correct. All that was necessary was to establish firm order in the rear, to persecute mercilessly all attempts by the landlords to restore their rights with punitive force, and most importantly to confiscate land from the landlords with proper compensation right away and to give it to the peasants. [. . .]

b) "Government agencies should be headed by individuals based on their merits and not their party affiliation. Only monsters from the right or the left are impermissible."

This principle is completely correct, but how correctly was it implemented?

You appointed [Aleksandr] Krivoshein,[46] who cannot possibly be called a monster from the right, only after "public activists" (mainly "Kadets"), having come to acknowledge their own impotence, talked you into agreeing to name Krivoshein (and [S. N.] Chaev), but this appointment occurred when it was too late to correct anything.

Again and again you avoid appointing outstanding individuals. [. . .]

c) Financial, commercial, and industrial matters.

Your principles: "Fiscal conservatism, combating the theft of state property, preserving grain and natural resources for Russia, rejection of foreign concessions."

Again, all of these principles are incontestable . . . but on the condition that it is feasible to regulate all these issues in a correct and healthy manner.

What happened in reality?

Given the aspiration to maintain *our own solid* currency, until recently it was in very short supply, leaving only pennies to fund the administration. As a result, people joined the civil service reluctantly, and most who did busied themselves with plunder and bribery, bringing hatred upon themselves and disorganizing the rear.

Protecting state property [. . .] was difficult in the Cossack regions, causing only hatred and acrimony.

The financial situation could have been improved through the taxation of commerce and by allowing natural resources to be exported abroad. This would have brought in manufactured goods, army uniforms, and hard currency.

---

46. The grandson of a peasant, Aleksandr Vasilievich Krivoshein (1857–1921) implemented the agrarian reforms of Prime Minister Piotr Arkadievich Stolypin (1862–1911) and served as Russia's minister of agriculture from 1908 to 1915. He headed the White general Piotr Wrangel's government in the Crimea in 1920.

A large-scale and correct resolution of this issue would have drawn the allies more fully to the cause of Russia's restoration, and their commercial interests intertwining with ours would have compelled them to help us more assiduously.

Yet fearing lest too much grain and too many natural resources should flow abroad and because of our inability to control the grain and natural resources from the Cossack regions, we failed to organize anything. [. . .]

The officer question. Very few of the idealistic officers who launched the [White] cause in 1917 and joined the Volunteer Army in 1918 remain.

The majority of the officers currently serving in our army are mediocre, have grown corrupt during the revolutionary period, and are far from being "idealistic." Still, your authority is high, and they believe in you.

Your appeals still make a strong impression on the officers.

But I repeat, few idealists remain, therefore serious attention must be paid to providing materially for the officers and their families.

Much has been done lately, but it is not enough. Remember that the ruble is now worth one-half kopek, and its value will continue to fall. [. . .]

It must not be forgotten that the majority of experienced officers are monarchists and that they blindly followed you only because you did not allow socialists and people like "Kerensky" to work with you. [. . .]

The officer corps fears the return of the reign of "Kerensky" and asks: "What are we shedding our blood for?"

It is impossible to explain everything to everybody, so doubts arise, which could lead to catastrophe. [. . .]

Generally, our work was unsystematic; everything was done hastily, based on the utter and *careless* conviction that by the summer (1920) we would be in Moscow and the rest would fall into place.

Now, if it's not too late, everything will have to be done from scratch, and most importantly, while advancing forward firm order and the garrisons must be established in the rear. [. . .]

It is with pain in my heart that I am parting with our dear army and with the sacred cause that we began together. I am asking you to view my letter not as an angry criticism, but as a desire to share my views candidly.

I hope that this letter will bring at least a bit of help.

I cannot work with socialists and the various scoundrels who have recently surfaced. I will remain in voluntary exile until the situation changes and I will again have the opportunity to work for the common cause and the benefit of the Motherland.

Please accept my assurances of complete respect and loyalty.

A. Lukomskii

PEASANTS IN REVOLT

121. Complaint by Peasants in Penza Province, March 1919   [16, pp. 72–4]

By summer 1918, as political parties opposed to the Bolsheviks, particularly the Mensheviks and Socialist-Revolutionaries, won majorities in many periodic elections to soviets, both urban and provincial, the authorities frequently called further, unscheduled, elections and manipulated them in a variety ways in order to achieve electoral success. Faced with increasing difficulties in securing control over the local soviets, the peasants often relied heavily on the more traditional rural institutions of self-government—village assemblies. The following document, a formal complaint against the Bolshevik government lodged by a village assembly in Penza province, suggests that peasants could possess a sophisticated understanding of legality, of the nature of representative government, and of their rights. It also shows that flimsy political arguments were unlikely to impress such rural dwellers.

[. . .] 1. How should we view the local Soviet authorities in the village of Mertovshchiny, who were elected by the Communist[47] cell without the consensus of the whole community? Are they lawful?

Response to the first question: The authorities established in the village of Mertovshchiny, who were selected solely by the Communist cell, should be viewed as unlawfully established, since the electoral commission, consisting of ten people, was chosen by them from among themselves, without the knowledge of the citizens of the village of Mertovshchiny. Thus the Communist cell proclaimed to the whole assembly that it was their business alone to choose the local authorities, and that's what they did.

2. Did this overly small cell consisting of eight people possess the legal right, having gathered the community into our local school building, to deprive us of the right to vote, solely on their own judgment and not with the

---

47. When the Bolsheviks added "Communist" to the name of their party, in early March 1918, to emphasize their commitment to a global communist revolution, many peasants came to believe that the relatively benign Bolsheviks were in fact superceded by the hostile and corrupt Communists.

~~consent of the~~ general assembly of citizens, as occurred in the elections of the present village authorities?

3. Did that cell have the right to threaten with execution those who failed to join it?

To the second and third questions: The Communist cell had no legal right whatsoever to deprive citizens of the right to vote solely on their own judgment and even less so to expel them from the building. Concerning the third question, even more so, it did not have the right to threaten with execution those who did not sympathize with it for any reasons. This outrageous act, which denigrates the Soviet power of people's commissars, shall be reported to the Gorodishchenskii district Soviet.

4. Did the local authorities chaired by [illegible] have a legal basis for hiding from the community the decrees of the Council of People's Commissars and especially the letter by Comrade Trotsky to middle peasants, which was published in a February 1919 issue of *Izvestiia vserossiiskogo VTsIK*?[48] That letter states in bold type that the Soviet power has not and will not violently force middle peasants to adopt the Communist system of agricultural production.

To the fourth question: The decrees of the Council of People's Commissars can under no circumstances be kept secret from the community, and the community would have been very thankful had the local Soviet made them public. Had the local Soviet made them public in time, and in particular, the letter by Comrade Trotsky to the middle peasants, then the conflagration, which took place on February 16 of this year, would absolutely never have occurred.

5. Did our local authorities under the direction of K. Lapshov have the right to destroy two breeding bulls without the knowledge of the community? Or to sell some of the beef (56 pounds) to the family of a member of the Gorodishchenskii district food office, Ivan Nikolaevich Evstifeev?

To the fifth question: The Soviet had no right whatsoever to destroy breeding stock, especially without the knowledge of the community. [. . .]

Footnote to the first response: The electoral commission comprised only Communists, of whom there are eight in the village of Mertovshchiny. This commission decided to hold new elections to the soviet and to allow every ten people to elect one voting delegate. Since the village of Mertovshchiny has a little over 1,200 souls, no fewer than 120 people should have become voting members. In reality, no more than 30–35 did. The discrepancy of 85–90 people was not recognized by anyone, which we consider illegal.

Chairman of the [Village] Assembly Sinichkin
Secretary I. Pilin.

---

48. *Izvestiia* of the All-Russian Central Executive Committee of Soviets (VTsIK) was the major official state newspaper.

122. A Bolshevik Official Demands Peasant Surrender, Simbirsk Province, March 1919   [16, pp. 127–8]

Peasant violence and rebellion first grew widespread during the summer of 1918 in response to Bolshevik grain-requisitioning policies. Simbirsk (later Ulianovsk) province, which is situated 400 miles east-southeast of Moscow, had a largely agricultural economy based on trade in grain, fish, cattle, and timber. In 1919 several peasant rebellions spontaneously broke out in the province, but were brutally suppressed by Bolshevik forces. One such rebellion took place near Sengilei, which was a district capital of Simbirsk province and an important center for grain distribution and flour milling, located on the right bank of the Volga River. The following conversation between Bolshevik official Vareikis and the rebels sheds light on the rebels' grievances, as well as on Bolshevik tactics in dealing with them.

Telegraph operator: This is Sengilei. For military reasons, clear the Simbirsk telegraph line.

Vareikis: This is Simbirsk: Iosif Vareikis, Committee of the Bolshevik Party, deputy chair of the provincial Executive Committee. Who is speaking?

Poruchikov: I am Poruchikov, chair of the township Soviet. What do you want?

Vareikis: First, give me an immediate response about the condition of your township and its mood; second, respond immediately about the number of the rebelling kulaks and deserters; third, be aware that I was sent specifically to investigate the culprits involved in this counterrevolutionary rebellion. Since an investigation can be conducted only on the basis of concrete evidence, I demand that you gather material and depart in two hours in order to report in person in Sengilei. That is all.

Poruchikov: We do not have, and never have had, any kulak rebellions. There are no counterrevolutionaries. [We] oppose the improper requisitions of grain and cattle. We hail the Bolshevik party and do not act against it. We are acting against the violence of the Communists. But there is no counterrevolution; we reject the incorrect requisition of grain and cattle. There is no kulak rebellion. All our peasants are laborers. The number of the rebels? Every village and all rural areas. We would like you to come to us yourself in order to see who exactly has risen up. The people want you to come here yourself, because the people do not want to send delegates. They are asking you yourself to come here. Comrade Vareikis, we are not saboteurs. We would like to speak with you, you will see for yourself that we are right, and the people will listen to you gladly. Please tell us right away if you are coming or not.

Vareikis; I am inviting. Are you there?

Poruchikov: I am listening.

Vareikis: I will not be coming for a while, because, first, the appropriate speakers must be sent: the artillery. Second, of course I will be there; otherwise I would not have come to Sengilei. Third, it is a mistake to trifle with us; you leave us no choice but to resort to military force. The counterrevolutionary mutiny, in which you, Poruchikov, are apparently taking part, gives us cause in the near future to root out all the bad apples. Our party and the provincial executive committee, which relies on the working peasant masses, must ensure their security. I am warning you that if you do not take all steps to liquidate [the rebellion] and do so immediately, then upon my arrival in your village you will. (*Poruchikov interrupts Vareikis.*)

Poruchikov: Comrade Vareikis. We are asking you not to say such things. Instead, tell us you will come and learn for yourself who is to blame. I, Poruchikov, cannot say anything myself. We are asking you to come. The peasants do not intend to harm you.

Vareikis: The same goes for me: I do not talk about such things: I do them. I will come on the condition that you lay down your arms.

Poruchikov: Comrade Vareikis, our assembly would like to meet with you in order to talk everything over, and then perhaps [the conflict] will be settled. We give you our word, comrade, that you will be safe. If you come alone, it will be better than the artillery. That would only anger the people. If you wish, come here and we will talk about everything.

Vareikis: I do not need your guarantees, since even without them no peasant comrades will lay a finger on me; that is quite clear. Second, what is better: artillery or me? For me, of course, artillery is better, and for you I am better. I am telling you that if you take steps forward and settle down, then I will do everything in my power to avoid bloody consequences. Tell this to the peasants. That's all.

Poruchikov: If you send the artillery, it will be in vain, because we do not fear it, but if you want to avoid bloodshed and want to go hand in hand with us peasants, then come yourself, if you are really just. Is that clear? I have finished.

Vareikis: I am through with negotiating, and I have understood from your words that action is needed.

Poruchikov: So you are not coming? That's too bad, because we are waiting for you to shed light on us. Come, Comrade Vareikis, and everything will be settled. We will express what is in our hearts and you will understand us.

123. Report on Bolshevik "Cossack Policy" in the Don Region, July 1919 [41, pp. 107–9]

The Don region, often referred to simply as "the Don," with its capital in Ros-
tov-on-the-Don and crisscrossed by the Don River, was an affluent grain-pro-
ducing area south of Moscow and north of the Caucasus Mountains populated
largely by the Cossacks. The Soviet Republic of the Don was proclaimed in
March 1918. As resistance to Soviet policies grew, in January 1919 the Polit-
buro decided "to carry out mass terror against the rich Cossacks, slaughtering
them all; to conduct merciless mass terror against all Cossacks who have dis-
played direct or indirect participation in the struggle against Soviet power."
The purpose of this policy, it seems, was to eliminate those Cossacks capable of
organizing resistance to the Bolshevik government. Using a typical colonizer's
method, the government also encouraged the migration of poor Russian peas-
ants to the Don region. By March 1919, Soviet military forces, which had oc-
cupied three-quarters of the Don region, launched a campaign of repression,
resulting in several thousands of dead. In response, the Cossacks themselves re-
belled and counterattacked, receiving support from Denikin's Volunteer Army.
In June, the Don Cossacks joined Denikin's final offensive against Moscow.[49]
At this point, the author of the following document, I. Reingol'd, a member of
the Bolshevik Don Regional Revolutionary Committee, urged the Bolshevik
leadership to adopt a more nuanced approach to subjugating the Cossacks.

The difficult condition of our Southern Front is an inevitable consequence
of the shortsighted policy which has been implemented in the Don [region]
in regard to the Cossacks.

It has to be noted, above all, that in general our Cossack policy since the
October Days has been distinguished by a lack of steadiness and consistency.
First we flirted with the Cossacks, giving them autonomy and an elected Soviet. We even agreed to establish the Republic of the Don, created a Cossack
military operational district, and issued a decree allocating benefits to the
Cossacks. Later, because of the successful offensive of the Red Army into
Rostov and Novocherkassk, our heads grew dizzy with success, and, having
deemed ourselves the victors, we threw down a challenge to the Cossacks,
by commencing their physical extermination. This was called de-Cossackization. We were hoping thus to renovate the Don, to make it, if not Soviet,
then [at least] submissive and obedient to the Soviet government. This was
done at a time when we were far from in control of the Don, when not a single Soviet organ on the Don had real power, when there were no garrisons

---

49. This offensive was halted only at Orel, 200 miles south of Moscow, in October.

ruffi*ri*.*.d)* *юong* tô feel capable of coping with the Cossacks and of suppressing the massive ferment and harsh resistance that the freedom-loving Cossacks would inevitably counterpose to the policy of de-Cossackization.

There can be no argument that our fundamental view of the Cossacks as an element alien to Communism and to Soviet ideology is correct.

The Cossacks, at least a huge segment of them, will sooner or later have to be exterminated, simply eliminated physically, but enormously careful tactics, the greatest caution, and every manner of diplomatic maneuvers with the Cossacks are needed here. Not for a minute should we forget that we are dealing with a warlike people, whose every village is a fortified camp and every household a fortress. The policy of their massive, indiscriminate extermination will make it impossible for us to win control over the Don, or at best only as the result of a long, bloody, and protracted struggle. [. . .]

The Central Committee and our party have always shown the greatest caution and sensitivity on the nationalities issue and in dealing with ethnic minorities, sometimes even excessively so. We have created a number of ethnically based republics, for foreign policy reasons, as well as in pursuit of domestic goals: to achieve the fastest possible elimination from the Soviet system of every manner of ethnic prejudice and misconception. Yet, for whatever reasons, we have not applied this approach consistently in regard to the Cossacks, despite the fact that it is precisely in their way of life and historical development that one finds the roots of their independence, separateness, and autonomous institutional existence. One cannot fight against such deeply held values and a caste-like separateness only by means of extermination. A whole system of measures has to be designed both to secure us against armed uprisings and attempts by the counterrevolutionary rabble to stir up the Cossacks and to allow us to destroy the entire old Cossack way of life with the hands of the Cossacks themselves. One cannot talk of poor Cossacks, since the Cossacks are almost entirely well-off and consist of kulaks and middle peasants. [. . .] The northern Cossacks have relatively small farms, while those of the southern Cossacks are very large. Therefore, it would be possible to develop an agricultural policy aimed at fostering disintegration in the Don Cossack milieu by dividing it into two mutually hostile camps.

Secondly, a lot can be achieved through agitation and educational work, especially among young Cossacks, with their much better attitude toward Soviet power than the old people, who are the most inert and counterrevolutionary element.

Finally, it is necessary in a timely fashion to issue an appeal to the Cossacks on behalf of the Council of People's Commissars or the Central Committee affirming earlier decrees proclaiming the autonomy of the Don or perhaps even its independence. It is also necessary in a timely fashion, the next time our forces enter the Don, to establish a Soviet Don Government composed of so-called Soviet Cossacks and people born there. Such an act would be of enormous significance, since it would make it impossible to complain about the influence of outsiders lacking ties to the Cossacks, which the revolutionary committees in point of fact were. [. . .]

Only under the formal banner of the Soviet Don Government should we implement red terror against the Cossack counterrevolution in the Don, by force of arms and words and agricultural-resettlement policies. Combining all these elements, we would achieve the "sovietization" of the Don much faster and with much less loss of life.

Member of the Don Revolutionary Committee, I. Reingol'd

124. An Appeal by the Altai Federation of Anarchists, Spring 1920 [5, p. 115]

Many anarchists initially supported the Bolsheviks before and after October and benefited from the new regime, seizing mansions, presses, and other property. But in early 1918 most adopted various positions of opposition or resistance. In April and May, government forces implemented repressive measures, killing dozens of anarchists and arresting hundreds more. They also seized or closed their publishing operations. Thenceforth, the anarchist movement splintered into several groups (like the Makhnovites in Document 117), which were active on all sides of the Civil War. The movement came to include peasant rebels, local warlords, and even regular criminals who claimed to be anarchists, but had a very limited understanding of anarchist doctrine.

COMRADE PEASANTS AND WORKERS.

The enemies of the revolution are falsely telling you that the Whites are approaching from the taiga and that they want to enslave you, but it is a lie. There are no Whites in the taiga, they all already turned red and sit in the cities in legislative institutions and issue harsh laws for you. It is your own brothers who are in the taiga, peasants and workers who have been persecuted equally by Nicholas, Kerensky, Kolchak, and the Soviet power that calls itself people's power. The power that calls itself that of the people strikes deals with the bourgeoisie and oppresses workers and peasants. That's why we workers and peasants have risen—openly risen against lies and injustice. We have risen for liberation and we cannot oppress peasants or workers; we cannot exploit. We are fighting for a complete liberation, for shaking off the bondage of the working masses, for self-government of the people them-selves in the localities. And since this is impossible under any power, we call upon you, peasant comrades to rise openly against any power with arms in your hands. Give not a single son to serve in the army, not a single pound of bread to spongers, but take arms and chase away all Commissar-Order-Givers. Take all the riches of nature in your own hands and build your life without nurses and mommy Commissars—these parasites, and scream out loud: "DOWN WITH ANY KIND OF POWER, WHATEVER IT IS, LONG LIVE ANARCHY—MOTHER OF ORDER"

125. Complaint of Dire Straits by Peasants in the Omsk Region, February 1921   [67, vol. 2, p. 211]

Throughout the Civil War, hundreds of peasant revolts broke out. Peasants of-ten fought against both Whites and Reds, though most feared the former more than the latter. When the Whites were defeated by mid- to late 1920, many more peasants, who were now in a desperate economic state, rebelled all across Russia, from western Siberia to the regions south of Moscow, seeking to drive out the Communist authorities. Their main desire was to be left alone. The following document, sent on February 17, 1921, to the chairman of the Siberian Revolutionary Committee, reflects this desire. It is written in a semi-literate and naive but very expressive, heartfelt, touching, and even powerful peasant language.

The present report is being submitted in order to elucidate public opinion in regard to current state policy. We are responding to the call of the Chair-man of the [Siberian] Revolutionary Committee as the sons of Great Russia who wish her well and wish her peace. Although we truly do see achievements, we also note deficiencies in the way she is governed. In this regard, we see quite clearly that neighboring villages (but not us) launched a rebellion because of the difficulties of existence under the current conditions of life.

1) The government's failure to carry out its own orders and words. Con-sequently, we were left not only without seeds but also without a crust of bread.

2) That the human being has ceased to be a person and has become like agricultural tools.

3) The peasant, reduced to guarding his land and foreseeing its inevitable perdition from the present conditions, becomes mentally deranged and therefore loses his balanced view of the state authorities.

This is just our worm's eye view, but it is deeply rooted in experience. We, as laborers of peaceful toiling life, desire to work, yet being unable, due to the problems of the moment, we become profoundly distressed. This is our truly sincere confession to the one who is stretching out his hand to us for the purpose of eliminating our discord.

To this we sign our names, as the Mokshino village Soviet certifies.

Chairman Bobykin
Secretary [illegible]

126. Demand That Peasant Rebels in Western Siberia Surrender, February 1921   [67, vol. 2, pp. 256–7]

The Bolsheviks, advancing on the former Kolchak strongholds, sought to capitalize on the hardships and abuses endured by the peasants under his rule. As the Red Army commander's appeal below indicates, they presented rebelling peasants with a simple choice: it is either us or Kolchak.

Comrades! We are speaking to all conscious[50] peasants and working Cossacks! We want to say a few words to you, who have been deceived, thrown into mutiny and instability, and disoriented by the Civil War. Preposterous and absurd rumors are being spread among you about seizures of power in Omsk, Cheliabinsk, and Ekaterinburg. You are being told about the fall of Soviet power, while the strength and tactical situation of the rebel movement are being misrepresented. They are making you believe all these untruths, making you fear us the way little children are afraid of a wood-goblin or a kikimora.[51] And who is doing all this? Look around and think carefully! It is none other than the hypocrite-kulaks who place their personal interests above the needs of the people and the state. It is the former officer-Kolchakites who have escaped from concentration camps and hate the Soviet power bitterly. And you know very well what Kolchakism is: for one and a half years you had to endure its tender mercies. You yourselves cast off the fetters and chains of the bourgeoisie. Do you really want to return to what you yourselves just destroyed? Do you really want again the power of the

---

50. Marxists use the term *conscious* to refer to the state in which people can see the true nature of exploitative capitalist economic relations and thereby allows them to perceive the necessity of struggling against them.

51. A malevolent spirit of Russian fairy tales said to dwell in and around people's homes.

priests[52] and the golden epaulettes [of former officers], because the priests give you orders as heads of the general headquarters and some Cossack rebel units wear golden epaulettes. Or perhaps you don't know this?

Spring is near, it is going to be warm soon, and sowing time will come. You need to begin peaceful agricultural toil, but your dwellings are destroyed; your fathers, brothers, and sons are killed or maimed or are hiding like wild beasts deep in the forest among the snow drifts, perishing from cold. It should be clear to everyone that fighting against us is futile and pointless, foolish and criminal. Presently the working masses of the whole world are stretching their arms to Soviet Russia. They await assistance from us, wishing themselves to bring low the power of the landlords and capital. World capital is defending its last positions, is still trying to strangle Russia, frequently taking advantage of your ignorance and lack of consciousness. Their tools everywhere are former tsarist stooges, priests, officers, and kulaks. And so you are involuntarily helping them, disrupting our rear, and forcing us to spill blood, which is often completely innocent, and to use brute force.

Comrades! It is in your power to stop all these horrors and to begin peaceful and creative work. Drop your weapons and surrender those inciting you before it is too late. Soviet power and the Communist Party know how to forgive and forget mistakes and failures, but it punishes severely and mercilessly all those who rise against it! Thus, before it is too late, return to your senses and rejoin the families you have abandoned and the farms you have left behind.

Commander of the defense group of the Petropavlovsk region,[53] N. I. Koritskii

Chief of Headquarters and Military Commissar, S. D. Lobanov-Volodarskii

52. The relations between priests and ordinary people in Russia were often strained. While most ordinary people were quite religious and observed the major church feasts and took the sacraments according to established practice, they sometimes held their priests in contempt for being poorly trained and venal. Communist propaganda played on these tensions by linking priests with Imperial Russian officers and big landowners.

53. Petropavlovsk is the capital of the Northern-Kazakhstan region, roughly 150 miles west of Omsk in western Siberia and 300 miles east of Cheliabinsk in the Ural Mountains.

127. Petition from 300 Tambov Hostages to the
All-Russian Cheka, November 25, 1921[54]   [45, pp. 294–5]

Already in November 1917, Trotsky advocated taking hostages among military cadets and shooting five of them "for every worker and every soldier" killed. In August 1918, Lenin mentioned designating hostages within population groups who would "answer with their lives" for any failure to deliver surplus grain to the state. With the launching of the Red Terror in September 1918, seizing hostages from the population became a systematic government policy. Then, in summer 1918, Bolshevik officials proposed setting up concentration camps to isolate "sinister agitators, counterrevolutionary officers, saboteurs, parasites, and speculators." Decrees issued in April and May 1919 by the All-Russian Central Executive Committee of Soviets called for creating a network of forced-labor camps to intern all sorts of dangerous persons, either as individuals or as categories. Each of the roughly thirty-eight provincial capital cities was henceforth required to build a camp able to confine 300 prisoners; the district capitals were authorized but not required to construct camps. All the camps were expected by law to exploit convict labor in order to cover their operating expenses. There were eighty-four concentration camps with some 50,000 inmates functioning in Soviet Russia by late 1920. The letter below was written by inmates of one such camp.

We, peasants of Kirsanovskii, Tambovskii, and Kozlovskii districts, were arrested in June this year.[55] It has been six months now that we, old people, pregnant women, and little children, are kept in unusually harsh conditions: we are starving and ill, and there have already been numerous fatalities among both the children and the adults. Being ignorant and uneducated we have no understanding whatsoever of why we were arrested. We also do not understand why those members of our families and other families who are healthier are at liberty, while we, sick old people, children, and their mothers, remain in the camps. Now the cold weather has come, and we have neither

---

54. At the time of the writing of the following petition, written on behalf of 300 hostages in the Kozhukhovskii concentration camp, an order had been issued freeing all hostages from Tambov in principle; though in practice they were to be held until December 15 at the latest.

55. The Tambov rebellion began in August 1920 when one village refused to hand over its grain to Bolshevik officials and killed several of them. The rebellion spread to other villages and in September found a charismatic leader in Aleksandr Antonov (1888–1922), a Left Socialist-Revolutionary who broke with the Bolsheviks in summer 1918 because of their confiscation of peasant grain. A brilliant organizer and tactician, Antonov built up a broadly based partisan movement that nearly overwhelmed the government authorities.

clothing nor shoes, since we were not allowed to take anything with us when we were arrested. Also, to be quite candid, we thought our detention would not be long at all, yet it turned out otherwise, and the causes for that are still not clarified to us. What is our guilt, why we were seized: as hostages? Because of the onslaught of Antonov's gangs or as scapegoats for the guilt of others? We really cannot understand any of this. We, as ever-toiling people, should have intensified our work toiling the land and in doing so provided substantial assistance in these hungry times for our worker-peasant power. But to our great regret, we cannot do so. They have turned us, true toilers of the land, into parasites, forced to remain without any use or guilt in the camps, which would seem impermissible, since we should be taking the most active part in the building of a new bright life for us, the laboring people, thus providing our posterity with an easier, joyful life.

Therefore, on the basis of the above, we strongly ask that you pay attention to our request: to speed up the consideration of our case and release us, to send us home. We are hoping for JUSTICE and MERCY from our worker-peasant power. We will be released, we will not be subjected to all the terrors of a cold and hungry life, and through our liberation we will be made into sincere helpers of the poor and the oppressed. [. . .]

THE BIRTH OF NEW NATIONS

128. The Turkestan Liberation Movement, 1917
[13, pp. 12, 14–5, 40–1]

*Born to an aristocratic Kazakh family in present-day Uzbekistan, Mustafa
Chokaev (1890–1941) graduated in law with distinction from the University
of St. Petersburg and spoke many languages. Immediately after the fall of
the Romanov dynasty, he took an active role in various Muslim movements,
political organizations, and short-lived governments in Central Asia and the
Caucasus region. Notably, he served as prime minister in the Provisional Government of Autonomous Turkestan, which existed from November 1917 to
February 1918, when Bolshevik forces crushed it. In 1920 he emigrated to
Turkey and then Western Europe where he was recognized as the leader of the
Muslim emigration from the Russian Empire. His purpose in writing his remi-
niscences, apparently in 1937 when they were first published in Turkish, was
"to show Turkestanis the difficulties we went through in those days" so that they
could "go forward with the hope of fulfilling our goal—the national independence of Turkestan." This name referred to a region of Central Asia, stretching
from Mongolia to the Caspian Sea, most of whose inhabitants spoke various
Turkic languages.*

We did not discuss Turkestan's autonomy at our congresses. But in the
depths of our national and regional committees it was the most frequent
topic of our conversations. We viewed autonomy this way: Turkestan should
have its own legislative body and an autonomous government. The central
all-Russian "federal" authority should be in charge of foreign policy, state finance, railroads, and the military. The local autonomous government should
exercise control over schools, local railroad construction, town and provincial institutions of self-government, the land issue—*we particularly emphasized this,* and the judiciary. We also wanted to introduce some substantial
reforms into the area of the formation of the army, namely, we envisioned
the creation of a *"territorial army,"* i.e., for Turkestanis to perform military
service in Turkestan, while remaining under a unified all-Russian command.
That was, of course, only principles, only a sketch. We did not go farther
into the details. Our main concern was the question of *Turkestani personnel.*
One can proclaim any principles, wish for anything at all, even for the moon

in the sky. Yet if adequate personnel are lacking, if there are no technical experts, no human resources, then all of these beautiful wishes will remain empty words, capable only of provoking the derision of enemies and misleading friends and the popular masses, on whose behalf and for whose good these principles are proposed and these beautiful slogans are proclaimed. I will not say that we did not have any such human resources, but they were extremely insufficient. [. . .]

I would like briefly to recount the last episode of our struggle. Kokand was already under fire. Machine guns and rifles were crackling. Hand grenades were exploding. Once in a while cannons boomed! The Bolsheviks sent us their first "parliamentarians" with the proposal to hand me over to the Kokand military revolutionary committee.[56] I received them in the presence of all the available members of the government. Without waiting for the opinion of my comrades, I responded that I was ready to surrender myself to the military revolutionary committee on the condition that the Bolsheviks immediately cease shelling the city and pledge not to apply repressive measures toward civilians. The Bolshevik parliamentarians left and returned only two days later. By that time Kokand was besieged from all sides. Bolshevik troops were arriving from Samarkand, Tashkent, and Fergana. Our people were also arriving, but they were armed with long iron-tipped pikes, sickles, axes, pitchforks, big knives, and, in the best cases, hunting rifles. Their most potent weapon was their hatred of the Bolsheviks. None could doubt the outcome of this struggle. I remember as if it were yesterday how at 11:20 a.m. new Bolshevik parliamentarians arrived with a new ultimatum. Now the Bolsheviks demanded: (1) the autonomous government's recognition of the Soviet government; (2) its issuing of an appeal to the population of Turkestan to obey the Soviet government; (3) disarming the population and handing over all of its weapons to the Bolsheviks; (4) disbanding the militia. And so forth. There were four members of the government present. [. . .] Our response was brief: we refused to accept the ultimatum. On behalf of my comrades I told the Bolshevik parliamentarians: "Strength is on your side. Except for our conviction that justice is on our side, we have none. We do not doubt that you will defeat us, but recognizing your right to rule, recognizing the Soviet government of Turkestan is something we cannot do!" [. . .]

---

56. The military revolutionary committees that Chokaev mentions were set up by the Bolshevik leadership on an ad hoc basis and endowed with almost complete autonomy and power to coordinate the seizure of power, to establish political organization, and to bring the October Revolution to every corner of the country. From late October 1917 to March 1918, the Bolshevik leadership created over 220 local military revolutionary committees. In many cases they were used to disband and reconstitute local soviets whenever elections returned non-Bolshevik majorities.

The Bolsheviks celebrated their victory. [. . .] Mass arrests and killings took place across Turkestan. [. . .]

At its only session [January 5, 1918], the Constituent Assembly had passed a law proclaiming Russia a federal republic, and on the morning of January 6 it was forcibly dissolved by the Bolsheviks.

The Constituent Assembly, the focal point of all the hopes of the people of Russia, perished, one must suppose, forever. Together with it our "federalist dreams" expired forever. We have entered the path of struggle for complete national liberation, for a free independent Turkestan, for the creation of a united TURKESTANI TURKIC STATE.

Long live free independent Turkestan!

129. Georgian and British Officials in Transcaucasia, September 1919   [62, pp. 165–8]

The Menshevik-dominated Democratic Republic of Georgia was established in May 1918 with its capital in Tbilisi, after the fall of the Transcaucasian Federation. The socialist government distributed most of the land to the peasantry and nationalized large-scale industry. The conversation below, between a worried Georgian government leader and a British official, took place shortly after British military forces left the region in August 1919, leaving the region vulnerable to a Soviet attack. The Georgians had good reason to be worried about their independence. In April 1920, Soviet military forces conquered Azerbaijan. The Polish-Soviet War, which broke out in the same month, stalled the Soviet offensive against Georgia, which resumed in December and was completed in March 1921 with the incorporation of Georgia into Soviet Russia.

E. P. Gegechkori.[57] I believe one of my main tasks is to inform you accurately about everything that has happened in Georgia recently. [. . .] To our sincere regret, the government of Georgia, in spite of every effort, has not yet been able to establish satisfactory contacts with the British military representatives in Transcaucasia. Having considering this fact carefully, I believe that the main reason for this phenomenon is the hostile information relayed by British military representatives. The most convincing argument against Georgia was the presence of German troops in the country, which created a sense of duplicity on our part. When at last, after many efforts, we dispelled these

---

57. Evgenii Gegechkori (1881–1954), a longtime Menshevik and deputy to the Third State Duma, was foreign minister of the independent Georgian government throughout its existence.

impressions, the [British] military commander would leave and be replaced by new ones, and our government had to repeat the same effort. [. . .] In general, the hostile information had its effect, and your generals upon returning to England undoubtedly spoke negatively about our country.

Sir Wardrop.[58] I must say that I met General Thompson before leaving England and based on my conversation with him came to the conclusion that he has very warm feelings for Georgia and for Transcaucasia in general.

E. P. Gegechkori. Nevertheless, I believe it may well have done so. Anyway, facts are facts, and we never had the opportunity to discuss with them the substance of the matter. All our efforts in that regard ran into a stereotypical response by the English generals: "We are merely soldiers. Politics is not our business. Our task is to preserve order." This resulted from their lack of authority to conduct political negotiations of any kind. That was the situation before you arrived. Now, I would like to present to you the position of my government: we understand perfectly that without a powerful ally it will be difficult for Georgia to secure the recognition of its independence, because even the relatively large states of Europe, which are more secure financially, cannot exist at the present moment without outside support. The government of Georgia is aware that it must rely on a strong state, and this awareness has dictated to us a particular orientation toward England. Of course, we know that such assistance on the part of the United Kingdom must be requited by us in one way or another. Regrettably, until now we have not received an answer to this question, which is so important to us. To sum up all I have said: under the current circumstances, Georgia cannot make it through the crucible of tribulations alone. It asks for assistance from England and would like to know what England would want in exchange. What I have expressed is the fruit of deliberations of the government, which experienced no disagreements on this issue. The current situation is being complicated by the departure of the British armed forces from Transcaucasia. This fact has preoccupied public opinion in Georgia. [. . .] we have officially asked the Peace Conference, London, and the British Command in Transcaucasia to leave at least some British troops here. We were promised a reply but as yet have not received one. [. . .]

I am now moving to the issue of finances. You know about our situation; we are still relying on our own resources. Unless we are able to establish commercial relations and unless we receive food assistance, our financial position has grown so unsound that, if aid is not immediately forthcoming,

58. Sir John Oliver Wardrop (1864–1948), who had spent considerable time in Georgia before the Revolution and studied the Georgian language, was the United Kingdom's first chief commissioner of Transcaucasia in Georgia.

then any help at all may become fruitless. We have been unable to establish trade relations with England, either because she was uninterested or has been overly preoccupied with more difficult issues. [. . .] The government of Georgia firmly believes that it will find points of common interest and a common language with England. Georgia as a pathway to Inner Asia must be of interest to Great Britain, and the latter will undoubtedly stretch out the hand of assistance to the Georgian people, which has carried the torch of culture and civilization thought many centuries. You know the history of our people so thoroughly that I find it unnecessary to point out these facts to you.

Sir Wardrop. I have not received definite instructions from my government, but I will immediately report to London all you have said and then will answer each question exhaustively. [. . .]

130. Kalmyks at the First Congress of the Peoples of the East in Baku, 1920 [25, pp. 35–7]

The Kalmyks are a Mongolian people who live on European Russia's southeastern frontier and are adherents of Tibetan Buddhism, the only such people in all of Europe. After the fall of the Tsar, the Steppe Region of the Kalmyk People was proclaimed. It became known as the Kalmyk Autonomous Region in 1920.

The First Congress of the Peoples of the East met in Baku, Azerbaijan, on September 1–7, 1920. There the Kalmyk delegation presented the following statement. The Bolsheviks organized the congress as a means to win support and promote revolution in the developing world and, apparently, in order to pressure England into making trade concessions. Many delegates at the congress repudiated "great Russian chauvinism." The Kalmyks' statement describes how local Russian colonist populations living in the former empire's periphery sometimes acted without regard for the interests of the indigenous peoples and in these actions could even receive support from local Bolshevik officials, if they presented them in terms of class struggle, of fighting "counterrevolution," or of hostility to religion.

[. . .] The February Revolution not only failed to improve, but indeed worsened the disenfranchised condition of the Kalmyks. Seizures and abuses that occurred under the tsarist regime under the guise of "legality" turn into undisguised plunder. The peasant colonists who previously had felt somewhat accountable to the law became completely unhinged in the days of the revolution. [. . .]

In such difficult times for the Kalmyks the October Revolution occurred and completely untied the hands of peasant invaders giving full room to their predatory instincts. The Kalmyk people experienced unbearable torment and a terrible drama. In the name of the October Revolution, the peasant kulaks took lands from the Kalmyks, grabbed their cattle, confiscated their property and money, and defiled the wedding bed by assaulting before their eyes the Kalmyks' wives, sisters, mothers, and daughters. They also defiled the holiest of the holies—the Buddhist religion—by destroying and attacking temples, ripping up sacred books, and shredding woven sacred images and using them for foot wraps. All of this was done under the banner of a struggle against counterrevolution by quasi-Communists from among local colonists and former tsarist officials. [. . .]

While the retreating units of the 11th and the 12th armies were passing through the Kalmyk steppes, they committed the same horrible acts of violence; plundering; seizures of horses, cattle, property, and money; and again the raping of women. [. . .] The slogan of the destruction of the old world was understood literally: all the tokens of prosperity built up during the prerevolutionary period were obliterated. [. . .]

The Astrakhan[59] provincial authority initially not only disregarded the Kalmyk Executive Committee, but in its blindness viewed peasant actions against the Kalmyks as a genuinely revolutionary movement of the poor.

[. . .] [T]he working Kalmyk people [. . .] nevertheless turned out to be fully capable of success and has firmly stood upon the path of new socialist construction.

For the successful and painless fulfillment of the promise of this endeavor, four things are necessary: first, the immediate granting of regional autonomy to the working Kalmyk people (attached is "The Declaration of the Rights of the Kalmyk People" adopted by the first All-Kalmyk Congress of Soviets); second, the central authorities' confidence in Kalmyk party and administrative institutions and their functioning under close Party supervision (but not tutelage) and with full cultural and material support; third, the absolute elimination of interference by the Astrakhan provincial authorities and the local Russian population; and fourth, the unequivocal implementation of the decrees on land tenure of the Kalmyk people and on the restoration and protection of Kalmyk cattle-breeding (copies attached).

Member of the Congress of the Peoples of the East
A. Amun Sanon

59. A city located near the mouth of the Volga River where it empties into the Caspian Sea, Astrakhan's population was 113,001 in 1897.

THE KRONSTADT REBELLION

131. Worker Unrest in Petrograd, March 4, 1921
[12, pp. 255–62]

By late 1920, the Polish-Soviet War and the Russian Civil War were over; the Bolsheviks were now firmly in power. With economic conditions dramatically worsening, many social groups hostile to government policies began to express their anger, disappointment, and opposition. Among these were industrial workers in Petrograd and sailors of the Baltic Fleet, especially those stationed at the fortress of Kronstadt. Beginning on February 28, strikes broke out in many factories in Petrograd. The crisis for the Bolsheviks' worker-oriented government was immense. Senior officials quickly provided necessary articles, such as warm clothing and boots, to workers in Petrograd but also, as the following document shows, tried to link the protesters with counterrevolutionary forces.

Minutes from a session of the Petrograd Soviet, March 4, 1921

Zinoviev [. . .] It is painful to admit, but I must say bluntly that the Baltic Plant[60] is a White Guard plant; it is an old Menshevik citadel. (*Voices: a disgrace.*) We have known this plant since 1905. Some old Petrograd workers have known it even longer—it has always been a fortress of Menshevism. A couple of months ago Comrade [Nikolai] Uglanov was there at a rally and he saw an old man speechifying. He recognized him as an old general. He went to the chairman and asked how this was possible. It turned out that this old general, who had formerly been a manager of the plant or a deputy manager, had now wormed his way into a draftsman's job, has become a supporter of democracy, etc. Quite a few such characters have wormed their way into the plant. To our shame such plants exist. We have shown them the greatest possible tolerance, because we understood that the situation was extremely difficult. [. . .] We must put an end to a situation when former generals are speechifying in our factories, when it is clear, like two plus two is four, that General A. N. Kozlovskii[61] was calling the shots in Kronstadt and that workers

60. Founded in 1856 in the southwest corner of Vasiliev Island in St. Petersburg, the Baltic Shipyard and Machine-Building Plant had built over ninety ships by 1917, including many of the country's mightiest naval vessels.

61. A former tsarist general, A. N. Kozlovskii served, but did not lead, the insurgents.

continue clocking off and engaging in "work-slowdowns." The Petrograd Soviet must adopt an iron-clad decision and at last put an end to all this. The Soviet Republic is now experiencing its most trying times. We do not deny this for a minute. Why the most trying? Because the longer the war lasted, the more difficult the situation became. It is clear that every extra month of war automatically meant an extra year of suffering for the people. Everybody understands that. [. . .] But we cannot permit ourselves the frivolity of surrendering Petrograd or any other city to the White Guards. We must conceive of some other way, wrack our brains, learn from the Kronstadt example. Misfortune helped, where fortune could not [Russian proverb]. From this example every non-party citizen will realize that to continue this game further will only help the White Guards to take advantage of the difficult moment and then Russia would be completely lost and the working class completely physically exterminated, because, comrades, they will not be asking who is a party member and who is not. Had the Whites been able to come here, under the banner of the SRs, who among you can doubt that hundreds and thousands of sailors would be hanging by the neck, while thousands and tens of thousands of workers of Piter would be exterminated, the way the Finnish bourgeoisie exterminated its workers. It is time to stop joking around. [. . .]

Iakovlev (from the Baltic Plant): The Baltic Plant elected me, and I have been working at the Baltic Plant for two years. It is claimed that the Baltic Plant is a White Guard plant and that a general is an agitator there. We do have a former naval captain, who was elected to the Petrograd Soviet. He works as a clerk and has not conducted any agitation. The workers remain revolutionary workers. The Baltic Plant is currently engaged in a work-stoppage but would like to return to work. [. . .] [T]he workers of the Baltic Plant request the release of non-party workers who have been arrested. In all, twenty-two were arrested, of whom two are Mensheviks, but regardless of that we asked for the release of all twenty-two. [. . .] We were told that after they are interviewed, they will be released. The workers refuse to return to work until those who were arrested are released; they will not recommence their work before that. Now they are gradually beginning to release the prisoners, but today again two people were arrested at the Baltic Plant. Because of that, the workers cannot settle down, so to speak, since once we begin to work, arrests occur right away. The workers will begin work immediately, once the comrades are released.[62]

62. On March 16, a revolutionary troika of Vasiliev Island issued orders to release the arrested Baltic Plant workers but to establish the "strictest" surveillance over them and "at the very first strike to expel the unacceptable elements from the plant."

132. Demands of the Kronstadt Rebels, March 6–16, 1921
[60, pp. 82–4]

The Baltic Fleet was hit hard in the economic crisis of 1920 due to poor mate-
rial conditions, excessively long terms of service for many sailors, and inept sen-
ior leadership. Morale had hit a low point by the winter of 1920–1921,
especially as the sailors received word of harsh living conditions from friends and
relatives living in Petrograd and in the countryside. Sailors aboard the warship
Petropavlovsk *docked at the Kronstadt naval base*[63] *learned immediately about*
the worker unrest in Petrograd and voted their solidarity with the workers. On
March 1, the sailors stationed at the Kronstadt Fortress rebelled. Once called
"the pride and glory of the revolution" by Trotsky, the Kronstadt sailors de-
manded "all power to the soviets and not to the parties," free and fair elections
to the soviets, civil rights, and freedom to buy and sell agricultural produce. The
document below reflects many of their key demands. The sailors were denounced
by the Bolshevik leadership as lackeys of international capital and foreign gov-
ernments and were mercilessly suppressed in the following weeks.

WHAT WE ARE FIGHTING FOR

In carrying out the October revolution, the working class was hoping to
throw off the yoke of oppression. Yet that revolution resulted in an even
greater enslavement of the human person.

The power of police-gendarme monarchism fell into the hands of the
conquering Communists, who instead of freedom gave the working people
the constant fear of ending up in a dungeon of the Cheka, whose horrors
have surpassed a gendarme station of the tsarist regime by many degrees.

[. . .] But what is more vile and criminal than anything else is the moral
servitude created by the Communists: they have violated even the interior
life of working people, forcing them to think only in the Communist way.

They chained workers to their machines with the help of official trade
unions, transforming their labor not into joy but into a new slavery. The
peasants, whose protests manifested themselves in spontaneous rebellions,
and the workers, who were forced by the very circumstances of their life to
go on strike, met with mass executions and the sort of bloodthirstiness the
tsarist generals were famous for.

[. . .] The long patience of the working people has reached its end.

[. . .] Here in Kronstadt the first stone of the third revolution has been
laid, a revolution that will break the last chains hobbling the working masses
and will open a new wide path for socialist creativity.

---

63. The Kronstadt Fortress was twenty miles from Petrograd out in the Gulf of Finland.

[. . .] The current takeover gives the working people an opportunity to finally have their own freely elected soviets working without any coercive party pressure and to revamp the official trade unions into voluntary associations of workers, peasants, and the working intelligentsia. At last the police club of the Communist autocracy has been broken.

133. Satirical Verse, Published by the Kronstadt Rebels, March 6–16, 1921   [60, pp. 178–9]

A SATIRICAL SKETCH:
KRONSTADT VERSE

> The All-Russian Commune
> Drove us into the poorhouse.
> The dictatorship of Communists
> Brought us to the brink.
>
> We drove away the landlords.
> We awaited dear freedom and land.
> We shook off all the Romanovs,
> And got the Communists instead.
>
> Instead of freedom and dear land
> They gave us the Cheka,
> And planted Soviet
> Farms right and left.
>
> They take the grain and cattle.
> The peasant is starving.
> They took a horse from Erema.[64]
> They even took the plough from Makar.
>
> With neither matches nor kerosene,
> Only thin torches give us light.
> Under the Bolshevik commune,
> Ration cards alone are left to eat.

64. Erema and Makar were common peasant names.

Five yards of red calico
Were sent to the village.
The commissars took it all.
Middle peasants got not an inch.

So across Russia
The peasants for land's sake rose.
And in *Izvestiia* they write:
"The Kulaks are rioting."

The Cheka operative arrives
Just like a tsarist general.
He covers the soil with blood
And steals everyone's last thread.

The serfs' duties are back in full.
Hey, peasants, don't you see?
The Bolsheviks alone today
Drink and eat like the lords of yore.

Rise up, peasant folk!
A new dawn is breaking—
Shake off the chains of Trotsky,
Throw down Lenin the tsar.

Down with the dictatorship.
Give workers their liberty.
All land, plants, and factories
To those who do the work.

Labor will establish equality
And workers' freedom forever.
Brotherhood there will also be
And so to live always and ever.

134. Official Statement on the Kronstadt Mutiny, March 8, 1921   [44, vol. 32, pp. 183–6]

Lenin delivered the report, from which this passage is excerpted, at the Tenth Party Congress held in Moscow on March 8–16, 1921. Security police intelligence of the preceding days indicated that the mutinous sailors were largely

anarchistic in outlook, that the main ideological instigators were Socialist-
Revolutionaries (and not White Guards), and that the factory workers in Pet-
rograd were extremely worked up and disgruntled themselves. In the report be-
low Lenin did not recognize any of this. He nevertheless went on to propose
what was essentially a yielding to the sailors' demand for the right of peasants
to sell their agricultural surplus on the market.

[. . .] I should now like to deal with the Kronstadt events. I have not yet received the latest news from Kronstadt, but I have no doubt that this mutiny, which very quickly revealed to us the familiar figures of White Guard generals, will be put down within the next few days, if not hours. There can be no doubt about this. But it is essential that we make a thorough appraisal of the political and economic lessons of this event.

What does it mean? It was an attempt to seize political power from the Bolsheviks by a motley crowd or alliance of ill-assorted elements, apparently just to the right of the Bolsheviks, or perhaps even to their "left"—you can't really tell, so amorphous is the combination of political groupings that has tried to take power in Kronstadt. You all know, undoubtedly, that at the same time White Guard generals were very active over there. There is ample proof of this. A fortnight before the Kronstadt events, the Paris newspapers reported a mutiny at Kronstadt. It is quite clear that it is the work of Socialist-Revolutionaries and White Guard émigrés, and at the same time the movement was reduced to a petty-bourgeois counterrevolution and petty-bourgeois anarchism. That is something quite new. This circumstance, in the context of all the crises, must be given careful political consideration and must be very thoroughly analyzed. There is evidence here of the activity of petty-bourgeois anarchist elements with their slogans of unrestricted trade and invariable hostility to the dictatorship of the proletariat. This mood has had a wide influence on the proletariat. It has had an effect on factories in Moscow and a number of provincial centers. This petty-bourgeois counterrevolution is undoubtedly more dangerous than Denikin, Yudenich, and Kolchak put together, because ours is a country where the proletariat is in a minority, where peasant property has gone to ruin and where, in addition, the demobilization has set loose vast numbers of potentially mutinous elements. No matter how big or small the initial, shall I say, shift in power, which the Kronstadt sailors and workers put forward—they wanted to correct the Bolsheviks in regard to restrictions in trade—and this looks like a small shift, which leaves the same slogans of "Soviet power" with ever so slight a change or correction. Yet, in actual fact the White Guards only used the non-party elements as a stepping stone to get in. This is politically inevitable. [. . .] Unrestricted trade [. . .] is still only the thin end of the wedge for the White Guard element, a victory for capital and its complete restoration. We must, I repeat, have a keen sense of this political danger.

It shows what I said in dealing with our platforms discussion: in the face of this danger we must understand that we must do more than put an end to party disputes as a matter of form—we shall do that, of course. We need to remember that we must take a much more serious approach to this question.

We have to understand that, with the peasant economy in the grip of a crisis, we can survive only by appealing to the peasants to help town and countryside. We must bear in mind that the bourgeoisie is trying to pit the peasants against the workers; that behind a façade of workers' slogans it is trying to incite the petty-bourgeois anarchist elements against the workers. This, if successful, will lead directly to the overthrow of the dictatorship of the proletariat and, consequently, to the restoration of capitalism and of the old landowner and capitalist regime. The political danger here is obvious. A number of revolutions have clearly gone that way; we have always been mindful of this possibility and have warned against it. This undoubtedly demands of the ruling party of Communists and of the leading revolutionary elements of the proletariat a different attitude to the one we have time and again displayed over the past year. It is a danger that undoubtedly calls for much greater unity and discipline; it undoubtedly requires that we should all pull harder together. Otherwise we shall not cope with the dangers that have fallen to our lot. [. . .]

CHAPTER 5
Revolution's Finale

In the face of huge popular uprisings, a disastrous economic breakdown across the country, and famine in broad swaths of territory, in early 1921 the Bolshevik leadership adopted a New Economic Policy (NEP) aimed at forestalling Russia's utter ruin and political collapse. This policy allowed small-scale private commerce, including trade in agricultural products, to develop with minimal restrictions, thus unleashing the efficiency of the free market. Still committed to Marxist ideology, however, the Bolshevik leadership viewed the NEP not as a permanent change in direction but as a temporary retreat on the "economic front." Therefore, this period also witnessed a tightening of control in the political and cultural spheres. At the same time, efforts to transform the country and to create a new, utopian society continued, for example through the partial abolition of money. By the end of 1922, a new country had been officially born (the USSR), and the struggle to succeed Lenin had begun.

The first section of this chapter, "The New Economic Policy and the Countryside" (Documents 135–139), opens with the frank admission by the party leadership of the economic hardship plaguing Russia and of the need to accommodate the largest segment of society—the peasantry—especially so long as revolution failed to erupt in any of the advanced capitalist countries of Western Europe. The concessions thus yielded were destined to return the country to prewar economic indices by the late 1920s. Yet as Document 136 makes plain, the government would resort to repression in dealing with those rural inhabitants who persisted in fighting against Bolshevik domination. The remainder of the section bears witness to the economic devastation and hard material conditions brought about by famine and ill-conceived government policies.

Retreating on the "economic front" did not mean allowing the political opposition to gain an advantage. "Political Consolidation of the Bolshevik Regime" (Documents 140–143) demonstrates that the Bolshevik leadership

Workers Studying at a School for the Underliterate, Moscow, 1922. RGAKFD. The Bolshevik leaders considered battling illiteracy a major task of their government.

aimed to tighten its control and increase its authority. There were three main "fronts" in this effort. The first involved banning factions, or caucuses, within the Bolshevik Party itself. Now that the Civil War was over, voices within the party began to call for changes in political direction. Banning factions was designed to silence these voices. A second front was opened against the Russian Orthodox Church, by far the country's most extensive institution, aside from the government itself. The church also retained some authority in the eyes of the majority of the country's population, especially among the peasantry. The third front was against the political organization that had pursued a very different vision of the Revolution and sought to represent peasant interests—the Socialist-Revolutionary Party. In fact, in the summer of 1922 the government orchestrated major "show trials" against leaders of both the church and the Socialist-Revolutionaries.

The Bolshevik revolution was intended to transform culture, society, economics, politics—all of life. Documents 144–150, in "The New Soviet Society," focus on some of these intentions. Not surprisingly, for a self-styled proletarian state, the laws and conditions of labor changed significantly. Workers were obligated to work and even encouraged to volunteer to work extra hours, but they also gained, at least de jure, the right to a job. Factory inspectors gained broad discretion in determining proper work conditions, while the government instituted means of keeping tabs on all employees throughout their careers. The days of rest and holidays were also changed quite radically. Another area that underwent a major transformation was domestic life. Divorce became readily obtainable: it sufficed for one party to express a will to end the union. Soviet Russia was also the first country in the world to legalize abortion. Education was an important sphere to the new leaders. They aimed to eradicate illiteracy, to inculcate broadly the principles of Marxism, and to train workers and peasants for positions of leadership. Finally, the government, at least initially, planned to abolish money entirely and to create a system that provided essential services to all—free of charge.

The Bolsheviks also claimed that they were opening up countless possibilities for cultural and artistic expression. The section "Soviet Culture: From Liberation to Subjugation" (Documents 151–156), provides an enthusiastic discussion of the achievements of young Soviet culture but also evidence of the efforts of the regime to control and restrict creative expression. Thus, the state set up elaborate plans to co-opt intellectuals even marginally sympathetic to the new regime and its ideals. Those clearly unwilling to compromise their own ideals and beliefs, however, faced banishment from the country or, should they remain inside Russia, assiduous censorship of their work.

In the final section of the book, "The Revolution's Heirs" (Documents 157–158), two topics are considered. The first is the creation of a new state born of successful efforts by the Bolsheviks to reestablish control over many former parts of the Russian Empire: the Union of Soviet Socialist Republics in late December 1922. The second is Lenin's so-called testament, of the same

The Union of Soviet Socialist Republics, 1922.

time period, in which he tries to reach out to the broader ranks of party activists and criticizes each and every possible successor to himself, thus setting the stage for the struggle that followed his death a year later.

By this point, the main structures, institutions, and norms of the Bolshevik regime were in place: parallel party and state authority with ultimate party control, strict censorship, a powerful secret police, utopian ideals of social transformation, informal leadership by individuals without constitutional checks or balances, few civil rights, highly restricted emigration, a universal labor obligation, and a huge multinational empire with cultural "affirmative action." The country had also embarked on an economic "retreat," the New Economic Policy, that would play out for several more years, allowing peasants and petty traders to achieve economic security and even well-being.

THE NEW ECONOMIC POLICY
AND THE COUNTRYSIDE

135. Announcement of the New Economic Policy, March 15, 1921   [44, vol. 32, pp. 214–8]

Lenin delivered the speech from which the following excerpt is taken at the Tenth Party Congress in the context of catastrophic economic collapse, disastrous harvests, and widespread peasant rebellions. Large-scale industrial production had fallen more than 80 percent from the 1913 level; grain production, by 40 percent. Consequently, urban centers emptied of population: St. Petersburg fell to a third its prewar size; Moscow, to half. The industrial workforce, in whose name the Bolsheviks had seized power, plunged from 3.6 to 1.5 million. Peasant uprisings, involving hundreds of thousands if not millions of insurgents, raged across Russia in 1921–1922, causing 237,908 casualties among Red Army soldiers alone. The harvests in 1920–1921 were meager. For example, in 1920 only 46.1 million tons of grain were produced in Central Russia compared to 80.1 million tons in 1913. Draconian seizures of grain—often well over half the total output—had spurred the peasantry to plant less. The nationalization of commerce and industry and resulting decline in industrial output left few goods the state could trade for grain. It was a vicious circle.

Not surprisingly, most party activists and leaders opposed Lenin's plan, propounded below, to restore free economic exchange, fearing it would lead to a restoration of capitalism. The plan was adopted only on the final day of the congress after stubborn resistance.

Comrades, the question of substituting a tax for surplus-grain appropriation is primarily and mainly a political question, for it is essentially a question of the attitude of the working class to the peasantry. We are raising it because we must subject the relations of these two main classes, whose struggle or agreement determines the fate of our revolution as a whole, to a new or, I should perhaps say, a more careful and correct re-examination and some revision. There is no need for me to dwell in detail on the reasons for it. You all know very well of course what totality of causes, especially those due to the extreme want arising out of war, ruin, demobilization, and the disastrous crop failure—you know about the totality of circumstances that has made the condition of the peasantry especially precarious and critical and was bound to increase its swing from the proletariat to the bourgeoisie.

A word or two on the theoretical significance of, or the theoretical approach to, this issue. There is no doubt that in a country where the overwhelming majority of the population consists of small agricultural producers, a socialist revolution can be carried out only through the implementation of a whole series of special transitional measures which would be superfluous in highly developed capitalist countries where wage-workers in industry and agriculture make up the vast majority. Highly developed capitalist countries have a class of agricultural wage-workers that has taken shape over many decades. Only such a class can socially, economically, and politically support a direct transition to socialism. Only in countries where this class is sufficiently developed is it possible to pass directly from capitalism to socialism, without any special countrywide transitional measures. We have stressed in a good many written works, in all our public utterances, and all our statements in the press, that this is not the case in Russia. For here industrial workers are a minority and petty farmers are the vast majority. In such a country, the socialist revolution can triumph only on two conditions. First, if it is given timely support by a socialist revolution in one or several advanced countries. As you know, we have done very much indeed in comparison with the past to bring about this condition, but far from enough to make it a reality.

The second condition is agreement between the proletariat, which is exercising its dictatorship, that is, holds state power, and the majority of the peasant population. Agreement is a very broad concept which includes a whole series of measures and transitions. I must say at this point that our propaganda and agitation must be open and above-board. We must condemn most resolutely those who regard politics as a series of cheap little tricks, frequently bordering on deception. Their mistakes have to be corrected. You can't fool a class. [. . .] [T]he small farmer does not want the same thing as the worker.

We know that so long as there is no revolution in other countries, only agreement with the peasantry can save the socialist revolution in Russia. And that is how it must be, I stated frankly, at all meetings and in the entire press. [. . .] The state of affairs that has prevailed so far cannot be continued any longer.

We must say to the peasants: "If you want to turn back, if you want to restore private property and unrestricted trade in their entirety, it will certainly and inevitably mean falling under the rule of the landowners and the capitalists. [. . .]"

Difficult as our position is in regard to resources, the needs of the middle peasantry must be satisfied. [. . .] On the whole, however, statistics show quite definitely that there has been a levelling out, an equalization, in the village, that is, the old sharp division into kulaks and cropless peasants has disappeared. Everything has become more equable; the peasantry in general has acquired the status of the middle peasant.

Can we satisfy this middle peasantry as such, with its economic peculiarities and economic roots? Any Communist who thought the economic basis, the economic roots, of small farming could be reshaped in three years was, of course, a dreamer. We need not conceal the fact that there were a good many such dreamers among us. Nor is there anything particularly bad in this. How could one start a socialist revolution in a country like ours without dreamers? Practice has, of course, shown the tremendous role all kinds of experiments and undertakings can play in the sphere of collective agriculture. But it has also afforded instances of these experiments as such playing a negative role, when people, with the best of intentions and desires, went to the countryside to set up communes but did not know how to run them because they had no experience in collective endeavor. The experience of these collective farms merely provided examples of how not to run farms: the peasants around either laughed or jeered.

You know perfectly well how many cases there have been of this kind. I repeat that this is not surprising, for it will take generations to remold the small farmer, and recast his mentality and habits. The only way to solve this problem of the small farmer—to improve, so to speak, his mentality—is through the material basis, technical equipment, the extensive use of tractors and other farm machinery and electrification on a mass scale. This would remake the small farmer fundamentally and with tremendous speed. If I say this will take generations, it does not mean centuries. But you know perfectly well that to obtain tractors and other machinery and to electrify this vast country is a matter that may take decades in any case. Such is the objective situation.

We must try to satisfy the demands of the peasants who are dissatisfied and disgruntled, and legitimately so, and who cannot be otherwise. [. . .] [I]t will take essentially two things to satisfy the small farmer. The first is a certain freedom of exchange, freedom for the small private proprietor, and the second is the need to obtain commodities and products. What indeed would free exchange amount to if there was nothing to exchange, and freedom of trade, if there was nothing to trade with! [. . .]

What is free exchange? It is unrestricted trade, and that means turning back towards capitalism. Free exchange and freedom of trade mean circulation of commodities between petty proprietors. All of us who have studied at least the elements of Marxism know that this exchange and freedom of trade inevitably lead to a division of commodity producers into owners of capital and owners of labor-power, a division into capitalists and wage-workers, i.e., a revival of capitalist wage-slavery. [. . .]

How then can the Communist Party recognize freedom to trade and accept it? [. . .] [C]an freedom of trade, freedom of capitalist enterprise for the small farmer, be restored to a certain extent without undermining the political power of the proletariat? Can it be done? Yes; it can, for everything hinges on the extent. [. . .] The peasants want to be shown in practice that the worker who controls the mills and factories—industry—is capable of organizing exchange with the peasantry. And, on the other hand, the vastness of our agricultural country with its poor transport system, boundless expanses, varying climate, diverse farming conditions, etc., makes a certain freedom of exchange between local agriculture and local industry, on a local scale, inevitable. In this respect, we are very much to blame for having gone too far; we overdid the nationalization of industry and trade, clamping down on local exchange of commodities. Was that a mistake? It certainly was.

In this respect we have made many patent mistakes, and it would be a great crime not to see it, and not to realize that we have failed to keep within bounds, and have not known where to stop. There has, of course, also been the factor of necessity—until now we have been living in the conditions of a savage war that imposed an unprecedented burden on us and left us no choice but to take wartime measures in the economic sphere as well. It was a miracle that the ruined country withstood this war, yet the miracle did not come from heaven, but grew out of the economic interests of the working class and the peasantry, whose mass enthusiasm created the miracle that defeated the landowners and capitalists. But at the same time it is an unquestionable fact that we went further than was theoretically and politically necessary, and this should not be concealed in our agitation and propaganda. We can allow free local exchange to an appreciable extent, without destroying, but actually strengthening the political power of the proletariat. [. . .]

I ask you to bear in mind this basic fact: it will take several months to work out the details and interpretations. The chief thing to bear in mind at the moment is that we must let the whole world know, by wireless this very night, of our decision; we must announce that this Congress of the government party is, in the main, replacing the surplus appropriation system by a tax and is giving the small farmer certain incentives to expand his farm and plant more; that by embarking on this course the Congress is correcting the system of relations between the proletariat and the peasantry and expresses its conviction that in this way these relations will be made durable. (*Stormy applause.*)

136. A Report on Fighting "Red Banditry," October 8, 1921   [5, pp. 189–93]

The years of Civil War tore apart the social fabric of the Russian countryside. Even though the Bolsheviks encouraged that process by promoting the rhetoric of class warfare, they could not fully control those who acted violently because of their hatred of the rich. As the document below indicates, the Bolshevik government had to look for ways to rein in such people, especially as it proceeded to implement the New Economic Policy in the countryside.

[. . .] The essence and the basic nature of red banditry can be best defined as the arbitrary action of certain groups of the population, which take upon themselves in one way or another the functions of government. The most frequent manifestations of red banditry are unsanctioned reprisals of one group of population embracing revolutionary ideals against a group it considers counterrevolutionary and publicly harmful. It was in this way, as a mass phenomenon, that red banditry first emerged. [. . .]

In its main and primary form, red banditry is a continuation of the civil war. By this means, one population group settles scores dating back to the times of Kolchak with another group: workers attack specialized professionals, [. . .] partisan elements of the village attack the kulaks and other counterrevolutionary village elements, or "scum" to use the expressive language of the red bandits. [. . .] Their own wishes are in essence to completely exterminate their political enemies, or at the very least to arrest and isolate all of them in prisons and concentration camps. [. . .] "Get the scum" is the main slogan of the red bandits in all of Siberia. But these attitudes and approaches of the red bandits reveal elements of dissatisfaction with the policies of Soviet power, which in their opinion is fighting "the enemies of the people" with insufficient vigor. [. . .]

Since spring 1921, red banditry has exhibited toward Soviet government policies a form of dissatisfaction with much deeper political and economic roots. The layer of the peasant population from which red bandits are recruited is either the poor or elements economically destroyed by Kolchak and thrown into the ranks of the poor. [. . .] With the abolition of *razverstka*[1] they have lost their economic support and have come to feel that they are just as deprived as they were under Kolchak. They sense that the new

---

1. The *prodovol'stvennaia razverstka* was a tax in kind imposed on all peasants starting on January 11, 1919. Poorer peasants benefited from this policy, which redistributed part of the rural wealth toward them.

course [i.e., the NEP] will inevitably lead to the strengthening of the elements
hostile to them and will diminish their own influence. These circumstances
are increasingly pushing them from mere discontentment toward sharp political hostility to Soviet power. They reject the new course. [. . .]

So what are the measures for fighting red banditry? [. . .]

1. The creation of a special fund in part to provide relief to impoverished
peasants and primarily for establishing them economically and for decreas-
ing their obligations to the state.

2. Increased political education among the worker and peasant masses
and abolishing political illiteracy among party members.

3. Strengthening the lower-level organs of Soviet power: the *township* executive committees and village soviets.

These measures cannot be implemented with Siberian resources alone.
Assistance from the Central Committee and the organs of central government is essential. [. . .]

By order of the Siberian Bureau of the Central Committee of the RKP, members Smirnov, Iaroslavskii, Iakovleva

137. Description of Famine Conditions in the Volga Region, 1921   [45, pp. 276–7]

*Little precipitation fell in much of Russia in late 1920 and early 1921;
drought followed. The Bolshevik policy of confiscating the peasants' "surplus" of
grain from 1918 into 1921, as well as the economic and recruitment burdens
of the Civil War, meant the people's margin of survival was extremely narrow
in many regions of the country. Much of Ukraine and the north Caucasus region, having avoided these confiscations during part of the Civil War, felt the
famine less severely than the central Volga region, especially the provinces of
Kazan, Ufa, Orenburg, and Samara. Overall, by early 1922 some 30 million
people were starving or close to starvation.*

*In July 1921, public activists organized and funded a voluntary association
called* Pomgol *(Committee for Famine Relief), which issued urgent appeals
abroad for monetary and logistical assistance. A month later at Lenin's sugges-
tion, this committee was disbanded and its leaders arrested, though foreign relief, especially from the United States, poured in from 1922 through most of
1923, saving millions of lives. The following report, describing effects of the
famine in the Volga region, was submitted by A. Novikov, a member of the
Famine Relief Commission of the Commissariat of Health, to the Central
Committee of the Russian Red Cross.*

Impressions during travel to the famine-stricken areas of the Tatar Republic, the Viatka region, the Mari region, and Ekaterinburg, Cheliabinsk, Ufa, and Simbirsk provinces, as well as the Bashkir Republic.

The horrible scenes of death by starvation among the population of the above-mentioned areas are indescribable. The bony hand of death seizes dozens of human victims daily. [. . .]

The districts of the Tatar Republic have suffered especially severely from starvation, and the population there is doomed to extinction. Infant mortality is staggering. The population feeds on coarse weeds like yellow dock and goosefoot, tree bark, wild mushrooms, and clay. These nutritional surrogates strongly affect the health of the population with fatal consequences. [. . .]

Conditions in the districts of the Tatar Republic in wintertime are particularly catastrophic, since they are located on the left bank of the Volga River, which is inaccessible by land. When the river freezes and navigation ceases, the population of these districts is doomed, for help becomes unavailable.

Before the river froze, the evacuation of children was speedy, and some of the little children were carried to safety, but the rest were left to their own devices. [. . .]

While traveling around the Bashkir Republic, I observed the following scenes: There is a cart on a country road, with a dead horse lying next to the cart and the dead owner lying on the cart. Both died from starvation.

A family is lingering in a small cabin, half destroyed, without a roof: a mother and two children. The mother in the last moments of her life pushes her children away, so as not to watch them dying from starvation. Soon they, too, are dead.

A little boy is dying from starvation under a bridge. He used to live off alms, but this help vanished, since the population of the whole village is starving. Someone took pity and brings him some milk, but the boy is already dead, lying with a hand stretched out. [. . .]

There are so many such scenes, one cannot describe them all.

Death by starvation is pitiless.

Strong, forceful, and organized assistance from abroad is needed.

The Soviet power of Russia is doing what is possible. Its heroic measures are innumerable, but it is powerless to achieve anything. [. . .]

138. Famine in the Countryside of Samara Province, December 1921   [45, p. 285]

The following telegram was sent from Grachevka village, Samara province, to the Samara provincial Union of the Russian Red Cross.

I report to you that the catastrophe of the famine in our region has reached such horrible and inexpressible proportions that adult citizens, wandering aimlessly and incapacitated by the famine, are collapsing in the middle of the streets and dying. An endless multitude of citizens are dying in various institutions, premises of buildings, courtyards, and the like. The sole evil causing these deaths is famine. Corpses of the dead are collected in streets and are stored by the authorities of some villages in empty barns until springtime, because digging graves is beyond the ability of citizens tortured by hunger. Some corpses are borne by citizens to cemeteries and are buried only in the snow, but the wind sweeps it away, exposing the corpses, which dogs snatch at. Therefore the citizens find themselves in the most hopeless and unbearable situation due to the famine and with their own eyes witness human remains torn to shreds. The heart of every citizen who passes by is broken by the sight. Because of this unprecedented and horrible condition, we urgently plead that you might send food for our adult citizens. Otherwise, owing to the horrible mortality of adult citizens, even of our administration, it will be impossible to work, and the direst panic will break out. In regard to food for children, there remains the most minimal quantity. We are today, December 31, sending a more detailed report by mail.

139. A Police Report on Political and Economic Conditions of the Peasantry, December 1922   [18, p. 46]

The Main Political Administration (GPU) replaced the Cheka in February 1922 and was supposed to mark a softening of the repressive apparatus by curtailing its power to impose administrative punishments. One of the chief functions of the GPU that was retained and even strengthened was to compile regular, systematic reports on the "political mood" of the population at all levels of society. One of thousands of such reports is provided below.

Top Secret
Urgent via courier.

Regular State Information Survey of the Zyrianskii[2] Regional Department of the GPU as of December 23, 1922

POLITICO-ECONOMIC CONDITION OF PEASANTRY

The mood of the peasantry is depressed because of the imposition of various taxes. Their attitude to Soviet power is indifferent, since the population of the Komi region is highly scattered and disorganized as well as depressed culturally, which makes it difficult to accomplish anything political in regard to them. In remote localities, especially because there are no good Soviet party workers, people understand almost nothing about the essence of Soviet power. As long as they are asked to pay fewer taxes, they do not care who is in power, and because of this depressed state local kulaks and priests often have influence on some individuals. [. . .] Certainly there is dissatisfaction with the open drunkenness of individual Soviet employees, such as food inspectors, militiamen, and quite often militia chiefs (instead of taking measures to liquidate drunkenness, the militia chief of the Viziginskii district, Istomin, having arrived in the township, typically engages in drunkenness together with several other militiamen. [. . .]) [. . .] The people's attitude toward the NEP is sympathetic because it provides an opportunity to expand agriculture and sell goods freely. [. . .]

Deputy Chief of Komi GPU Rasputin
Troika: Shchebenev, Ezet, Nikiforov

2. The Zyrianskii oblast is in the Ural region near Perm.

POLITICAL CONSOLIDATION OF THE BOLSHEVIK REGIME

140. Draft Resolution on Party Unity, March 1921
[44, vol. 32, pp. 241–4]

As the last Socialist-Revolutionaries and Mensheviks were purged out of the soviets, legitimate political dissent in Soviet Russia could exist only within the confines of the Bolshevik Party and its program. In 1920, several party activists led by Aleksandr Shliapnikov, chairman of the Russian Metalworkers' Union, and the feminist Alexandra Kollontai banded together in a Workers' Opposition faction to campaign against bureaucratization in government institutions and for the increased influence of trade unions and industrial workers in the country's economic life. The Tenth Party Congress in 1921 adopted some proposals of the Workers' Opposition, such as party purges and improved material conditions for workers. Yet the faction's main concern, trade-union influence, was not addressed, and factions themselves were banned.[3] The banning of factions created an extremely narrow concentration of political power within the leadership of the party. Lenin firmly insisted on the need to ban factions in the speech below, which he presented at the Tenth Party Congress.

1. The Congress calls the attention of all members of the Party to the fact that the unity and cohesion of the ranks of the Party, the guarantee of complete mutual confidence among Party members, and genuine team-work that really embodies the unanimity of will of the vanguard of the proletariat, are particularly essential at the present time, when a number of circumstances are increasing the vacillation among the petty-bourgeois population of the country.

2. Notwithstanding this, even before the general Party discussion on the trade unions, certain signs of factionalism had been apparent in the Party—the formation of groups with separate platforms, striving to a certain degree to segregate and create their own group discipline. Such symptoms of factionalism were manifested, for example, [. . .] by the so-called Workers' Opposition group, and partly by the so-called Democratic Centralism group.

3. The disbanded faction's leaders suffered persecution in the 1920s; several, including Shliapnikov, were executed during Stalin's Terror in the late 1930s.

All class-conscious workers must clearly realize that factionalism of any kind is harmful and impermissible, for no matter how members of individual groups may desire to safeguard Party unity, factionalism in practice inevitably leads to the weakening of team-work and to intensified and repeated attempts by the enemies of the governing Party, who have wormed their way into it, to widen the cleavage and to use it for counterrevolutionary purposes.

The way the enemies of the proletariat take advantage of every deviation from a thoroughly consistent Communist line was perhaps most strikingly shown in the case of the Kronstadt mutiny, when the bourgeois counter-revolutionaries and White Guards in all countries of the world immediately expressed their readiness to accept the slogans of the Soviet system, if only they might thereby secure the overthrow of the dictatorship of the proletariat in Russia, and when the Socialist-Revolutionaries and the bourgeois counterrevolutionaries in general resorted in Kronstadt to slogans calling for an insurrection against the Soviet government of Russia ostensibly in the interest of the Soviet power. These facts fully prove that the White Guards strive, and are able, to disguise themselves as Communists, and even as the most left-wing Communists, solely for the purpose of weakening and destroying the bulwark of the proletarian revolution in Russia. Menshevik leaflets distributed in Petrograd on the eve of the Kronstadt mutiny likewise show how the Mensheviks took advantage of the disagreements and certain rudiments of factionalism in the Russian Communist Party actually in order to egg on and support the Kronstadt mutineers, the Socialist-Revolutionaries, and the White Guards, while claiming to be opponents of mutiny and supporters of the Soviet power, only with supposedly slight modifications.

3. In this question, propaganda should consist, on the one hand, in a comprehensive explanation of the harmfulness and danger of factionalism from the standpoint of Party unity and of achieving unanimity of will among the vanguard of the proletariat as the fundamental condition for the success of the dictatorship of the proletariat; and, on the other hand, in an explanation of the peculiar features of the latest tactical devices of the enemies of the Soviet power. These enemies, having realized the hopelessness of counterrevolution under an openly White Guard flag, are now doing their utmost to utilize the disagreements within the Russian Communist Party and to further the counterrevolution in one way or another by transferring power to a political group which is outwardly closest to recognition of the Soviet power. [. . .]

4. In the practical struggle against factionalism, every organization of the Party must take strict measures to prevent all factional actions. Criticism of the Party's shortcomings, which is absolutely necessary, must be conducted in such a way that every practical proposal shall be submitted immediately,

without any delay, in the most precise form possible, for consideration and decision to the leading local and central bodies of the Party. [. . .] Analyses of the Party's general line, estimates of its practical experience, check-ups of the fulfillment of its decisions, studies of methods of rectifying errors, etc., must under no circumstances be submitted for preliminary discussion to groups formed on the basis of "platforms," etc., but must in all cases be submitted for discussion directly to all the members of the Party. [. . .]

5. [In regard to] every practical proposal concerning questions to which the so-called Workers' Opposition group, for example, has devoted special attention [. . .] the Party will unceasingly continue—trying out new methods—to fight with all the means at its disposal against the evils of bureaucracy, for the extension of democracy and initiative, for detecting, exposing, and expelling from the Party elements that have wormed their way into its ranks, etc.

6. The Congress, therefore, hereby declares dissolved and orders the immediate dissolution of all groups without exception formed on the basis of one platform or another (such as the Workers' Opposition group, the Democratic Centralism group, etc.). Non-observance of this decision of the Congress shall entail unconditional and instant expulsion from the Party. [. . .]

141: Metropolitan Veniamin[4] on Church-Supported Famine Relief, March 5, 1922   [11, pp. 67–8]

In the midst of a famine affecting up to 30 million people, the Bolshevik leadership laid plans to seize church valuables (including chalices, icons decorated with silver foil, and silver and gold crosses) ostensibly to help feed the hungry. On February 23 orders went out to local officials to organize confiscation campaigns. Patriarch Tikhon proposed at this point to collect money equivalents and to donate nonconsecrated church valuables, but his offer was rejected. As tensions grew, Metropolitan Veniamin issued the statement excerpted below, explaining the church's position. As government officials began to implement their orders, clashes with believers on March 11–16 left several people dead and many wounded in a half-dozen localities. On March 19, Lenin sent a notorious "top secret" letter to the Politburo in which he claimed that it was precisely then, "when in the starving regions people are eating human flesh,

---

4. Metropolitan Veniamin (born Vasilii Pavlovich Kazanskii in 1874) served as a bishop from 1909 and was elected to his post in Petrograd in 1917, after the fall of the Tsar. Extremely popular among the laity for his humaneness and compassion, on a number of occasions he resisted Bolshevik attempts to harass the church.

and hundreds if not thousands of corpses are littering the roads" that it was necessary "to smash the enemy" (i.e., the church) and confiscate its valuables, without which "no government work in general, no economic construction in particular, and no defense of our position in Genoa especially is even conceivable." Lenin added that the more counterrevolutionary priests who could be executed in the course of the confiscation campaign, the better. Veniamin became one such priest. Even though on April 10 he issued an appeal to his flock urging them to comply with the confiscation campaign without resistance, he was arrested and executed on the night of August 26, 1922, along with three others.[5]

* * *

The entire Russian Orthodox Church at the call and blessing of its Father, the Most Holy Patriarch, in August of last year (1921) with all zeal and readiness responded to the cause of aiding the starving. However the work that began at that time in Petrograd churches on my instructions was at the very outset terminated by order of the Soviet authorities.

At the present time the government is again offering the Church the right to begin aiding the starving. Once the opportunity to work for the starving emerged, I did not wait a single day and re-launched the activities of the Church Aid Committee issuing to all of my parishes a vigorous appeal and plea to provide the starving with monetary, material, and food aid. In addition, the Most Holy Patriarch urged the clergy and parish councils to donate for the sake of the starving, with the consent of the faithful, precious church items not being used in worship.

Yet the decree of 23 February recently published in the Moscow *Izvestiia* on the confiscation of church valuables for the needs of the starving, apparently indicates that the Church's sacrifice on behalf of the starving is deemed insufficient.

Drawing attention to this matter, I as senior pastor consider it my sacred duty to state that the Orthodox Church, following the testaments of Christ the Savior and the example of the great holy men [*sviatiteli*], has always manifested high Christian love in times of calamity, sacrificing all of the church's property, even the sacred vessels, for the sake of saving people from dying.

But when sacrificing for the salvation of the starving its most sacred and precious treasures, which are cherished because of their spiritual, not material value, the Church must have confidence:

5. The three other victims were a priest and former member of the State Duma, a university professor, and the legal counsel of the Alexander Nevskii Monastery.

I. that all other means and ways of aiding the starving have
been exhausted,

II. that the sacrificed holy items will be used exclusively for
the purpose of helping the starved,

III. that the Supreme Church Authority has blessed and
granted permission for sacrificing these items.

Only on these principal conditions, carried out in a manner leaving no
doubt to the people of faith about the sufficiency of the needed guarantees
can I call upon the Orthodox people to sacrifice sacred church objects, while
the treasures themselves are to be turned into bullion with my direct participation in accordance with the holy fathers' directions and the examples of
ancient Church leaders. Only in the form of bullion can these treasures be
donated and not as vessels, which according to church rules no unsanctified
hand can touch.

When the people sacrificed money and food for the sake of the starving,
they did not have to ask (and did not ask) where and how this money would
be appropriated. But when the people sacrifice sacred items, they have the
right to know how their church treasures will be used, since Church canon
law allows them to be used only for aiding the starving and bailing out prisoners and only then in exceptional cases.

At the present time, with the blessing of the Most Holy Patriarch, we are
calling upon churches to sacrifice only those valuables that do not have rit-
ual value. At the same time we decisively reject the forced confiscation of
church valuables as an act of blasphemy and sacrilege. According to canon
law, a layman participating in such an act can be excommunicated and a clergyman can be stripped of his priesthood.

                        Veniamin, metropolitan of Petrograd and Gdov

142. Trotsky on Fostering a Schism within the Church, March 1922   [11, pp. 81–3]

*Beginning as early as 1920, the Cheka set up local offices aimed at recruiting
agents within the clergy and winning support for the new government among
what a secret police report called the small but significant segment of "progressive, pro-reform, even revolutionized" priests. The government saw its chance
to divide the entire clergy during the confrontation over the campaign to seize
church valuables. Trotsky, who was the secret mastermind behind the campaign, sent the following letter to Politburo members on March 30 proposing
a broad strategy.*

1. [. . .] There is no doubt that since the establishment of Soviet Power the church hierarchy, seeing itself "persecuted" (because it is no longer privileged), has been preparing to take advantage of an advantageous situation. There are certain counterrevolutionary activists in its milieu, and religious influence is used to project political influence.

2. The European church passed through the Reformation. [. . .]

3. Here opposition to church dogmatism never moved beyond various sects. [. . .]

4. Therefore, the church, which is permeated with a serf-owning and bureaucratic mentality and never even underwent bourgeois reform, is now facing the proletarian revolution. What can its fate now be? There are two trends: one is openly counterrevolutionary and infused with a Black-Hundred[6]-monarchist ideology; the other is "Soviet." The ideology of the "Soviet" clergy appears to resemble the "changing signposts"[7] ideology and is therefore bourgeois-collaborationist in nature.

5. Had this slowly shaping bourgeois-collaborationist changing-signposts wing of the church developed fully and grown strong, it would have become much more dangerous to the socialist revolution than the church in its present form: taking upon itself a protective "Soviet" coloring, the "progressive" clergy create for themselves opportunities to penetrate those progressive layers of the working people, which constitute or should constitute our base of support.

6. Therefore the changing-signposts clergy should be viewed as the most dangerous enemy of tomorrow. But only tomorrow. Today we need to topple the counterrevolutionary part of the clergymen who de facto run the church. In this struggle we have to rely on the changing-signposts clergy without aligning with them politically, much less as a matter of principle. [. . .]

7. The more decisive, abrupt, furious, and violent the breakup between the changing-signposts wing of the church and the Black-Hundred one, the more advantageous it will be for our position. [. . .]

8. For this purpose, the famine campaign is extremely advantageous, since it focuses attention on the fate of church treasures. We should, first, force the changing-signposts priests openly and completely to link their fate to the issue of the confiscation of church valuables; second, force them to

---

6. See p. 45, n. 12.

7. *Smena vekh* (*Change of Signposts*) was a compendium of articles and a periodical edited by Nikolai Ustrialov in July and starting in October 1921, respectively. The title echoed the 1909 compendium *Vekhi* (*Signposts*), which had criticized the Russian intelligentsia's alleged infatuation with the idea of revolution. Ustrialov argued that since the Bolsheviks were building up the Russian state, they deserved the support of Russian nationalists. The Bolshevik government provided funding to the *smenovekhovtsy* beginning in November 1921.

use this campaign to bring about a complete organizational breakup with the Black-Hundred church hierarchy and then to convene their own church assembly in order to elect new church leaders.

9. During this campaign we should allow the changing-signposts priests to openly speak along specific lines. There is no more furious haranguer than an oppositionist priest. Even today, in our newspapers, some of them accuse specific bishops of being sodomites and other sins. I believe we should allow them and even convince them of the need to have their own press organ, say, a weekly, in order to prepare the convocation of a church assembly by a certain date. We would thereby receive invaluable agitation material. [. . .]

10. Meanwhile, in the period leading up to the assembly, we should prepare a campaign of theory and propaganda against the renewed[8] church. Since it is impossible to simply leap over the bourgeois reformation of the church, we must cause it to miscarry. [. . .]

143. Speech by Abram Gots, Trial of Socialist-Revolutionaries, August 6, 1922   [66, vol. 3, pp. 908–10]

Abram Rafailovich Gots (1882–1940) was condemned to death for revolutionary activity in 1907 and was in a hard-labor prison when revolution broke out in 1917. He then headed the Socialist-Revolutionary (SR) faction of the Petrograd Soviet and the Central Executive Committee of the Soviet but vehemently rejected the Bolshevik takeover. Gots helped organize both armed resistance and terrorist acts against the Bolshevik government. Repeatedly arrested and released, he ended up in prison in 1920. In March 1921, Trotsky proposed mounting "show trials" of the anarchists and Socialist-Revolutionaries as a method of propaganda against them "much better than leaflets." In summer 1922, Gots, along with eleven other men and two women, all Socialist-Revolutionaries and long-term fighters against the Imperial Russian regime, were "tried" in Moscow, without any due process, for their militant opposition to the Bolshevik regime in 1918, despite an amnesty granted to them in February 1919 following a promise by party leaders to cease fighting in the Civil War. This trial, along with another undertaken against church leaders also in summer 1922, were Soviet Russia's first show trials and thus prefigured the infamous Moscow show trials of 1936–1938. The chief prosecutor gave the defendants a chance to "repent" and when they refused, twelve death sentences,

---

8. The "renewed" (*obnovlennaia*) church was the name chosen by advocates of radical ecclesiastical reform and support for the Bolshevik state.

a foregone conclusion, were issued but later commuted to terms of prison on condition of good behavior. Freed in 1925, Gots worked in a Soviet agency in Simbirsk but also faced frequent persecution. He was condemned to 25 years in prison in 1939 and died in a labor camp the following year.

In a few more hours, this episode of great political contention between the S-R party and the party of Communists, which has dragged on since the beginning of the revolution, will pass. [. . .]

I find it necessary to dwell on only one question posed to us today by the chairman of the tribunal: "What would you do if you were free to go today?" [. . .]

What we would do in the area of foreign policy? We would fight against all masked forms of intervention and blockade, we would insist on the necessity for capitalist Europe to immediately recognize the Soviet government, and we would assist the Soviet government in its struggle against predatory claims of foreign capital. As long as the government's policies in this area follow the interests of the working class and the whole country, we will support it. And we will decisively fight against it to the extent its policies deviate from those interests.

What would we do in the area of domestic policy?

Here our main task would be organizing the broad working masses of the city and the village in order to prevail over the Bolshevik dictatorship, as the central issue currently on the agenda and for the purpose of fighting reaction, which is currently threatening the working class not from without, but from within, from those new social forces, which are growing on the soil of your economic policy.

That's our brief answer. [. . .]

I wanted to mention one more thing.

All the rebuttals against us from the prosecutorial benches usually ended with one triumphant refrain, one jubilant rejoicing: "We are the victors! We crushed you in an open fight, and now we judge you by the right of the victor."

I don't know how valuable such an argument is before the judgment of history. History often judges victors and judges them harshly! Nevertheless, in the context of the present day this argument sounds convincing and weighty.

Now we can oppose to it only the consciousness of our moral and political righteousness, the righteousness of the cause, which we serve and have given all our strength, for which we have been fighting all our lives.

Yes—alas! We did not make a pact with victory and in return must make a pact with death.

We have fulfilled all the obligations that result from such a pact with the courage of revolutionaries who know how to stare death in the eyes.

THE NEW SOVIET SOCIETY

144. Communist Saturdays   [70, vol. 2, p. 180]

In early May 1919, at the height of the Civil War, the Central Committee of the Communist Party of Russia appealed to workers to seek "new methods of productive labor and of replacing the old habits that had been transmitted by capitalism with new revolutionary customs." By May 17, Pravda *reported that almost immediately workers of the Moscow-Kazan Railroad pledged to devote 6 hours of voluntary labor every Saturday until "the final victory over Kolchak has been gained." A year later, in March 1920, the press reported that "At more and more industrial institutions the workers have volunteered to work twelve hours of the day," something that they would have refused to do under the Tsars. "Communist Saturdays," described below in a Soviet propaganda periodical, became a regular feature of Soviet life and were increasingly driven by government officials rather than grassroots initiative.*

The Soviet press [. . .] reports many examples of heroic deeds performed by soldiers of the Red Guard. In the defense of the accomplishments of the revolution against Kolchak, Denikin, and other hirelings of the landed proprietors and capitalists, workers and peasants have repeatedly achieved wonders of valor and endurance.

Not less worthy of admiration are the heroic efforts of the workers in the rear. In this connection, the establishment of Communist Saturdays by the workers, on their own initiative, is of far-reaching importance.

The introduction of the "Saturdays" has barely begun, and yet the institution is already of immense importance. It is the beginning of a new revolution, of a revolution which is a workers' revolution in the highest measure, which is more material, more radical, and more significant than the mere overthrow of the bourgeoisie, for it signifies nothing less than a victory over indolence, over disorder, over petty bourgeois egoism, a victory achieved by the working class themselves, a victory over all the bad habits bequeathed to the workers and peasants as a legacy of the capitalistic anarchy. Only the solidification of this victory may secure the creation of a new public, socialistic discipline, and render impossible a return to capitalism by making Communism invincible.

145. Soviet Russia's Code of Labor Laws, 1919
[70, vol. 2, pp. 193–4, 197–8]

The laws included in the labor code of 1919 underwent various revisions over the following years, but most of those excerpted below remained constant through much of the Soviet period. These included a universal labor obligation, the right to work, and rudimentary protections of workers.

ARTICLE I: On Compulsory Labor

1. All citizens of the Russian Socialist Federated Soviet Republic, with the exceptions stated in sections 2 and 3, shall be subject to compulsory labor.[9]

2. The following persons shall be exempt from compulsory labor:

   (a) Persons under 16 years of age;
   (b) All persons over 50 years;
   (c) Persons who have become incapacitated by injury or illness.

3. Temporarily exempt from compulsory labor are:

   (a) Persons who are temporarily incapacitated owing to illness or injury, for a period necessary for their recovery.
   (b) Women, for a period of 8 weeks before and 8 weeks after confinement.

4. All students shall be subject to compulsory labor at the schools. [. . .]

ARTICLE II: The Right to Work

10. All citizens able to work have the right to employment at their vocations and for remuneration fixed for such class of work.

Note. The District Exchange Bureaus of the Department of Labor Distribution may, by agreement with the respective unions, assign individual wage earners or groups of them to work at other trades if there is no demand for labor at the vocations of the persons in question. [. . .]

ARTICLE V: Transfer and Discharge of Wage Earners

42. The transfer of a wage earner to another enterprise, establishment, or institution situated in the same or in a different locality, may be ordered by the corresponding organ of management with the consent of the Department of Labor Distribution. [. . .]

---

9. The Russian Constitution of July 10, 1918, established the duty of every citizen to work, according to the motto: "He who does not work will not eat."

46. The discharge of wage earners from an enterprise, establishment, or institution where they have been employed is permissible in the following cases:

(a) In case of complete or partial liquidation of the enterprise, establishment, or institution, or of cancellation of certain orders or work;
(b) In case of suspension of work for more than a month;
(c) In case of expiration of term of employment or of completion of the job, if the work was of a temporary character;
(d) In case of evident unfitness for work, by special decision of the organs of management and subject to agreement with the respective professional unions;
(e) By request of the wage earner. [. . .]

ARTICLE IX: Protection of Labor

127. The protection of life, health, and labor of persons engaged in any economic activity is entrusted to the labor inspection—the technical inspectors and the representatives of sanitary inspection. [. . .]

132. The officers of labor inspection are authorized to adopt special measures [. . .] for the removal of conditions endangering the lives and health of workmen, even if such measures have not been provided for by any particular law or regulation, instructions or order of the People's Commissariat of Labor or of the Local Department of Labor. [. . .]

APPENDIX TO SECTION 80: Rules Concerning Labor Booklets

1. Every citizen of the Russian Socialist Federated Soviet Republic, upon assignment to a definite group and category [. . .] shall receive, free of charge, a labor booklet. [. . .]

2. Each wage earner, on entering the employment of an enterprise, establishment, or institution for employed paid labor, shall present his labor booklet to the management thereof. [. . .]

3. All work performed by a wage earner during the normal working day as well as piece work or overtime work, and all payments received by him [. . .] must be entered in his labor booklet.

Note. In the labor booklet must also be entered the leaves of absence and sick leave of the wage earner, as well as the fines imposed on him during and on account of his work.

146. Proletarian Holidays   [70, vol. 2, p. 569]

The Bolsheviks harbored no sympathies for the traditional Russian holidays, especially since most of them were tied to the Russian Orthodox Church. The revolutionary transformation of society meant not only that the way people worked but also the way they spent their leisure time had to change completely. Following the practices of the French Revolution, the Bolsheviks thus proceeded to develop a whole new set of holidays based on a very different set of values and beliefs. The rules laid out below were adopted by the All-Russian Central Executive Committee in March 1920.

1. In every branch of labor one day a week is to be set aside as the day of rest.

2. This day is decided upon by the People's Commissariat of Labor in agreement with the Supreme Council of National Economy, and the All-Russian Council of Trade Unions. [. . .]

4. All workers of the Russian Socialist Federated Soviet Republic must observe the set days of rest. This excludes establishments mentioned in the 6th article of these regulations. The local branches of labor, in agreement with the local councils of trade unions, may set various days of rest for various regions and establishments or groups thereof, in accordance with local conditions and the composition of the population.

5. When setting the day of rest for the workers of enterprises and establishments, the workers of each branch of commerce are divided into groups and each group is to observe a different day of rest which does not coincide with that of any other group.

6. In establishments, the activity of which is continuous, the work may be carried on during the general days of rest, and instead of the general holidays, special days are set for each group of workers.

Note. The order in which the days of rest are taken by various groups is established by the institutions mentioned in Article 4 of these regulations.

7. No work is to be done on the following holidays, dedicated to certain historic and social events:

   a) January 1st—New Year;

   b) January 22d—the 9th of January (old Russian calendar, 1905);[10]

   c) March 12th—the overthrow of autocracy;

---

10. "Bloody Sunday," when soldiers fired on protesting workers. See also p. 35, n. 2.

d) March 18th—the day of the Paris Commune;[11]
e) May 1st—the day of the Internationale;[12]
f) November 7th—the day of the Proletarian Revolution.

8. The local Councils of trade unions, with the consent of the People's Commissariat of Labor, may set special days of rest (besides the above mentioned); but no more than ten per year and in accordance with the general days of rest, with local conditions, and with the composition of the population. Such special days must be announced in advance for the information of the public at large, and they are not to be paid for.

Chairman of the All-Russian Central Executive Committee: J. Sverdlov
Secretary of the All-Russian Central Executive Committee: V. Avanessov

147. Soviet Domestic Relations Law
[70, vol. 2, pp. 477–8, 501]

The leading Bolsheviks viewed the proletarian revolution as profoundly liberationist and transformative of society in a host of ways. Following Marx and Engels, they believed that marriage and family life had been deeply corrupted by capitalism and market relations and that all of culture would change radically once the economic system itself changed. Under socialism, marriage for example would become a purely consensual relationship of two people who loved each other. Religious conceptions of marital obligation would vanish; couples would remain together only so long as both parties remained in love. The Domestic Relations Law excerpted below reflects these views.

[. . .] 52. A civil marriage registered with the office for the recording of documents relating to civil status shall create rights and duties of husband and wife as provided in the present title. A marriage contracted by a religious

---

11. Marx hailed the Paris Commune, when radicals seized power in Paris in late spring 1871 and then were crushed by the government of the Third Republic, as "a working class government . . . the political form at last discovered under which to work out the economic emancipation of man."

12. The International Workingmen's Association, or the First (Communist) International, was founded in 1864. The movement's anthem was composed in 1870 and entitled the *Internationale*. The May 1st workers' holiday was first celebrated in the United States in 1886.

ceremony performed by a clergyman, shall create no rights or duties for the parties to such marriage unless the same shall be registered according to law. [. . .]

72. The monastic state, priesthood, or deaconhood shall not be considered impediments to marriage.

73. A vow of celibacy even if taken by a member of the white or black clergy shall not be considered an impediment to marriage. [. . .]

87. Mutual consent of the husband or wife or the desire of either of them to obtain a divorce shall be considered a ground for divorce.

88. A petition for the dissolution of marriage may be presented orally or in writing and an official report shall be drawn thereon. [. . .]

104. The change of residence by one of the parties to a marriage shall not impose an obligation upon the other party to follow the former. [. . .]

107. A party to marriage unable to perform any work and being in a state of need (e.g., unable to provide the minimum living expenses) shall be entitled to receive a support from the other party provided the latter shall be able to afford this support.

148. The Legalization of Abortion, November 1920
[63, pp. 82–4]

Soviet Russia was the first country in the world to make abortion legal. When the Soviet government adopted this decree, the people's commissar of public health, Nikolai Semashko (1874–1949), explicitly denied that it would establish an individual right to abortion. He also warned that the legalization of abortion could lower the country's birthrate and therefore should be resorted to only in extreme cases. In practice, by the mid-1930s the number of abortions nearly equaled the number of births in the Russian Federation and greatly exceeded it in major cities. Abortion was therefore re-criminalized in 1936.

ON THE PROTECTION OF WOMEN'S HEALTH

During the past decades the number of women resorting to artificial discontinuation of pregnancy has grown both in the West and in this country. The legislation of all countries combats this evil by punishing the woman who chooses to have an abortion and the doctor who makes it. Without leading to favorable results, this method of combating abortions has driven the operation underground and made the woman a victim of mercenary and often ignorant quacks who make a profession of secret operations. As a result, up to 50 per cent of such women are infected in the course of the operation, and up to 4 per cent of them die.

The Workers' and Peasants' Government is conscious of this serious evil to the community. It combats this evil by propaganda against abortions among working women. By working for socialism, and by introducing the protection of maternity and infancy on an extensive scale, it feels assured of achieving the gradual disappearance of this evil. But as the moral survivals of the past and the difficult economic conditions of the present still compel many women to resort to this operation, the People's Commissariats of Health and Justice, anxious to protect the health of women, and considering that the method of repressions in this field fails entirely to achieve this aim, have decided:

(1) To permit such operations to be made freely and without any charge in Soviet hospitals, where conditions are assured of minimizing the harm of the operation.

(2) Absolutely to forbid anyone but a doctor to carry out this operation.

(3) Any nurse or midwife found guilty of making such an operation will be deprived of the right to practice and tried by a People's Court.

(4) A doctor carrying out an abortion in his private practice with mercenary aims will be called to account by a People's Court.

People's Commissar of Health N. Semashko
People's Commissar of Justice, Kurskii

149.[13] Eradication of Illiteracy in Cherepovets[14]

[70, vol. 2, p. 638]

Doing away with illiteracy had been a major goal of the Russian government from the late 19th century on. The number of primary schools quadrupled from 1878 to 1911. Thus, the total literacy rate of the country had increased from 25.6 percent in 1887 to 42.8 percent in 1917 (and from 37 to 57.6 percent for males). The Bolsheviks sought to spread literacy with great vigor, viewing it as an essential prerequisite for Communist enlightenment. In December 1919, the Bolshevik government issued a decree "On the eradication of illiteracy among the population of RSFSR." This policy relied on mostly voluntary

---

13. This article appeared in the newspaper *Pravda* on April 17, 1920.

14. During the period 1918–1927, the city of Cherepovets was the capital of a province 200 miles north of Moscow. In 1920, it had roughly 700,000 inhabitants.

anti-illiteracy campaigns, since little state funding was available. Thus, the rate of literacy rose only to 51.1 percent (66.5 percent for males) by 1926, even as official press reports like the one below hailed the policy as a complete success.

The months of February and March were entirely devoted to the preliminary work necessary in insuring the success of the general campaign to do away with illiteracy which it was decided to bring to an end by January next.

During those two months a census of the entire population of the province was taken in accordance with a uniform plan, classifying them into illiterates, literates, public school, and high school graduates, etc.

In each of the five districts of the province, three-day conferences were held, in accordance with a definite program, for the instruction of teachers of the first and second grade schools. As many as 350 teachers attended these conferences, each county [i.e., volost] having sent two.

The latter, upon their return, called two-day county conferences of all the teachers in their county, rendering reports on the work performed by the district conferences. Thus the teaching staff of all counties in the province attended these conferences.

For immediate work in eradicating illiteracy among the population of the province, 10,000 young men and women—graduates of the elementary or higher schools—were mobilized for compulsory service, and upon the completion of a three-weeks' special course of instruction, formed the ranks of the new teaching staff.

Professional teachers are, as a rule, assigned as instructors in the campaign to abolish illiteracy and are utilized to prepare new teachers. For the same purpose thirty-six students of the People's Institute of Education were mobilized, and after three days of special preparation were assigned throughout the province as inspecting instructors for the Provincial Department of Education.

With a view to bringing about a more systematic, uniform, and speedy eradication of illiteracy in the counties, districts, and throughout the province, extraordinary committees of three are being formed by the local offices of the People's Commissariat of Education, composed of representatives of the Department of Education, the Executive Committee, and the party organizations. Upon these committees rests all the responsibility for the successful and prompt execution of the work of doing away with illiteracy.

From April 1 to May 15, 10,000 schools for illiterates were functioning in the province. The schools are open for two hours daily, including holidays. The new teaching staff comes from the ranks of the laboring masses.

From May 15 to October 1, attendance at these schools is compulsory on Sunday only, but it is desirable that students attend them also on other holidays lest they forget what they have learned.

From October 1 to the end of the school year, the schools will be open as usual for two hours daily until the entire course has been completed—180 study periods of one hour each.

By the end of the year, illiteracy will be eradicated in the [province] of Cherepovets, and the entire population of all five districts of that province will be literate, unless some unforeseen or extraordinary circumstances intervene.

150. Preparing for the Abolition of Money, January 1921
[70, vol. 4, p. 16]

Even after the Civil War had ended, by late 1920, the Bolshevik leadership continued to pursue radical economic policies aimed at achieving the Marxist definition of Communism: "From each according to his abilities, to each according to his needs." Among these policies were the provision of basic social services free of charge and the elimination of money, as outlined in the press report below. The New Economic Policy, which partially reestablished a market economy, put an end to these experiments, as did the creation of the State Bank in October 1921.

[. . .] In one of its most recent sessions, the Small Council of People's Commissars [. . .] adopted a resolution [. . .] which commissions the People's Commissar of Finance to submit within one month [. . .] proposals for carefully elaborated decrees on the abolition of money payments for all products that are issued by the People's Commissar for Provisions, to the workers, employees, and their families, as in general to bearers of cards of the first and second categories, as well as for the abolition of money payments for rent on dwellings of workers, clerks, and their families, living in national or municipal lodgings, and finally for fuel of all kinds that is provided to workers and clerks in institutions according to the plans of the Fuel Section. Also for gas, electric current, telephone, water supply, drainage, etc. At the same time, a commission was formed in the Council of People's Commissars, which was instructed to consider within one month the question of a complete abolition of money payments [. . .] even between the productive Soviet enterprises and institutions.

In this way, very probably not later than January 1, this new, and as a principle, important improvement in the organization of the order of life of Soviet Russia will enter into force. Simultaneously, from January 1 on, our second regulation also will go into force,—the abolition of fees for railway transportation of all freight, and of almost all passengers, provided for by a decree approved August 24 by the Council of People's Commissars. This would include fares now paid by workers and clerks who are on leave or are traveling to their work, to their schools, to their congresses, or with excursions of their unions.

SOVIET CULTURE:
FROM LIBERATION TO SUBJUGATION

151. Education and the Arts, an Official Report, 1921
[70, vol. 4, pp. 287–91]

Of all those who welcomed the Bolshevik revolution, perhaps no one was more excited about the prospects of a new Communist culture than Anatolii Lunacharskii. He became the head of the Commissariat for Education, or, as the Bolsheviks called it, the Commissariat of Enlightenment. This title reflected their firm belief that the masses could only create a new and superior culture if they enlightened themselves not only with basic education but with the teachings of Marxism. Enlightened culture, no longer concerned with profits or dependent on the capitalist classes for support, would allow the human spirit to soar to endless heights, or so people like Lunacharskii believed. Lunacharskii's report below conveys this sense of optimism. In practice, shortages of paper, popular resistance to the new teachings (especially in the countryside), and ordinary people's ignorance of basic political concepts made it difficult for the government to spread its message and promote its values.

ART IN SOVIET RUSSIA
(From the Report of the Commissariat of Education)

In Tsarist Russia the enjoyment of art in all its forms was exclusively the privilege of the ruling classes. The "nation" only got wretched crumbs as a substitute. Knowing what a powerful means of agitation the theater is for the masses, the State kept a vigilant eye upon the so-called people's theaters, fencing them round with censorship, and entirely subjecting them to the police authorities. Education, both musical, theatrical, and artistic, was quite inaccessible to the masses.

It became the aim of the Soviet Government to make art accessible to all, to bind it up in the life of the laboring masses, to put it on a new foundation, so that it should draw new forces from the proletariat.

At the same time, while working persistently towards the creation of a new, purely proletarian art, we endeavored to familiarize the proletariat with the best achievements of former art.

At the start, in the realization of this task, we met with our principal difficulty, which was the lack of talented forces in the art world, who could understand the tasks confronting Soviet Russia and could see them carried out. Only recently have we been able to make progress among the workers, and they have given us a number of prominent men and helped us to put art on a sound basis.

Theatrical World. Much has been done in democratizing the theater. The repertoire of the theaters has been greatly improved; in this we are still working to acquaint the workers with the best models of the classic theater. By a recent regulation a uniform price for seats in all theaters has been established; this measure is a step towards the complete abolition of all pay for theatrical shows. Considering the theater an instrument of education and propaganda, we should make it free of charge, as we do the school. Parallel with the classical repertoire, there is slowly coming up a new revolutionary repertoire, which we are endeavoring to foster by means of competition in the studios and workshops.

On the other hand, among the working masses themselves, such a tremendous striving towards theatrical creation is evident that it has proved extraordinarily difficult to manage and direct all the theaters and groups that sprang up so naturally.

The Musical World. In the musical field our path was generally the same as in the theatrical sphere, i.e., we aimed at drawing the wide laboring masses to appreciate works of genuine musical art; extensive musical education was given and wide facilities for the production of new music, growing out of the proletariat itself and corresponding to the spirit of the times.

We are accomplishing the first task by creating a number of state orchestras, from our best orchestral forces. The Musical Department has formed five large symphony orchestras, about fifty small orchestras, and two orchestras of national instruments. These orchestras, during 1919 and the beginning of 1920, gave in the provinces about 170 symphonic concerts from chosen works of classical music, 70 concert-meetings, and over 170 concerts of various kinds. These concerts enjoy invariable success among the workers and Red Army men.

The work in the field of musical education is conducted along two lines; the musical education of the wide masses is attained by the establishment of a network of national musical schools, whose number at the present time is 75 (before the Revolution there was one); on the other hand the Musical Department of the Commissariat of Education is working extensively in schools and children's homes. Thus in Petrograd up to 500 schools and 600 children's homes have included in their curriculum the systematic teaching of music. Choir singing has been introduced in 80 per cent of all the schools;

the practice of music in 60 per cent; the nurseries all have a musical staff attached to them.

The second line is the creation of professional music schools, the number of which is already 200, with an attendance of 26,000. The percentage of worker and peasant students in the national schools is 70 per cent, in the vocational schools of the First and Second grades about 55 per cent, and in the higher musical schools it is not more than 30 per cent, which is naturally to be explained by the fact that a corresponding cadre of workers and peasants has not yet been prepared for the high schools.

Apart from this the Musical Department is engaged in the production of musical instruments; it is at present giving most attention to the revival of the noblest of Russian national instruments,—the "Dombra." The nationalization of instruments and of music enabled the Musical Department to adopt measures for the correct distribution of this stock, and to take stock of especially valuable old instruments, of which a collection has been formed. Thus we possess the only collection of the famous Stradivarius violins in the whole world; these are not hidden in museums, but are given, on competition, to the use of the best violinists, who are obliged to let the masses hear good execution on the famous instruments.

The problem of realizing a new proletarian music is, of course, not going to be decided by means of decrees or by personal effort. In this regard our hope is with the proletarian youth who are training in our musical schools, and every spark of talent is supported by us by all possible means.

Fine Arts Department. This department carries on extensive work of a practical nature. Having made the industrial principle the basis of its work, it has spread a wide network of workshops, both of a purely artistic type and of industrial art where on the one hand it strives in general to develop the artistic taste of the working masses, and awaken talent amongst them, and on the other hand directly introduces the principles of art and style in industrial work. With the latter aim, workshops have been set up for chintz work, woodwork, stonework, printing, pottery, and toy-making, etc. There are 35 such workshops in different parts of Russia. The total number of people in these workshops is 7,000.

Besides this the Department is organizing, both in Moscow and in the provinces, art exhibitions whose aim it is to acquaint the workers with all the tendencies of art in general. That fine art is not declining with us is proved clearly not only by the productivity, but by the quality of the work in our porcelain factories, whose productions are highly valued abroad. They now employ widely the watchwords and emblems of the times in their work. The State has given full freedom of development to all tendencies in the sphere of art, for it believes that its ever-growing contact with the working masses serves as the surest regulator for putting art on a firm and true foundation.

The occasionally apparent preponderance of one tendency in art over another finds its explanation in the fact that energy and impetus is at times displayed by young art groups, which discover enthusiastically new ways or achievements. We regard this calmly and without apprehension. We are sure that the new artist, the proletarian-artist who has graduated from our art schools, will at the proper moment deliberately sweep away all that is superfluous and superficial; he will use all that is valuable and will give to the world an art that will be unequaled for its vividness and expressiveness.

Museum Department. One of the most brilliant pages in our artwork is the activity of the Commissariat for Education in the sphere of safeguarding the monuments of art and of the past.

Since the Revolution, our museum collections have been growing all the time. All the treasures that had been hidden from the eyes of the masses in palaces and manors have been collected and placed in museums, being the property of all the workers. [. . .]

OUT-OF-SCHOOL EDUCATION

From the very first day of its existence, the Commissariat for Public Education was confronted by the problem of out-of-school education, or, according to the present terminology, of political-educational work.

We have to deal with a country in which the percentage of illiterates is enormous, a country which it was the policy of the Tsarist regime to keep in darkness and ignorance, a country which was in the power of the most fanatical prejudices.

The Out-of-School Department, now the Political-Educational Department of the Commissariat of Public Education, faced the problem of organizing public libraries, schools of all types for adults, clubs, people's houses, excursions, etc. The task was to broaden this activity and give it a communist direction.

In the field of library work the results were the following: In 32 provinces there were 13,500 libraries in 1919. In 32 provinces there were 26,278 libraries in 1920. [. . .]

Very characteristic are the figures showing the growth of the library matter in Petrograd: Before the Revolution there were 23 libraries with 140,000 volumes; after the Revolution 59 libraries with 865,000 volumes.[15] [. . .]

All over the Republic an enormous number of literacy schools have been opened; 10,000 schools were opened by the middle of Spring in the province of Cherepovets alone; in the province of Tambov—6,000 schools, which were attended by 48,000 pupils in the month of April; in the province of

15. The authorities confiscated vast numbers of books from private homes and organizations and concentrated them in the major cities and in local public libraries.

Simbirsk—6,000 schools, in the province of Kazan—5,000 schools, which were attended by 150,000 pupils; in the province of Viatka—4,000 persons were attending literacy schools, even before the decree was issued. [. . .]

It is interesting to point out the compulsory measures, which are practiced in different parts of the Republic: In the province of Kazan, those who refuse to attend the literacy schools are subject to a 5,000-ruble fine, to 3 months of compulsory labor, and the loss of their food cards. In Petrograd those who refuse to attend the schools are reduced to a lower food category; they are tried in a people's court, and are excluded from the trade union. In the province of Tambov a signature for an illiterate has no validity. [. . .]

152. Senior Cheka Officials Oppose Cultural Elites Traveling Abroad, May 1921   [2, pp. 18–9]

The overwhelming majority of educated Russians greeted the February Revolution favorably but also vehemently rejected the Bolshevik seizure of power. Within 3 years of that event, at least 1 million elites emigrated, most illegally. Among these were most of Russia's leading cultural figures, including Sergei Rachmaninov, Ivan Bunin (Nobel Prize for Literature, 1933), Igor Stravinsky, and Vladimir Nabokov, to name only a few. The document below shows that the Bolshevik leadership tried hard to prevent such people from leaving the country.

In re: Politburo resolution of May 7, 1921, no. 23, paragraph 16

Reiterating its first statement [of April 19], the All-Russian Cheka once again must direct the attention of the Central Committee to the totally unacceptable attitude of the Commissariat of Enlightenment toward the question of artists traveling abroad. There is no doubt that the great majority of actors and artists who travel abroad are lost for Soviet Russia, at least for the immediate future.

Moreover, many of them, once abroad, wage an overt or a covert campaign against us.

Of those who have traveled abroad with the permission of the Commissariat of Enlightenment only five have returned; the remaining nineteen have not; and one ([Konstantin] Balmont)[16] is waging the most vile campaign against Soviet Russia.

---

16. Konstantin Balmont (1867–1942), a leading symbolist poet, was a major figure in Russia's artistic Silver Age. A resident of Paris from 1905 to 1916, he greeted the Febru-

As to the First Studio of the Artistic Theater, the All-Russian Cheka can say with confidence that it will not return. All of the [other] actors of the Artistic Theater who are presently abroad have enjoyed great success and live splendidly in material terms.

Moreover, a number of well-known actors (such as Sukhachev) are closely linked to foreign embassies in Moscow, and there is reason to believe that these relations are not solely of a personal nature.

> Politburo resolution no. 34, paragraph 5, May 28, 1921
> Request of the First Artistic Studio for
> permission to travel abroad is denied.

153. Handling Russia's Cultural Elites, June 1922
[2, pp. 36–7]

As the Bolshevik leaders sought to develop and refine their policies toward the country's cultural elites, Trotsky submitted the following report to the Politburo on June 30, 1922, sharing his ideas on this matter.

We are undoubtedly running the risk of losing young poets, artists, etc., who are gravitating toward us. No attention is being paid to them or almost none. More precisely, attention is being paid to individuals by individual Soviet officials randomly or in a purely amateurish way. [. . .]

We must set ourselves the task of approaching young representatives of Soviet art carefully and in an individualized fashion. For this purpose it is necessary to:

1. Seriously and carefully register poets, writers, artists, etc. Concentrate this work in the Main Censorship Agency in Moscow and Petrograd. Maintain a file on every poet with his biographical information and his current literary, political, and other relations. This information should be gathered so as to:

a) guide censors in determining whether to authorize publications;
b) help party literary critics in formulating positions concerning the poets in question;
c) help specify which young writers and others should receive material support.

---

ary Revolution enthusiastically but rejected the Bolshevik coup of October. He received permission to travel abroad in June 1920 and settled in Paris never to return, despite profound nostalgia.

2. Draft immediately a short list of writers who are clearly gifted and clearly sympathetic to us yet whom the struggle to survive is pushing toward the bourgeoisie and may soon push into the camp of our enemies or of those hostile to us. [. . .]

3. Order the editorial boards of the most important party publications (newspapers, magazines) to mention these young authors in a more "utilitarian" fashion, i.e., in such a way as to exert a certain impact and influence on each such young person of letters. [. . .]

4. Our censors should also adopt the above-mentioned pedagogical slant. It is necessary to manifest *severity*[17] toward publications displaying obvious bourgeois artistic tendencies. It is necessary to manifest *ruthlessness* toward those artistic and literary groups that are dominated by Mensheviks and Socialist-Revolutionaries. At the same time, an attentive, careful, and gentle approach is required for works and authors that, even while containing countless prejudices, are clearly developing in a revolutionary direction. [. . .]

5. The question of support for young poets should receive separate consideration. [. . .]

6. In any case, a certain amount of money will have to be allocated for this purpose.

7. The same measures should be applied to young artists. But here a separate discussion is necessary to decide which institution should maintain the personnel files and who should be personally responsible for this work.

154. Official Denunciation of Non-Communist Intellectuals, August 1922   [55]

In May 1922, Lenin gave orders to GPU officials to carefully study the publications of writers and professors in preparation for a mass exiling of intellectuals. As part of this operation, Politburo members were supposed to spend 2–3 hours a week browsing through non-Communist publications; those found "untrustworthy" would need to supply written justifications of their positions. Over the summer, a few hundred names of intellectuals across the country were compiled. From August to December, as many as 160 were exiled, mostly to Germany. Many of the scholars were in the humanities; by contrast, scientists were often denied the right to emigrate. This endeavor was part of a broad assault by the Soviet press, which published articles attacking intellectuals, like the one below.

---

17. Italics in original, here and below.

Kadet-style and Socialist-Revolutionary-style circles of the intelligentsia, having imagined that the NEP is giving them a new basis for counterrevolutionary work, began to conduct such work intensely, maintaining close ties with the White Guards abroad. Soviet power having shown too much patience, has finally issued a first warning: the most active counterrevolutionary elements from among professors, doctors, agronomists, etc., are being exiled partly abroad and partly to the northern provinces. For workers and peasants all of this serves as a reminder that they need to develop their own worker-peasant intelligentsia as soon as possible. [. . .]

After the victory of Soviet power over the White Guards, after the liquidation of the fronts and the bandit rebellions, these groups [of intellectuals] found themselves in a dead end. But in the conditions of the NEP [. . .] they sought to adjust themselves, to consolidate themselves, and to gain influence primarily over students, then over the petty-bourgeois philistine population in general. They sought to use "legal" opportunities under Soviet power in order to continue stubbornly and over the long haul the same work that resulted in the failure of the counterrevolution in its open struggle against Soviet power. [. . .]

They found several bases for their anti-Soviet work. Higher education, which was scarcely affected by the October coup, was their most important citadel. Learned professor-intriguers with every step stubbornly resisted Soviet power, which began reforming higher education and massively bringing workers and peasants into the *rabfaks*.[18] [. . .] [T]hey have even dared to engage in open struggle, for example this spring during an academic strike by professors.

These groups have organized a number of journals, published mostly in Petrograd, where, though rather cautiously, yet stubbornly, viciously, and consistently, they have sought to discredit all the initiatives of Soviet power, subjecting them to pretended scholarly criticism. They have pursued the same course in journalism. Imaginative literature put out by these circles is also of an anti-Soviet nature. In the field of philosophy they have preached mysticism and religious superstition, loading up numerous private publishers with a modernized ideology of the Middle Ages. A group of anti-Soviet-minded doctors diligently fabricated anti-Soviet public opinion in its sphere, which was so clearly manifested at the recent Doctors' Congress.[19] Counterrevolutionary elements among the agronomists conducted the same work in their area

18. *Rabochie fakul'tety* were remedial departments established, beginning in 1919, to prepare workers and peasants lacking secondary education for college.

19. A report by Nikolai Semashko, people's commissar for Public Health, pointing to "dangerous and harmful currents" at the Second All-Russian Congress of Doctors held in May 1922, outraged Lenin.

seeking support from student circles and pro-Socialist-Revolutionary kulak elements. In the cooperative movement the same work was led by Kadet-style and Socialist-Revolutionary-style elements, which have always been strong in our cooperative movement. Finally, some groups within these anti-Soviet elements have sought a rapprochement with the counterrevolutionary part of the clergy that actively opposed the confiscation of church valuables.

Finally, all of these groups were in close contact with our White-Guard emigration, which receives money from the bourgeois governments hostile to us and has sought to discredit in every way all actions of Soviet power in the international arena. From among these groups, correspondents of foreign White-Guard newspapers have been recruited to provide the foreign press with false and libelous information. [. . .]

[. . .] If these gentlemen do not like living in Soviet Russia, let them enjoy all the benefits of bourgeois freedom outside of its borders. [. . .]

There are almost no prominent figures among those who are being exiled. For the most part these are professorial elements engaged in political intrigue, who are much better known for their affiliation with the Kadet party than for their scholarly merits. [. . .]

155. Fedor Stepun Is Expelled from Soviet Russia
[73, pp. 617–23]

Fedor Stepun was among the dozens of intellectuals expelled from Soviet Russia in 1922. He taught and published in Germany until expelled by the Nazis from Dresden's Higher Technical School. He miraculously survived the bombing of Dresden during World War II and occupied a chair in Russian studies at the University of Munich from 1947 till 1960. In the memoir excerpt below, he explains why after initial reluctance he agreed to leave Soviet Russia.

[. . .] Exile to free Europe, however enticing, did not elicit joy. In the course of the revolutionary years my soul became deeply attached to Ivanovka,[20] to the house, the garden, all of the village's inhabitants, with whom we shared so many experiences, both difficult and horrible but also joyful and bright. I was also certain for some reason that if we were exiled, neither my mother, nor Natasha's parents would be alive by the time we returned. [. . .]

---

20. Ivanovka was a village near Moscow.

Upon my arrival in Moscow, I happened to run into Nikolai Aleksandrovich Berdiaev. After a quick greeting he told me in agitation, more joyful than fearful, that preparations were under way for the exile abroad of a whole group of religious philosophers, economists associated with the cooperative movement, and some other individuals, not well known in our circles. [. . .]

Finally, I was brought into a small room, from which two full hours later I was taken to an adjacent room, where a rather simple man was sitting behind an office desk. [. . .] After the usual procedure establishing one's date of birth, origin, and education, he presented me a sheet with three questions I was already familiar with printed on it: (1) What is your attitude toward Soviet power; (2) What is your attitude toward capital punishment; (3) What is your attitude toward emigration?

I had already thought through the spirit, the style, and to a certain extent the content of my answers. I decided to respond quite candidly, but gently, without fervor or any sort of sharp remarks, not like a political fighter, since I had not viewed myself as one since the failure of [the] February [Revolution], but as a passive, honest, and incorruptible observer of the unfolding events.

Adhering to this decision, I wrote the following:

(1) As a citizen of the Soviet Federated Republic, I accept the government and all [political] parties unconditionally; as a philosopher and a writer, however, I consider Bolshevism to be a grave disease of the people's soul. That soul is ill, and I cannot but wish its speedy recovery;

(2) I cannot protest against the application of capital punishment in transitional revolutionary times, since I myself defended it in the military commission of the Soviet of Workers' and Soldiers' Deputies. Even so, my confident belief that the Bolshevik government will end up turning capital punishment into a conventional method of governing the country makes it impossible for me either to be involved in this government in any way or to accept it personally;

(3) As to emigration, I am against it: one should not abandon one's own mother on her death bed. To remain at that bed is the natural duty of every son. If I had been for immigration, I would have left Russia long ago.

I do not remember whether my answers resulted in any displeasure or surprise on the part of the investigator, if he was in fact an investigator. He posed two more questions verbally, without, it seems, any personal interest, just as a matter of official duty. One was about my view of Marxism; the other concerned the task of the Russian intelligentsia.

As I remember, my answer boiled down to what I had been thinking about Marxism back then and still think about it now: Marx's *Capital* is an acutely thought-through and generally correct sociological analysis of the capitalist system of Europe, but there is no sense or basis in turning the sociological doctrine of Marxism into a historiosophical doctrine applicable to all times and peoples. In Russia, incidentally, Marxism triumphed not as an abstract philosophical doctrine, but as a false faith, which had captured the people's soul. The task of the Russian intelligentsia is to untangle this mess. One has to believe in God, not in Karl Marx; the Marxist analysis of the historical sins of the capitalist system should be used for building a freedom-loving socialist society.

Perhaps I am mistaken, but I think my thoughts were to my investigator's liking. Something sparked between us; something even brought us closer, and at the end of the interrogation we were conversing rather amicably about the front and about the tragedy of the soldiers' revolution. [. . .]

After the interrogation I was given two documents to sign: One stated that were I to return illegally to the RSFSR I would be subject to capital punishment. The other inquired whether I preferred to travel at my own or, as they said in the old days, at official expense. [. . .]

[. . .] First of all, it was absolutely necessary to extend the [one week] deadline [of my departure]. Thus, I decided to go to the German embassy the very next day and to tell them everything as it was and tearfully entreat them not to issue me a visa, until I told them I was ready to depart. At the embassy, I was very kindly received by a certain Dr. G., whose name I thankfully keep in my memory. [. . .]

Accompanied by a respectful servant, I entered a warm, bright, newly remodeled living room [in the embassy]. I felt not without some surprise the extent to which I had lost the feel for what had formerly been my life too, how simplified my life had become, and even how low I had sunk in the course of long years of sitting in the trenches and of moving from place to place in cold, often noxious rooms with hungry rats and village roaches. About five to six people were invited to attend a simple dinner, which seemed to me at that time incredibly luxurious. [. . .]

[. . .] After the dinner we moved to the study. Wine and cigars appeared, a blue, aromatic smoke filled the room, the firewood began cracking in the fireplace, and everyone's thoughts became somewhat sharper and tongues grew more loose. I was asked about many things, which to the foreigners seemed incomprehensible, even incredible. I answered not without certain circumspection, which had already entered my flesh and blood, but honestly and candidly. I was surprised that there were still people in the world, whom one barely knows but with whom it is possible to share one's thoughts without fear, trusting that they will not denounce you [to the authorities]. This was a totally new and very significant experience for me. In the course of animated conversations in the German embassy I for the first time during my Soviet life realized that I had been living in a prison, where only the closest relatives and friends can whisper and send messages to each other, naturally considering all others to be their potential enemies or betrayers.

When I returned home, I told Natasha in detail about my evening at the embassy. Having talked through the night again we decided by morning that however sad it was to leave what was ours and those who were ours, Russia and Ivanovka, we should nevertheless sincerely thank fate that the prison doors were opened in front of us and that we already were breathing the air of freedom, without which one cannot live. [. . .]

156. The Institutionalization of Soviet Censorship, December 2, 1922   [6, pp. 36–7]

Already in October 1917, the arbitrary closing of non-Bolshevik periodicals began and censorship grew stricter over time. A few opposition socialist newspapers continued to appear intermittently into 1919. In 1920, the government ordered the creation in libraries and archives of limited-access secret vaults for "sensitive" imprints and documents. An order of October 17, 1921, established an expansive range of "state secrets," which included road conditions, unrest in military units, epidemics, the country's gold reserves, regular criminality, peasant resistance to the grain tax, and unrest in concentration camps and prisons. An institution to implement strict censorship, the Main Literature Administration (Glavlit), was created by a decree of June 6, 1922. The following directive spelled out Glavlit's responsibilities and functions.

The Rights and Functions of Glavlit and Its Local Agencies

Glavlit and its local agencies carry out all categories of censorship (military, political, ideological, etc.). All publishers are obligated to submit all printed material for preliminary screening. Censorship of printed material consists of:

a. not allowing articles openly hostile to the Communist Party and Soviet power;

b. not allowing any kind of printed material that conveys a hostile ideology on fundamental issues (public life, religion, economics, the field of art, etc.);

c. deleting from articles the most critical passages (facts, figures, characterizations) that might discredit Soviet power and the Communist Party.

Glavlit has the right to temporarily suspend individual publications, to decrease their circulation, as well as to shut down publishers in the event of an openly criminal activity and to bring the responsible executives to court or to refer their files to the local GPU.

The GPU's Political Control Section provides Glavlit with technical assistance in maintaining surveillance over printing presses, the book trade, and the importation and exportation of printed material from abroad and out of the Republic.

The Literary Subsection:

1. carries out political and military censorship of all materials for print (periodical and non-periodical publications, playbills, posters, etc.);

2. comrades conducting censorship and political editing work divide the books they read by content: those versed in economic issues read the books of an economic nature, and those with an interest in fiction read poetry, fictional prose, etc.

Each "appraisal" should conform to a special format and contain a brief and clear political evaluation of the given work, including a general political evaluation, [. . .] a precise indication of the most unacceptable passages, and a checking of the text against "The list of information not to be revealed in print."

The Literary subsection compiles lists of prohibited and authorized books.

The Administrative-Inspection Section carries out control functions of surveillance over publishers, printing presses, bookstores, and libraries. The section keeps a detailed register of all the publishers in [each] province (private, trade union, and governmental, etc.), identifying the members of their governing and editorial boards and the authors, individuals, and public groups that collaborate with them, finance them, and inspire them. As a matter of practice, these functions are carried out through the GPU.

Glavlit Chief Lebedev-Polianksii
GPU representative Ashmarin

THE REVOLUTION'S HEIRS

157. The Formation of the Union of Soviet Socialist Republics, December 1922   [25, pp. 65–6]

The First Congress of Soviets of the USSR, which met in Moscow's Bolshoi Theater on December 30, 1922, ratified the Declaration and Treaty on the Formation of the Union of Soviet Socialist Republics (USSR). The new state comprised the Russian and Transcaucasian Soviet Federated Socialist Republics and the Ukrainian and Byelorussian Soviet Socialist Republics. The latter three included former parts of the Russian Empire that the Bolsheviks brought back under Moscow's control. The idea to create a union of formally equal republics was strongly advocated by Lenin, who thus prevailed over Stalin's desire to integrate these Soviet republics back into Russia. The declaration below explains the reasons for the creation of the USSR and describes the underlying Soviet worldview.

From the moment of the formation of the Soviet republics, the countries of the world have split into two camps: the camp of capitalism and the camp of socialism.

Out in the camp of capitalism, there are national enmity and inequality, slavery and jingoism, national oppression and pogroms, imperialistic atrocities and wars. Here, in the camp of socialism, there is mutual trust and peace, the freedom and equality of nations, peaceful coexistence, and brotherly cooperation of peoples. [. . .]

The bourgeoisie has proved incapable of organizing the cooperation of peoples.

Only in the camp of the Soviets, only in the conditions of the dictatorship of the proletariat, which has consolidated around itself the majority of the population, did it become possible to root out national oppression, to create an environment of mutual trust, and to lay the foundations for the brotherly cooperation of peoples.

Only these circumstances permitted the Soviet republics to repulse the attack of both internal and external imperialists of the whole world, only these circumstances permitted them to win the civil war, to secure their survival, and to begin peaceful economic construction. [. . .]

[. . .] [But] reconstruction of the national economy proved to be impossible with the republics existing separately.

Moreover, the instability of the international situation and the danger of new attacks render inevitable the creation of a united front of the Soviet republics in the face of capitalist encirclement.

Finally, the very structure of Soviet power, which is internationalist given its class-based nature, draws the working masses of the Soviet republics toward unification into a single socialist family.

All these circumstances imperatively demand unification of the Soviet republics into one united state capable of securing both external safety and internal economic achievements, as well as freedom for the national development of peoples.

The will of the peoples of the Soviet republics, who recently convened congresses of their soviets and unanimously approved a motion to form the Union of Soviet Socialist Republics, serves as a reliable guarantee that this Union is a voluntary association of peoples equal in their rights, that each republic is guaranteed the right to secede freely from the Union, that entry into the Union is available to all socialist Soviet republics, those in existence today and those to emerge in the future, that the new unified state will be a worthy crowning to the foundations of peaceful cohabitation and brotherly cooperation of peoples laid back in October 1917, and that it will serve as a reliable bulwark against world capitalism and a new decisive step on the path of unifying the laboring people of all countries into a Global Socialist Soviet Republic.

158. Lenin's "Testament," December 1922 to January 1923 [44, vol. 36, pp. 593–7, 603]

Lenin's "testament" was a letter, severally amended, which he intended to be read at the Twelfth Party Congress in April 1923. He dictated it to two staff secretaries, Lidiia Fotieva and Mariia Volodicheva, on several occasions from December 23, 1922, to January 3, 1923, after he suffered a second stroke. That night paralysis set in on the right side of his body. He stated repeatedly to Volodicheva that the text was "to be considered categorically secret" and given only to his wife, Nadezhda Krupskaia. After a third stroke deprived Lenin of the faculty of speech in March 1923, Krupskaia kept the document hidden, revealing it to party leaders only upon his death in January 1924. Her request that delegates to the Thirteenth Party Congress in May 1924 be given the document was not fully honored: regional leaders read it to their individual delegations, note taking was forbidden, and no mention was made of the "testament" in the plenary meeting of the congress. Lenin's intention to telegraph his misgivings directly to the rank and file, whom he considered to be the revolution's heirs, and over the heads of the party leaders was thwarted. Thus, the document had very little impact.

Letter of December 23, 1922

I would urge strongly [. . .] an increase in the number of Central Committee members to a few dozen or even a hundred. [. . .]

I think it must be done in order to raise the prestige of the Central Committee, to do a thorough job of improving our administrative machinery, and to prevent conflicts between small sections of the C.C. from acquiring excessive importance for the future of the Party. [. . .]

Such a reform would considerably increase the stability of our Party and ease its struggle in the encirclement of hostile states, which, in my opinion, is likely to, and must, become much more acute in the next few years. [. . .]

Continuation of the notes, December 24, 1922

[. . .] I have in mind stability as a guarantee against a split in the immediate future, and I intend to deal here with a few ideas concerning personal qualities.

I think that from this standpoint the prime factors in the question of stability are such members of the C.C. as Stalin and Trotsky. I think relations between them make up the greater part of the danger of a split, which could be avoided, and this purpose, in my opinion, would be served, among other things, by increasing the number of C.C. members to 50 or 100.

Comrade Stalin, having become Secretary-General, has unlimited authority concentrated in his hands, and I am not sure whether he will always be capable of using that authority with sufficient caution. Comrade Trotsky [. . .] is personally perhaps the most capable man in the present C.C., but he has displayed excessive self-assurance and shown excessive preoccupation with the purely administrative side of the work.

These two qualities of the two outstanding leaders of the present C.C. can inadvertently lead to a split, and if our Party does not take steps to avert this, the split may come unexpectedly.

I shall not give any further appraisals of the personal qualities of other members of the C.C. I shall just recall that the October episode with Zinoviev and Kamenev was, of course, no accident, but neither can the blame for it be laid upon them personally, any more than non-Bolshevism can upon Trotsky.

Speaking of the young C.C. members, [. . .] Bukharin is not only a most valuable and major theorist of the Party; he is also rightly considered the favorite of the whole Party, but his theoretical views can be classified as fully

Marxist only with great reserve, for there is something scholastic about him (he has never made a study of the dialectic, and, I think, never fully understood it).

December 25

As for Piatakov, he is unquestionably a man of outstanding will and outstanding ability, but shows too much zeal for administrating and the administrative side of the work to be relied upon in a serious political matter.

Both of these remarks, of course, are made only for the present, on the assumption that both these outstanding and devoted Party workers fail to find an occasion to enhance their knowledge and amend their one-sidedness.

Addition to the letter of December 24, 1922

Stalin is too rude and this defect, although quite tolerable in our midst and in dealing among us Communists, becomes intolerable in a Secretary-General. That is why I suggest that the comrades think about a way of removing Stalin from that post and appointing another man in his stead who in all other respects differs from Comrade Stalin in having only one advantage, namely, that of being more tolerant, more loyal, more polite, and more considerate to the comrades, less capricious, etc. [. . .]

Taken down by L. F.
January 4, 1923

Continuation of the notes, December 26, 1922

The increase in the number of C.C. members to 50 or even 100 must, in my opinion, serve a double or even a treble purpose: the more members there are in the C.C., the more men will be trained in C.C. work and the less danger there will be of a split due to some indiscretion. The enlistment of many workers to the C.C. will help the workers to improve our administrative machinery, which is pretty bad. We inherited it, in effect, from the old regime, for it was absolutely impossible to reorganize it in such a short time, especially in conditions of war, famine, etc. [. . .] It is enough that in five years we have created a new type of state in which the workers are leading the peasants against the bourgeoisie; and in a hostile international environment this in itself is a gigantic achievement. [. . .]

Continuation of the notes, December 29, 1922

In increasing the number of its members, the C.C., I think, must also, and perhaps mainly, devote attention to checking and improving our administrative machinery, which is no good at all. For this we must enlist the

services of highly qualified specialists, and the task of supplying those specialists must devolve upon the Workers' and Peasants' Inspection. [. . .]

If the number of C.C. members is increased in the appropriate way, and
they go through a course of state management year after year with the help
of highly qualified specialists and of members of the Workers' and Peasants'
Inspection who are highly authoritative in every branch—then, I think, we
shall successfully solve this problem which we have not managed to do for
such a long time. [. . .]

GLOSSARY

All-Russian: Adjective connoting the whole Russian territory; see *Russian.*

All-Russian Central Executive Committee (VTsIK): Executive branch of government in Soviet Russia.

anarchists: Any of various political activists, allied in several parties, who rejected the state and advocated cooperative political structures; frequently supported political terrorism.

Bolshevik Party: More radical fraction of the Social Democratic (Marxist) Party; dominated by Vladimir Lenin.

Cheka: Secret police.

Comintern: Communist International; the Moscow-controlled union of worldwide Communist parties founded in 1919.

commissar: Government official charged with a particular assignment, in imitation of the French revolutionary *commissaires.*

Cossacks: Peoples of Russian, Ukrainian, and other ethnic backgrounds who began settling on Russia's southern frontiers in the 1300s and formed communities from the mid-1500s. Gradually incorporated into the Russian state, they enjoyed greater autonomy than other subjects of the Tsar and in exchange provided loyal military service.

Council of People's Commissars (SNK): Soviet government or Council of Ministers under the Bolsheviks.

democracy (*demokratiia*)/democratic: (Of) the popular masses.

district: See *uezd.*

duma: Representative political assembly (either a town council or the parliament) in late Imperial Russia.

Executive Committee of the Soviet (Ispolkom): Main governmental body at the district and provincial level.

fraction: A sub-group of a political party; sometimes by extension referred to an entire political party.

GPU: The successor to the Cheka, or secret police.

Kadet Party: Liberal Constitutional Democratic Party; advocated civil rights, the rule of law, and constitutionalism.

kulaks: Rich, or allegedly rich, peasants; from the Russian word meaning "fist."

Left Socialist-Revolutionary Party: Split from the Socialist-Revolutionary Party in fall 1917 and allied with the Bolsheviks until summer 1918.

Menshevik Party: More orthodox and moderate fraction of the Social Democratic (Marxist) Party; strict adherents to Marx's conception of the economic stages of history.

344

Octobrist Party: Moderate political party founded to work with the government to implement the promises of the October Manifesto of 1905, which granted Russia civil liberties and a limited parliament.

People's Commissar: Head of a Bolshevik government agency.

Piter: St. Petersburg, Petrograd; pronounced "peeter."

pood: Unit of weight equal to 36 pounds.

precinct: See *chast'*.

prodotriad: Grain-confiscation brigade.

Progressist Party: A moderate liberal party founded in 1908.

proletariat: The industrial-worker class.

raion: Ward; district of a city during the Soviet period.

Revkom: Revolutionary committee.

Russian: Can mean both *russkii* (cultural meaning) and *rossiiskii* (state or territorial meaning).

Social Democrats: Political activists who espoused Marxist ideology.

Socialist-Revolutionary Party: Pro-peasant political party with a terrorist wing; Russia's largest political party; championed redistribution of all large estates among the peasants.

soviet: Council in Russian; representative bodies at various levels of society and administration in Soviet Russia from factories and military units to cities and provinces, consisting of delegates elected by workers, peasants, and soldiers.

township: See *volost*.

troika: Unit of three leaders, often representing the party, soviet, and security police.

Trudoviks: Laborers' Group (*Trudovaia gruppa*), a State Duma faction composed of diverse pro-peasant socialists.

Tsar: Emperor.

Tsarist: Imperial Russia; the term was often used by critics of the government and dynasty.

uezd: District; the political units into which a province was divided.

verst: English version of *versta;* a unit of measure equal to 1 kilometer or 0.6 miles.

volost: Township; political units into which a district was divided.

ward: See *raion*.

White [Guard(ist)]: Broad term applied by the Bolsheviks to their nonsocialist opponents, implying their association with the Old Regime.

zemstvos: Institutions of rural self-government at the provincial and district level, mostly dominated by educated elites.

CHRONOLOGY OF WAR
AND REVOLUTION

1914

June–July: Mass strikes in St. Petersburg

15/28 July: Austria declares war on Serbia

17/30 July: Russian order for general mobilization

19 July/1 August: German declaration of war

30 July: Creation of All-Russian Zemstvo Union for aid to sick and wounded soldiers

8 August: Duma meets one day, votes almost unanimously for war credits, and dissolves itself

14 August: Creation of All-Russian Union of Town Dumas

10–16/22–29 August: Russian offensive in East Prussia; after initial success, crushed at Tannenberg

6 November: Arrest of five antiwar Social Democratic Duma deputies

1915

Military supply crisis (insufficiency of shells and or equipment)

10/23 May: Russian troops suffer defeats and start retreat from Galicia

26–29 May: Anti-German pogroms in Moscow destroy 800 businesses and residences

13 June: War minister Sukhomlinov resigns amid accusations of corruption and espionage

July–August: Formation of liberal Progressive Bloc in Duma

19 July: Duma meets, demands "ministry of confidence"; Russia evacuates Warsaw

26 August: Nicholas assumes supreme military command against advice of his ministers

1916

Gradual disorganization of railroad system; grave fuel and food shortages; massive inflation

20 January: Boris Shtiurmer appointed prime minister

13 March: pro-Duma General Polivanov dismissed as minister of war

22 May/4 June: Brusilov Offensive begins, dealing powerful blow to Austria; seizure of Galicia

Fall: Harvest down by 40 percent compared to 1915

18 September: Protopopov, former Duma deputy, appointed acting minister of interior

1 November: Miliukov excoriates Shtiurmer in Duma and cites reports that people close to Alexandra sympathize with Germans; speech banned from publication but circulates illegally

10 November: Shtiurmer removed, replaced by A. F. Trepov
17 December: Rasputin is murdered
27 December: Trepov dismissed, replaced by Prince N. D. Golitsyn

1917

9 January: Mass demonstration in Petrograd
27 January: Arrest of Workers' Group of War-Industries Committee
14 February: Duma session opens
18 February: Strike begins at Putilov Works
22 February: Nicholas leaves for General Headquarters in Mogilev
23 February: Spontaneous demonstrations in Petrograd caused by bread shortage in stores
24–25 February: Demonstrations grow; reserve troops reluctant to suppress them
25 February: Nicholas orders suppression of demonstrations
26 February: Arrest of 100 revolutionary activists; troops begin to switch sides
27 February: Petrograd declared in state of siege; mass troop mutiny in Petrograd; Tsar rejects Prime Minister Nikolai Golitsyn's request to disband cabinet and form new government; Provisional Committee of Duma formed; Petrograd Soviet of Workers' Deputies convoked by party leaders; sailors of Baltic Fleet mutiny, murder officers
28 February: Council of Ministers resigns; prisoners liberated; police stations looted; revolution in Moscow; Nicholas departs Mogilev for Petrograd
March: Formation of soviets in cities, factories, military units, and countryside; hundreds of revolutionaries and political activists return from exile
March–June: Increase in peasant uprisings and attacks on landlords' property
1 March: Petrograd Soviet's Order No. 1 abolishes military chain of command; Tsar's train diverted to Pskov; all former ministers arrested
2 March: Provisional Government formed; Nicholas abdicates in Pskov in favor of his brother Mikhail
3 March: Mikhail renounces crown; formation of Provisional Government announced; amnesty for mutineers; release of political prisoners
4 March: Zemstvo activists replace governors; security police and censorship apparatus abolished; creation of Ukrainian Rada (parliament)
8 March: Nicholas departs for Tsarskoe Selo under arrest
9 March: United States recognizes Provisional Government
10 March: Police Department abolished
12 March: Freedom of association declared; abolition of capital punishment
16 March: Nationalization of crown lands; Polish independence recognized
20 March: Provisional Government abolishes ethnic and religious discrimination
25 March: Establishment of state grain monopoly
Early April: All-Russian Central Executive Committee of Soviets established
3 April: Lenin return to Petrograd from Switzerland with dozens of revolutionaries
4 April: Lenin's "April Theses" calls for a deepening of revolution
14 April: Red Guards begin to be formed

21 April: Creation of land committees to prepare land reform

30 April: Miliukov and Guchkov forced to resign from government

1–11 May: First All-Russian Muslim Congress in Moscow proposes federal structure for Russia

2–5 May: Government crisis leads to inclusion of Soviet leaders in First Coalition Government; socialist Kerensky becomes minister of war

4–28 May: First All-Russian Congress of Peasant Soviets

1 June: Women admitted to the bar

3–24 June: First All-Russian Congress of Workers' and Soldiers' Soviets

4 June: Kronstadt sailors rally in support of Bolsheviks on Mars Field

18 June–14 July: Failed offensive against Germans; troops mutiny

3–6 July: Demonstration of armed reservists under slogan of "All Power to the Soviets" in Petrograd, joined by 20,000 armed sailors from Kronstadt (July Days); arrest of several Bolshevik leaders; Lenin and Zinoviev flee to Finland to avoid trial for aid to Germans

8 July: Kerensky becomes prime minister

12 July: Capital punishment restored at front

18 July: General Kornilov appointed supreme commander

20 July: Women 20 years and older acquire vote

26 July–3 August: Sixth Bolshevik Congress votes for armed insurrection

5 August: Abolition of Holy Synod; creation of Ministry of Faiths

5 August: Women granted full rights of entry to civil service

15 August: Russian Orthodox Church Council begins work, elects patriarch in November

21 August/3 September: Germans seize Riga

25–31 August: Alleged mutiny by Kornilov (Kornilov Affair)

27 August: Kerensky imposes martial law in Petrograd, declares Kornilov traitor

31 August–9 September: Bolsheviks win majority in Petrograd Soviet, take control of Presidium

1 September: Provisional Government declares Russia a republic; directory created with Kerensky as supreme political and military leader

September–October: Apogee of peasant uprisings

14–22 September: Democratic conference meets in Petrograd and is mired in endless debates

15 September: Bolshevik leaders reject Lenin's demand for power seizure

23–26 September: All-Russian strike of railroad workers

25 September: Trotsky elected chair of Petrograd Soviet

1 October: Lenin's third letter urging power seizure

7 October: Preparliament meets; Bolsheviks walk out

10 October: Bolshevik Central Committee votes in favor of armed uprising

12 October: Petrograd Soviet forms Military Revolutionary Committee (Milrevkom)

20 October: Milrevkom dispatches "commissars" to military units in and near Petrograd

22 October: Mass demonstrations in favor of soviets taking power

24 October: Pro-government units occupy key points in Petrograd, close Bolshevik newspapers; pro-Soviet units seize postal and telegraph offices; few military units support government

25 October: Lenin declares Provisional Government overthrown; flight of Kerensky; pro-Soviet troops and Red Guards take control of city

25–26 October (night): artillery fire from Cruiser *Aurora* and Peter-Paul Fortress; capture of Winter Palace; arrest of ministers; opening of Congress of Soviets; Right Socialist-Revolutionaries (SRs) and Mensheviks walk out; Bolshevik-dominated congress passes decrees on peace and land and creates Council of People's Commissars (SNK) headed by Lenin

25 October to 3 November: Bolsheviks seize power in Moscow

26 October: Cossack commander Kaledin declares himself supreme authority in Don region

27 October: SNK outlaws opposition press (Press Decree)

29 October: Resistance of military cadets crushed; Railroad Workers Union (Vikzhel) rejects SNK monopoly on power

30 October: Clash between Cossacks and pro-Bolshevik sailors and Red Guards near Petrograd suburb of Pulkovo

Late October–November: Soviet power spreads across country and through military units

2 November: Declaration of Rights of Peoples of Russia; abolition of religious privileges

4 November: SNK obtains formal authority to legislate by decree without approval of VTsIK

5 November: Tikhon elected patriarch of Russian Orthodox Church in Moscow

10 November: Estate and civilian ranks abolished

14 November: Bank and state employees refuse to carry out SNK's orders; worker control over production instituted

15 November: Transcaucasian Commissariat formed with leftist and nationalist representatives as regional, anti-Bolshevik government

17 November: Nationalization of private enterprise; Bolshevik troops seize State Bank funds

19–20 November: Seizure of Military Headquarters, murder of Supreme Commander Nikolai Dukhonin; Generals Alekseev and Kornilov flee to south

22 November: Decree on elective courts and revolutionary tribunals

23 November: Finland declares independence from Russia

December: Establishment of All-Russian Council for Economy (VSNKh)

2 December: Russia and Germany sign truce in Brest-Litovsk

7 December: Extraordinary Commission to Fight Counterrevolution and Sabotage (Cheka) set up

10 December: Formation of coalition government of Bolsheviks and Left SRs

11 December: Creation of Soviet Ukraine government in Kharkov

14 December: Nationalization of banks

16 December: Decree on democratization of army; decree on no-fault divorce

18 December: Decree on civil marriage; SNK recognizes right to self-determination of Finland

27 December: Formation of anti-Bolshevik Volunteer Army in Novocherkassk

1918

Spanish flu widespread in Russia

2 January: Decrees on "laborers' rights" and on universal labor obligation

5–6 January: Constituent Assembly opens with 25 percent Bolsheviks; anti-Bolshevik majority refuses to ratify decrees of Second Congress of Soviets; Lenin orders armed shutdown of assembly; in several cities troops fire on protestors supporting Constituent Assembly; several are killed

11 January: Ukrainian Central Rada proclaims Ukraine independence

15 January: SNK decrees establishment of Red Army

19 January: Patriarch Tikhon anathemizes Bolsheviks

20 January: Separation of church and state proclaimed

21 January: Repudiation of all state debts

23 January: Confiscation of private banks and merchant fleet

1/14 February: Gregorian calendar instituted (February 1–13, O.S., deleted)

18 February: Following Russia's refusal to sign peace treaty, Germany and Austria abrogate truce and begin broad offensive against Russia

21 February: Cheka granted right to shoot internal enemies "on the spot"

3 March: Treaty of Brest-Litovsk signed; Germany gains most of Ukraine, Byelorussia, Baltic; Turkey claims part of Caucasus; pogroms against Armenians leave 25,000–30,000 dead

4 March: Supreme Military Council created; Trotsky becomes commissar of war

6–24 March: British landing in Murmansk with Bolshevik approval

8 March: Bolshevik Party renamed Russian Communist Party

10–12 March: Government moves to Moscow

14–16 March: Extraordinary Congress of Soviets approves moving capital to Moscow and ratifies Treaty of Brest-Litovsk; Left SRs quit government in protest

27 March: Uprising of Don Cossacks against Bolsheviks

5 April: Allied military intervention begins in Far East: Japanese, American, and British troops land in Vladivostok

8 April: Creation of Red military commissars

10–13 April: Volunteer Army offensive in Ekaterinodar

11–12 April: Mass arrests of anarchists in Moscow and Petrograd

13 April: Kornilov killed by stray shell; General Denikin assumes command of Volunteer Army

22 April: Foreign trade nationalized; establishment of universal military training; independent Transcaucasian Federation (led by Nationalists and Mensheviks) proclaimed in Tbilisi

27 April: Abolition of right to inheritance

May–June: Elections to urban soviets; Bolsheviks often lose majorities, reimpose them by force

13 May: Decrees on fighting "peasant bourgeoisie" and on food detachments seeking mass grain extraction from peasants; beginning of "War Communism"

25–26 May: Czechoslovak Legion (30,000 soldiers) refuses Bolshevik order to disarm; by late July, with help of anti-Bolshevik forces, they control much of Siberia and Urals

26 May: Transcaucasian Federation divides into three independent republics: Georgia, Armenia, and Azerbaijan

28 May: Martial law instituted across country

29 May: Universal military draft

June: Redistribution of housing (*uplotnenie*) begins in Moscow

8 June: Czechs occupy Samara; Committee of Constituent Assembly (Komuch) formed, immediately begins armed struggle against Bolsheviks

11 June: Decree on forming committees of village poor (*Kombedy*)

13 June: Establishment of Revolutionary Military Council and Eastern Front

16 June: Introduction of capital punishment

18 June: SNK establishes Commissariat of Enlightenment (Narkompros)

20 June: Volodarsky, commissar for propaganda and agitation in Petrograd, chief censor of Petrograd, assassinated by a Socialist-Revolutionary

26 June: Lenin urges mass terror reprisals

28 June: Nationalization of all heavy industry, railroads, and steam plants

July–August: Numerous peasant revolts

4–10 July: Fifth All-Russian Congress of Soviets ratifies first Soviet Constitution limiting rights of "former people"

6–22 July: Uprisings in Iaroslavl, Murom, and Rybinsk, led by SR Savinkov and anti-Bolshevik officers, are suppressed

6–7 July: Left SRs assassinate German ambassador; their uprising is suppressed

16–17 July: Execution of Imperial family in Ekaterinburg

23 July: Volunteer Army takes Stavropol and by December entire Kuban region

25 July–August: Czechs take Ekaterinburg, Simbirsk, Ufa, Kazan, Irkutsk, Chita

29 July: Compulsory military training introduced; officers of Imperial Army ordered to register

2 August: Allies occupy Archangelsk

6 August: Czechs seize gold reserves in Kazan; anti-Bolshevik worker rebellion begins in Izhevsko-Votkinsk

14 August: Baku occupied by British; they depart on 15th at approach of Turkish forces, which set up Musavatist government

26 August: Abolition of right to own urban real property

30 August: SR terrorists kill Petrograd Cheka head Uritskii, wound Lenin

2 September: Decree declaring country a single military camp

5 September: Decree on mass terror against "class enemies"

6 September: Creation of Revolutionary Military Council of Republic

10 September: Kazan captured by Red Army

16 September: Decree on marriage, family, and guardianship

23 September: Ufa Directory established to replace Komuch

5 October: Decree that bourgeois can receive food rations only for work; food rations for all at minimal level for wartime; decree on obligatory registration of artworks and antiquities

8 October: Capture of Samara by Red Army

10 October: Decree on new orthography

21 October: Able-bodied citizens required to register with government employment agencies

11 November: Armistice ends World War I

13 November: Annulment of Treaty of Brest-Litovsk; Red Army begins occupation of Ukraine, Byelorussia, and Baltic

18 November: Admiral Kolchak proclaims himself "supreme ruler" after coup in Omsk; Czechoslovaks no longer take part in Civil War

21 November: Ban on all retail and wholesale commerce

November–December: French and British land in Sevastopol, Odessa, and Novorossiisk

30 November: Creation of Council of Worker and Peasant Control with absolute power in war effort

10 December: Labor Code establishes universal labor obligation for people aged 16–50

14 December: Ukrainian nationalist forces commanded by Petliura occupy Kiev

1919

Typhus epidemic strikes broadly in population; increased role in Civil War of peasant rebels, forces led by Makhno, Petliura, Grigoriev; mass violence against Jews in Ukraine

4 January: Bolsheviks open Ukrainian Front, and by February occupy much of Ukraine, including Kiev

11 January: *Prodrazverstka* (confiscatory tax in kind) instituted across entire country

24 January: Central Committee Directive on mass terror against Don Cossacks

8 February: All-Russian Congress on defense of childhood declares family "dying institution"

14 February: Decree on forming first *sovkhozy*, Soviet state farms

2–6 March: First Congress of Comintern, Communist International

3 March: Decree on fighting desertion

4–14 March: Kolchak forces enter Volga region and seize Ufa

6 March: Decree on establishing *Osobye otdely* in all armies and fronts

16 March: Nationalization of consumer cooperatives; all citizens must join them

6 April: Red Army takes Odessa

11 April: Decree on creating first forced labor camps

12 April: First *Subbotnik* (voluntary work on Saturday)

13 May: Iudenich begins offensive against Petrograd; seizes Pskov by the 25th

June: Denikin's Volunteer Army occupies all of Don region, Donbass, and part of Ukraine

21 June: Commencement of expulsion of Kolchak's forces from Urals

12 July: First general amnesty

11 August: Turkestan front created

31 August: Denikin takes Kiev

11 September: Decree on creating worker departments in universities (Rabfaki)

13 October: Denikin forces seize Orel, threatening Moscow

16 October: Iudenich nears Petrograd

20 October: Red Army retakes Orel

21–24 October: Red Army repulses Iudenich and captures Tobolsk and Voronezh

14 November: Red Army takes Kolchak's capital Omsk

19 November: General offensive of Red Army begins in south and southeast

28 November: Statute on militarization of state institutions and enterprises

1920

Majority of large and medium factories strike; 15 percent of population contracts typhus, of whom 20–30 percent die; fuel crisis deepens

3–10 January: Red Army retakes Rostov, Novocherkassk, Azov, Taganrog, and Tsaritsyn

15 January: Decree on creation of labor armies

17 January: Capital punishment officially abolished

30 January: Allies decide to evacuate their forces from Far East

February: Red Army takes Kiev, Poltava, and all Right-Bank Ukraine

4 February: Massive anti-Bolshevik peasant uprising breaks out in Volga region

7 February: Kolchak executed in Irkutsk; Worker-Peasant Inspectorate created, with Stalin as head

21 February: Creation of Committee on Electrification of Russia

March–April: Peasant rebellions in Kazan and Saratov provinces

13 March: Red Army captures Murmansk, ending anti-Bolshevik operations in north

25 March: Toward abolition of money: Soviet institutions get free mail, telegraph, and phone service

29 March–5 April: Party congress votes to abolish private property and to militarize economy

April: Council of Defense transformed into Council of Labor and Defense

2 April: Completion of American departure from Soviet territory

4 April: General Wrangel replaces Denikin as chief commander of anti-Bolshevik forces in south

24 April: Poland begins anti-Soviet offensive: Polish-Soviet War begins

28 April–1 May: Red Army takes Baku, proclaims Azerbaijan Socialist Republic

30 April: Universal food-rationing system instituted for all laborers

2 May: Fares on public transportation abolished

22–25 May: Workers opposition denounces party bureaucratization at party conference

July-September: Peasant uprising in Saratov province

8 July: USA lifts trade embargo on Soviet Russia

14 July: Soviet forces take Vilnius, Minsk, Kovno; Bolshevik Commander Sapozhkov launches anti-Bolshevik rebellion in Volga region

20 July: Soviet and public institutions and organizations prohibited to use money for purchases

21 July–6 August: Second Congress of Comintern

23 July: Commencement of Soviet offensives toward Warsaw and Lvov

30 July: Decree to "liquidate" saints' remains across country
15 August: Tambov peasant uprising under Antonov begins
15–16 August: Polish forces begin counteroffensive
2 September: Congress of Toilers of East opens in Baku
12 October: Peace treaty signed with Poland, ceding portions of Ukraine and Byelorussia
14 November: Wrangel's forces evacuate Crimea and retreat to Turkey
18 November: Abortion legalized
29 November: Soviet troops proclaim Armenian SSR; nationalization of small businesses
4 December: Food to be distributed for free

1921

27 January: Payment for housing abolished
11 February: Decree on creating Red Professorate
22 February: Creation of State Planning Commission (Gosplan)
25–27 February: Red Army invades Georgia and establishes Georgian SSR
28 February–11 March: Strikes in Petrograd
28 February–18 March: Kronstadt sailors rebel "for Soviets without Communists"
8–16 March: Tenth Party Congress bans factions; condemns Workers' Opposition and bureaucratization of party; proclaims New Economic Policy (NEP), including freedom of trade, small-scale production, hiring of labor; *prodrazverstka* replaced by grain tax
16 March: Anglo-Soviet Trade Agreement
17 May: Start of partial denationalization
28 May–20 June: Antonov uprising crushed by Red Army
Summer: Famine begins in Volga region and southern Ukraine (1.5–2 million die)
16 June: Party forbids courts to try Communists without party sanction
July: Journal *Change of Signposts* is launched in Prague by pro-Bolshevik émigré leaders
9 and 18 July: Payment reestablished for transportation and postal-telegraph services
18 July: Creation of Central Commission on Famine Relief (Pomgol)
20 August: American Relief Administration begins work on famine relief
27 August: Private relief organization disbanded, leaders arrested
12 September: Establishment of State Bank
16 September: State institutions forbidden to refer to Central Committee decisions in minutes
27 October: State enterprises permitted limited trade of products at market prices
30 December: Decree on disbanding labor armies

1922

5 January: Banishment from country of ten anarchist leaders
19 January: In Moscow first "purge" (intimidation) of poets
6 February: Cheka recast as Main Political Agency (GPU)

23 February: Decree on confiscation of church valuables
2 March: Introduction of uniform tax in kind
11 March: After international protest, Menshevik leaders released from prison and exiled abroad
19 March: Secret letter of Lenin calling for "decisive attack" on church
3 April: Stalin elected general secretary of Central Committee
10 April–19 May: International conference in Genoa
16 April: German-Soviet treaty on economic and military cooperation signed in Rapallo
26 April: Trial against fifty-four religious leaders begins in Moscow
5 May: Arrest of Patriarch Tikhon
19 May: Young pioneer organization founded
22 May: Legalization of leasing of land
25 May: Lenin's first stroke
1 June: Adoption of Criminal Code
6 June: Creation of Glavlit, main censorship agency
8 June–7 August: Trial against thirty-four Right SR leaders
11 June-5 July: Trial against eighty-six church leaders
18 June: House of Scholars opens in Moscow
11 August: Secret military agreement between RSFSR and Germany
Fall: Expulsion of 160 scholars, philosophers, professors—flower of Russia's intelligentsia
19 September: Opening of Communist University of National Minorities in Petrograd
8 October: First Soviet automobiles produced in Moscow
20–21 October: Georgian Communist Party collectively resigns in protest against pressure from Stalin and Ordzhonikidze to join USSR
31 October: VTsIK ratifies Civil Code strengthening state's exclusive right to property
December: Left Front of Art (LEF) founded in Moscow
23 December: Lenin's health deteriorates, right arm and leg paralyzed; Lenin begins dictating "Testament" (through 29th)
30 December: First Congress of Soviets of USSR affirms Treaty on Formation of USSR

WORKS CITED

[1] Alekseyev, V.V., ed. *The Last Act of a Tragedy (New Documents about the Execution of the Last Russian Emperor Nicholas II)*. Translated by B. Ye. Zarubin, Ye. V. Alekseyeva, and W. H. Schettler. Yekaterinburg: Urals Branch of Russian Academy of Sciences, 1996.

[2] Artizov, A., and O. Naumov, eds. *Vlast' khudozhestvennaia intelligentsia*. Moscow: Mezhdunarodnyi fond "Demokratiia," 2002.

[3] Babkin, M. A. *Rossiiskoe dukhovenstvo i sverzhenie monarkhii v 1917 godu: Materialy i arkhivnye dokumenty po istorii pravoslavnoi tserkvi*. Moscow: Indrik, 2006.

[4] Balk, A. P. "Poslednie piat' dnei tsarskogo Petrograda, 23–28 Fevralia 1917 g.: Dnevnik poslednego Petrogradskogo Gradonachal'nika." A. Balk Collection. Hoover Institution Archives. Stanford, California.

[5] Bezrukov, G. N., ed. *Partizanskoe i povstancheskoe dvizhenie v Prichumyshie, 1918–1922. Dokumenty i materialy*. Barnaul: Regional Legislative Assembly and Altai Regional Administration: 1999.

[6] Blium, A. V., ed. *Tsenzura v Sovetskom Soiuze, 1917–1991, Dokumenty*. Moscow: ROSSPEN, 2004.

[7] Bonch-Bruevich, Vladimir Dmitrievich. *Na boevykh postakh fevral'skoi i oktiabr'skoi revoliutsii*. 2nd ed. Moscow: Federatsiia, 1931. [First ed: 1930.]

[8] Browder, Robert Paul, and Alexander Kerensky, eds. *The Russian Provisional Government, 1917: Documents*. 3 vols. Stanford: Stanford University Press, 1961.

[9] Chaadaeva, O. "Soldatskie pis'ma v gody mirovoi voiny (1915–1917)." *Krasnyi arkhiv* 65–66 (1934): 118–63.

[10] Chalmaev, V. A., ed. *Pod sozvezdiem topora. Petrograd 1917 goda—znakomyi i neznakomyi*. Moscow: Sovetskaia Rossiia, 1991.

[11] Cherepnina, N. Iu., and M. V. Shkarovksii, eds. *Sankt-Peterburgskaia eparkhia v dvadtsatom veke v svete arkhivnykh materialov, 1917–1941*. St. Petersburg: Liki Rossii, 2000.

[12] Cherniaev, V. Iu., ed. *Piterskie rabochie i "diktatura proletariata." Oktiabr' 1917–1929. Ekonomicheskie konflikty i politicheskii protest*. Sankt-Peterburg: Russko-Baltiiskii informatsionnyi tsentr BLITZ, 2000.

[13] Chokaev, Mustafa. *Otryvki iz vospominanii o 1917 g.* Tokyo and Moscow: Russian Academy of Sciences, 2001.

[14] Chugaev, D. A., ed. *Petrogradskii voenno-revoliutsionnyi komitet. Dokumenty i materialy*. 3 vols. Moscow: Nauka, 1966.

[15] Danilov, Iu. N. "Moi vospominaniia ob Imperatore Nikolae II-om i Vel. Kniaze Mikhaile Aleksandroviche." In *Arkhiv russkoi revoliutsii*. Edited by I. V. Gessen. 22 vols. Berlin, 1934. Vol. 19, 212–41.

[16] Danilov, V., and T. Shanin, eds. *Krestianskoe dvizhenie v Povolzhie, 1919–1922. Dokumenty i materialy*. Moscow: ROSSPEN, 2002.

[17] Denikin, General A. *The White Army.* English translation, 1930; Gulf Breeze, Fla.: Academic International Press, 1973.

[18] Dobronozhenko, G. F., ed. *VChK-OGPU o politicheskikh nastroieniiakh severnogo krest'ianstva, 1921–1927 gody.* Syktyvkar: Syktyvkarskii gosudarsvtennyi universitet, 1995.

[19] Ehrenburg, Ilya. *Na tonushchem korable.* Petersburg: Peterburgskii pisatel', 2000.

[20] "Fevral'skaia revoliutsiia v dokumentakh." *Proletarskaia revoliutsiia,* no. 1 (1923): 262–3.

[21] Fuhrmann, Joseph T., ed. *The Complete Wartime Correspondence of Tsar Nicholas II and the Empress Alexandra, April 1914–March 1917.* Westport, Conn., and London: Greenwood Press, 1999.

[22] Gal'perina, B. D., ed. *Sovet Ministrov Rossiiskoi Imperii v gody pervoi mirovoi voiny. Bumagi A. N. Iakhontova (zapisi zasedanii i perepiska).* Saint-Petersburg: Dmitrii Bulanin, 1999.

[23] Gal'perina, B. D., and V. I. Startsev, eds. *Petrogradskii Sovet Rabochikh i Soldatskikh Deputatov v 1917 godu.* 5 vols. Moscow: ROSSPEN, 2002.

[24] Golder, Frank, ed. *Documents of Russian History, 1914–1917.* New York: The Century Company, 1927.

[25] Golovizin, M. V., ed. *Tetradi po istorii rabochego i revoliutsionnogo dvizheniia. Daidzhest zhurnala "Cahiers du movement ouvrier" na russkom iazyke.* Moscow: NII "Geodeziia," 2006.

[26] Gootnik, Abraham. *Oh Say, Can You See: Chaos and a Dream of Peace.* Lanham, Md: University Press of America, 1987.

[27] Gordienko, I. *Iz boevogo proshlogo (1914–1918).* Moscow: Gospolitizdat, 1957.

[28] Graves, William S. *America's Siberian Adventure, 1918–1920.* New York: Peter Smith, 1931.

[29] Gruiznskaia, N. P. "zapiski knotrrevoliutsionerki." In *1917 god v sud'bakh Rossi ii mira. Fevral'skaia revoliutsiia. Ot novykh istochnikov k novomu osmysleniiu.* Edited by P. V. Volobuev. Moscow: Institut rossiiskoi istorii RAN, 1997: 347–66.

[30] Igritskii, I. V., and A. Ia. Iakovlev, eds. *1917 god v derevne.* Moscow: Politizdat, 1967.

[31] Inozemtsev, M. "Iz istorii rabochego dvizheniia vo vremia mirovoi voiny." *Krasnyi arkhiv* 6 (1934): 5–27.

[32] Institut Marksizma-Leninizma, ed. *Pobeda Velikoi Oktiabr'skoi sotsialisticheskoi revoliutsii. Sbornik vospominanii uchastnikov revoliutsii v promyshlennykh tsentrakh i natsional'nykh raionakh Rossii.* Moscow: Gospolitizdat, 1958.

[33] Isakov, S. G., ed. "Neizvestnye pis'ma M. Gor'kogo k Leninu." *Revue d'Études slaves* 64, no. 1 (1992): 143–56.

[34] Katagoshchina, M. V., and A. V. Emel'ianov, eds. "Moskva v noiabre 1919 goda: Sochineniia uchashchikhsia nauchno-populiarnogo otdeleniia Universiteta im. A. L. Shaniavskogo." *Rossiiskii arkhiv,* no. 2–3 (1992): 362–76.

[35] Kerensky, A. F. *The Prelude to Bolshevism: The Kornilov Rising.* New York: Dodd, Mead and Company, 1919.

[36] Kokoreva, N. S. "Okhrana materinstva." In *"Bez nikh my ne pobedili by."* Edited by M. O. Levkovich et al. Moscow: Politizdat, 1975.

[37] Kollontai, Alexandra. *Selected Writings of Alexandra Kollontai.* Translated with an introduction and commentaries by Alix Holt. Westport, Conn.: Lawrence Hill and Company, 1978.

[38] "Krov' za krov'." *Krasnaia gazeta* (August 31, 1918).

[39] Kruglov, S. *Put', ozarennyi Leninym. Vospominaniia.* Moscow: Moskovskii rabochii, 1965.

[40] Kulakov, A. A., L. P. Kolodnikova, and V. V. Smirnov, eds. *Obshchestvo i vlast': Rossiiskaia provintsiia, 1917 - seredina 30-x godov.* Vol. 1 of *Obshchestvo i vlast': Rossiiskaia provintsiia, 1917–1980-e gody (po materialam nizhegorodskikh arkhivov).* Edited by A. A. Kulakov et al. 3 vols. Moscow, Nizhni-Novgorod, and Paris: Institut rossiiskoi istorii RAN, 2002.

[41] Kvashonkin, A. V., et al., eds. *Bol'shevistskoe rukovodstvo: Perepiska, 1912–1927: Sbornik dokumentov.* Moscow: Rosspen, 1996.

[42] Larina, L. I., ed. *Istoriia otechestva v dokumentakh 1917–1993 gg.* Part II: *1921– 1939 gg. Khrestomatiia dlia uchashikhsia starshikh klassov srednei shkoly.* Moscow: ILBI, 1994.

[43] Lemke, Mikhail. *250 dnei v tsarskoi stavke (25 sent. 1915–2 iulia 1916).* Peterburg: Gos. izd., 1920.

[44] Lenin, V. I. *Collected Works.* 47 vols. Moscow: Progress Publishers, 1964.

[45] Livshin, A. Ia., and I. B. Orlov, eds. *Pis'ma vo vlast', 1917–1927.* Moscow: ROSSPEN, 1998.

[46] Makarov, E. I., et al., eds. *Piterskie rabochie i "diktatura proletariata," oktiabr' 1917–1929: Ekonomicheskie konflikty i politicheskii protest: Sbornik dokumentov.* St. Petersburg: BLITs, 2000.

[47] Mayakovsky, Vladimir. Comic strip distributed by the Russian Telegraph Agency, #241, August 1920.

[48] *Nauchno-informatsionnyi biulleten',* no. 4. Moscow: RTsKhIDNI, 1994: 38–54.

[49] Negretov, P. I., comp. *V. G. Korolenko: V gody revoliutsii i grazhdanskoi voiny, 1917–1921: Biograficheskaia khronika.* Benson, Vt.: Chalidze Publications, 1985.

[50] Nielsen, Jens Petter, and Boris Weil, eds. *Russkaia revoliutsiia glazami petrogradskogo chinovnika. Dnevnik 1917–1918 gg.* Oslo: Univ. i Oslo, Slavisk-baltisk institutt, 1986.

[51] Notovich, F., ed. "Soldatskie nastroeniia nakanune mirovoi voiny." *Krasnyi arkhiv* 64 (1934): 79–80.

[52] Okunev, N. P. *Dnevnik moskvicha, 1917–1924.* 2 vols. Moscow: Voennoe izdatel'stvo, 1997.

[53] Papernikov, Ia. "Fevral'skaia revoliutsiia v Irkutske." *Katorga i ssylka* 30 (1927): 93–98.

[54] Pavlov, D, R ed *Nauchnee oppozitsionnoe dvizhenie v bol'shevistskoi Rossii, 1918 g. Sobraniia upolnomochennykh fabrik i zavodov. Dokumenty i materialy.* Moscow: ROSSPEN, 2006.

[55] "Pervoe predosterezhenie." *Pravda* (August 31, 1922).

[56] Petrograd: Izd. Sev. Obl. i Petrograds. Kom. Partii Levykh S.–R. (Internatsionalistov), 1919. "Obrashchenie k matrosam i krasnoarmeitsam, predlozhennoe rabochimi lev.s.-r. 19 marta 1919 g."

[57] Pirozhkov, V. P., ed. *V. I. Lenin and VChK.* Moscow: Izdatel'stvo politicheskoi literatury, 1987.

[58] "Po Rossii." *Novoe vremia* (September 19, 1916).

[59] Potapenko, V. *Zapiski prodotriadnika, 1918–1920 gg.* Voronezh: Tsentral'nochernozemnoe Knizhnoe izdatel'stvo, 1973.

[60] *Pravda o Kronshtadte.* Prague: Volia Rossii, 1921.

[61] Raskolnikov, F. F. *Tales of Sub-Lieutenant Ilyin.* Translated by Brian Pearce. London: New Park Publications, 1982.

[62] Sef, Semen. "Demokraticheskoe pravitel'stvo Gruzii i angliiskoe komandovanie." *Krasnyi arkhiv* 21 (1927): 122–73.

[63] Semashko, N. A. *Health Protection in the U.S.S.R.* London: V. Gollancz, 1934.

[64] Senin, A. S., ed., *V. B. Stankevich: Vospominaniia, 1914–1919. Iu. V. Lomonosov: Vospominaniia o Martovskoi revoliutsii 1917 goda.* Moscow: RGGU, 1994.

[65] Sharikova, O. A., ed. *Fevral'skaia revoliutsiia, 1917. Sbornik dokumentov i materialov.* Moscow: RGGU, 1996.

[66] Shelokhaev, V. V., ed. *Partiia sotsialistov-revoliutsionerov. Dokumenty i materialy.* 3 vols. Moscow: ROSSPEN, 2000.

[67] Shishkin, V. I., ed. *Sibirskaia Vandeiia.* 2 vols. Moscow: Mezhdunarodnyi fond "Demokratiia," 2001.

[68] Sidorov, A. L. *Revoliutsionnoe dvizhenie v armii i na flote v gody pervoi mirovoi voiny, 1914—fevral' 1917: Sbornik dokumentov.* Moscow: Nauka, 1966.

[69] Sokolov, A. K., ed. *Protokoly Prezidiuma Vysshego Soveta Narodnogo Khoziaistva. 1920 god. Sbornik dokumentov.* Moscow: ROSSPEN, 2000.

[70] *Soviet Russia.* Vols. 2–6 (1920–1922). New York: The Russian Soviet Government Bureau.

[71] Stalin, Joseph. *The Road to Power.* New York: International Publishers Co., 1937.

[72] Stasova, E. D. *Stranitsy zhizni i bor'by.* 3d ed. Moscow: Politizdat, 1988.

[73] Stepun, F. *Byvshee i nesbyvsheesia.* Moscow: Progress-Litera and St. Petersburg: Aleteiia, 1995.

[74] Strel'tsov, B. V., ed. *V bor'be za Sovetskuiu vlast'.* Minsk: Belarus', 1967.

[75] Sukhanov, N. *Zapiski o revoliutsii.* 3 vols. Berlin, Petersburg, and Moscow: Izdatel'stvo Grzhebina, 1922.

[76] Sukhanov, N. N. *The Russian Revolution, 1917: A Personal Record.* Edited by Joel Carmichael. London: Oxford University Press, 1955.

[77] Sworakowski, Witold S. "A Churchill Letter in Support of the Anti-Bolshevik Forces in Russia in 1919." *Russian Review* 28 (1) (January 1969).

[78] "Sytye i golodnye." *Bednota* (April 10, 1918).

[79] Tolstoi, V. P., ed. *Agitatsionno-massovoe iskusstvo. Oformlenie prazdnestv.* Moscow: Iskusstvo, 1984.

[80] Trotsky, Leon. *My Life: The Rise and Fall of a Dictator.* London: Thornton Butterworth, Limited, 1930.

[81] Trukan, G. A., et al., eds. *Rossiia antibol'shevistskaia. Iz belogvardeiskikh i emigrantskikh arkhivov.* Moscow: Institut rossiiskoi istorii RAN, 1995.

[82] Tukhachevskii, M. N. *Pokhod za Vislu.* Moscow: Novosti, 1992.

[83] Vakunov, S., ed. "'Zato teper' svoboda': Pis'ma krest'ian i gorodskikh obyvatelei v Uchreditel'noe sobranie i obzor khoda izbiratel'noi kampanii." In *Neizvestnaia Rossiia XX vek.* Vol. 2. Moscow: Istoricheskoe nasledie, 1992.

[84] Verstiuk, V. F., ed. *Nestor Ivanovich Makhno.* Kiev: RIF "Dzvin," 1991.

[85] Volkov, I. M., ed. *Sbornik dokumentov i materialov po istorii SSSR sovetskogo perioda (1917–1958 gg.).* Moscow: Izdatel'stvo Moskovskogo universiteta, 1966.

[86] Volobuev, P. V., ed. *1917 god v sud'bakh Rossii i mira. Fevral'skaia revoliutsiia. Ot novykh istochnikov k novomu osmysleniiu.* Moscow: Institut rossiiskoi istorii RAN, 1997.

[87] von Mohrenschildt, Dimitri Sergius, ed. *The Russian Revolution of 1917: Contemporary Accounts.* New York: Oxford University Press, 1971.

[88] Wells, H. G. *Russia in the Shadows.* London: Hodder and Stoughton, 1920.

[89] Youssoupoff, Prince. *Rasputin: His Malignant Influence and His Assassination.* Translated by Oswald Rayner. Guernsey: The Star and Gazette Company Ltd., 1927.

[90] Yun-An, Liu, ed. *Kitaiskie dobrovol'tsy v boiakh za sovetskuiu vlast' (1918–1922 gg.).* Moscow: Izdatel'stvo vostochnoi literatury, 1961.

[91] Zelov, N., ed. "Pis'ma iz 1918 goda." *Oktiabr',* no. 11 (1987): 168–77.

[92] Zenzinov, Vladimir. *Deserted: The Story of the Children Abandoned in Soviet Russia.* Translated by Agnes Platt. Westport, Conn.: Hyperion Press, Inc., 1975.

[93] Ziornov, V. D. *Zapiski russkogo intelligenta.* Moscow: Indrik, 2005.

TEXT CREDITS

Selections from the Correspondence of Nicholas and Alexandra from Joseph T. Fuhrmann, ed., *The Complete Wartime Correspondence of Tsar Nicholas II and the Empress Alexandra, April 1914–March 1917* (Westport, CT, and London: Greenwood Press, 1999), pp. 574–5, 577, 582, 601–2. Copyright © 1999 by Greenwood Press. Reproduced with the permission of Greenwood Publishing Group, Inc., Westport, CT.

"A Socialist Describes the Creation of the Executive Committee of the Petrosoviet" from N. N. Sukhanov, *The Russian Revolution, 1917: A Personal Record,* ed. Joel Carmichael (London: Oxford University Press, 1955; Princeton NJ: Princeton University Press, 1984), pp. 40–1, 76–86. Copyright © 1984 Princeton University Press. Reprinted by permission of Princeton University Press.

Viktor Chernov, "Russia's One-Day Parliament," January 5, 1918, from Dimitri Segius von Mohrenschildt, *The Russian Revolution of 1917: Contemporary Accounts* (New York: Oxford University Press, 1971), ISBN 0195014200, pp. 268–72. By permission of Oxford University Press, Inc.

"Ukrainian Declaration and the Provisional Government's Reply, June 1917" from Robert Paul Browder and Alexander Kerensky, eds., *The Russian Provisional Government, 1917: Documents,* 3 vols., 1:383–6; "Resolutions of the First All-Russian Muslim Congress," May 1–11, 1917, 1:409–11; "What Is a Revolution?" *Novoe Vremia,* March 12, 1917,

1:200; "Newspaper Editorials on the Abolition of the Death Penalty," March 1917, 1:200–2; "Finance Minister Andrei Shingarev on the Food Crisis," May 21, 1917, 2:632–3; "Russian Message to the Allies Following the July Days," July 19, 2:1123–24; "Alexander Kerensky at the Front," July 7, 1917, 3:962–6. Copyright © 1961 by the Board of Trustees of the Leland Stanford Jr. University; renewed 1989.

Alexandra Kollontai, "Communism and the Family," 1920 from Alexandra Kollontai, *Selected Writings of Alexandra Kollontai,* trans. Alix Holt (Westport, CT: Lawrence Hill & Co., 1978), pp. 250–60. Used with permission of Lawrence Hill Books.

"The Tragedy of Abandoned Children in Civil War Russia" from Vladimir Zenzinov, *Deserted: The Story of the Children Abandoned in Soviet Russia,* trans. Agnes Platt (Westport, CT: Hyperion Press, Inc., 1975), ISBN 9780883551905, pp. 9–25.

"Violence and Daily Life in a Jewish Community during the Civil War" from Abraham Gootnick, *Oh Say, Can You See: Chaos and a Dream of Peace* (Lanham, MD: University Press of America, 1987), ISBN 0819163120, pp. 74–8, 103–9. Reprinted by permission of University Press of America.

"Launching the Volunteer Army, 1917–1918" from General A. Denikine, *The White Army,* trans. Catherine Zvegintzov (Paris, 1929; English translation, 1930; Gulf Breeze, FL: Academic International Press, 1973), pp. 22–35. Reprinted with the permission of Academic International Press.

"Supreme Commander of the Red Military Forces, Leon Trotsky" from Leon Trotsky, *My Life: The Rise and Fall of a Dictator* (London: Thornton Butterworth, Ltd., 1930), pp. 351–60.

"Winston Churchill Urges French Support for Anti-Bolshevik Forces, late 1919" from Witold S. Sworakowski, "A Churchill Letter in Support of the Anti-Bolshevik Forces in Russia in 1919, " *Russian Review* vol. 28, no. 1 (Jan., 1969), pp. 77–82. Reprinted by permission of Wiley Blackwell.

"America's Intervention in Siberia, 1918–1920" from William S. Graves, *America's Siberian Adventure, 1918–1920* (New York: Peter Smith Publisher, Inc., 1931), pp. 71, 81–2, 92, 97. Reprinted by permission of Peter Smith Publisher, Inc.

"A Bolshevik Account of the Constituent Assembly" from F.F. Raskolnikov, *Tales of Sub-Lieutenant Ilyin*, trans. Brian Pearce (London: New Park Publications, 1982), pp. 1–20. Beekman published an edition in 2001 (Index Books ISBN 0-861510-25-9). Reprinted with the permission of Index Books.

INDEX

Page numbers in italics refer to illustrations. An expanded version of this index is available at http://www.hackettpublishing.com.